Christian Missions in Bihar and Jharkhand till 1947

Christian Missions in Bihar and Jharkhand till 1947

A Study by P. C. Horo

Edited by

Jose Kalapura

Christian World Imprints™

&

Gossner Theological College

First Published in 2014 by

Christian World Imprints(TM)
Christian Publishing & Books from India
H-12 Bali Nagar, **New Delhi-110015**
info@christianworldimprints.com
www.ChristianWorldImprints.com
Phone: +91 11 25465925 Fax: +91 11 25173055

&

Gossner Theological College
Main Road, **Ranchi-834001**
gtcranchi@rediffmail.com
Phone: +91 651 2350005

ISBN-13: 978-93-5148-038-9 (HB)
ISBN-13: 978-93-5148-039-6 (PB)
ISBN-10: 93-5148-038-0 (HB)
ISBN-10: 93-5148-039-9 (PB)

Cover Description:

Four oldest churches in Bihar and Jharkhand against the map of undivided Bihar which included Jharkhand.

1) Catholic Church, at Padri ki Haveli, Patna City, 1779
2) Church of North India St. Luke's Church, Danapur, 1845
3) Gossner Evangelical Lutheran Church, Christ Church, Ranchi, 1851
4) St. Mary's Cathedral (Catholic), Ranchi, 1890

Cover design and layout: Jose Kalapura and Tapeshwar Prasad

Cover map: Not to be Scaled

Printed at Chawla Offset Printers

In the memory of Prof. Prem Chand Horo (1915-2011), who endeavoured to recount the story of the Christian Missions and Missionaries who laboured in love for the development of Bihar and Jharkhand.

Contents

Foreword

I feel honoured to have been asked to write a Foreword to the book entitled *Christian Missions in Bihar and Jharkhand till 1947: A Study by P.C. Horo*, edited by Jose Kalapura. Late Prof. Prem Chand Horo, was Head of the Department of History at St. Columba's College, Hazaribagh, presently, a constituent College of Vinoba Bhave University, Hazaribagh. While being the Pro-Vice Chancellor of Ranchi University, he got his Ph. D. degree in History from Patna University, in 1976. His long years of experience in teaching History, his will power, tenacity and commitment to the cause of Christian Missions enabled him to complete the study even at the age of 60.

The present book comes out of his Ph. D. thesis entitled "Christian Missions and Communities in Bihar". Having spent so many years in teaching History in the College, Prof. Horo undertook his doctoral research in the fag end of his teaching career, on the advice and inspiration of his own eminent History Professor, Dr. Kali Kinkar Datta, of Patna University.

Due to heavy and multiple responsibilities Dr. Horo could not revise and get his thesis published. Being a member of the Gossner Evangelical Lutheran Church, Horo was particularly close to Gossner Theological College and to me. He shared with me his dream of getting the thesis published. On 3rd August, 2006 Prof. Horo handed over his Ph. D. thesis to the GEL Church Commission on Mission History in the presence of Bishop C. H. Hansda, the then Moderator of GEL Church in Chotanagpur and Assam. The Central Council of GEL Church resolved to publish the work and authorized Gossner Theological College, Ranchi, to translate the dream of Horo into a reality. But that could not be done till his death in 2011.

It was a coincidence that I met Dr. Fr. Jose Kalapura in 2010 who came to Ranchi in connection with the writing of a History of Christianity in Bihar, Jharkhand and Chattisgarh, a project of the Church History Association of India. I am glad and thank him for accepting to edit the book, at my request. A life member of the Indian History Congress, he has efficiently done the work by editing, checking the facts and rectifying any methodological drawbacks, without altering the content of the Thesis, to make it relevant, readable for students, researchers and general readers. He has also added an informative Appendix on the Missions besides a suitable Introduction to the book which gives an overview of the Church till the present day. I also thank Prof Horo's daughter, Dr. Bina Tiru, who partially shouldered the financial responsibility in the publication of this book.

The writing of history of the Missions in Bihar and Jharkhand very much comes from the life experience of Dr. Horo. The history of exploitation of his own people and the liberation mediated by the Christian Missions seem to have been the main motivating factors in undertaking a study on Christian Missions. Besides, from the side of researchers and students of History, there has been a growing demand for History books particularly of this region. The present book is the first of its kind covering entire undivided Bihar including Chotanagpur. The book covers the history of the Christian Missions from their beginnings till the time of Indian Independence. Several colleges and Universities including the Senate of Serampore College (University) have in their syllabus Regional Church History as a subject. It is hoped that the present book will serve the demand of researchers, students and those interested in the history of the Christian Missions in Bihar and Jharkhand.

Rev. Dr. Manmasih Ekka
Principal, Gossner Theological College, Ranchi;
Secretary, GEL Church Commission on Mission History

Preface and Acknowledgements

Christianity in India is as old as Christianity itself. Scholars have classified the arrival and development of Christianity in India in four waves. The first was by Apostle Thomas and the missionaries of the Eastern Church who came to Malabar (Kerala) and founded the St. Thomas Church there. The second was begun by European Catholic missionaries beginning with Franciscan missionaries in early 13th century and later, under the Portuguese Colonial powers in early 16th century. Vigorous evangelization was undertaken in the next two centuries in various parts of India spearheaded by Religious Orders such as Franciscans, Dominicans, Jesuits, Augustinians, etc.

A third wave was inaugurated at Tranquebar in South India, by Danish Protestant missionary Bertholomeus Zeigenbalg in early 18th century and in like manner, by William Carey, at Serampore, in North India in end 18th century. The third wave picked up momentum in the 19th century, thanks to Charter Act 1835 during British Colonial rule, but seems to have declined in mid-20th century. The involvement of both Catholic and Protestant Missions hastened the development of Christianity in India during this period.

Finally, the fourth wave, characterized by the Pentecostal movement, began in early 20th century, and seems to be sweeping India for the past 30-40 years, influencing not only the mainline Catholic and Protestant Churches, but also Non-Christians.

This book is an attempt to study the impact of the third wave in Bihar and Jharkhand. Christian presence in Bihar, begun first in 1620, was short-lived, but became continuous since 1706 thanks to the Catholic Capuchin missionaries. Missionary movement from Bengal expanded to Bihar, particularly in Chotanagpur, in mid-19th century under the aegis of the Gossner Mission, the Jesuit Mission and others, who came from Europe and America.

Christian Missions in Bihar and Jharkhand till 1947: A Study by P. C. Horo is a detailed description of some 17 Christian Missions established by different missionary organizations in undivided Bihar from 1620 to 1947. This book has emerged from the doctoral study of Prof. Prem Chand Horo whose painstaking efforts at reconstructing the story of these Christian Missions had not, unfortunately, seen the light of day till his death in 2011. However, it was his dream to highlight the contribution of the Christian Missions in Bihar and Jharkhand toward nation building. Enormous data from various Mission archives in India and abroad and Government sources were collected by Prof. Horo during early 1970s. The description of events and persons has been substantiated with data drawn from historical sources. I am sure Prof. Horo would be delighted in his heavenly abode that his research study is taken to its logical end.

While working on the study of Christianity in Bihar, Jharkhand and Chattisgarh, with the mandate of the Church History Association of India, I came across with the thesis of Dr. Horo, thanks to Rev. Manmasih Ekka, who then requested me to edit it for publication in book form.

It may be noted that an earlier version of this research work was published in 1976 as a chapter of a multi-volume work published in 1976, entitled, *The Comprehensive History of Bihar, Volume III, No. 2,* edited by Horo's own Professor, Dr. Kali Kinkar Datta, of Patna University. Horo had submitted his thesis in 1976 and had wanted to revise this doctoral thesis for publication in book form, but the task had to wait some 38 years.

I gladly accepted the idea and initially thought that the data in the thesis should be updated to the present time. But, it needed enormous time and resources and so the idea of updating was shelved. So the main narrative in ten chapters deals with the history up to 1947. But in my introductory chapter, I have attempted to update the data and interpret it from a historian's perspective up to the turn of the 21st century. The chapters have been re-arranged and edited to make it more readable and relevant for students of history, researchers, and the general readers. The original title "Christian Missions and Christian Communities in Bihar" had to be modified because Chotanagpur was carved out of Bihar and attained Statehood in 2000. That aside, as the title of the book indicates, it is the story of the Christian Missions, which is only a part of the full story of the Christian community. The contemporary orientations in history writing give much importance to the people who were evangelized by these Missions, making the history, community-oriented. Nevertheless, the book has highlighted the benign presence of hundreds of dedicated missionaries and their heroic work among the poor, the marginalized and the sick wherever they operated, effecting significant transformation in the Christian community in particular, and the wider ambient society, in general.

From my part, I consider this as an aspect of telling the Good News which God has done among His people through the Missions, missionaries and the native collaborators who laboured in the mission field of Bihar and Jharkhand.

This work is in your hand's because of the collaboration of so many people to whom I owe great debt of gratitude. First, I thank Rev. Dr. Ekka, who on behalf of the Gossner Church Commission on Mission History, placed his trust and confidence in me to edit, revise and reconstruct the narrative keeping the data intact. I also thank Mrs. Horo, Prof. Dr. Catherine Rani, and family who took equal interest in the task.

Clerical and technical assistance was received from the staff of my own Institute, Xavier Institute of Social Research, Patna: the manuscript was digitalized by Ms Anju Kumari, and other assistance was received from Ms Rajani Roseline and Mr. Surendra Manjhi and Mr. Tapeshwar Prasad. Profuse thanks to all of them. Whatever mistakes have remained in the text, though inadvertent, are mine.

I also thank Mr. Sudhanshu Kanda, of Christian World Imprints, for doing a wonderful job in transforming the manuscript into a presentable book in a short time. I also thank the co-publisher Rev. Dr. Ekka, the Principal of Gossner Theological College, Ranchi.

Facts and events bygone are dead unless they are recovered. Recovering the past and interpreting it is the task of a historian. Thus, the past comes alive, so that the present can learn from it, and build up the future. I am happy to present this book to you, our esteemed readers: to be informed, inspired, and transformed. Have a great reading.

Jose Kalapura
Director
Xavier Institute of Social Research, Patna
Sept 20, 2014

Profile of Prof. Prem Chand Horo

Prof. Prem Chand Horo was one of the few people whose achievements cannot be assessed by the amount of books and articles produced. His life time commitment was to teaching and educational administration in various capacities. He spent more than 50 years in the educational field as a teacher of History and in administrative posts in the University. Inspite of these responsibilities he found time to do his doctorial study, though at the fag end of his teaching career. That shows his commitment to research. The topic of his research was his first love: love for History and love for the Church. Hence this book, *Christian Missions in Bihar and Jharkhand till 1947: A Study by P. C. Horo.*

Life and Early Career

Prem Chand Horo was born on June 30, 1915 in village Kathkunwari, Ranchi District. His father Mr. Hardugan Horo and mother Smt. Halyani Horo belonged to a traditional tribal farmer family. However, they decided to educate their son Prem Chand and made every effort to provide him with the needed resources even making sacrifices: the family's agricultural land was sold and the rice farm mortgaged. Prem Chand also did not make futile his parent's efforts. He maintained utmost simplicity in life, and did hard work. Time to time he received financial support from the Government, which reduced his burden and that of the parents.

Prem Chand passed his Lower Primary School examination in 1925, Matriculation in 1935, and Intermediate Arts Examination in 1937. After the Intermediate Examination, Bihar Government offered him Aboriginal Junior Scholarship which enabled him to continue his study. He made his family and village proud: he was the first person in his village and vicinity who passed the Intermediate Examination.

He had many ups and downs in his life, but he continued his study. Despite the scholarship, he often had to face financial crises. Many times, while waiting for scholarship money to come, he had to face starvation. He graduated from Patna College in 1941 and continued the Post Graduate study. He was a student of the famous Historian, Prof. K. K. Datta of Patna University, author of the well-known book, "*A Comprehensive History of Bihar*". His Professors admired the academic interest of Prem Chand in History.

An interesting fact in his life was his love for hockey. Many a time, in his student days, he had represented Patna College in Inter-State competition of Hockey. Nevertheless, in this area he did not go much further. Ultimately, he chose the teaching profession as his main career. But, he went beyond the duty of a teacher. He combined teaching with concern, particularly for marginalized students. He paid special attention to the neglected and tribal community members.

Due to financial constraints he had to take a job. In September 1941, he was appointed teacher at a School of the Santal Mission of the Northern Churches in Kaerabani village in Santhal Parganas. Thereafter, on 1st December 1943, he became a Lecturer at St. Columba's College, Hazaribagh, a premier institution founded by the Dublin University Mission. It was the only Christian College in undivided Bihar at that time. This was a dream of Prem Chand. It was the first event in the history of Bihar, that a son of an *Adivasi* became a Lecturer.

Contribution in Educational Administration

Dr. Prem Chand retired from College teaching on 1st July 1977. Life after retirement was not spent in leisure. From time to time he joined highly responsible administrative posts. It is not necessary to say that he fulfilled his duty with dedication. Earlier, on December 10, 1971 he became a member of the University Service Commission, Bihar and on June 26, 1975 he became its Chairman. In 1977, he worked as the Pro-Vice Chancellor of Ranchi University, Ranchi. In 1979, he became a member of the Managing Committee of the Indian Institute of Management, Bangalore. In addition, he worked on many responsible key positions. And thus, he maintained an active life, till the last moment of his life.

Committed Teacher, Inspiring Guru

Prof. Prem Chand was a committed teacher and he cared for his students. A great number of his students lived up to his expectations and made him proud. Many of his students are now holding important positions in public life. These included academicians, politicians, social workers, doctors and Church dignitaries such as Mr. Raymond Bhengra (Govt. Bureaucrat), Dr. Walter Horo and Dr. Stephen Murmu (Physicians), Rt Rev. Z. J. Terom (Moderator of CNI), Prof. Narmadeswar Singh and Dr. Chitaranjan Paty (Prof. of History) and many others. They wished to recall some aspects of their guru P. C. Horo. His student, Dr. Azariah U. Hans, former Principal of the same College recalled: "Prof. P. C. Horo, even after retirement would turn-up at the campus on a particular day every year remembering his joining the College as a Lecturer. This he did almost without fail, a gesture perhaps to show gratitude for his vocation. Subsequently, many lecturers followed his manner and method of his teaching". Many others recall the diverse aspects of his life as their tutor and guide. His devotion to duty aside, his former students recall his manners and self-presentation, especially his impeccable suit and tie.

Similarly many others had admiration for P. C. Horo. Dr. Dilbar Bhengra an illustrious former student was doing Post Graduate studies in History at Patna staying with Rev. T. S. Cyril Hans, who had just returned from Europe. Both recalled interesting anecdotes of Prof. P. C. Horo, their guru as "a loveable person". Dr. Bhengra went on to become the Director of the Archaeological Survey of India (Jharkhand Branch) and wrote a book entitled "*Archaeology of the Chotanagpur Division*". He gives much credit to his mentor P. C. Horo for his inspiration in undertaking serious academic pursuits.

Dr. P. C. Horo inspired many people. He supervised the Ph.D. thesis of a person who was refused by all others due to the latter's social background. One of his former students and later on his colleague Prof. Shiv Dayal Singh, the former Principal of Markham College, Hazaribagh, narrated P. C. Horo's life as a "laborious, commitment to service and as such motivated many people". Another former history student of St. Columba's College, Rev. Dr. Marsalan Bage, who was the Rector, Vice Principal of Serampore College, and later Director-Principal of Gurukul Lutheran Theological College, Chennai, said: "I would not have studied in the College if Dr. P. C. Horo had not supported and inspired me to do so."

Interestingly, inspite of his busy schedule he loved to go to his ancestral village Kathkunwari along with his family. The Bengali *Zemindar* (landlord) of the village had given the title of *Mahato* to his family.

Appreciation of Christian Missions

There is no doubt that his special concern for the poor emerged from his own personal experience of the plight of the poor. The various Christian institutions where he worked seem to have imbibed in him, the spirit of service to humanity. This, indeed, was the reason why he chose a topic, the Christian Missions for his doctoral study. Besides, his familiarity with Christian institutions, and of their history, made him aware of the significance of the Missions in nation building. He always wanted to know more and more about these organizations, their policies, objectives, methodologies, and achievements. He was closely associated with some Churches and institutions. This made him undertake a significant task in the form of an exploratory research on the history of the Christian Missions.

He regularly attended Church Services and encouraged church members to become dedicated in life and worship. He took active interest in his Church, the Gossner Evangelical Lutheran Church and was a member for one term, of the Church's highest administrative body the GEL Church Council. He regularly contributed articles on Church History in the Gossner Evangelical Lutheran Church Magazine, *Ghar Bandhu*. Inspired by his personality I was also encouraged to complete my Ph.D. in Mundari Language under the guidance of the well-known Hindi scholar, Dr. Dineshwar Prasad. He also saw to it that all his children did well in their studies and career: Daughter (Dr.) Bina Tiru became Associate Professor of History, Ranchi Women's College; son Mr. Paul Horo became Chief Mechanical Engineer, Indian Railway Service; daughter (Dr.) Telani Meena Horo became Senior Assistant Professor, Political Science Dept, Magadh Mahila College, Patna University; son Mr. Peter Horo became Assistant Administrative Officer, National Insurance Company; and son Mr. John Horo became Executive Engineer, Water Ways Division, Hazaribagh.

On January 3, 2011, Dr. Horo passed away at the ripe age of 96 leaving a noble example of dedication to humanity and a significant contribution to scholars on Christianity.

Prof. (Dr.) Catherine Rani Horo
W/o (Late) Prof. P. C. Horo
Retd. Professor, Dept. of Hindi
K. B. Women's College
Hazaribagh (Jharkhand)

Christian Centres in Undivided Bihar

(Map not to scale)

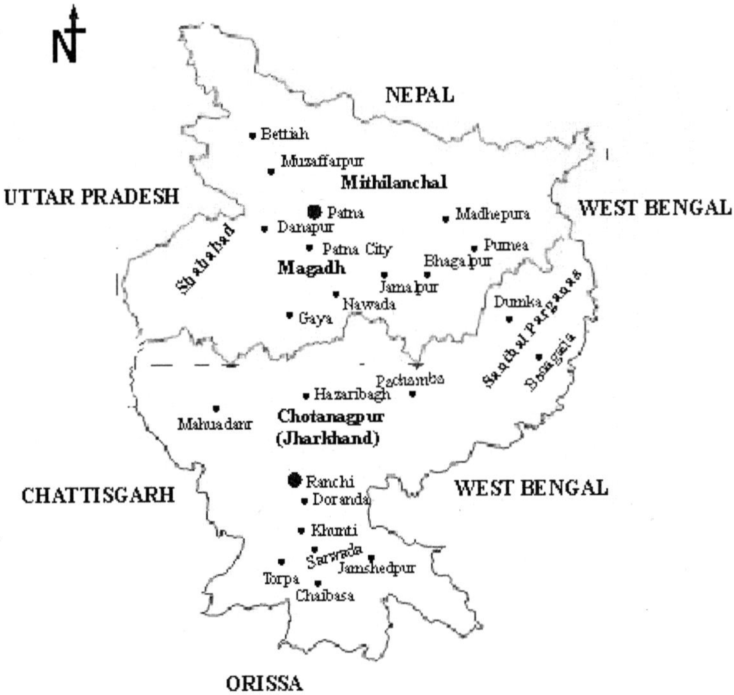

Introduction

A Historical Overview of the Church in Bihar and Jharkhand at the Turn of the 21st Century

– Jose Kalapura

Christianity in India is nearly two millennia old. Along with Hinduism and other prominent minority religions such as Islam, Buddhism, Jainism, and Sikhism, it has become a part of the religious heritage of India, which is known for its religiosity and religious diversity. Therefore, the History of Christianity in India is a part of the History of this land. So also, the History of the Christian community[1] is an aspect of the general history of the people of this country.

This book deals with the History of Christianity in Bihar and Jharkhand till the year of Indian Independence, in 1947. However, in this introductory chapter, an attempt is made to give a brief overview of the 20-century-old Christianity in India, along with a discussion on the Church in Bihar and Jharkhand and its impact on society, in the post-Independence era as well, till the turn of the 21st century. The thematically inter-linked sections below are the following: 1) a note on periodisation of Christian History and Christian Historiography, 2) an overview of Christianity in India in ancient, medieval and modern periods, and 3) a discussion on Christianity in Bihar and Jharkhand (Chotanagpur)[2].

1. Christian History of India and Historiography

The History of Christianity in India can be classified into various periods based on the arrival of the evangelizing agents through whom sections of Indians were Christianized. From this perspective the 20 centuries of Catholic Christianity in India has been classified into five periods: 1) Christianity in ancient period spread through Apostle St. Thomas, 52-1320, 2) Christianity in medieval period spread by European missionaries, 1320-1502, 3) Christianity in medieval period spread under Portuguese *Padroado*[3], 1502-1622, 4) Christianity in medieval period spread through the Propaganda Fide, 1622-1886, 5) Christianity spread through agents under the Indian Hierarchy, 1886 ff. Using the same criterion, Protestant Christianity in India can be classified into two periods: 1) Protestant Christianity under Danish Mission (Tranquebar) and William Carey (Serampore) prior to the Charter Act, 1813, 2) Protestant Christianity after the Charter Act, 1813, particularly after the Act of 1835.

It may be noted that this is a functional classification which underscores the main trends. This is not a neat demarcation of Mission periods. There might have been several agencies during a particular period, and the end of the period does not mean end of a Mission agency. Besides, Christianization in India has been a continuous process in which together with the external missionary agents, the community's own members have played the role of the messenger of the Gospel and have attracted members to their fold. One may also note that widespread and concerted efforts at evangelization took place in India from early 16th century thanks to the arrival of the Catholic missionaries under the Portuguese Padroado, and Protestant missionaries mainly from Northern Europe and America since mid-19th century.

1.1 Trends in Indian Christian Historiography

Historiography on Indian Christians began when European missionaries began to 'inscribe' India.[4] By and large, Christianisation of Indians after the 16th century was characterised by westernisation and naturally, histories of Indian Christians were written from European perspectives. There are six categories of literature in the Christian historiography in India.[5] First, is a body of literature, couched in essentialist terms, written by European missionaries from the 16th to early 20th centuries. Embedded exclusively in the European experience of Christianity, those writers tended to underplay the significance of culture and lived religion of the converts, as if the latter lived in a void without religion. Early missionary writings on India, with few exceptions, generally ignored a vast array of forms and religious practices of the ancient St. Thomas Christians in India and treated these with disdain, dismissing them as corrupt accretions resulting from the moral lassitude of the Indian Christians.[6]

Similarly, in the 19th century, when Protestant Christianity began to spread far and wide, thanks to various European and American missionaries, there appeared a body of missionary literature on India and its peoples which generally reflected the agenda of the British Colonial administrators, namely 'civilising the Indians'.[7] On the other hand, in recent times more histories have been noted highlighting the Indian resistance to the Portuguese hegemonisation of the Church, particularly by the Thomas Christians in Kerala and some individuals in Goa.[8] The literature of the 17th to 29th centuries reflects these internal discourses. Within the Protestant Church circles too, similar internal discourses were generated by nationalist Indians and European sympathisers on one hand, and the dominating European authorities, on the other. These discourses became more pronounced during and after the Indian freedom struggle and the literature of both types fall in the second category.[9]

A third category of writings are those that appeared in the period from late 19th century to mid-20th century which was characterised by many apologetic discourses which tended to devaluate Indian religions on the one hand, and uphold Christianity, on the other.[10] Among the recent works on Christianity in India is the fourth category, having the largest number of writings on Christian missionary work in different regions and among diverse people groups, highlighting the Church's work in education, development, social welfare and so on.[11] Some of these also study the process of Christianisation from the perspective of cultural encounter.[12] The fifth category of writings on social change of Christian communities which appeared since the 1960s, use contemporary sociological, anthropological and historical perspectives, and view Indian Christianity as part of India's religious tradition.[13] Finally, more recent times have seen several themes in history writings such as community development, fight for justice, continuity-discontinuity characteristics in convert communities, Pentecostal movements, Subaltern and Dalit Christianity.

1.2 Subaltern History

Among the above-mentioned categories Dalit Christian Histories are generally included in the sixth category.[14] But, some of these can be further classified under an emerging category, the Subaltern History. Subaltern perspective is an attempt to bring about the subjectivity of the subalterns in developing their history. It is a methodology through which the subalterns do not just become the objects of history but the very subjects themselves. Subaltern Studies is an effort to hear the people and their voices which have been silenced in the dominant discourses; it is an effort to make the Subaltern people speak in their own language, a language of protest, resistance and negation. In India, the term subaltern was brought to the centre of critical scholarship by the 'subaltern studies collective.'[15] V.V. Thomas' recent work on understanding Subaltern History is an excellent contribution in this line.[16]

Despite many attempts no substantial Historical study from the subaltern perspective has yet been made on the conversion movements in India.[17] However, a few noteworthy works are available and many are in the process. Some examples are the works by Dick Kooiman, Manikam Sunder Raj, Walter Fernandes, Geoffrey Oddie, Frederick Downs, John C. Webster, and so on.[18]

Perusing some 720 titles in Christian Historiography, it was found that only 103 works are related to Subaltern History, of which 79 are related to subaltern issues. George Oommen and John C. B. Webster have listed some 42 in their recent book on Dalit Christian History.[19] It must also be mentioned that there are only 70 works which focus on the community.[20]

The need of the hour is to make efforts to develop a subaltern perspective to the study of Christian history, because a large number of those people that responded to the Gospel and flocked to the Church were Dalits, Tribals, and Fisher folk whose community history has largely gone unrecorded.[21]

1.3 Community-oriented History

In Indian Christian Historiography, the role of the missionaries has been much empahsised almost ignoring the role of the converts. Mission history has been written from the stand-point of the 'shepherds' and too little from that of the 'flock.'[22] In such histories, the people were painted as having no religious culture and traditions of their own and what they had were devalued as 'pagan'. This betrays a lack of proper understanding of the people, their history, culture, customs and values. To develop a proper community-oriented Christian History one must look for the local people who played important roles in the whole process of change and transformation.[23] The initiative usually came from the converts and not from the missionaries as has been highlighted by K. G. Daniel[24] and T. S. Samuel Kutty.[25] Particularly appreciative is the work by F. Hrangkhuma which highlights, the struggle for liberation by many subaltern communities.[26] Since the 1970s there have been earnest attempts to understand the people anthropologically, and a few studies have appeared appreciating people's history, culture, indigenous customs and values.

In this context, the re-orientation given by the Church History Association of India (CHAI), an association of scholars on Christianity, is clearly towards community-based history, not missionary-based. The CHAI has envisaged that the history of Christianity in India should be written in the context of the social, political and cultural history of the Indian people rather than as an extension of Christianity from the West. The cultural and regional diversities had to be borne in mind, yet treated as a part of the national matrix.[27]

At this point, I must point out that P. C. Horo's study of the Christian Missions and Christian communities, also is very traditional, and focuses on the missionaries rather than the people.[28] The people are pictured as mere beneficiaries of the Missions. Hence, I must point out that the history depicted in this book is only partial and should be supplemented with the rest of the story, the story of the converts whose lives were impacted by the Missions. A study of the depth of impact on the converts belonging to different castes or tribes, the process of their becoming an indigenous, local, Christian community from being a group of converts, is the whole story.

Therefore, both parts, integrated together, would make the complete history of Christianity in Bihar and Jharkhand. It may be noted that the title of the book clearly spells out its limited scope namely, Christian Missions and not Christian communities.

2. Christianity in India in Twenty Centuries

2.1 Christianity in Ancient and Medieval Periods

Christianity in India is as old as Christianity itself. According to tradition, St. Thomas, one of the apostles of Jesus Christ, after preaching to the inhabitants of Socatra, Parthia and in the Kingdom of Gondophares, North-Western India, landed at the ancient port of Cranganore, in Malabar (Kerala) in 52 A.D.[29] Recent studies point out that Apostle Thomas was only trailing the Jewish migrants' path to India before the Christian era.[30] He preached the Gospel and established seven Churches on the Malabar Coast. Almost all the records confirm that St. Thomas founded the Churches at Cranganore, Palur, North Parur, South Pallipuram, Niranam, Nellakul and Quilon.[31] The Christian community emerged from his ministry calls itself St. Thomas Christians (or *Nasranis*: followers of Jesus of Nazareth). From Malabar the saint proceeded to Mylapore, on the Coromandal Coast,[32] where he died as a martyr for the faith at a place near Chennai known as San Thome.[33]

Much controversy was raked up by European scholars on the claim of St. Thomas Christians (Syrian Christians)[34] of the apostolic origin of their Church.[35] But, scholars are less skeptical of it at present than they were fifty years ago.[36] Dr. J. N. Farquhar's verdict (in 1972) may be taken as typical of the attitude of a number of scholars on the subject at the present time: "Thirty years ago, the balance of probability stood absolutely against the story of the apostolate of St. Thomas in India; today the balance of possibility is distinctly on the side of historicity."[37] Further, in recent times oral histories are taken seriously by historians.[38] The community has a very strong oral history tradition which highlights their living faith in the past 20 centuries. Though written historical evidences are few, they are significant to establish the historicity and Christian heritage of this community.

The community grew naturally, through conversions, intermarriages with the native people, and in-migration. About the year 345 A.D., a certain Thomas Cana, a merchant, came to Travancore with some 400 Christians from Syria, probably fugitives from the terrible persecution of the Persian King Sopor-II of Persia.[39] In the last quarter of the fifth century, Nestorian missionaries were said to have made strenuous attempts to persuade the Indian Christians to accept their doctrines, but failed. The historical evidence regarding the existence of a Church in Kerala can be found in a book written by an Alexandrian merchant Cosmas Indicopleustes (*Cosmas, The Voyage to India*), who visited India in the second quarter of the sixth century AD.[40]

Though there are no detailed written evidence about the Thomas Christians in the subsequent centuries, till the arrival of the Latin Monks at the close of the 13th century, travel accounts of visitors point to an active community in Kerala. Certain inscriptions and accounts of visitors from the West as well as archaeological evidence point to the fact that there were different waves of migration from Western Asia to the Malabar coast and that the immigrants received a cordial reception at the hands of the ruling princes of Kerala.[41] Certain copperplates, probably belonging to the ninth century, and containing charters of privileges granted by these princes testify to the high position enjoyed by the Christians as well as the Jews among the people of the land. The Persian crosses (or the so-called 'Thomas' crosses) with inscriptions in Pahlavi (one found in St. Thomas Mount, Madras, and two in a church in Kottayam in Travancore), are evidence of the connection of the Malabar Church with the Church in Persia, which eventually came to be known as the East Syrian or Nestorian Church or the Church of the East.[42]

Among the visitors to the Malabar Church in the middle ages may be mentioned the names of Marco Polo, the Venetian traveller (1293), John of Monte Corvino, a Franciscan friar (1292-93), Friar Jordan of Toulouse, a Dominican (1302), and John de Marignolli (1348). From all the evidence that is available, we may infer that, during this period, the Christians on the Malabar coast established themselves as good traders as well as patriotic soldiers and administrators.[43]

The Syrian Church in Malabar was aligned to the Church of Rome through its patriarch in Syria who represented the community at the ecumenical Council of Niceae in 325 AD. The Church of Rome came into contact directly with the Malabar Church since early 13th century.[44] This contact was made when the first western Catholic missionary Father John of Monte Corvino, an Italian Franciscan who was appointed Papal Legate to China, came to Malabar. He was accompanied by a Dominican, Nicolas of Pistoia.[45] Arriving in India, the two missionaries landed at Mylapore, the city hallowed by the martyrdom of Apostle St. Thomas. For some reason, their departure for China was delayed by thirteen months. During the period of their stay, the missionary baptized a hundred persons.[46] Further, in response to the touching appeal of friar Jordan, five Dominicans were sent to various Mission stations in Kanara, Mysore, and Malabar. According to Jordan's own words, before he left for Europe in 1328, there were about ten thousand Christians. Earlier in 1330s Quilon [Kollam] in central Kerala was made the first Latin Diocese in Asia.[47]

Also, when Marco Polo passed through Mylapore on his way to Europe, he found some Christians there. Church historians are of the opinion that these Christians whom Marco Polo found were the early Christians converted by St. Thomas. After the martyrdom of Jordan, the Catholic community languished on the eastern coast. The contact of the Malabar Christians with the Patriarchate in the East got disrupted due to the Islamic aggression, capture and decimation of most of the Christian centres in the Middle East. So also, the land route of the Latin missionaries who came through Persia, was blocked because of which the contact of the Syrian Church with the Western missionaries was also practically cut off during late 14th to 15th centuries.

2.2 Portuguese Period, 1500-1773[48]

The arrival of Vasco da Gama in Calicut, in 1498, may be taken as a landmark not only in the history of the Church, but also in the political and cultural contacts of India with the West. From this time European nations were attracted towards India, and several of them attempted to establish themselves in this land of pepper and spices. Franciscan and Dominican missionaries, supported by the Colonial Government of Portugal, followed the traders: Franciscans in 1502, and Dominicans in 1503. Cochin was the headquarters of the both the Portuguese Colonial power and the missionaries. Later, Goa, captured in 1510, was made the headquarters of the Portuguese viceroy as well as the seat of a Bishopric in 1534. The Portuguese Colonial empire in India was at its peak of power by mid-16th century, and the same century saw also the heyday of prosperity for the Roman Catholic Missions in India and in many parts of Asia where the Portuguese established their enclaves. With Goa, Cochin, and Tuticorin as their bases, Portuguese missionaries preached the Gospel to the fisher folk in the coastal regions in the first instance, and later penetrated into the interior.[49]

Francis Xavier (1506-52), known as the Apostle of the Indies, was the first Jesuit missionary to arrive in India, and has rightly become celebrated as one of the greatest in the whole history of the Church. Following the footsteps of Xavier, the Jesuits founded hundreds of Mission centres, churches, and some 22 well-known Educational Institutions in India till the Jesuit Society was suppressed in 1773. The Jesuits established Missions not only in Goa, but along the north and south Konkan coast, Kerala, Fishery Coast, Madurai, Corromandel coast, Bengal and even in the Mughal capital, Agra, at the invitation of Emperor Akbar. During this period of Mission history, some well-known Jesuit scholar-missionaries and scientist-missionaries have left lasting contributions in Indian literature, travelogues, scientific establishments, astronomical contributions, and geographical maps.[50] The first printing presses were brought to India from Europe by the Jesuits in 1550, and they printed Christian literature in Indian languages since 1556.

An important aspect of the Padroado-supported Portuguese Church administration in India was the souring of the relationship with the Syrian Christians. Though the relations between the two were at first friendly, they became gradually strained to the breaking point. A crisis was reached during the visit of Alexio de Menezes, Archbishop of Goa, in the summer of 1599. At the Synod of Diamper (Udayamperoor), mostly through circumstances beyond its control, the Syrian Church was obliged to promise obedience to the Pope through the Portuguese-crown controlled Church authority.[51] But, thanks partly to the conquests of the Dutch, who were friendly to the Syrians and hostile to the Portuguese, the tide soon turned in favour of the Syrians, and in 1653 large numbers of them took a solemn oath in 1653 to renounce the authority of the Portuguese and the Jesuit missionaries, but obey only the Pope. This is known as the Coonen Cross Declaration.[52] As Bishops from Eastern patriarchates were blocked from coming to Malabar, some of the Syrian Christians organized themselves under a Bishop sent out by the Jacobite Patriarch of Antioch, and thus forged a new link with another of the historic Church of the East. Realizing the gravity of the situation, the Pope sent Carmelite prelates to win back the seceded Syrians back to the Roman Church. However, this was only partially successful. Thus the St. Thomas Christian community became divided between those aligned to the Roman Church and those aligned to Orthodox Church in Antioch. Subsequent divisions among the Orthodox section caused the emergence of a few more Churches. Overall, the Syrian Christians, numbering nearly 8 millions, are today divided into 7 denominational Churches.

At the close of the 18th century, Roman Catholic Christianity was in decay and the outlook was very grim, partly because of the orphaning of the Missions after the Suppression of the Jesuits and partly because of the declining power of the Portuguese. On the other hand, the period saw the entry of European Protestant missionaries into the Mission field. Overall, while the 16-18th centuries saw vigorous Catholic missionary movements, the 19th and 20th centuries saw vibrant Protestant missionary ventures in India.

2.3 Protestant Missions in India, 18th-20th Centuries

Tranquebar near Trichinopoly has gained the honour of being 'the birth-place of Protestant Christianity in South India', as Serampore in Bengal is of the North. In this sea-coast town, which was once a flourishing seaport, landed, in 1706, the first Protestant missionaries of India, German Lutherans, led by Bertholomeus Zeigenbalg, sent out under the protection of the king of Denmark to his Indian possessions.[53]

The arrival of William Carey in Bengal in 1793 opens a new chapter in the history of Christianity in India. With him begins, according to Dr. Latourette, "a new era in Protestant Missions not only in India, but also in the entire world."[54] Though there were missionaries in Bengal before his time, like John Kiernander of Sweden (1758-86), who built the Old Mission Church in Calcutta (presently, Kolkata) with the help of Lord Clive, William Carey was the first missionary to be sent out by a missionary society from the West. His pioneering work in the field of Bible translation, primary education, and journalism, apart from his work as a preacher of the Gospel, gives him a unique place in the history of modern Bengal as well as in that of the Christian Church in North India. Serampore College, which he founded in 1818 for the promotion of 'piety and learning', has one of the oldest University charters in Asia.

Carey and his colleagues had to fight hard against heavy odds from the British East India Company, which held the reins of power at the time, and was not friendly towards Mission work, for the Directors feared it might affect their dividends. Until 1812, no Christian missionary had been granted a licence by the Company to reside in its settlements. But pressure was brought to bear by the British Parliament and people upon the Company at the time of revision of its Charter in 1813. As a result of this, an ecclesiastical establishment, with an Episcopal see at Calcutta, came into being (1814), which eventually paved the way for the organization of a branch of the Church of England in India.[55]

The Charter of 1833 threw the way open for Non-British Missions to enter India. Some of the earliest missionaries were American Baptists and Lutherans who worked respectively at Nellore (1840) and Rajahmundry (1848). By 1850, there were to be found not only missionary societies from Great Britain, but also from various parts of Europe and America.

One of the latter ones to take advantage of this was the Church of Scotland, whose first missionary, Alexander Duff landed in Calcutta in 1830. He gave a new turn to missionary work by making education an evangelist's agency.[56] The educational programme of Missions received an impetus from the policy adopted by the Government, under Lord William Bentick, of imparting English education in schools and colleges in accordance with Lord Macaulay's Minute of 1835.[57] Subsequently, missionaries from America, Canada, Australia, New Zealand, and from the continent of Europe, followed in the wake of those who hailed from Great Britain.[58]

By 1850's Protestant Christianity was displaying a fairly rapid growth.[59] They opened many Educational Institutions some of which became very well-known over the years for educating Indian youth over several generations.[60] Societies and missionaries were increasing, converts were multiplying and a beginning in training Indian leadership had been made. Preaching, education and humanitarian works of the missionaries attracted many converts from many castes, particularly the Lower castes, Dalits, and Tribals.

3. Christianity in Bihar and Jharkhand

3.1 Beginnings in Bengal

Bengal was the launching board of many missionary enterprises. As noted earlier, the Colonial Government in Bengal did not permit missionaries to evangelize in its territories. But the Catholic missionaries had been working there since the Portuguese period, in early 16th century. Jesuits, Dominicans, Franciscans and other missionary societies were active in undivided Bengal (which included the present-day Bangladesh), right from Chittagong to Balasore in Orissa. It was from Bengal that missionary societies expanded to Orissa, Bihar and Chotanagpur. It was from Bengal that the first Jesuit Mission set out in 1620 to Patna, capital of Bihar. Even the Capuchin missionaries who came to found a new Mission centre at Patna in 1706, set out from their base at Chandernagar, the French enclave on the banks of Hooghly river. The Gossner missionaries made Calcutta, a stepping stone to launch out to Chotanagpur. Similarly, the Jesuit missionaries who launched the first Catholic Mission in Chotanagpur set out in 1868, from Calcutta, headquarters of the second Jesuit Mission (Belgian Jesuit Mission) which was established in 1859.[61] Also, a few other societies pitched their tents first at Calcutta and then ventured out to outlying areas.[62]

3.2 Christianity in Bihar

One of most densely populated part of the "Hindi heartland", Bihar is India's third most populated State with 103 million people, and accounts for one-seventh of India's population below the poverty line.

Demographically, the caste-class equation in Bihar has remained almost the same over the years: the upper castes generally comprise the upper class and likewise for the middle and lower castes, like in many other States. However, politically the Middle Castes or Backward Castes (52%) have wrested power from the High Castes (15%) for over 15 years. The Dalits (15%) being numerically fewer and oppressed in all aspects of life, are helpless in the present-day caste-polarized scenario wherein they are generally targeted in organized caste/class battles by upper-caste or middle caste *senas* (private armies). After the bifurcation of Jharkhand from Bihar, the tribal population in Bihar was reduced to less than one percent.

The Christian community comprises only 0.3% (over 250,000 Christians: of whom nearly 70% are Catholics) of the total population, the majority of whom are Hindus (82%), followed by Muslims (16%) and other tiny minority communities, which have numerically fewer members than the Christian community.

Recorded Christian presence in Bihar begins in 1620, when a Jesuit Mission was founded at the old city of Patna, capital of Bihar. As the Mission was abruptly wound up in a year, the beginning of active Christian work began only around 1706 when Italian Capuchin missionaries came to work in their newly founded Mission, the Tibet-Hindustan Mission whose territory comprised of Northern India (Hindustan), Nepal and Tibet. Among the several Church organizations working in Bihar since then, the Catholic section is the oldest and has the largest following.

The three major ethnic Christian communities in Bihar are: the *Bettiah Christians, Tribal Christians,* and the *Dalit Christians,* mainly located respectively in West Champaran District in North Bihar, Purnea and Bhagalpur Districts in Eastern Bihar and the Central plains of Bihar, south of the Ganges. Numerically, the largest community is the Tribal Christians (Santals and other tribals), followed by Dalit Christians and the Bettiah Christians. Migration due to a variety of reasons has led to settlement of all the three ethnic groups outside their Districts and outside Bihar.

3.2.1 Mission among the Bettiah Christians

Since the Capuchins were pre-occupied with their Tibet Mission they did not undertake any major work in Bihar except building a Church (1713) at Patna City, which remained as their transit point from Europe to Tibet.[63] In fact, it was the short-lived Tibet Mission (1707-1745) that paved the way for the founding of the oldest Christian community in Bihar, the *Bettiah Christians* at Bettiah, West Champaran District. Having had contacts with the European traders at Patna, the Hindu Raja of Bettiah, Dhurup Singh, came into contact with a charismatic, healing Priest, Capuchin Father Joseph Mary Bernini, then at Patna. The Raja invited the Priest to his kingdom, extending patronage to establish a Christian Church at his capital, for which he obtained the necessary permission from Pope Benedict XIV in 1741.[64]

The Bettiah Mission, founded in 1745, became home of a new Christian group, which gradually drew its membership from ten caste groups (upper and trading castes) from far and near Bettiah town. Individual converts were settled within the Capuchin Mission compound and the community grew in an enclosed quarter which still bears the name "Christian Quarter", within the walled capital of the Bettiah Raj in Bettiah.[65] Nearly after 100 years the Bettiah Christians began to migrate to other cities in north India, particularly Calcutta, the Colonial capital which offered jobs for them, and to Asansol, Patna, and other cities in Bihar. The total number of Bettiah Christians, at Bettiah and elsewhere in India and outside comprise some 15,000.[66]

From its first centre at Patna City, the Capuchin Mission expanded to several other places besides Bettiah: Chuhari, Chakhni, Rampur, Ramnagar, Motihari, Muzaffarpur, Samastipur, Morpa, Latonah, Chanpatia, Purnea, Bhagalpur, Bankipur, Danapura, Khagaul, Jamalpur, etc.[67] The Capuchin Mission was succeeded by American Jesuit Mission in 1919 which opened some 60 Mission stations in central and north Bihar by the end of the 20th century.[68]

Christian Mission work among the Santals of Purnea had started in late 19th century by the Bengal Jesuits. The work was carried on by other missionary bodies in the 20th century. The Santals in Bhagalpur District was begun by Patna Jesuits in 1925 and has expanded under other missionary societies, especially the Franciscan Third Order Regular. In terms of numbers, the Santals (50,000 members) and other tribals together comprise the largest ethnic Christian community in Bihar as well.[69]

3.2.2 Protestant Missions in Bihar

Several Protestant societies also worked in Bihar since mid-19th century. The details of their work have been described in the various chapters of this book. The prominent Missions which worked in Bihar were the Baptist Mission Society (1812), the Church Missionary Society (1826), Gossner Evangelical Lutheran Mission (1838) whose members were assimilated into other Protestant groups gradually, the Santal Mission of the United Free Church of Scotland (1878), the Fellowship of Christian Assemblies Mission (1880), the Zenana Bible and Medical Mission (1882), the Methodist Church (1885), the Anglican Mission (1902), the Brethren of Christ Mission (1914), and the Assembly of God (1914). Numerically the Catholic section is the largest among the diverse denominations.

3.2.3 Mission among the Dalits

Christian Mission among the Dalits in Bihar began with the Protestants who established Mission centres in Patna, Gaya, Arah and other places and had some converts among them in early 20th century. However, the Dalits' response to Christian evangelization became a 'mass movement'[70] in Bihar only in mid1930s, following Catholic (Jesuit) missionary involvement in rural central Bihar.

The castes which entered the Catholic Church are *Chamars*, followed by *Dusadhs,* and *Musahars,* whereas Dusadhs form a majority, followed by Chamars and Musahars, in the Protestant Churches. Certain Protestant groups (especially some 40 recent Pentecostal ones) have claimed that Bihar has some 68,000 Dalit Christians (excluding the 50,000 Dalit Catholics) from 17 Scheduled Caste groups.[71] In contemporary times, the Catholic section of the Dalit

Christians, the majority (95%) of whom are Chamars, are largely in Patna and Buxar Dioceses which together have some 60 Mission centres in the 16 Districts of central Bihar.[72]

3.2.4 Impact of Christianity and Social Transformation

An understanding of the impact of Christianity in Bihar can be had by reviewing the development of Church Institutions. This may indicate the volume of humanitarian works done by the Christian Churches in the area on the one hand, and the extent of mobility achieved by the target Christian communities, on the other. Although Church membership in the State is less than one percent of the total population, the community's presence has been very visible through its educational and humanitarian institutions and the Mission personnel. The vast majority of the beneficiaries of the Christian institutions have been non-Christians. The Catholic community alone runs 3 Colleges, some 50 High Schools, 160 Middle and Primary Schools, 25 Vocational training institutes, 15 Non-formal training centres, 15 Hospitals, 100 Health care centres, a few Old age homes, Leprosaria, over 40 Social welfare centres, in 280 Mission centres, with the help of 1800 Church personnel and thousands of lay collaborators.[73]

Christian impact on the Bettiah Christians has been significant in two key areas: Education and Occupation. In Education, the change is reflected in a high level of literacy: from a non-literate culture to literate culture resulting in a near total literacy among the Bettiah Christians, by the 1990s. The community also responded to a substantial improvement in life chances: employment-generating training and activities such as knitting, tailoring, composing, and type-setting; employment as peons, clerks, catechists, teachers and supervisors in the Mission's own institutions in Bettiah and elsewhere in north India; and financial institutions such as credit societies, artisanal co-operative societies and mutual help societies for help in various needs, including housing.[74]

The change in the Bettiah Christians' occupations has been mainly due to educational mobility. Occupations have changed from traditional to non-traditional ones: clerical, teaching, blue and white collar jobs, and so on.[75] As for the Dalit Christians, the Mission, with its multi dimensional, spiritual and temporal programmes covering preaching, educational service, medical service, humanitarian works and the like, affected the Dalits, who adopted Christianity, and to a lesser extent, the wider ambient society. Besides, spread of general awareness of the socio economic problems of their society, creation of forums in parishes and villages where their problems could be discussed and the like, gave the converts psychological and moral support.[76] These were supplemented with supportive, foundational Christian principles, insights and doctrines so that the converts' psyche would discard some of the hitherto unquestioned dicta, which chained them to perennial low status: towards re-discovering their lost dignity.[77]

In practice, the Mission sponsored the education of the Dalit children, facilitated alternative, more remunerative and higher status employment. By the 1990s, a large number of them were holding blue and white-collar jobs, indicating significant change in their socio- economic life.[78] The number of Dalits who received the benefit of education and who obtained higher status jobs could be taken as a measure of their vertical status and psychological mobility or liberation from a subaltern mind set. In central Bihar, the rate of literacy among the Christian Chamars is over 60 percent, whereas the corresponding rate among the Dalits in Bihar is only 28.5 percent.

Similarly, the Santal tribal Christians have been facilitated by the Mission to ascend the occupational ladder thanks to educational mobility with the result that thousands have been migrating to urban centres in the State and outside, being employed in better-paid jobs.

3.3 Christianity in Jharkhand (Chotanagpur)[79]

3.3.1 Socio-political and Economic Context

The term 'Chotanagpur' was used in all Government and Ecclesiastical records till the re-christening of the region into 'Jharkhand' (literally, hill tract) when it was made a separate State bifurcated from Bihar State in 2000. Though the State is considered a 'tribal State', the percentage of tribals is only 27.67 in a population of nearly 33 millions.[80] Some of the major tribes among the 30 tribal communities are the Santals who comprise 35.7% of the total tribal population in the State, followed by the Oraons, the Mundas, the Hos, besides the Bhumij, Kharia, Kharwar, Lohra, and others.[81]

The extreme economic backwardness of Jharkhand is indicated by its low per capita income and high poverty ratios in both rural and urban areas. Formerly the indigenous agrarian systems (*Khuntkatti* and *Bhuinhari*) generally ensured economic autonomy to the tribals until these were manipulated by the intruding "*dikus*" (outsiders--moneylenders, landlords, zamindars, etc), who appropriated much power from the tribals since the Mughal period.[82] The end of the 235-year-long British Colonial rule (since 1765) witnessed debilitating disintegration of the tribal system. Overall, the tribals and indigenous peoples of Jharkhand have suffered double colonialism: external colonialism of the British and internal colonialism of the dikus. The internal colonialism and marginalization of the tribals have continued even after Independence.

The exploitation and oppression of the tribals by the *diku* ruling class led to the migration of thousands of Adivasis from their villages to other places like Calcutta, or reduced them to landless labourers. Land alienation, social oppression, and suppression raged during early British Colonial rule. Tribals--Mundas, Hos, Oraons, and Santals protested and rebelled against the oppressive and exploitative systems prevailing among them in the 19th century. Several revolts took place in Chotanagpur: the *Kol Vidroh* (Kol Revolt) in 1831-32, the Bhumij Revolt in 1832-33, the *Santal Kul* (Santal Insurrection) in 1855-56, the *Sardar Larai* (Sardar Fight) from 1859-95, and *Birsa Andolan* (Birsa Revolution) from 1895-1900.[83] The Missionaries arrived among the Adivasis when the latter's socio-economic and political conditions were disturbed and they were losing confidence in their traditional religions.[84]

3.3.2 Missionary Engagement in Jharkhand

The arrival of Christian missionaries in Chotanagpur was an event of great importance in the history of Chotanagpur. Christian presence in Jharkhand began with the chaplaincy service by Anglican pastors from 1814. Their missionaries opened a Mission centre among the Paharias in Santal Parganas in 1826. By 1842, the Anglicans had established a Church at Hazaribagh. Wanting to move into more receptive tribal communities in Chotanagpur, the Gossner Evangelical Lutheran (GEL) Mission, which had already begun work in Bihar in 1838, came to Ranchi and founded a Mission centre there in 1845. The Catholic (Jesuit) missionaries started operations in 1869, followed by others.

The main Missions which worked in Chotanagpur are the Anglican Mission (1842), the GEL Mission (1845), the Santal Mission of the Northern Churches (1866), the Church Missionary Society (1868), the Catholic Mission, (1869), the Santal Mission of the United Free Church of Scotland (1869), the Fellowship of Christian Assemblies Mission (1880), the Methodist Church (1884), the Dublin University Mission (1892), the Seventh Day Adventist Mission (1898), the British Churches of Christ's Mission (1909) and the Assembly of God (1927). In the Post-Independence era, several denominational groups such as Christian Brethren, Watch Tower Mission, Mennonite Mission and scores of Pentecostal sections in very recent times, have begun Mission work in Jharkhand.[85]

Among these missionary groups, it was the GEL Mission and the Catholic Mission which were able to make a powerful, positive impression of Christianity among the tribals by offering them liberation from oppression by the landlords who were perceived to be hand in glove with the Colonial rulers. Receiving baptism was seen as a means to obtain agrarian security and social protection. Thousands of tribals sought baptism and this inaugurated a mass movement.[86]

Conversions generally followed ethnic or kin lines, facilitated by the converts themselves. For instance, Mundas facilitated Munda conversions in villages where they were concentrated. So also, Oraons, Kharias, Santals, and so on, facilitated conversions among their respective ethnic groups. This has had its limitations too: even after 150 years, only less than ten tribes among 30 tribes in Jharkhand have become members of the Church. The spread has been too limited by intra-tribe relations.

The mass movement in Jharkhand picked up momentum in late 1880s after the arrival of a zealous, hardworking, ingenious Jesuit missionary, Father Constant Lievens in Jharkhand. Already by 1885, there were eight stations in Chotanagpur run by the Belgian Catholic missionaries.[87] He championed the cause of the aboriginals against the landlords and money lenders, helping the oppressed win their cases at court.[88] He learned the Munda system, their traditional rights and claims which were sanctioned by their laws and customs. He made up his mind to help them, but at the same time to be prudent so as not to antagonize the Government.[89] Gradually, there began a 'mass movement' from the aborigines, seeking baptism. Besides the tribals belonging to native religions, hundreds of Lutherans also went over to the Catholic Mission.

Unfortunately, in 1891, the great missionary was attacked by tuberculosis and had to return to Belgium, where he died in 1893. But, before his death, there arrived new missionaries, such as John Baptist Hoffmann, Louis Van Hoeck, and others to carry on the work. Father Hoffmann began his missionary life in the Munda country of Sarwada, which made him keenly aware of the grave problems of injustice by the diku landlords, the lease holders and the moneylenders. And he rendered the greatest service to Chotanagpur through his extraordinary knowledge of the language and customs of the Mundas.[90] He wrote the *Encyclopedia Mundarica* which is a signal literary contribution. Hundreds of Schools, practically in all Catholic Villages, were established thanks to the leadership of Father Van Hoeck, who was the Director of Schools in the Chotanagpur Mission of the Jesuits.

Along with the Jesuits, several religious societies of Women (sisters/nuns) came to work in Jharkhand. Some of the earlier ones were the Loreto Sisters (1890), Daughters of St. Ann, which was founded in Ranchi (1897), Order of the Sisters of St. Usruline (1903), etc.

By 1935, when the Mission celebrated golden jubilee, the membership in the Catholic Church had become nearly 300,000. As per Census 2001, the Christian community comprises only 4.1% of the State population (33 millions) and is largely found in three Districts--Ranchi, Gumla and Simdega. Oraon, Munda, Kharia, Santal and Ho tribes comprise the largest tribal groups in the Christian community. A modest estimate of the numerical strength shows there are at least 18 lakhs tribal Christians (Catholics 12 lakhs and

Protestants 6 lakhs) who are spread not only in Jharkhand State, but also in the Andaman and Nicobar Islands, Assam, Bihar and several urban centres in North India.[91] From the perspective of rapidness of spread and rootedness of Christianity, one can say that Chotanagpur tribal Christian community is presently one of the most flourishing ethnic Christian communities in the World.[92] Overall, by early 1950s, the Chotanagpur Mission including the contiguous areas of Raigarh, Jashpur and Ambigapur in north-eastern Chattisgarh State, had grown into a well-founded Church in Eastern India.[93]

3.3.3 Factors that Facilitated High Growth of Christianity

The Christian missionaries in Chotanagpur may be credited for having created a landmark in the socio-economic life of the people of this area and opened up altogether a new chapter in which the activities of the missionaries made profound impact on the socio-economic and cultural life of the tribals in a number of significant ways.[94] Aside the evangelical efforts by the missionaries, there were major socio-economic, agrarian and legal factors which accelerated the growth of Christianity in Chotanagpur.

Studying the conversion movements in Chotanagpur, K. N. Sahay says that there were several positive and negative factors that led to conversion in large numbers. First, the condition of extortion and exploitation of the tribals by the landlords and others in the pre-missionary days, and the subsequent embracing of the Christian faith by the tribals can be seen as a bid to safeguard their age-long economic and social rights. The exploitation of the aboriginals, the infringement on their tenant rights and the demand of excessive *begari* labour were the most important factors which gave a favourable push to Christianity. "The people were subject to oppression for centuries and gradually a psychological background was created in which the people were ready to follow anyone who would help them in their troubles. The missionaries came at the right moment and the natives found in them a great defender of their rights and comforts."[95]

Sahay argues that Christian missionaries had been successful because of the support of the British Colonial Government. However, the fact of the matter is that except for the few Anglican and British missionaries, there was no direct support by the Colonial

Government. Certainly some individual Colonial administrators did sympathize with the oppressed tribals and encouraged the missionaries to undertake liberative work among them.

Tribal religions are usually animistic and belief in spirits, witchcraft and witch-doctor play an important role. Some sections of the people were chronically suffering from the dread of malevolent spirits and practiced witchcraft. They were compelled to sacrifice fowls and goats to appease the spirits and to satisfy the witch-doctors, which indeed was taxing on their resources. When the missionaries came to Chotanagpur they offered complete emancipation and exemption from such fears and superstitions. They assured the people that a spirit could not harm a Christian. The natives were thus impressed and convinced themselves that the only way to become free from the horror of spirits and witchcraft was acceptance of Christianity.[96]

To ameliorate the sufferings of the people, hospitals, dispensaries, and Leprosoria were opened by various Missions. Opening of schools, hostels, orphanages, vocational institutions, co-operative societies and other social works were other methods adopted in Christian conversion. Though these institutions were meant for the Christians, non-Christians also benefited from their services. The missionaries attached great importance to education as they realised that the progress of a society lies in moulding the character of young people.

According to Sahay, the method of Christian conversion created some controversies, providing a point of attack on the Christian missionaries in general. He argues that there was no doubt that a "handful of tribals" might have been genuinely moved by the preaching of Christianity but for a majority of them it was not the preaching, but protection and defense from the landlords and other such privileges, that motivated them to 'accept' the Christian faith.[97] Similarly, other critiques such as Ravi Bhushan Pandey have interpreted that these works were 'coercion', 'bluff and deception', or 'inducements' to elicit conversions.[98] By the same argument they tend to discredit the tribals' ability to make decisions by themselves, and to exercise freedom of conscience. Data on the impact of Christian institutions on Non-Christian students show that a vast majority of the beneficiaries have been Non-Christians and few among them were converted. The fact of the matter seems to be that Christian missionaries tried to bring salvation, of both body and soul, to the tribals. In other words, preaching Christianity included 'love of neighbour' in both material and spiritual terms.

3.3.4 Impact of Christian Missions

A significant and far reaching step towards making the tribals self-sufficient was the introduction of certain socio-economic measures such as establishing the Catholic Co-operative Credit Society (1909), Chotanagpur Co-operative Stores (1913), and Mutual Help Societies.[99] Influencing the Colonial Government to enact adequate laws, Father Hoffmann drafted the Chotanagpur Tenancy Act (1908), which was accepted entirely and enacted by the Government as an Act that empowers the tribals to prevent alienation of tribal land to non-tribals.[100] While other economic programmes of the Church did promote better paddy cultivation, use of green manure and so on, neither the missionaries, nor the tribals ventured into commerce and trade: two areas in which the non-tribal communities have dominated and the tribals have not proved themselves.[101]

A large network of schools at various levels was established which mediated the educational upward mobility of the tribals who were largely illiterate earlier. An estimate of the institutional services of the Catholic Church may be had from the following statistics (for late 1990s): eight Catholic Dioceses in Jharkhand had served several million people, especially lakhs of students, through 860 educational institutions (from kindergarten to college), 137 vocational and non-formal training centres, 186 health care centres, and 59 welfare centres, located under 645 Church centres using some 3200 voluntary Church personnel.[102]

Obviously, educational mobility led to occupational mobility, which entailed higher upward status.[103] Thousands of tribals hold well-placed Government jobs in urban centres all over India today. Better employment has led to out-migration and settlement in urban centers. Since the past two decades, employed tribal men and women comprise a considerable Christian population in several cities of north India. Besides, a large segment of Church leadership, in terms of clergy and nuns, including many Bishops serving in many dioceses in North and Eastern India, has come from the Church in Chotanagpur.

On the cultural front, Christianization in Chotanagpur did not entail any rupture in the cultural life of the tribals as it happened in Goa, during the Portuguese period of evangelization.[104] Religio-cultural values such as gender equality, dignity of women, consensual procedure in community actions, etc., were retained and encouraged. Cultural expressions such as singing, music, etc., were retained. Cultural identity markers such as traditional apparel, language, cuisine, art, etc., were continued.[105] That the Tribal Christians in Chotanagpur were not de-tribalised is evident in the retention of their nominal identity.[106] They have remained rooted in their tribal identity and indigenous culture even after change of religion.[107] In fact, tribal Christians in the region have been re-discovering some of the abandoned traditions and festivals to become fully indigenous Christians.[108] In recent times, with the impetus given for inculturating Christianity, they have been carefully studying the meanings behind these feasts and festivals and tend to integrate these in their life.[109] Of course, the recent re-evaluation and retention of certain indigenous practices and festivals by Christian tribals have been opposed by some Non-Christian tribals apparently under the influence of certain Hindutva organizations which, on the one hand, have been trying to divest the Christian tribals of their tribal identity, and Hinduize the Non-Christian tribals, on the other. Apparently, they latter want to create a wedge between Christian and Non-Christian tribals, whereas ethnically and culturally they were united.

Perhaps an area of life, which has not been adequately attended to, is political life. Entrenched in secluded life for centuries, the tribals in Chotanagpur were first brought into national political administration in the 17th century by the Mughals and later, by the British Colonial administrators. During the period of Christian influence, the tribals' political participation tended to be more pro-active and positive during the period, 1920-1960.

Political participation of the tribals as Christians can be traced to the early 1920s. What was founded (1920) by the Protestants, the *Unnati Samaj* (Development Society) also enlisted Catholic members in the beginning.[110] Smelling danger to the faith of the Catholics, the clerical leaders made the Catholics dissociate with the Samaj and eventually founded the *Catholic Sabha* (Catholic Association) in 1935. In 1939, under Jaipal Singh (a Non-Catholic Christian), the *Adibasi Mahasabha* was formed with the objective of creating a separate State of Jharkhand. This non-denominational political party was supported by Catholics and Non-Catholics alike. The Jharkhand Party was founded in 1950 as the political wing of the *Adibasi Mahasabha* with the aim of attracting the people of Chotanagpur and Santal Parganas into a wide political organization.[111] During the Post-Independence election in 1952 the Party fared well with many elected representatives of the people. But, the decline set in from 1962 when it merged into the then ruling Congress party, which led to the creation of a new Jharkhand Party under the leadership of N. E. Horo, a Lutheran.[112] However, due to inter-tribe and intra-tribe dissensions party members could not remain united. Given the fact that Christian tribals are more educated than their Non-Christian brethren, they should have had more leadership in politics. The trend seems to be to shy away from politics.

Within the Christian community there have been denominational characteristics: Protestants, though numerically less, have had larger political visibility than the Catholics. Further, due to a variety of reasons (as for example, high motivation to move out of an agrarian society into a bureaucratic society, advantages of remunerative employment in cities, dislike for troublesome political career, displacement .of natural tribal leadership by clergy and religious, etc.) seem to have made the Catholics prefer employed occupations to politics.[113]

Overall, the Christian presence in Chotanagpur has been dynamic, transformative and has effected tremendous socio-economic, educational and religio-cultural changes among a large segment of the tribal population. Through its substantial service-oriented institutions, the Church has been an agent of social change in the wider society as well.

4. Sources and Chapterisation

This study is based on authentic sources, both Mission/Church and Government, as can be noted in the classified Bibliography.

An exhaustive list of secondary sources has also been given in the Bibliography. Besides, the Appendix-1 is envisaged to facilitate a researcher to familiarize with some of the rare Church sources.

This being a book of Christian History, chronological sequence, beginning with the first Mission to the last, has been followed in the chapterisation. Chapter 1 deals with the first Christian Mission in undivided Bihar—the Catholic Mission in Bihar, followed by the Catholic Mission in Jharkhand, in Chapter 2. It is observed that the present-day Catholic Church in Bihar was nourished by two missionary societies, namely the Capuchins (1703-1919) and the Jesuits (1919-ff). Along with these leading societies, were some of the Congregations of women such as the IBMV Sisters, the Holy Cross Sisters, the Loreto Sisters, the Sisters of St. Joseph of Champery, the Sisters of the Sacred Heart, the Medical Mission Sisters, the Apostolic Carmel Sisters, the Sisters of Charity of Nazareth, and the Notre Dame Sisters, who began to work in Bihar before 1950.

The leading Catholic Mission organization which worked in Jharkhand was the Ranchi Jesuit Society, which was an extension of the Bengal Jesuit Mission. The leadership role played by the Belgian Jesuits to establish a strong, large, self-sufficient Catholic community in Jharkhand is a powerful example of capacity building, human resource management and religious philanthropy. The Jharkhand Catholic community is one of the most flourishing and lively Christian communities in the world today.

Chapter 3 gives details of the earliest Protestant Mission society in Bihar: the Baptist Church, which is numerically second largest in Bihar, after the Catholic Church. The Baptists are still active in Bihar. Chapter 4 describes the early founding and development of the Church Missionary Society, which operated in both Bihar and Jharkhand. Chapter 5 studies in detail the second largest Church in Jharkhand, namely the Gossner Evangelical Lutheran (GEL) Church, which was also one of the first Christian Missions to enter that State (1845). Closely related to the GEL Church is the Anglican Church (Chapter 6) in Jharkhand, a majority of whose members emerged out of a split in the GEL Church in 1868. At the time of its formation in 1869, its membership consisted of nearly 50% of the total converts of the GEL Church.

In Chapters 7 and 8 we get the details of two Mission organizations respectively, the Santal Mission of the Northern Churches and the Santal Mission of the United Free Church of Scotland. As the nominal identity of the organizations indicates they focused on the Santals of Jharkhand and Bihar. Both organizations contributed to the development of the Santals, the largest tribal community in India. Among the two, the first society was noted for its work among the diaspora Santals in Assam, as well as among the Boros there. Though limited in numerical strength of missionary personnel, it achieved wonderful progress both in attracting a large number of Santals to Christianity and in making lasting contributions to Santali language and literature. Similarly, the latter Mission also made some valuable contribution to Santali language and literature.

Chapter 9 deals with the Dublin University Mission which earned the unique distinction of starting the first Christian college (St. columba's college) in undivided Bihar, in 1899, at Hazaribagh. Being born in a University campus in Ireland, this Mission was oriented to higher education from the beginning. Finally, Chapter 10 describes the activities of seven smaller Missions which worked in Bihar or in Jharkhand or in both. Notable among them was the Zenana Bible and Medical Mission from England which earned the unique distinction of being in health service, particularly to women. The Methodist Church also did pioneering work in Bihar, being the first Christian missionary society to work among the Dalits in Bihar. The concluding section gives a summary of the ten chapters with some interpretations.

Endnotes and References

1 At the outset I would make some conceptual clarifications regarding 'Christian community' and 'Christian Mission' as these terms are used frequently in this book. While the former means the community of Christians including both the lay members and the clerical or religious leaders besides their church/parish organization, institutions, etc., of a local church/parish/diocese/nation, the latter means a missionary society which initially establishes Mission centres and the related church institutions such as a church (building) for community worship,

schools, hostels, hospitals, etc. An organized missionary society which is affiliated to a particular Christian denomination (as for instance, the Catholic Church, the Gossner Church, the Baptist Church, etc) is indicated by the term 'Mission' (with a capital M), and is to be differentiated from 'mission' which means the objective of a missionary. So also, a Church (with Capital C) is a distinct denomination within the Christian religion, whereas 'church' means the physical structure of worship of the Christian community. A Church may, thus, send a Mission with a mission to evangelize a people group in a particular region, to baptize those who are desirous of becoming members of that Mission/Church and to build up a local Christian community of that Church (denomination). As the title of the book indicates, the narrative in this book is predominantly of the various Christian Missions which started their respective Christian institutions and gathered their respective groups of converts, who, eventually matured to become a local Christian community.

2 In this book, the term 'Chotanagpur' and 'Jharkhand' are interchangeably used to indicate the present-day territory of Jharkhand State. In some old records one may notice the bifurcation of 'Chotanagpur' into 'Chota' and 'Nagpur' which reduces the unity of the term.

3 *Padroado* literally means patronage. It was an institution for Christian evangelization instituted in late 15th century. Two most powerful Catholic countries (Spain and Portugal) undertook the task of evangelization, with the permission of the Pope, in 1493. The authority of *Padroado* implied assuming complete responsibility for governance including financial support of the missionaries and institutions of the Catholic Church which may be founded in those areas wherever these Colonial powers established themselves, besides jurisdiction over the Missions in these parts. Thus, the Eastern World (means, Africa and Asia) was assigned to the Portuguese *Padroado* and the West (of the Iberian Peninsula: the Americas) was assigned to the Spanish *Padroado*. Eventually, the *Padroados* appropriated much of the authority of the Missions across the world so much so that the pope became powerless to exercise his spiritual and religious authority over the Catholics in Padroado areas. Hence, the pope himself created a new department for evangelization, known as *Propaganda Fide* (Propagation of the Faith) in 1622, which sent its own missionaries independently. This created much clash in the Mission fields in India and elsewhere between the two institutions in late 17th-late 19th centuries. This unsavoury relation between the Portuguese *Padroado* in India and the Vatican created

rift among the Catholic communities as well and erupted into open clashes in Churches within the Latin Rite communities and between the Goa-based Latin authority and the Syrian Church in Kerala: see Jonas Thaliath (1958), *The Synod of Diamper;* Dr. Scaria Zacharia (ed.) (1994), *The Acts and Decrees of the Synod of Diamper, 1599;* and notes #7, below.

4 The idea of India was constructed from a European perspective through a series of writings. Teltscher's study of these writings are noteworthy. Kate Teltscher's (1995), *India Inscribed: European and British Writing on India, 1600-1800.*

5 This is a broad classification based on major themes of some 150 works. Some categories may have overlapping themes. More rigorous criterion of classification may find several additional themes: Jose Kalapura (2009), "Christianity and Marginalised Communities in India," in *Indian Church History Review,* Vol. XLIII, No. 1, June, pp. 7-36. Also see two recent studies on Christian Historiography: John C.B. Webster, *Historiography of Christianity in India*, Oxford University Press, New Delhi, 2012; Chad M. Bauman (2011), "Indian Christian Historiography from Below, from Above, and in Between", *Church History*, Jan. 2011, pp. 622-629: Available at: http://works.bepress.com/chad_bauman/37 , accessed May 1, 2013.

6 For instance, Abbe Dubois (1995), *Letters on the State of Christianity in India: To which is Added A Vindication of the Hindu Male and Female*; Ines G. Zupanov (1998), "The Prophetic and the Miraculous in Portuguese Asia: A Hagiographical View of Colonial Culture," in Sanjay Subramaniam (ed), *Sinners and Saints: The Successors of Vasco da Gama,* pp. 135-169; Teltscher (1995), op. cit.

7 The body of literature of this period can also be categorised into the first one. However, there were works of ethnographic value in this category: Rev. M. A. Sherring (1884), *The History of Protestant Missions in India: From Their Commencement in 1706 to 1881*; J. J. Weitbrecht (1844), *Protestant Missions in Bengal Illustrated: Being the Substance of a Course of Lectures Delivered on India Missions.*

8 On resistance in Kerala, see Jacob Kollamparambil (1981), *The St. Thomas Christians' Revolution in 1653*; Francis Thonippara, CMI (1999), *Saint Thomas Christians of India: A Period of Struggle for Unity and Self-Rule* (1775-1787); A. M. Mundadan, CMI (1984), *Indian Christians Search for Identity & Struggle for Autonomy*; on protest in Goa, see Dr. Pratima Kamat (2013), "Priestly Protests against the Portuguese 'Pigmentocracy': The Case of the first Goan Bishop, D.

Matheus de Castro" *Indian Church History Review,* Vol. XLVII, No. 2, pp. 118-140; Pratima Kamat (1999), *Farar Far- Local Resistance to Colonial Hegemony in Portuguese Goa, 1510-1961.*

9 For a discussion on nationalist struggle of Christians in India against Colonial and European Church administrators, see George Mathew (1979), *Christian Indians and Indian Nationalism, 1885-1950.* Also there were instances, when the movement of Indians was supported by European missionaries: see C. F. Andrews (1908), *Handbook of English Church Expansion: North India*; George Studdert-Kennedy (1998), *Providence & the Raj: Imperial Mission and Missionary Imperialism.*

10 For instance, see Fr. Jerome D' Souza (1957), *Sardar Panikkar and Christian Missions.*

11 For instance, P. C. Jain (1995), *Christianity, Ideology and Social Change Among Tribals*; Dasarathi Swarno (1990), *The Christian Missionaries in Orissa: Their Impact on Nineteenth Century Society*; Augustine Kanjamala (1981), *Religion and Modernisation: A Case Study of Northern Orissa*; S. K. Bhattacharya (1999), *Christian Missions, Missionaries and Indian Society: A Socio-Economic Study*; Dick Kooiman (1989), *Conversion and Social Equality in India: The London Missionary Society in South Travancore in the 19th Century*; K. P. Sengupta (1971), *The Christian Missionaries in Bengal, 1793-1833*; Frederick S. Downs (1992), *History of Christianity in India, Vol. V, Part 5 (North East India in the 19th and 20th Centuries).*

12 For instance, the anthropological study of cultural process: see K. N. Sahay (1986), *Christianity and Culture Change in India*; S. Estborn (1959), *Our Village Christians: A Study of the Life and Faith of Village Christians in Tamil Nadu.*

13 Some of these are on themes of change while some others are change and continuity. C. J. Godwin (1972), *Change and Continuity: A Study of Two Christian Village Communities in Suburban Bombay*; Rowena Robinson (1998), *Conversion, Continuity and Change: Lived Christianity in Southern Goa*; Olivinho J. F. Gomes (1987), *Village Goa, A Study of Goan Social Structure and Change*; Elsie Baptista (1967), *The East Indians: Catholic Community of Bombay, Salsette and Bassein, Bandra*; G. A. Oddie (ed) (1991), *Religion in South Asia: Religious Conversion and Revival Movements in South Asia in Medieval and Modern Times*; John C. B. Webster (1976), *The Christian Community and Change in Nineteenth Century North India.*

14 Kalapura (2009), "Christianity and Marginalised:" op. cit.

15 The subaltern group of scholars have produced a 12-volume work which is scholarly and totally from a subaltern perspective on Indian history. For a discussion on 'subaltern' see Ranajit Guha (ed.) (1982), *Subaltern Studies* 1: *Writings on South Asian History and Society*, (Preface), p 8.

16 V. V. Thomas (2006), *Understanding Subaltern History: Theoretical Tools.*

17 Ibid., pp. 1,38-44

18 On conversion and social equality India: Dick Kooiman (1989), *Conversion and Social Equality in India: The London Missionary Society in South Travancore in the 19th Century*; On the social settings of Christian conversion in South India: Manickam Sundararaj (1977), *The Social Setting of Christian Conversion in South India: The Impact of the Wesleyan Methodist Missionaries on the Trichy–Tanjore Diocese with Special Reference to the Harijan Communities of the Mass Movement Area* 1820-1947; Walter Fernandes (1981), "Caste and Conversion Movements India", *Social Action,* Vol. 31, No. 3, pp 261-290; On religious conversion as social protest: Oddie (ed), (1991), op. cit; Downs (1992), op. cit; John C. B. Webster (1992), *The Dalit Christians: A History.*

19 See bibliography in George Oommen & John C. B. Webster (2002), *Local Dalit Christian History*, pp 147-150.

20 For a list of studies related to conversion, protest movements and change, one may refer to the select bibliography compiled by M. R. Mac who lists some 424 works (books and articles). M. R. Mac (1989), Conversion, *Protest Movements & Change: A Select Bibliography (With Special Reference to Christianity in India),* Centre for Social Studies, Surat. Also the bibliography of Satyaprakash is worth examining as sources for Christian Historiography. Many works on Christianity have been published since the publication of this book: See Satyaprakash (1986), *Christianity: A Select Bibliography.*

21 This is a reflection on the discussion that was held at the concluding seminar on "Mission and Evangelism Study Project," at the Centre for Rural Health and Social Education, Yelagiri Hills, Tamil Nadu, from June 22-27, 1998, organised by the Study Programme of the Ecumenical Charitable Trust founded by the late Dr. M. M. Thomas: see Thomas (2006), op. cit. p 35.

22 Emmanuel, David (1986), "History of Christianity in India: Changing Perspective," *Indian Church History Review (ICHR)*, 30 (No. 1) p. 5.

23 The Church History Association of India's attempt at writing a series on the *History of Christianity in India* proposes to take a people's perspective

approach. But for a critique, see Felix Wilfred (2009), "Historiography of Indian Christianity", *Vidyajyoti Journal of Theological Reflection*, Vol. 73, No. 10, Oct., pp. 737-751. Also, Thomas (2006), op. cit. p. 47

24 K. G. Daniel (1998), *Let the Hills Rejoice: The Conversion of the Hill Arayans of Kerala and Its Effect on Evangelism.*

25 Rev. T. S. Samuelkutty (2000), *The Place and Contribution of Dalits in Select Pentecostal Churches in Central Kerala from 1922 to 1972.*

26 F. Hrangkhuma & C. H. Sebastian Kim (Ed.) (1999), *The Church in India: Its Missions Tomorrow.*

27 Mathias Mundadan (2001), *History of Christianity in India, Vol. I: From the Beginning to the Middle of the Sixteenth Century (up to 1542),* p viii.

28 P. C. Horo (1976), **"**Christian Missions and Communities in Bihar**"**, in Kali Kinkar Datta (ed), *The Comprehensive History of Bihar* Vol-III, Part-II, (Historical Research Series Vol. XIV), K. P. Jayaswal Research Institute, Patna, pp. 109-292. This long article seems to be a version of his doctoral thesis which was submitted to Patna University in June 1976.

29 George Mark Moraes (1964), *A History of Christianity in India from Early times to St. Francis Xavier: AD 52-1552*, p. 25.

30 It is well-known that the Jewish community in India (in Kerala) had migrated during the Roman occupation of Palestine. Based on archaeological, anthropological and etymological evidences, Abraham Benhur says that some of the first converts in Kerala were Jews: See Abraham Benhur (2011), *The Jewish Background of Indian People.*

31 Moraes (1964), op. cit., p. 26.

32 A. C. Perumalil (1952), *The Apostles in India,* p. 71.

33 Arab merchant Suleiman mentioned this in A.D. 851: see C. E. Abraham (2004), "The Rise and Growth of Christianity in India" in *Cultural-Religious Heritage-India,* Vol. 8, p. 18.

34 It may be noted that 'Christians of St. Thomas' was the name usually applied to these people who in more modem times are known as Syrian Christians, on account of their connection with the Syriac-speaking Churches in the East, and the use of Syriac as their ecclesiastical language.

35 A. Mathias Mundadan, C.M.I. (1984), "*Indian Christians*", op. cit..

36 Abraham (2004), op. cit., p. 18; Benedict Vadakkekara (2007), *Origin of Christianity in India: A Historiographical Critique*; George Nedungatt, SJ (2008), *Quest for the Historical Thomas Apostle of India: A Re-reading of the Evidence.*

37 J. N. Farquhar (1972), "The Apostle Thomas in South India", pp. 32 ff, A more recent historian makes the following comment on the St. Thomas tradition: The tradition of the Malabar Christians is so ancient and continuous as to deserve a reasonable share of probability: D. Ferroli (1951), *The Jesuits in Malabar,* Vol. I. p. 58.

38 For instance, community histories or peoples' histories can be largely dependent on oral traditions, as for instance, the tribal or indigenous communities who may have non-literate, non-written cultures. Can we deny that they existed on this earth for thousands of years before the historical periods? See Laurice Mercier & Madeline Buckendorf (1992), *Using Oral History in Community History Projects.*

39 Perumalil (1971), op. cit, p. 150.

40 Abraham (2004), op. cit., p. 19.

41 Ibid., pp. 19-20.

42 Perumalil, H. C. and E. R. Hambye (1972), *Christianity in India: A History in Ecumenical Perspective.*

43 J. de Marignolli, who stayed at Quilon for over a year, writes: 'On Palm Sunday (1348) we arrived at a very noble city of India called Quilon, where the whole world's pepper is produced ... Nor are the Saracens the proprietors, but the Christians of St. Thomas, and these latter are the masters of the public weighing office from which I derived as a perquisite of my office as Pope's Legate, every month a hundred gold fanams and a thousand when I left ...: see Ferroli, S. J. (1951), *The Jesuits in Malabar,* Vol.I, p. 66.

44 Daniel D'souza, *A History of the Catholic Church in North India* (Till 1757), p. 15.

45 Moraes (1964), op. cit, p. 85.

46 Ibid., p. 88.

47 This was brought under the Diocese of Funchal in Portugal in 1515, and later suppressed when the Diocese of Goa was created in 1534.

48 The Portuguese power was at its peak in the 16th and 17th centuries. But in the 18th century, their power declined politically, while other European powers such as England, France, Netherlands emerged as bigger powers. The decline of the Portuguese also negatively affected the Padroado-supported evangelization in India. Besides, in 1759, the Portuguese authorities blatantly suppressed the Jesuit Society in their empire and colonies which affected Mission work in India. They and other powers ensured that the most powerful missionary society of the period, the Jesuit Society, was suppressed world-wide in 1773 which

put a stop to some 3000 Mission centres in the world. Hence the year 1773 can be considered a landmark in Mission history.

49 Abraham (2004), op. cit. pp. 22-23.

50 Among the Jesuit scholar-missionaries were Robert De Nobili, Constantius Beschi, Earnesto Hanxladen, Thomas Stephens, Henry Roth, and others. Among the scientist-missionaries were Jean Francois Pons, Gaston Coeurdoux, Joseph Tieffenthaller, Johann Grueber, Claude Boudier, Gabelsberger and others who contributed much to Indian astronomy, mathematics, science and geography. See a study by Jose Kalapura (2006), "East-West Interaction and Development of Modern Science in India: Jesuit Mediation during 16-19th Centuries," pp. 493-513.

51 Jose Kalapura, 2012, "Christianity, Colonial Globalization of Culture: An Indian Experience with Special Reference to Malabar Christians," in George Menachery & Oberland Snaitang (eds.), *Christianity and Cultural Encounter*, pp. 178-198.

52 Abraham (2004), op. cit., p 21.

53 Ibid., p. 24.

54 Ibid., p. 36, quoting Kenneth Scott Latourette (1940), A History of the Expansion of Christianity, Volume-VI; William Carey (1888), A *Missionary Tour in the Hughli and Howrah and Districts.*

55 Abraham (2004), op. cit., pp. 24-25.

56 Ibid., p. 37.

57 Dharmaraj, J. S. (1993), Colonialism and Christian Mission.

58 Abraham (2004), op. cit., p. 38.

59 Latourette (1971), op. cit, p. 110.

60 Some of the best known colleges are, Madras Christian College, Wilson College (Bombay), Women's Christian College (Chennai), Malabar Christian College (Calicut), CMS College (Kottayam), Ewing Christian College (Allahabad), American College (Madura), St. Stephen's College, Delhi, etc. There were also famous Catholic Colleges: St. Joseph's College, Trichinopally, St. Xavier's College, Kolkata, St. Xavier's College, Mumbai, Loyola College, Chennai, etc.

61 For a detailed study of the early history of the Catholic Mission in Chotanagpur, see H. Josson, S.J.(1993), *The Mission of West Bengal or The Archdiocese of Calcutta*, Belgian Province of the Society of Jesus, Trans by L. Clarysse.

62 Robert E. Frykenberg (2008), *Christianity in India: From Beginnings to the Present*; Samuel H. Moffett (1992), *A History of Christianity in Asia*, Vol. I; Samuel H. Moffatt (2006), *A History of Christianity in Asia, Volume 11: 1500-1900.*

63 A. J. Osta (1959), *Tibet-Hindustan Mission.*

64 Jose Kalapura (2000), "King, Fort, Zamindaris and Missionaries: The founding of Bihar's Oldest Christian Community, 1745," in *Proceedings of the Indian History Congress,* p. 1011-1028.

65 Fulgentius Vannini (1981), *Hindustan- Tibet Mission.*

66 Jose Kalapura (1999), *Religion and Community: The Making of the Bettiah and Ravidasi Christians in Bihar.*

67 Fulgentius Vannini (1979), op. cit.

68 Henry Pascual Oiz (1991), Blessed by the Lord, A History of the Patna Jesuits, 1921-1981.

69 About 50 percent of the 23,000 Catholics in Purnea Diocese and 50 percent of the 80,000 Catholics of Bhagalpur Diocese could be Santals, the rest being other tribals: see *Catholic Directory of India, 2005-06* (2006).

70 *Mass movement,* a term coined by the Protestant missionaries to mean mass conversion to Christianity which began in the 1870s. Waskom J. Picket (1938), *Christian Mass Movements in India.*

71 Vasantraj Albert (1992), *Bihar Church and People Groups.*

72 *Directory of Patna Diocese* (1998).

73 *Directory of Patna Diocese* (2004).

74 Jose Kalapura (2011), “Christianity in Bihar: Origin, Development and Challenges”, in Joy Kaipan, sdb (ed), *Studies on the History of the Church in India*, pp. 77-97.

75 A majority of the working men, till about the 1940s, was active in carpentry, blacksmithy and carting, irrespective of their pre-conversion caste-based occupations. However, by the 1990s, Bettiah Christians had moved out of carpentry, blacksmithy, carting, etc.,-a vast majority (80%) of them being in blue and white-collar jobs, particularly teaching (34%). See Jose Kalapura (2006), "Cooperatives and Community Development: A Study of Champaran in Bihar," *Jharkhand Journal of Development and Management Studies,* Vol. 4, 1: pp. 1805-1818.

76 Swapan Kumar Nandi (1976), "Impact of Christianity on the Chamars of Majhwaja, a Bhojpur Village," *Journal of Social Research,* Vol. 19, no. 1; Also, Nicholas J Pollard (1936), "Whither Outcaste India?" in *Patna Mission Letter*, Aug-Sept, 1936.

77 Jose Kalapura (2006), "Dignity Re-discovered: Christians in Eastern India," in *Indian Christian Directory,* pp. 124-129.

78 Jose Kalapura (1999), "Change of Socio-Economic Structure: A Paradigm of Dalit Mobility: A Case Study of the Ravidasis of Bihar,"

in *Dalits and Peasants: The Emerging Caste-Class Dynamics,* ed. Ashish Ghosh (hereinafter, *Dalit Mobility*), pp. 166-202.

79 The entire Chotanagpur plateau was considered as one unit because similar social and ethnic identities of the tribes there. The original Chotanagpur included 18 districts of Bihar, 3 districts of West Bengal, 4 districts of Orissa, and 2 districts of Eastern Madhya Pradesh. When the new State was created only the 18 districts of Bihar was carved out.

80 As per *Census of India 2011.*

81 Nadim Hasnain (1992), *Janjatiya Bharat*: 3rd Edition.

82 Mangobinda Banerjee (1993), *An Historical Outline of Pre-British Chotanagpur*, p. 150.

83 See detailed study of the Tribal revolts in Sunil Kumar Singh (2005), *Inside Jharkhand,* pp. 39-69.

84 Nirmal Minz (1998),"Christianity among the Mundas, Oraons, and Kharias of Chotanagpur" in Hrangkhuma (ed), Christianity in India, p. 22.

85 Jose Kalapura (2011), "Church in Jharkhand: Mediating Social Transformation among Tribals", in Joy Kaipan, sdb (ed*), Studies on the History of the Church in India,* p. 135; *Ranchi Catholic Archdiocese,"*(1995); Vasantharaj Albert (1992), *Bihar Church and People Groups.*

86 Dr. S. Mahto (1971), *Hundred years of Christian Missions in Chotanagpur since 1845*, p. 37.

87 Clarysse, L.(1985), *Father Constant Lievens.*

88 Fidelis De Sa (1975), *Crisis in Chotanagpur;* Latourette (1971), p. 85.

89 Peter Tete S.J. (1986), *A Missionary Social Worker in India*: Fr. J. B. Hoffmann: The Chotanagpur Tenancy Act and the Catholic Co-operatives, p. 26.

90 Ibid., cover page.

91 Kalapura (2011), "Church in Jharkhand", op. cit., p. 134.

92 Kalapura (2006), "Dignity Re-discovered", op. cit., pp. 124-129.

93 Christianity spread in these regions from Ranchi: Boniface Tirkey (2001), *Jashpur mein Isaai Samudaya ka Prarambhik* (The Beginnings of the Christian Community in Jashpur).

94 Sahay (1986), op. cit., p. 81.

95 Ibid., pp. 94-96.

96 Ibid., pp. 96-98.

97 Ibid., pp. 97-103.

98 Ravi Bhushan Pandey (2005), *Christianity and Tribes in India,* especially Chapter 6, pp. 175-222 and Chapter 7, 223-240: Pandey seems to have subscribed to the views of K. N. Sahay in interpreting humanitarian works as inducements.

99 Michael Vanden Bogaert (1986), "Social Transformation of a Tribal Society: Fallout of Evangelization in Chotanagpur," *Sevartham,* Vol. 11, pp. 26, 30.

100 T. Van Der Schuerer (1928), *Moral & Intellectual Uplift of the Aboriginal Races of Chotanagpur.*

101 Kalapura (2011), "Church in Jharkhand", op. cit., p. 142.

102 *The Catholic Directory of India 2005-06* (2006), pp. 35-41.

103 Jose Kalapura (2003), "Church in Chotanagpur: Mediating Change through Education," in Beni Ekka, H. K. Singh, V. P. Sharan, & Anirudh Prasad (eds), *The Catholic Church in Jharkhand: A Mediator of Change,* pp 197-221.

104 Portuguese missionaries tried to westernize Indian converts by imposing their culture on them in every aspect of life. This was called Lucitanization because when Portugal was under the ancient Roman rule, it was known as Lucitania.

105 While the earlier foreign missionaries insisted on giving up many indigenous customs and festivals, along with spirit-worship and witchcraft, later on those aspects of culture and religion were permitted which did not go against the values of Christianity. See Minz (1998), op. cit., pp. 14-38.

106 Retention of surnames such as Ekka, Minz, Tete, Soren, Tirkey, etc.

107 Kalapura (2011), "Church in Jharkhand", op. cit., p. 145.

108 For a discussion on the process of Christianization among the Chotanagpur tribals, see Sahay (1986), op. cit.

109 Jose Kalapura (2010), "Margins of Faith": Dalits and Tribal Christians in Eastern India", in (eds) Rowena Robinson & Joseph Marianus Kujur, *Margins of Faith: Dalit and Tribal Christianity in India,* pp. 75-96.

110 Mahto (1971), op. cit.

111 G. S., Munda (2000), *Caste Dynamics and Tribal Society,* pp. 24-37.

112 For a discussion see Nirmal Minz (2007), "Understanding Tribal Identities in Jharkhand," in (eds) Joseph Marianus Kujur & Sonajharia Minz, *Pearls of Indigenous Wisdom,* pp. 41-49.

113 Kalapura (2010), "Church in Jharkhand", op. cit., p. 146.

Chapter 1

The Catholic Mission in Bihar

1. First Phase: Jesuit Mission, 1620

The earliest Christian Mission to enter Bihar was the Catholic Mission which made Patna the centre of its missionary work. It was, therefore, known as Patna Mission.[1] It was a Jesuit Mission (Mission organized and managed by the members of the Society of Jesus).

In 1620, Emperor Jahangir appointed one Nawab Mukarrab Khan as the Viceroy of Patna.[2] Nawab Mukarrab Khan had previously been the Mughal ambassador to the Court of Portuguese Governor Don Aleixo de Meneses at Goa. While at Goa, this ambassador was baptized in the Catholic faith by Fr. Nicholas Pimenta, S. J., in the Jesuit College of Goa.[3]

On his next appointment as Viceroy of Patna, Mukarrab Khan or Lord John summoned friendly Portuguese traders[4] there and from them, learned of the presence in Bengal of a few Jesuit Priests. He desired to have these Priests with him at his Court as they were present in the Court of the Mughal Emperor Jahangir[5] at Delhi at that time, and he wrote them letters of invitation.

Accordingly, Jesuit Fr. Simon Figuieredo, S.J., came to Patna from the Jesuit centre in Bengal and was received with much pomp and ceremony.[6] According to Paul Dent, the Nawab invited the Priest to look for a proper site for a church. "He also requested him to kindly submit to a custom in use among the Nobles and Viceroys of the Moghul Empire. It was their custom he said, to offer a splendid banquet to their guests. Thereupon, he pressed on the father's acceptance a purse containing a hundred rupees....Out of civility the Father acquiesced, and retired to one of the houses along the Ganges which the Nawab had caused to be prepared for his lodgings. The apartments were adorned with great luxury and spread with carpets of the highest price.... He assigned for the support of the Father the income of a village which yielded at least 500 tangams a year...."[7]

"The following day the Viceroy came in person to visit the Father. Drawing him into a secret apartment he told him that he was a Christian. It was he who was at Goa in the time of Ray Larenco, Viceroy of India, and there he was baptized. He added that he had sent for him to make his confession and to have a church built that he might live like a true Christian."[8]

Fr. Simon Figuieredo was given full freedom to preach Christianity. So long as the Father remained in the city, the Portuguese merchants would frequent it, and the Viceroy did not object to trading with them. He also said that he did not profess openly to be a Christian because he was afraid of losing his position as Governor.[9]

However, the Father encountered much opposition from the Muslim gentry.[10] After four people were converted, his residence was attacked by a young Muslim fanatic, who killed the door-keeper, a Bengali Catholic named Amadore, and then, a young Catholic named Gonsalvo who had come out to rescue Amadore and finally wounded the Father himself very badly. The Viceroy inflicted death penalty on the murderer and this caused even more opposition to the Father's work in the city. Due to growing hostility by the Muslim gentry, the Father left Patna in 1621.[11] Thus, the Jesuit beginnings of Patna Mission was short-lived.[12] After the Mission was abandoned, a few Jesuit missionaries occasionally visited the city. No other priest is reported resident in the city until 1707, when the second Patna Mission commenced, not by Jesuits, but by Capuchins.

2. Second Phase: Capuchin Mission, 1703-1919

2.1 Tibet-Hindustan Mission

In 1703, the *Propaganda Fide*[13] erected the new Prefecture of Tibet[14] which included the Kingdom of Tibet and the surrounding territories. This was entrusted to the Franciscan missionaries (Capuchins) of the Italian Province of Picenum in Ancona.[15] A Prefect, Fr. John Francis of Camerino, was then chosen, with five companions to assist him: Frs. Felix of Mustachio, Joseph of Ascoli, Francis Mary of Tours, Joseph Mary of Fossombrone and Bro. Fiacre of Paris. The team left Rome in 1704 and started on a trying journey by land and sea via Alexandria, Palestine, Mesopotamia, Persia and Surat, arriving at last in 1706 at the French colony of Chandernagore in Bengal. All could not reach the destination. Prefect Fr. John Francis himself became ill and he died in Mesopotamia. So Fr. Felix of Mustachio was made Prefect and Superior in his place.

From Chandernagore, Fr. Joseph of Ascoli and Fr. Francis Mary of Tours pushed on to Patna, at that time a good month's journey distant.[16] On January 11, 1707 (the very year the last great Mughul Emperor, Aurangzeb, died), the team went on towards Lhasa and reached there five months later, after an arduous journey mostly on foot through Darbhanga in north Bihar, Katmandu and Kuti. In the same year (1707), fresh recruits came from Europe. Coming on to Patna, they met Fr. Francis Mary of Tours who was then there and took one of the new Fathers to Lhasa. After five months' stay at Lhasa, Fr. Francis Mary of Tours returned to Patna.[17]

Since the Mission of the Capuchins was Tibet, they set up only a transit house at Patna only as a transit centre. The first two Fathers who began to reside at Patna were Fr. Joachim da Loreto and Fr. Pietro da Petrona.[18] When they reached Patna, they found Fr. Felix of Montecchio caring for the few Catholics in the city, mostly European traders and their native servants. In 1713, they set up a house and built a church at Patna.[19] This small church, known as Padre-ki-Haveli, in

Patna City (old capital of Bihar)[20] continued to serve Patna until the opening of the present Cathedral on December 8, 1779.

Frs. Joseph of Ascoli and Francis Mary of Tours seem to have died before 1717. In 1734, Fr. Joachim of San Anatolia is reported to have been in charge of Patna where he served some six or seven hundred Catholics, traders and soldiers coming and going in the city.[21] In 1739, Fr. Joseph Mary[22] arrived at Patna from Chandernagore. He knew German, Portuguese, French and other languages and he was very keen in studying Hindi. He was also a skilled medical practioner and the reputation of his healing went far and wide.

2.2 Founding of the Bettiah Mission, 1745

The Capuchin Mission in Bihar founded a new centre at Bettiah town, Capital of the Kingdom of Bettiah in North Bihar, which had a flourishing Christian community later on. The story of its founding is as follows. In Bettiah, perhaps late in 1739, the Raja Dhurup Singh quarreled with his brother, and cut off his head "near a tree in front of the palace".[23] The Brahmans accused him of irremissible sin which would bring down ruin on his whole family. They pointed out that the spirit of his murdered brother was living in that tree and would constantly molest the royal family. Therefore, he would have to build a temple near the tree and also erect near the same several houses for Brahmans who would offer daily sacrifices for the soul of his brother in order that it might leave the royal family in peace. It was done by the Raja.

Then the Rani fell ill[24] and it was thought that she was being tormented by the spirit of the dead prince. The Raja omitted nothing in order to cure her but all in vain. In the meantime, he heard about the Christian Priests (Fathers) at Patna. He sent messengers to Patna requesting the Fathers to come to Bettiah assuring them that their journey would not go unrewarded. Twice they refused his request as they were new to the country and they did not know the local language. The Raja sent his servants for the third time begging the Fathers to visit Bettiah and cure the sick queen.

Fr. Joseph Mary, a healer-Priest, then made up his mind to go, and taking an interpreter along, arrived at Bettiah after five days in 1740.[25] The Raja embraced him and told him about the trouble through the Interpreter. The Rani suffered merely from a few cancerous ulcers in her throat. The Father prescribed a medicine which completely cured her of throat ailment in a fortnight to the great joy of the Raja and the whole royal family.[26] The grateful Raja begged him to remain in Bettiah and build a Mission house there.

Fr. Joseph Mary refused and advised the Raja to seek the permission of the Church authorities in Rome for a Mission in Bettiah.[27] He then returned to Patna. He frequently visited Bettiah after that. It is said that during his two years in Patna, Father Joseph Mary visited Bettiah seven times at the request of the Raja there.

Sometime in 1741, Fr. Vito[28] passed through Bettiah, probably enroute to Patna from Bhatgaon or Katmandu, and the Raja called him to his presence. He made the same request for establishing a Mission in Bettiah and the reply was as before. The Raja at last said that he would himself write and request the Pope to bid the Fathers do as he desired. The letter was written, and Fr. Vito sent it off with a translation.[29]

In 1742, Father Joseph Mary left Patna to take up a new assignment in Lhasa.[30] On his way, he passed through Bettiah and the Raja informed him that he had already written to the Pope at Rome for his permission. In Tibet, Fr. Joseph Mary found six Fathers and a group of Nepali and Tibetan Christians suffering severe persecution for their faith. At the end of two years, in 1744, word reached the Fathers at Lhasa that the Congregation of Propaganda at Rome left it to the prudent discretion and zeal of the Fathers to remain on at Lhasa or return to India, while the persecution lasted.[31]

At the same time came a letter of Pope Benedict XIV from Rome to the Raja of Battiah,[32] in which he approved of the Raja's offer to open a Mission in Bettiah, and ordered that Fathers be sent for this purpose.

Closing down their Tibet Mission, the Fathers, led by Fr. Horace Tranquillo, left Lhasa for Nepal, on Easter Monday, April 20, 1745.[33] The Tibetan authorities didn't allow any Tibetan to accompany them. So they had to leave their new Christians behind and make the journey with only one Nepali Catholic, Michael by name. On the way, Fr. Horace died at Patan town in Nepal. Fr. Joseph Mary waited for the monsoon to end before he proceeded to a new Mission in Bettiah. Thus, the closing down of the Tibet Mission coincided favourably with the opening of new Mission at Bettiah.

Fr. Joseph Mary was considered to be the most acceptable missionary at Bettiah. On December 7, 1745, Fr. Joseph Mary, accompanied by Michael, the Nepali Catholic, reached Bettiah.[34] The Raja Dhurup Singh received them very warmly, conversed with them for several hours with the kindest familiarity, expressing his gratitude that the Pope had permitted the Fathers to come to Bettiah, and that Fr. Horace Tranquillo had sent the very man he wanted, Fr. Joseph Mary, and put a house at their disposal. Thus, began the Bettiah Mission.

Fr. Joseph Mary worked very hard but soon fell ill. He was taken to Patna and from there, he was sent to Chandernagore. Fr. Edward da Cingoli[35] was transferred from Patna to Bettiah to continue the work begun by Fr. Joseph Mary. Fr. Cassian was made in charge of the Patna Mission. Fr. Joseph Mary did not like the atmosphere at Chandernagore, and in 1750, he was sent back to Bettiah.[36] He reached Bettiah in December 1750, escorted with honour by the Raja's troops. Fr. Joseph Mary, the 'Apostle of Bettiah' and founder of the Bettiah Mission, carried on the Mission work until his death on January 19, 1761.[37] Fr. Marco della Tomo[38] came to Bettiah late in 1761 to take charge of the Mission work there at the death of Fr. Joseph Mary.

All did not go well with the Bettiah Mission. In 1762, the Nawab of Patna[39] waged a war on the eighty-year old Bettiah Raja, Dhurup Singh, besieged the city and later conquered it and took the Raja as prisoner to Patna where he died shortly after. Fr. Marco and three other Priests were for three days without food or water. Then they were in derision led naked through the city and freed.[40]

In 1763, a war broke out between the English East India Company and Mir Qasim, the Nawab of Bengal. After being defeated, Mr. Qasim fled to Patna, where, at his orders, 150 English prisoners were brutally murdered by a Catholic soldier under him, named Sumroo, on June 25, 1763.[41] The Patna Mission House at Padri-ki.-Haveli was sacked, and the three Priests who were there, were stripped, beaten, humiliated and taken prisoners. Sumroo intervened and secured their freedom. The missionaries returned to the Church to find it in ruins, and all archival records of the sixty years of apostolate in Tibet, Nepal and India were completely destroyed.[42] Soon after their release, they began to restore the Mission.

In 1766, the Bettiah Mission had to suffer again. The new Raja of Bettiah refused revenue to the English, who had now become masters of the land after the defeat of the Mughal Nawab at Buxar in 1764. The British forces attacked, occupied and plundered Bettiah. The Bettiah Mission suffered loss during the siege, and by way of compensation, Sir Robert Barker, who was in command of the forces, assigned to the Catholic Mission about 60 bighas within the fort and also a plot of land outside Bettiah called Dusaiya Padri measuring over 200 bighas for the support of themselves and their converts.[43] According to Rev. Paul Dent, S.J., the English Commander offered Fr. Marco a large village, probably Jagadishpur. But, due to scruples that he might be receiving far more than he had lost, the Father took instead a smaller village, Chuhari.[44]

In 1768, another Muslim conqueror, seeking revenge on the English, surprised Bettiah, forced its gates and, for the fourth time within seven years, gave it over to plunder. This time, Fr. Marco, who was ill, did not wait for outrages, but gathering his altar vessels and vestments and a few books, fled secretly to Patna.[45]

Meanwhile, in late 1760s the Capuchin Mission in the Nepal Valley had to face hostilities from the new rulers of Nepal, the Shah Kings of Katmandu. Beginning from 1715, the Capuchin missionaries had set up four mission centres in Nepal. In 1769, the new ruler of Nepal, Raja Prithwi Narayan Shah began to look with disfavour on the Catholic Mission working in Nepal. The Fathers being foreigners, he thought, would help the English at Patna against him. He refused to continue the royal subsidies granted for the Mission support by the previous rulers. The Fathers and their followers had no alternative but to abandon their work in Nepal. On February 10, 1769, five Fathers, 62 Nepalese Christians, and five catechumens (under instruction for baptism) left Nepal for Bettiah.[46] A week later, they reached Bettiah. In 1770, they were settled down in Chuhari village, where, as already stated, some land had been granted to the Bettiah Mission in compensation for the losses suffered when the English forces took Bettiah.

Fr. Joseph da Rovato, Prefect of the Mission,[47] on his arrival at Patna from Nepal, found the church (built in 1713) in a very bad condition and too small for the ever increasing congregation. He proposed to build a new one. The old church was demolished in 1772, and the existing church at Padri-Ki-Haveli was built. The foundation stone was laid by Fr. Joseph da Rovato on October 8, 1772. It was he who solemnly blessed it at its completion on December 8, 1779. The architect of the church was a Venetian named Signor Tiretta. It was dedicated to the Blessed Virgin Mary.

In 1782, Bahadur Shah, son of King Prithwi Narayan of Nepal, and a friend of the missionaries being tutored by them, presented the Fathers with a large bell bearing his name. The inscription on the bell reads: *Bahadur Shah Prithvinarain Regis, Nepal, Anno 1782, 'Maria'*[48] Maria is the name of the bell. Since it cracked during the earthquake in 1934, it is installed presently from two pillars on the ground beside the church. The church is still used by the small Catholic community at Patna City, as many members have moved out to the new city of Patna at Bankipur and surroundings.

2.3 Two Mission Extensions: Bhagalpur and Purnea

According to one record the first church was built at Bhagalpur in 1779 by Fr. Marco Della Tomba,[49] who came to India in 1756 and later became Prefect Apostolic of the Tibetan Mission. In 1806, there were at Bhagalpur a presbytery and only thirty Christians, and they were looked after by a visiting missionary from Patna. In 1817, Bhagalpur was visited by Fr. Julius Cæsar of Caravaggio, one of the three lonely missionaries who had to work in the whole of Northern India. The earliest extant registers-back to 1829-show only 20 converts and 28 baptisms of infants of Catholic parentage, during Fr. Florian's tenure.

Fr. Florian's flocks were mostly indigo planters and their employees. Fr. Florian worked in Bhagalpur from the beginning of 1836 to at least the end of 1843. Owing to his ill health he was sent to Europe; but he died at the end of his journey, at Paris.

The records for the next 60 years are silent about the work by the Capuchins at Bhagalpur. In those early days, the Priest used to come from Allahabad to minister to the Catholic personnel and officials stationed at Gokhla.

In 1846, one Rev. Damasus of Turin made a long and tedious journey to Bhagaplur to establish a residence from which to administer the Sacraments to the 150 plus Catholics who were residing in Bhagalpur town.[50] The tomb stones give silent but eloquent evidence that this town had a representative and vivified Catholic life from all walks of life. The early indigo planters had establishments in the vicinity of Bhagalpur and records show that not a few were of Catholic ancestry.

The small church built by Fr. Marco Della Tomba was renewed by Fr. Cesary, a secular priest of Patna Mission, who was in charge of Bhagalpur from 1885 to 1901. It was destroyed by the great earthquake of 1897. In 1898 Bhagalpur was given a resident priest in the person of Fr. John of Anzola.

Fr. John at once set about collecting funds for a new chapel-the cost of which was estimated at rupees 8,000--, and in December, 1902, Bhagalpur's third and present church was blessed and dedicated to the Immaculate Conception by Dr. Charles Gentili. Eleven years later the present Mission Bungalow was also erected.

In 1911, Fr. John secured for his station the services of three IBMV Sisters of Bankipur, chiefly for the Bhagalpur Hospital and for dispensary work out in the nearby villages. As there was no house Fr. John built one for them.

Unhappily later information is not at hand, but for the first two months of their work they cared for 1,497 patients, visited 64 villages and baptized 27 dying infants. Three years later their Superior, Mother Monica, was presented with the *Kaisar-i-Hind* medal of the second class for "Excellent work in the General Hospital". The work of the Sisters is again highly commended by the Civil Surgeons concerned.

Purnea, headquarters of the District in north Bihar, became an important British centre since 1771 as many European indigo planters and traders settled there. In 1836, Bishop Pezzoni of Agra sent there Fr. Florian, a Polish priest, who built a small chapel and a cell for himself near river Saura. Later on, due to floods, the locality was infected with malaria and so the faithful were compelled to change their residences to a place about three miles away. As the church now became too far from the new locality, a new church was built by Bishop Hartmann in 1849, with a house for the Priest, in the new locality. Two notable Capuchins who served there were Fr. Raphael and Heliodorus. In the re-organization of Mission territories between Patna and Calcutta, Purnea, Hazaribagh and Darjeeling Districts became part of Calcutta Diocese in 1887. Thereafter, Jesuit missionaries of the Bengal Mission began to evangelise the Santals of Purnea District about which we shall see in Chapter 2.

2.4 Capuchin Mission under Patna Vicariate, 1845

Since the Capuchin missionaries had to withdraw from Tibet in 1745 and Nepal in 1769, their Mission now consisted only of Bihar. As noted earlier, the Jesuit Mission begun at Agra in 1593 was constituted as a Vicariate, named Vicariate of the Grand Moghuls. However, when the Jesuits were suppressed by the Pope in 1773, this Mission was handed over to the Carmelites who managed it for ten years (1774-84). In 1784, the Capuchins from Bihar were asked to shoulder its responsibility, and later in 1826, Agra was made a separate Vicariate which included the region of Bihar and the whole of Hindustan (North India).[51] From their headquarters at Agra, they continued the work in their centres in Bihar (Patna, Bettiah, Chuhari, and Bhagalpur).

In 1779, a church was built at Bhagalpur[52] for the indigo planters and their servants, as well as one each in Purnea and Monghyr. In the Patna area, the large cantonment of soldiers at Danapur and the presence of numerous traders in the city brought the Catholic population to nearly 700.[53]

At Chuhari, where 62 Nepalese Christians settled in 1769, Fr. John Gualbert built its first chapel of straw. He remained there until his death there in 1796. He made no converts and his little community numbering 312 souls in 34 houses in January 1802 continued for many years, to live rather as Nepalese than as Indians.[54] The Christians at Bettiah increased in number, mostly otherwise than by conversion.

From about 1824, the Catholic Mission in Bihar became more active. Some new recruits came and the number of missionaries rose to six.[55] Their arrival enabled Fr. Anthony Pezzoni, who had just moved from Bettiah to Lucknow, to visit Rome to report on the Mission. Fr. Pezzoni was a great scholar. At Rome, when Pope Leo XII learnt of Fr. Pezzoni's nearly 20 years' work in the Mission and inspected his manuscript translations into Hindustani of the Gospel, the Epistles and the Psalms, he chose him as Bishop. He was consecrated Bishop in Rome in February 1826 and he returned to India as Vicar Apostolic of the whole Capuchin Mission in India.[56] He was no longer young and his Mission was immense. To help him, Msgr. Borghi came from Rome in 1829 as a Coadjutor. Msgr. Pezzoni returned to Italy in 1842 and died soon. After his death, his Hindustani writings were published. These were, besides a long and widely used Catechism, a Prayer Book (1847) an Italian-Hindustani Grammar (1870) and Lives of Forty-four Saints (1873).[57]

In 1846, the Bihar sector of the Mission in North India was separated from Agra Vicariate and constituted into Patna Vicariate.[58] On March 15, 1846, Fr. Anastasius Hartmann[59] was consecrated at Agra as the first Vicar and Bishop of Patna Vicariate. When he arrived at Patna city, a few days later he felt unhappy about the pathetic management of the Mission.[60] The Mission House was in ruins. There were no schools any where in the whole Mission, no Sisters and no Brothers. There were only four Priests - Fr. John Baptist of Melegnano, caring for some 1400 Christians of Bettiah and Chuhari; Fr. John Baptist of Giglia at Bhagalpur, Fr. Damasus at Purnea and Fr. Lawrence with the troops at Danapur Cantonment.

Bishop Hartmann laid great stress on education. With eight stations - Bettiah, Chuhari, Patna City, Danapur, Monghyr, Bhagalpur, Purnea and Darjeeling - and about 2000 Christians, he had no where a single Catholic school.[61] He set to work at once to found Catholic schools throughout his territory. In 1849, through a Catholic Judge R. S. Loughnan,[62] he secured some five acres of land at Bankipur, where he laid the foundation of a chapel on September 23, 1849. After trying for five years, he succeeded in obtaining the services of the Sisters of the Institute of the Blessed Virgin Mary (hereinafter, IBMV Sisters)[63] from Munich, Germany.[64] Two Sisters came by boat from Calcutta, others by bullock-cart and boat from Bombay, and the present St. Joseph's Convent School was established in 1853 with nine students, three boarders and six orphans.[65] It served both the Christian and Non-Christian communities as a school and an orphanage, for many years and continues its services even today. On April 16, 1854, the St. Stephen's Church at Danapur was opened for divine service.[66]

During the 'Sepoy Mutiny' (First War of Independence) 1857, Bankipur and Danapur were affected. The Sisters and children of Bankipur fled to Danapur or Calcutta for the protection of their lives.[67]

In 1858, a piece of property was purchased further west at Kurji for a residence for the Bishop.[68] The Fathers at first conducted a small school for candidates for the Catholic Priesthood. It slowly developed into a Middle School in charge of laymen. At Jamalpur, a railway town near Monghyr, he built a church with the help of Fr. Raphael. Bishop Hartmann was transferred to Bombay for the period from 1850-56. During his second stint as Bishop of Patna from 1860-66, he invited the Irish Christian Brothers from Calcutta in 1864 to take charge of the Middle School at Kurji.[69] Bishop Hartmann died of cholera at Patna on April 23, 1866.[70] He is famous for his Hindustani *New Testament*, published in Roman characters in 1864 and in Urdu or Persian 15 years later.[71]

2.5 Patna Vicariate made Allahabad Diocese, 1866

The Catholic Mission had, by now, expanded to many places in Hindustan. In 1866, Allahabad, a city more centrally situated, was made the headquarters of the Vicariate, elevating it to a diocese. Bishop Hartmann was succeeded by Bishop Paul Tosi.[72] More schools were opened as more Sisters came from Europe. Improvements were made in the school at Bettiah. New buildings were erected. The Christians were taught some useful trades such as blacksmithing and carpentry, besides giving them land for cultivation. A large number of famine orphans were given not only shelter and boarding, but also means of independent livelihood.[73]

In 1874, the IBMV Sisters were asked to set up another school for girls at Bettiah.[74] Three Sisters reached Bettiah in end 1874 on a bullock cart and started a girls' school there, which later, became St. Theresa's High School. Two years after their arrival in Bettiah, the town was ravaged by famine and plague and the number of the orphan children dependent upon the Bettiah Mission became so great that more land was purchased at Fakirana, where the same Sisters began a home for the orphan girls.[75] An Indian Sisterhood, the Sisters of St. Clare (locally known as *Clara Bahins*) was started at Chuhari. The famine and plague forced the authorities at Bettiah to move the boys' orphanage to Chuhari. Here also, a first class Middle School and a handicraft school for boys were conducted by the Fathers, while the girls were instructed in the school conducted by the Sisters of St. Clare.[76]

In 1881, Bishop Tosi was succeeded by Bishop Francis Pesci, who was the last Vicar Apostolic of the Patna Vicariate.[77] In 1883, a large plot of land was acquired in Chakhni, a village 30 miles north-west of Bettiah, where 14 couples, who had been brought up as orphan children by the Mission, were settled.[78] A Middle School was built there and the charge was given to the Sisters of St. Claire.

2.6 Bettiah Prefecture, 1892-1919

In 1886, the Austrian Tyrolese Capuchins were invited to share the work of the Italian Capuchins in North Bihar.[79] These at once opened an Apostolic School for preparing Indian candidates for Priesthood. In 1892, Bettiah was made the headquarters of a newly carved out Prefecture Apostolic of Bettiah and Nepal,[80] consisting of North Bihar. Fr. Hilarian Abtei, the Prefect and Superior of this Mission, secured a piece of land at Darbhanga and the Apostolic School was transferred there from Bettiah in 1895. Under the leadership of Fr. Hilarian, several Mission stations (such as Darbhanga, Motihari, Morpa, Ramnagar, Rampur, Muzaffarpur, Samastipur, Latonah, Khoria, Champatia, Someshwar, etc.) were founded in the Prefecture for the next 25 years.

Until the transfer of the Apostolic School to Darbhanga the Catholic Christians there had been looked after by Fr. Cajetan Casary,[81] born at Bettiah, the first son of Bettiah Christians to become a priest in 1860. He was transferred to Jamalpur, where Fr. Raphael of Livorno had founded a church in 1869. An indefatigable worker, he built a school there and established schools at Bhagalpur, Monghyr and Samastipur, which he staffed with Catholics whom he regularly visited and supervised. He was assisted by Fr. Joseph[82] in founding a school for the Santal children of the District of Monghyr in 1883 but this work did not prosper at that time.

After 20 years of management, the IBMV Sisters handed over the school and orphanage at Bettiah and Fakirana, to the newly arrived Sisters of the Mercy of the Holy Cross (in short, Holy Cross Sisters)[83] from Switzerland, in 1894. Meanwhile, the Indian Sisters of St. Claire had opened girls' schools in Bettiah, Chuhari and Chakhni. They were assisted in administration by the Sisters of the Holy Cross.

At Latonah,[84] now in the Saharsa District, Fr. Pius founded a mission on the land purchased from a European indigo planter in 1897. There he built a church and a school. The School was staffed by the Sisters of St. Clare from Bettiah. Capuchin Brother Ammon conducted a dispensary for the poor at the residence of the Fathers.

In Ramnagar,[85] to the north of Bettiah, Fr. Jerome began a school sometime in 1895, for the indigenous Indo-Nepali tribe called Tharus. His successor, Fr. Cosmas, completed the school and built a church and an orphanage. The School and Orphanage were staffed by the Sisters of St .Clare. The Sisters followed up this work in Ramnagar with similar undertakings at Rampur, a village near Nepal border. In course of time, the School at Rampur took precedence over the Ramnagar School and, in 1907, the two Schools were combined at Rampur, where there was sufficient land to settle the orphan children as they grew up.

Fr. Florian, founded a school in 1900, at Chanpatia,[86] where in addition to the regular curriculum, the children were taught weaving and basket-making.

In 1899, Fr. Hilarian rented a house in Muzaffarpur[87] to provide a chapel for a group of Catholics, resident in that area. He later placed the house at the disposal of the Holy Cross Sisters for an English School for girls. This failed after a year and the house once more became a residence and chapel for Fathers.

In 1907, the Fathers were offered some land in Morpa in the District of Muzaffarpur. Fr. Plus and a lay-brother went there and established a small congregation of Catholics around their church and bungalow. The Sisters of St. Clare were later brought in to conduct a small school there.[88]

In Bettiah, the Holy Cross Sisters, besides conducting their girls' school, took up, in 1911, the task of nursing administration in the Bettiah Government Hospital, at the invitation of the local Government. They were eminently successful and won the gratitude of the people and high praise of Government officials.[89] At Patna, another group of Sisters of St. Joseph of Champery from Sagar in Madhya Pradesh came to take up the care of the sick in the Patna General Hospital in 1910. Also, in 1911, they took charge of the nursing service at the Government Hospital at Bhagalpur. Those Sisters continued their service until 1925, when they returned to Sagar.[90]

At the beginning of the First World War, the Austrian Tyrolese Fathers working throughout Bihar were interned and a year later, expatriated.[91] During this period, a Belgian Capuchin from Lahore, Fr. Felix, as Prefect Apostolic, came to Bettiah which had the largest Christian community in Bihar.[92] He was assisted by six Indian priests, natives of Bettiah, who had been ordained between 1907 and 1914. They were Frs. Alban, Patrick, Constantine, Joachim, John Baptist and Benedict.[93] They looked after the 13 churches then in the Prefecture.

Aside the Mission centres of the Bettiah Prefecture, the Capuchins had the following centres in the south of Ganges in Bihar: Bhagalpur, Monghyr, Jamalpur, Patna City, Bankipur, Kurji, Danapur, and Khagaul. All these stations had a church and a Priest's residence each and a few Christians converts besides a few migrant Christians such as Europeans, Anglo-Indians and Bettiah Christians.

3. Third Phase: Jesuit Mission Again, Patna Diocese, 1919-ff

During the World War-I period (1914-18) the Christian centres were almost orphaned due to dearth of missionaries. At the end of the War, the Roman Catholic authorities in Rome decided to hand over the Mission in Bihar to another Religious Society with independent charge. Thus, the entire Bihar region including Bettiah Prefecture along with Nepal, was separated from Allahabad

Diocese, and was created into a new diocese called Patna Diocese, in 1919.[94] Its geographical areas in Bihar comprised of all the Districts in north and central Bihar, excluding Chotanagpur (south Bihar). The Mission was handed over to American Jesuits of the Missouri Province, who were to work under the newly appointed Bishop of Patna, Bishop Louis Van Hoeck,[95] a Belgian Jesuit of Ranchi Mission which was then under the Bengal Mission. On March 16, 1921, five American Jesuits, Frs. William Eline, Henry Milet, Edward Anderson, Thomas Kelly and Patrick Troy, from the USA,[96] reached Patna. Besides, another American Jesuit Fr. Henry Westropp, who had been working earlier in the Bombay-Pune Jesuit Mission, joined the Patna Mission.

Fr. William Eline, the Superior, at once took up the task outlined by Bishop Van Hoeck which was to intensify Catholic education throughout the Diocese.[97] More recruits came to man the schools and churches in the north and south of the Ganges. At the old Church in Patna City, Bishop Van Hoeck promoted an Apostolic School under the direction of Fr. Benedict, an Indian Priest, but in 1927, Fr. Benedict died and the school was shifted to Chuhari.[98]

After building the Pro-Cathedral at Bankipur (1925), Bishop Van Hoeck went to the U.S.A. to secure funds and more personnel for the Diocese. On his return, he founded in 1926, a new congregation of Catholic Sisters, the Sisters of the Sacred Heart,[99] who were to be trained to expand the work in the girls' schools in the Diocese and to take up the nursing work done in hospitals by the Sisters of St. Joseph of Champery, who had returned to Sagar in 1925. The Sisters later conducted schools, orphanages and dispensaries in many mission stations.

At Bettiah, the Jesuit Fathers took over the Middle School for boys, which was founded in 1860. Soon it became the largest Middle School in the District. It was decided to found a High School, and in 1928, at Turhapatti in the southern side of Bettiah, the foundation-stone of the beautiful and imposing Khrist Raja High School was laid.[100] Hostels for boys were constructed at K. R. High School, and at Chuhari, where students from many Mission centres as far away from Shahabad and Santal Parganas Districts studied. The Chuhari Girls' School too was improved with new buildings.

On February 15, 1928, Bishop Van Hoeck[101] was made the Bishop of the newly-constituted Diocese of Ranchi. American Jesuit Right Reverend Bernard Sullivan was chosen as successor and was consecrated Bishop of Patna on March 17, 1929.[102] School expansion was given the top priority in Bishop Sullivan's programme. Bishop Sullivan also took much interest in the evengelisation of the Santals in Bhagalpur District which was already begun in 1925. In 1930, a school for Santals was opened at Bhagalpur. Later, it was transferred to Gokhla in the same District. The IBMV Sisters also opened a school for Santal girls there.[103]

In 1934, Fr. P. J. Sontag replaced Fr. Eline as Superior and the programme of opening new schools in new sectors was accelerated. Fr. Henry Westropp secured a large tract of land at Gajhi village in Monghyr District where he introduced the Santals to cottage industries.[104] The ministry to the Santals was one of the most successful missionary undertakings of the Patna Jesuits. During the first decade (1925-35), more than 10,000 Santals had converted to Catholicism in the area.

The earthquake of January 15, 1934, damaged many schools and church buildings of Patna Diocese. Soon the work of reconstruction and expansion were taken up. One aspect of the expansion was evangelization of the Depressed Classes (former out-castes) in Bihar, who began to respond to Christian preaching in mid-1930s. Already, since 1910s, many of them had begun to convert in groups. More and more missionaries were appointed to carry out this pioneering work. Two pioneering missionaries, (Fr. Marion Batson in the central Districts east of Patna, and Fr. Westropp, in Shahabad District, west of Patna), super headed a sort of movement among the Chamars, who responded to Catholic preaching in large numbers. Together with conversions, schools, hostels, priests' residences and churches were founded in many villages in these Districts. The first was at Mokama, where a building was erected to serve both as a church and residence. A primary school was started there with arrangements for boarding poor boys. With Mokama as headquarters, Fr. Batson moved about the areas around and established Mission centres and schools at Barbigha, Nawada, Biharsharif, Gulni, Bakhtiarpur and Sheikhpura.[105] Similarly, in Shahabad District, Fr. Westropp opened new mission stations at Arah, Piro, Shahpur, Buxar, and Itarhi, and brought the Sisters of the Sacred Heart to conduct a school and an orphan home for girls at Buxar and a widows' home at Arrah.[106] In 1934, he started a school for boys at Arah. Also, at Padri-ki-Haveli in Patna City, a Middle School and an orphan home for boys were started by Fr. Sontag.[107]

The Jesuit Fathers had been visiting Gaya[108] from Patna for many years to take care of the Catholics who were engaged in the railway services. A resident Priest was stationed there since 1936. In 1938, the IBMV Sisters opened a Middle School there, which quickly prospered. However, the Sisters being German nationals, had to withdraw from there because of the restrictions placed on them at the outbreak of the Second World War, and their place was taken by the Sisters of Loreto from Calcutta, who opened a school on the Cambridge system.

In 1939, invited by the Patna Jesuits, the Society of Medical Missionaries[109] from Philadelphia in the USA came to work in the Patna Mission. A generous Father Sontag, the Superior, allowed them to occupy the Middle School for boys, in the Old Cathedral compound of Patna City. There they started a hospital, called the Holy Family Hospital. In 1942, the Sisters started a Nursing School which obtained Government approval. This was followed by a School of midwifery and pharmacy. From the beginning a dispensary served out-patients. In-patients were also treated by the hospital. The Holy Family Hospital at Patna City proved too crowded and plans were made for a new and larger building at Kurji, west of Bankipur.

In 1938, the Jesuit Fathers rented a house on the Exhibition Road in new Patna town where they opened a hostel for college students. It was here that Fr. Marshall Moran inaugurated the first classes of St. Xavier's Cambridge School,[110] while new buildings were being erected on the present site of the school just west of the Gandhi Maidan formerly known as Bankipur Lawn. The stately built new school and residence were dedicated by the Governor of Bihar in January 1940.

The need for a college for women in Patna was keenly felt at this time. In 1940, at the invitation of Bishop Sullivan, the Sisters of the Apostolic Carmel of Mangalore arrived to start such a college, the first College for Women in Bihar, the Patna Women's College.[111] To provide buildings for the College, the Bishop surrendered his newly built Episcopal residence in Bankipur. The newly erected guest house served as College Hostel. Land was acquired near Patna High Court for a new and suitable building for this College. The construction began in 1946.

In 1946, Bishop Sullivan returned to the U.S.A. and appointed Fr. Batson, as the Administrator Apostolic of the Diocese of Patna. Fr. Batson invited the Sisters of Charity of Nazareth, from Kentucky, USA, to work in the Diocese.[112] They came in the following year and opened the Nazareth Hospital, which Fr. Batson had built meanwhile, at Mokama. New schools were opened at Maner by Fr. Jacob Kunnunkal (diocesan Priest), at Jehanabad by Fr. Alphonse Goveas, at Gulni by Fr. Mathew Mezhukanal (diocesan Priest) and at Muzaffarpur by Fr. John Meyer.[113]

On June 12, 1947, Right Reverend Augustine F. Wildermuth was appointed Bishop of Patna.[114] In 1947, Fr. Meyer started a school at Muzaffarpur with the help of a lay staff. Patna Diocese cannot ignore the great builder and pioneer, Fr. Frank N. Loesch, the builder of St. Xavier's School and Patna Women's College.[115] After the completion of the latter, he began to build the Loyola Industrial School at Kurji. From here, he provided plans, equipments, personnel and fabricated materials for the construction of many churches and schools in the Patna Diocesan area and outside.

Patna Mission had a printing press, the Catholic Mission Press, founded at Bettiah in 1897, by the Capuchins during the leadership of Fr. Hilarion.[116] In publishing books and magazines on the Christian religion, and in doing odd job printing work for planters and merchants in Bettiah, the Press had given employment to a good number of Catholics and had trained them in the printing trade. All the public utility institutions run by the Mission--schools, hospitals, and the College--were open to all, Christians and Non-Christians.[117]

3.1 Jesuit Mission to Santals in Purnea and Bhagalpur

Santals the largest tribal community in India, are presently settled in various States in Jharkhand, Orissa, Chattisgarh, West Bengal,

Assam, Bihar and even in Nepal. It is not clear whether they migrated from the District of Santal Parganas (in Jharkhand today), which is considered their home. It may be noted that evangelization among the Santals and Paharias was first undertaken by the Protestant missionaries in undivided Bihar which included Jharkhand: among the Paharias in 1820s, among the Santals in 1850s, by the Church Missionary Society (see Chapter 4). Catholic missionaries also worked among the Santals, but from late 19th century. Their areas of work were Purnea and Bhagalpur Districts where a significant number of Santals were settled. This work was undertaken by Jesuit missionaries belonging to two societies: the Bengal Jesuit Mission and Patna Jesuit Mission.

Already in 1879, Jesuit Fr. Charles Schaff of the Bengal Mission was in contact with migrant Santals at Jhargram (Midnapur) in West Bengal. In that year, he visited Santal Parganas to explore the possibility of evangelization of the Santals in their home land. In 1887 Fr. John Schafer from Calcutta made an attempt to begin a Mission station there. In 1900 Jesuit Fr. Leopold Knockaert[118] was made chaplain at Purnea. He also made some attempts to visit Santal Parganas and eventually, in 1918, he founded a Mission centre in Santal Parganas in present day Jharkhand State. We shall see in Chapter 2 how the Santal Mission in Santal Parganas developed by the Belgian Jesuits followed by Maltese Jesuits in the Santal land.

Work among the Santals settled in Bhagalpur District in Bihar began in 1925, by Patna Jesuits. In 1928, Jesuit Fr. James Creane of Patna took up residence at the Bhagalpur Presbytery.[119] Soon after his arrival, he set up a boys' school for Santals on an experimental basis. When he found that the school work was making an impression on the people, he invited the IBMV Sisters from Bankipur to start a school for Santal girls in a nearby compound.

During the 1934 earthquake, some of the Mission buildings in Bhagalpur were destroyed. Not long afterwards, a suitable property was purchased in Gokhla village,[120] near Mirzachowki. The 177 boarders from Bhagalpur were moved to this place, and, on August 15, 1934, the new Stanislaus Middle School for boys was formally opened by Fr. J. Bohn S.J. In another compound, not very far from the boys' school, the St. Michael's Middle School for girls was opened some months later. These two schools were open to students of all castes and creeds. St. Michael's Middle School was managed by the IBMV Sisters. There were a dispensary and a 15 bed hospital under the care of certain Dr. D. Dias.

As the Mission expanded there was need for more Mission personnel. So Bishop Sullivan invited the American Franciscan Missionaries of the Third Order (TOR Fathers) to shoulder responsibility of the Santal Mission. In a few years' time this was made a separate Prefecturate under the care of the TOR missionaries, who continued the legacy of the Patna Jesuits and expanded the Santal Mission further, founding several Mission centres in Bhagalpur District.

4. Conclusion

In this overview of the Catholic Mission in Bihar we have noted that there were three phases in its development: first, the Jesuit Mission in 1620-21, which was short lived, secondly, the Capuchin Mission which began in 1703 and ended in 1919. This Mission had its beginning at Patna, extended to Tibet and Nepal both of which had to be closed down due to external factors. With its headquarters at Patna its territory extended from Darjeeling to Allahabad at one time. Later, the Patna Vicariate was made a new Diocese with its headquarters at Allahabad in 1866. Gradually certain regions were bifurcated as for example, Darjeeling, Purnea, Santal Parganas and Hazaribagh sections were handed over to Calcutta Archdiocese in 1886, North Bihar was made a separate Prefecture in 1892. Eventually, the present Patna Diocese was created in 1919 with the remaining civil territory of Bihar (minus Purnea, Santal Parganas, and Hazaribagh). Thirdly, when the Capuchins had to withdraw, the management of this Diocese was given to the American Jesuit Mission (third phase: second Jesuit Mission in Bihar). Meanwhile, the Chotanagpur region of the undivided Bihar was evangelized since 1868 by the Jesuit missionaries of the Bengal Mission, about which we shall see in Chapter 2.

Overall, the Catholic missionary engagement in Bihar catered to two segments in society: a) the convert communities, and b) the general society. Evangelization and conversion aside, the missionaries attempted to develop the Christian communities through education, health care, vocational training, industrial training, etc. Their care was extended in a special way to the marginalized sections of society, particularly orphans, Dalits and Tribals. They were also involved in humanitarian activities during natural calamities such as floods and famine. It may be noted that all the missionary institutions were public utility structures which were available to the general public, but preferentially to the Christians. The most significant achievement of the Catholic Mission in Bihar was the founding of three Christian communities: 1) the Bettiah Christians, centred at Bettiah since 1745, 2) the Santal Christian community in Bhagalpur division since 1925, and 3) the Dalit Christian community in central Bihar since 1930s. The story of the development of these communities, their transformation from convert groups into distinct Church communities, their socio-economic, educational, occupational and religious development, etc., warrants a separate study.

Endnotes and References

1 Paul Dent, *A Brief History of Patna Mission* (typed, bound and unpublished), p. 1.

2 Ibid., p. 1; C. P. Saldanha, *Roman Catholic Church in Bihar* (hereinafter, *RCC, Patna*) – (typed and unpublished), p. 1.

3 The Jesuit *Annual Letter* from Cochin, for 1620 and 1621, translated by Fr. Henry Hosten, S.J., into English, vividly describe the baptism of Nawab Mukarrab Khan and the beginning of the Patna Mission with his support. The Nawab or Viceroy of that city is called Lord John (Signore Giovann). He was baptized by Fr. Nicholas Pimenta, S.J. in the College of Goa, when he came thither as Ambassador of the Mogor (Mughal) to the Governor Don Aleixo de Meneses": Dent, p. 1; See *Bombay Examiner* (1912, pp. 117-118) and the *Calcutta Herald* (1906, p. 804), quoted by Paul Dent; Saldanha, *RCC, Patna*, p. 1.

4 Dent, p. 1; Saldanha, *RCC, Patna,* p. 1; Extract from *Catholicus* (official newsletter of the Catholic Sadan, of Allahabad Diocese), nos. from Dec. 1921 to Jan. 1922, quoted in *Patna Mission Letter,* No. 2, Feb. 1922, p.b-2a.

5 The Jesuit Mission to the Court of the Mughals was begun in 1580 when Emperor Akbar invited them from Goa. The Mission was wound up in 1583, re-started in 1590, but closed again in 1591. The third

Mission started in 1593, again at the invitation of Akbar, continued throughout the Mughal period, until the Jesuits were suppressed in 1773. During this period, the Jesuits founded a few churches in the Mughal cities such as Fatehpur Sikri, Agra, Delhi, Lahore, Peshawar, Sambhar, Bhopal, etc.

6 He was given a grand welcome. Escorted by the Nawab's retinue the Father arrived at the palace. The Viceroy who had been waiting, received him with extraordinary signs of joy. Throwing his arms around him he said he was happy to have the Fathers of the Society in his dominions, and added that it was with deep regret he had quitted the court of the Great Moghul at Agra: Dent, p. 1; Saldanha, *RCC, Patna,* pp. 1-2.

7 Dent, p. 1.

8 Saldanha, *RCC, Patna,* p. 2; Dent, p. 2.

9 Ibid., p. 2.

10 Dent, pp. 2-3; Saldanha, *RCC, Patna*, p. 2.

11 Saldanha, *RCC, Patna,* p. 2.

12 Dent, p. 4.

13 The *Propaganda Fide* (Congregation for the Propagation of the Faith), founded by the pope in 1622: the Department of Evangelization in the Vatican.

14 Prefecture: Church's elementary administrative unit under a prefect, prior to its elevation as a Vicariate (under a Vicariate Apostolic) and eventually as a Diocese under a Diocesan Ordinary (Bishop).

15 Dent, p. 4; Also, Extract from *Catholicus:* quoted in *Patna Mission Letter* No. 2, Feb. 1922, p.b-2a.

16 Dent, p. 4; Saldanha, *RCC, Patna,* p. 2.

17 Dent, pp. 4-5.

18 Dent, p. 6, Extract from *Catholicus*: quoted in *Patna Mission Letter* No.2, Feb. 1922, p. b-2a.

19 Dent, p. 5; A. Gille, S.J., *A Record of the Inscriptions at the Catholic Church at Patna* (1917), p. IV; Saldanha, *RCC, Patna,* p. 2.

20 Dent, p. 6.

21 Saldanha, *RCC, Patna,* p. 2.

22 Dent, p. 30; Saldanha, *RCC, Patna,* p. 2; L. S. S. O' Malley, *Bihar and Orissa District Gazetteers, Champaran* (1907), pp. 42-43.

23 Dent, p. 30.

24 Ibid., p. 31.

25 Ibid.

26 Ibid; Saldanha, *RCC, Patna,* p. 2; L. S. S. O' Malley (1907), p. 140.

27 Dent, p. 31.

28 Dent, p. 41.

29 The letter, in English translation, runs thus:
Your Holiness,
I am well and I hope that you are well. I have heard that the Missionary Fathers are sent out to do good to the world. To make sure of this for myself I called them to me. Having thereby convinced myself of their assertion that work consists entirely in charity, I have ordered them to remain in my Kingdom. But they told me that they are unable to obey my orders without the consent of the High Pontiff. Therefore, I request this High Pontiff to order some Missionaries to stay in my Kingdom. I shall esteem this as the highest favour...Dhurup Singh: Quoted in Dent, p. 41.

30 Saldanha, *RCC, Patna,* p. 2.

31 Ibid., pp. 2-3.

32 Letter cited by Paul Dent, p. 43; Saldanha, *RCC, Patna,* p. 3

33 Saldanha, *RCC, Patna,* p. 3.

34 Dent, p. 43; Saldanha, *RCC, Patna,* p. 3.

35 Dent, p. 44.

36 Dent, p. 45.

37 Ibid.

38 Ibid., p. 47.

39 Ibid.

40 Ibid.

41 Dent, p. 47-48; Saldanha, *RCC, Patna,* p. 3; Extract from *Catholicus*: quoted in *Patna Mission Letter* No.2, Feb., 1922, p.b-2a.

42 Dent, p. 48.

43 L. S. S. O'Malley (1907), p. 141.

44 The title deed of the three plots given as *zamindari* possessions was given in 1786: Catholic Church Office Files, Bettiah; Paul Dent, p. 48.

45 Dent, p. 48.

46 Dent, p. 49; Saldanha, *RCC, Patna,* p. 3.

47 A. Gille (1917), p. iv; Dent, p. 50; Extract from *Catholicus*: quoted in *Patna Mission Letter* No. 2, Feb. 1922, pp. b-2a.

48 The translation is: Bahadur Shah, son of Prithvinarain, King of Nepal, presented this in the year 1782: A. Gille, p. 2; Extract from *Catholicus*: quoted in *Patna Mission Letter,* No. 2, Feb. 1922, p. b-2a; Saldanha, *RCC, Patna,* p. 3.

49 According to another record Fr. Marco della Tomba, the undisputed builder of this Church was in Europe from 1774 to 1781 or 1783. There is no Church record earlier than 1829.

50 Monsignor Urban McGarry (1960), *The Catholic Mission in the Bhagalpur District and Adjacent Santal Areas* , p. 1.
51 Dent, p. 50; Saldanha, *RCC, Patna,* p. 4.
52 Saldanha, *RCC, Patna,* p. 4; Dent, p. 50.
53 Saldanha, *RCC, Patna,* p. 4.
54 Dent, p. 50.
55 Ibid., p. 51.
56 Ibid.
57 Ibid., p. 52.
58 Ibid., p. 55.
59 Ibid.
60 Ibid; Extract from *Catholicus*: quoted in the *Patna Mission Letter,* No. 2, Feb. 1922, p. b-2a.
61 See Dent, for a description of all the Churches he founded.
62 Dent, p. 56; Saldanha, *RCC, Patna,* p. 4.
63 IBMV acronym from its Latin rendering, but presently known as Sisters of the Congregation of Jesus-CJ.
64 Saldanha, *RCC, Patna,* p. 5.
65 Saldanha, *RCC, Patna,* p. 4; Dent, p. 58.
66 Dent, p. 58.
67 Ibid.
68 Ibid., p. 60; Saldanha, *RCC, Patna,* p. 5.
69 Dent, p. 65.
70 Ibid., p. 61.
71 Ibid., p. 59.
72 Ibid., p. 62.
73 Saldanha, *RCC, Patna,* p. 5.
74 Ibid., p. 5; Dent, p. 64.
75 Saldanha, *RCC, Patna,* p. 5; Dent, p. 64.
76 Saldanha, *RCC, Patna,* p. 5.
77 Dent, p. 64.
78 Saldanha, *RCC, Patna,* p. 6.
79 Dent, p. 64; Saldanha, *RCC, Patna,* p. 6.
80 Dent, p. 70; L. S. S. O'Malley (1907), p. 141.
81 Saldanha, *RCC, Patna,* p. 6.
82 Ibid.
83 Dent, p. 71.
84 Ibid. p. 73; Saldanha, *RCC, Patna,* p. 6.
85 Dent, p. 76; Saldanha, *RCC, Patna,* p. 6.
86 Saldanha, *RCC, Patna,* p. 7; Dent, p. 77.

87 Dent, p. 76; Saldanha, *RCC, Patna,* p. 7.
88 Saldanha, *RCC, Patna,* p. 7; Dent, p. 78.
89 Saldanha, *RCC, Patna,* p. 7.
90 Ibid., p. 7; Dent, p. 68.
91 Saldanha, *RCC, Patna,* p. 7; L. S. S. O'Malley (1907), p. 141.
92 Saldanha, *History Sketch of Patna Diocese for our field* (hereinafter, *History Patna Diocese*), p. 1.
93 Ibid.
94 Ibid.
95 Saldanha, *RCC, Patna,* p. 7.
96 Saldanha, *History Patna Diocese,* p. 1.
97 Ibid.
98 Saldanha, *History Patna Diocese*, p. 2; also, Saldanha, *RCC, Patna,* p. 8.
99 Saldanha, *RCC, Patna,* p. 8; Saldanha, *History Patna Diocese*, p. 2.
100 Saldanha, *RCC, Patna*, p 8.
101 Saldanha, *History Patna Diocese*, p. 2.
102 Ibid.
103 Ibid., Saldanha, *RCC, Patna,* p. 9.
104 Saldanha, *History Patna Diocese*, p. 2.
105 Ibid; Also, Saldanha, *RCC, Patna,* p. 9
106 Saldanha, *History Patna Diocese*, p. 3; Saldanha, *RCC, Patna,* p. 10.
107 Saldanha, *RCC, Patna,* p. 9; Saldanha, *History Patna Diocese*, p. 3.
108 Saldanha, *RCC, Patna,* pp. 9-10.
109 Ibid., p. 10; Saldanha, *History Patna Diocese*, p. 3.
110 Ibid., p. 11; Saldanha, *History Patna Diocese*, p. 3.
111 Saldanha, *History Patna Diocese*, p. 3; Saldanha, *RCC, Patna,* p. 11.
112 Ibid.
113 Ibid.
114 Ibid.
115 Saldanha, *RCC, Patna,* p. 12.
116 Paul Dent, p. 71; Saldanha, *RCC, Patna,* p. 12.
117
118 Henry Holsten, SJ (1920), *Inscriptions on Christian graves and memorial tablets in the Purnea District,* Bihar and Orissa, Patna, pp. 8 & 71; p. 1.
119 Monsignor Urban McGarry (1960), *The Catholic Mission in the Bhagalpur District and Adjacent Santal Areas,* p. 1.
120 Monsignor Urban McGarry (1960), *The Catholic Mission in the Bhagalpur District and Adjacent Santal Areas,* p. 3.

Chapter 2

The Catholic Mission in Jharkhand

1. The Beginnings in Bengal

The Roman Catholic Mission began missionary activity in Chotanagpur (Jharkhand) in 1868, through the "Bengal Mission" that had been entrusted to the Jesuits (members of the Religious Order, Society of Jesus) of Belgian Province in 1859. The Jesuit Bengal Mission's first missionaries reached Calcutta at the end of the same year to take charge of a College and a Parish.[1] In 1864, the whole Vicariate Apostolic of Bengal was formally made over to the Belgian Province, and a Vicar Apostolic appointed who belonged to that Province.[2] Calcutta became the centre of Bengal Mission, and, from there, the first Jesuit missionary to enter Chotanagpur was Fr. Stockman,[3] who, unlike the Gossner and Anglican Missionaries, made a start, not at Ranchi, but at Chaibasa in the District of Singhbhum.

2. Entry into Chotanagpur

It was almost casually that in 1868 Bishop Steins, the Vicar Apostolic of Bengal Mission in Calcutta, heard from a British officer, stationed in Chotanagpur, about the aboriginals of Chotanagpur and the possibility of success of missionary activities there. Bishop Steins had no man free for the task, and he, therefore, asked Fr. Stockman, then at Midnapore, to proceed at once to investigate the possibility of starting a Mission station in the area.[4] Fr. Stockman reached Chaibasa on November 24, 1868.[5] After spending some time at Chaibasa, he felt there were no hopes for a new Mission, and he returned to Midnapore on December 10, 1868.[6]

Bishop Steins, however, asked Fr. Stockman, in the following year, to return to Chaibasa to start a Mission there.[7] With his arrival at Chaibasa on July 10, 1869, the Roman Catholic Mission in Chotanagpur actually began.[8] The Gossner Mission was already there and the Anglican Mission had just started. There he built a residential house and a chapel in 1871.[9] He worked entirely among the *Hos* and the *Mundas.* It was the Mundas who expressed interest in Christianity and sought baptism on November 9, 1873.[10] Bishop Steins baptized 28 Mundas - the charcoal burners – of whom 24 were adults and 4, infants. These ware the first Catholics among the aboriginals of Chotanagpur.

3. Early Expansion

From Chaibasa, missionary activity moved towards the north and, in 1874, a new Mission station was built at Burudih,[11] near Baddgaon, in Ranchi District for settling the Catholic Munda converts of Chaibasa. It was the first Catholic village. There the first Catholic chapel in Ranchi District was built. Progress was very slow. By 1876, there were only 160 Catholics, some of whom were former Lutherans.[12] Doranda was the next station to be opened. Since 1873, the Catholic soldiers in the cantonment at Doranda had been visited by military chaplains. A Catholic clergyman, Fr. De Cock,[13] who had been a military chaplain there, finally settled at Doranda in 1877 and began missionary work around. In 1878, another station was established in a village called Buruma.[14] Here there were six Catholic families, of which four had been baptized at Burudih. Burudih and Buruma were both in a forest region. The missionaries knew of the disputes between the zamindars and the tenants, but they decided to keep clear of these troubles. By 1881, the Catholic Mission had 371 followers, many of whom were former Lutheran Christians.[15]

As more Jesuit missionaries arrived, more Mission stations were established: at Sarwada (1881), Jamgain (1882), Dolda, Bandgaon and Doranda (1884).[16] By 1885, the Catholic Mission in Chotanagpur had eight stations, seven of them being among the Mundas.[17] Fr. De Cock was made the Director of the Mission. Progress was very slow. In 1885, after sixteen years of hard labour, the Munda country had yielded only 1,837 Christians[18] to the Roman Catholic Mission in Chotanagpur. From Doranda, attempts were made to penetrate into the *Oraon* region in the direction of Dighia and Lohardaga.

4. Legal Aid to the Oppressed Tribals

With the arrival of a young and energetic missionary, Fr. Constant Lievens,[19] popularly known as 'Libin Saheb' at Doranda on March 14, 1885, the Catholic Mission in Chotanagpur underwent remarkable expansion followed by mass conversion. The Superior appointed him to Jamgain with instructions to study the people and to see if he could find a more successful method of conversion than the one used by his predecessors. For this task, he was given an opportunity which none of his predecessors had. His duty was to get into contact with the people and their way of living in order to acquire for his future apostolate sufficient knowledge of the languages, customs and usages of the aboriginals.[20] He was to stay provisionally at Jamgain under Fr. De Cock and reconnoiter. On March 19, 1885, Fr. Lievens first settled down at Jamgain.[21] It lay in the Munda country but it was very close to the Oraon country too. Within five months, he learnt the Munda and Oraon languages.[22]

On November 23, 1885, Fr. Lievens, with the approval of the Vicar Apostolic, settled at Torpa in the Munda country and built a new station.[23] At that time, a widespread and serious agrarian unrest prevailed in Ranchi District on account of the exploitation of the illiterate aboriginals--Mandas, Oraons and Kharias--by their alien landlords, money-lenders and tax-collectors. The biggest struggle of the aboriginals was against the landlords who demanded high rents and many kinds of services. Lievens rightly realised that in such a situation direct preaching to the people could not attract their attention: they needed help in their agrarian struggle against their landlords.[24] It is said that an Indian police officer advised him to take up the defence of the people on questions of rent and services.[25] He decided to follow his advice. He at once studied the local land tenure laws, the traditional rights of the aboriginals on their lands and the rights and duties of the landlords.[26]

Fr. De Cock, the Director of the Mission was against the missionaries helping the people in their land disputes.[27] Fr. Lievens resolved to champion the cause of the aboriginals. He mixed freely with them as friends and openly helped them against the injustices of their landlords. He told the people who came to him that he had come not only for their eternal happiness but also to make them happy in their earthly life.[28] Thus, there was a complete change of the policy so far followed by the Catholic Mission in Chotanagpur.

5. Christian Mass Movement

As a result of this policy, he did not have to go to the oppressed people. They themselves came to him for aid and advice, and, of their own, showed their willingness to embrace Christianity.[29] Many people and villages joined the Catholic Mission. Fr. Lievens admitted many Lutheran and Anglican Christians also to the Catholic told.[30] The news of the help that he rendered to the people spread far and wide. The number of converts increased rapidly. In September 1886, there were 2,000 followers.[31] New stations were built at Ranchi and Dighia in the same year. By 1887, the Catholic Mission had 5,000 baptized Christians and 10,000 catechumens (beginners who are taught the rudiments of Christianity before baptizm) in 400 villages.[32] According to Fr. Lievens, the Torpa Mission alone had 10,000 Christians,[33] many of whom were receiving instructions. In the same year, Fr. Motet moved the Central Mission station from Doranda to Ranchi.[34]

With Torpa as centre, the missionary movement, in 1888,[35] spread south-west towards Palkot (nearly 10,000 people in 40 Oraon and Kharia villages came over *en masse*), then north-east towards

Karra and Doroma (5,000 were converted in 11 days) and north-west towards Dighia and Mandar in the Ranchi District. By August 1888, the Catholic Mission had 11,291 baptized Christians and 39,060 catechumens in 832 villages.[36] In January 1888, the Torpa Mission counted about 25,000 adherents, in March there were 40,000, and early in October, the total was 56,000.[37] Here too, many of them must have been catechumens.

This remarkably rapid success was mainly due to the efforts of one man - Fr. Lievens - whose zeal for Mission work was unbounded. He was assisted by a band of devoted missionaries like Frs. Van Severen, Haghenbeck and Huyghe who arrived in January 1888 and Fr. Grosjean, the Secretary- General of the Bengal Mission. In June 1888, Fr. Grosjeen arrived at Ranchi for an annual visit. He named Fr. Motet, the local Supervisor at Ranchi, as Superior of the District and made Fr. Lievens the District Director.[38] The functions which should have been carried out by one man were divided between two: Fr. Motet as religious Superior and Fr. Lievens in charge of mission work. Fr. Grosjean evidently prevailed upon Bishop Goethals of Calcutta, who had, in 1878, succeeded Bishop Steins, to accept the new arrangements. Bishop Goethal in a circular letter of August 27, 1888,[39] appointed Fr. Lievens the Director of the entire Mission field in Chotanagpur and fixed his powers. He became the responsible intermediary between the missionaries and the Bishop for all matters concerning the mission work. The missionaries were to follow his advice and direction in the matter. They were also to have recourse to him in judicial and other matters to be treated at Ranchi with civil authorities. All the money sent by the Bishop to Chotanagpur, was, in future, to be sent to Fr. Lievens who was to distribute it equitably and send a monthly report to the Bishop on its use. Thus, Fr. Lievens was given full control over mission work and the missionary activities of the Fathers in Chotanagpur.

Fr. Lievens shifted his headquarters from Torpa to Ranchi in September 1888. Ranchi was the capital of Chotanagpur and the seat of Government. It was easier for Fr. Lievens to meet the people and help those who had cases in the court at Ranchi.[40] He carried on the mission work with the same zeal in Biru and Barway in Ranchi District, in Chechari in Palamau District and at Purulia in Manbhum

District.[41] He asked for more missionaries to look after the newly-baptized Christians. Among the new missionaries, who came to assist him were Fr. Cardon, Fr. Dehon and Fr. Lauvent. Mission stations were opened at Karra (1888), Noatoli (1890) and Khunti (1891).[42] In 1892, Fr. Lievens had a severe attack of tuberculosis and he was sent back to Belgium for treatment, where he died on November 7, 1893,[43] at the young age of 37. By 1893, the Catholic Mission had 50,000 baptized Christians.[44]

The period of rapid expansion was followed by a short period of hardship and sharp decline.[45] Fr. Lievens was dead. The conversion movement had been too fast. There were not enough missionaries and workers to look after and sustain the new converts. More than half a dozen missionaries died of sickness and exhaustion. Several converts returned to their original faith or joined the Birsa movement of 1895. The number of Catholic Christians in Chotanagpur went down to 33,500 in 1896.[46]

Paradoxically enough the terrible famine of 1897, the wide-spread epidemic cholera in 1898, and the reappearance of a severe famine in 1899, were to mark the beginning of a new period of expansion of the Mission.[47] These caused immense and indescribable suffering and distress to the people of Chotanagpur. Large scale relief was needed. The Catholic Mission conducted relief operations in several places and saved many lives from death from starvation.[48] It also built churches at Nawatoli, Torpa, Khunti, Katkahi, Mahuadanr and other places and gave employment to famine-stricken people. This humanitarian service of the missionaries drew many to the Catholic told. A new station was founded in 1896 at Mahuadanr in Palamau District.[49] By1900, the number of Catholics in Chotanagpur rose to 62,300.[50]

6. Further Expansion

The first decade of the 20th century witnessed consolidation and further expansion of the mission work.[51] Stations were opened at Rengari, Tongo, Soso (1901), Kurdeg and Samtoli (1908) - all in Ranchi District.[52] The main church (future Cathedral) at Ranchi was consecrated on October 3, 1909. The mission work in Biru and Barway was properly organised to serve as a base for further expansion westward towards the neighbouring Native States of Jashpur and Gangpur.[53] In 1909, the Catholic Mission had 1,47,366 converts of whom 72,943 were catechumens.[54] Out of this total number as many as 91,345 belonged to Ranchi District, 1763 to Singhbhum District, 6230 to Palamau District, and 35,791 and 18,222, to the two native States of Jashpur and Gangpur respectively.[55]

The outbreak of the First World War put a stop to the coming of new missionaries and caused great financial hardship. [56] At the end of the War, situation gradually improved and missionary activities went on vigorously. In 1920, the Catholic Mission had altogether 1,75,000 Christians.[57] This number rose to 2,33,000 in 1927.

7. Ranchi becomes Autonomous Mission

The year 1928 opened a new chapter in the history of the Catholic Mission in Chotanagpur.[58] So long, it was under the control and direction of the Belgian Jesuits of the Bengal Mission with headquarters at Calcutta. Its activities had now become so vast and varied and were expanding so rapidly, that it was found very difficult to manage the missionary activities of Bengal proper and of Chotanagpur from one centre. The *Newsreel* reported that it had been found impossible to continue administering both the over expanding Ranchi section and the simultaneously flourishing Mission in Bengal proper, from distant Calcutta.[59] The Archbishop Perier of Calcutta applied for relief in his overwhelming duties to Pope Pius XI, who sanctioned the opening of a separate suffragon Diocese of Ranchi.[60] The Bengal Mission was renamed as Calcutta-Ranchi Mission. On June 28, 1928, Bishop Louis van Hoeck, who had been a missionary in Chotanagpur since 1908, and was the first Bishop of Patna since January 1921, was transferred to Ranchi, when Ranchi was made a Diocese.[61] The new Diocese was comprised of seven Districts: Ranchi, Khunti, Biru, Barway and Nawatoli in Chotanagpur, Jashpur in Madhya Pradesh and Gangpur in Orissa.[62]

In 1930, Hazaribagh became a resident Mission station. Catholic chaplains had been rendering service to the military personnel and other settler Christians there since 1865. In 1931, the work at Chaibasa was reopened and a new Mission station was built at Lohardaga. In 1933, the Ranchi Mission had opened a

Jesuit training College—St. Stanislaus College—at Sitagarh village, near the town. In the same year, two tribals of Chotanagpur, Peter Shanti Nawarangi and Martin Topno were ordained priests at the Jesuit theologate, St. Mary's College, at Kurseong in West Bengal. On April 30, 1933, Bishop Van Hoeck died.[63] The Catholic Mission had its presence in seven districts, having 32 parishes and 2,82,987 Christians.

Bishop Van Hoeck was succeeded by Bishop Oscar Sevrin on July 25, 1934.[64] Next year (1935), the Catholic Mission in Chotanagpur celebrated its Golden Jubilee from March 14 to March 17 at Ranchi.[65] The celebration was presided over by the Papal Nuncio (Representative of the Pope in India) and was honoured by the presence of ten Archbishops and Bishops besides some 15,000 Delegates. The Catholic monthly magazine published from Ranchi, *Nishkalanka*, brought out two issues in April and May, as Jubilee Special Issues. The Catholic Mission had then altogether 2,95,802 Christians. In March 1935, the Jesuit Mission at Ranchi was made an autonomous Region, independent of the Jesuit Mission of Bengal.[66] New stations were opened at Chandwa in Palamau District, Anandpur in Singhbbum District and Banabira in Ranchi District.[67]

8. Mission to the Santals by Bengal Jesuits and Patna Jesuits

As noted in Chapter 1, in 1879, Jesuit Fr. Charles Schaff of the Bengal Mission was in contact with migrant Santals at Jhargram (Midnapur) in West Bengal. In that year, he visited Santal Parganas in Jharkhand State, to explore the possibility of evangelization of the Santals. In 1887 Fr. John Schafer from Calcutta made an attempt to begin a Mission station there. In 1900 Jesuit Fr. Leopold Knockaert[68] was made chaplain at Purnea from where he made some attempts to visit Santal Parganas. Eventually, in 1918, he founded a Mission centre in Santal Parganas. He retired in 1922 and was succeeded by Fr. De La Croix.

On April 16, 1923, Fr. J. B. Anselmo[69] entered Santal Parganas and made many converts among the Santals. In 1924, the Santal Mission was handed over to the Maltese Jesuits of Cecily Province by Archbishop Perier of Calcutta. Appointed Superior of the Mission, Fr. De Bono[70] focused on laying a strong foundation for a flourishing

Santal ministry. A number of Fr. Knockaert's converts of Purnea District lived around a village called Majlispur in the Kishanganj sub-division. Fr. De Bono built a bungalow there in 1929, and a church and convent, in 1930. The Sisters of Charity of St. Capitano were called to work at Majlispur. In course of time, Fr. Cauchi, Fr. Grech-Cumbo and Fr. Cordaro arrived to assist Fr. De Bono.

At the end of 1929, the Superior appointed Fr. Cauchi[71] to start mission work in the four sub-divisions of Santal Parganas: Dumka, Jamtara, Rajmahal and Pakur. On April 12, 1930, Fr. Cauchi shifted to a village called Kasturi.[72] Kasturi proved too small for a permanent residence. Fr. Cauchi and Fr. Cordaro moved to another village called Monglapara.[73] There they were joined by Fr. J. D' Espierres, S.J., and Fr. A. Trussart, S. J. Many came for instruction and were baptized. They opened the Mission's first Upper Primary School with 150 pupils. They had been invited by Misir Murmu, the headman of the village. On October 11, 1932, Misir Murmu died of snake-bite, and his brother, who became the headman, was accused before the Sub-Divisional Officer of having transferred his land to non-tribals (missionaries). The missionaries lost the case, and, they had to demolish the Mission house and the Church in October 1933.[74] They were advised to settle elsewhere. The Fathers shifted their abode to Torai, a village two miles from Monglapara, which was outside the domain. Fr. Cauchi purchased land at Guhiajari.[75]

In Sahibganj, a railway colony, where many Anglo-Indians and some Santals lived, a new church (Our Lady of Mercy Church) was built and blessed by the Archbishop of Calcutta on February 15, 1932. In 1933, a bungalow was bought at Dudhani, one mile from Dumka, a major town. Another bungalow close to it was purchased and changed into a convent for the Sisters of Charity of St. Capitanio. Fr. Cauchi was appointed the first Parish Priest. The church, dedicated to St. Paul, was blessed in 1934. Lands were purchased at Torai and near Tinpahar. At the end of 1935, the number of Christians in the Mission, which was only 80 in 1925, increased to 7,700.[76]

During 1936-1939, churches were built and blessed at Guhiajori, Torai and Tinpahar. Fr. Grech Cumbo became the first Parish Priest of the congregation near Tinpahar.[77] There a school was opened. Soon Fr. B. Bugeja, S.J., Fr. J. Milanes S.J. and Fr. J.

Portelli S.J. joined the Mission staff. During the Second World War, Mission work was much constrained. However, things improved at the end of the War. In 1946, Madhupur was made a separate parish. The number of Christians of the Santal Catholic Mission rose to 13,324.[78] New Jesuit Fathers like T. Roussos, Y. Laferla and A. Grech joined the Mission staff and began to shoulder some of the heavy responsibilities of the pioneer missionaries. The Daughters of St. Anne, a Congregation of Indian Sisters founded at Ranchi, came to Torai and Tinpahar and started schools and dispensaries. Subsequently, mission work spread to many areas in the District facilitated by the availability of more Mission personnel and resources, to cater to an ever increasing Christian community.

Patna Jesuits also ventured into the Santal land from their base at Bhagalpur. In the early months of 1930, American Jesuit of Patna Mission Fr. James Creane visited the Deputy Commissioner of Santal Parganas at Dumka and obtained permission to acquire land in the Godda sub-division of Santal Parganas. A modest church with a residence was built at Narainpur. From there, another piece of land for a church and residence was purchased at Baromasia,[79] where a large two-storied building was constructed, and a school, a dispensary and a leprosy clinic were opened.

In Godda, the Mission possessed a piece of land since 1900, and built a bungalow with an attached chapel.[80] A piece of land was acquired in Gorhi Village, to the west of the town, where a house with a church was built. During 1944-45, a big church was built in a nearly village called Sundarnagar. Another Mission station was founded at Poreyahat,[81] almost due south of Godda, during 1929-30. A bungalow with a church was built and a dispensary was opened there. Some Village Schools were also opened from this centre.

A Mission station was also founded in the Mandar Hill area near the Rajapokar Bungalow. This Mission, known as Holy Cross Mission, and a school were opened at Harimorha.[82] In course of time, a dispensary and a leper clinic were opened. Harimorha exercised control over the sub-stations at Drumria, Chakapather and Babumahal.

9. Native Clerical Leadership and Women Religious Societies

Then began the Second World War in 1939, which put the Mission into financial and personnel crunch. For five years the Catholic Mission in Chotanagpur had to manage without aid from abroad.[83] A few Jesuits, considered as 'hostile' by the British, were taken to concentration camps, while others were sent out to the army as chaplains.[84] The situation in a way helped increase recruitment and ordination of more Indians and of Europeans within India, as Belgian missionaries were unable to come out to India on account of the outbreak of the War. Almost every year, priests were ordained for the efficient working of the Diocese. In 1941, seven Fathers, including Fr. Camille Bulcke, who became well-known as a Hindi pandit, were ordained at Kurseong and six others, at Ranchi. Next year, 17 priests including six Jesuits were ordained priests. In 1943, Fr. P. Kerketta was ordained priest at Kurseong. The statistics on the Roman Catholics as given in the *Nishkalanka* in that year was 2,92,331 baptized and 23,366 catechumens in 41 parishes.[85] In July, 1944, 29 tribal priests were working in the Diocese of Ranchi. Even during the War, the number of Catholic Christians went on increasing. At the end at the War (1945), the number rose to 3, 27,226.[86] In 1947, the Catholic Mission in Chotanagpur had 3, 56,903 adherents.[87]

During the period from 1868 to 1947, many Jesuit missionaries came to work in the Mission. Some died after a few years, and some, after several years, in the Mission field and they were buried at Doranda, Ranchi, and in other Mission stations in the interior. They considered Chotanagpur their second home land. The names of Fr. Hoggor (d. 1895), who helped the pioneer missionary, Fr. Stockmann, Fr. Desnoy (d. 1899), Fr. Dahon (d. 1905), Fr. De Gryse (d. 1908), Fr. Bodson (d. 1922), Bishop Van Hoeck, Fr. Emelen (d.1936), an eminent Mundari scholar who assisted Fr. Hoffmann in compiling his famous *Encyclopedia Handarica*, Fr. Bretendean (d. 1942), one of the earliest missionaries, Fr. Grignard (d. 1942), an eminent scholar of the Oraon language and author of the *Oraon Dictionary*, the *Oraon Grammar* and the *Oraon Folklore*, Fr. Cardoes (d. 1946) and Fr. Turkenbergh (d. 1946), the manager and printer of the Catholic Press, Ranchi, may be mentioned in this connection.

The Catholic Mission in Chotanagpur received most valuable assistance, from 1899 onwards, from different organisations of European and Indian Sisters[88] such as the Lorreto Sisters, the Daughters of the Cross, the Daughters of St. Anne, the Sisters of Charity, the Sisters of Mercy of the Holy Cross, the Apostolic Carmel Sisters and the Medical Mission Sisters, particularly in educational and medical spheres. Like the Jesuit Fathers, many lady missionaries of these organisations, working as Superiors (Mothers) and Sisters, served the Mission for many years, earned reputation and admiration and died in Chotanagpur. The names of Mother Josephine (d. 1928), Mother Antoine (d. 1935), Mother Sophia (d. 1936), Mother Veronica (d. 1940) and Mother Mary Antoinott may be mentioned in this connection. Mother Antoine and Mother Mary Josephine were awarded the *Kaiser-i-Hind* medals for their remarkable educational services.

The Catholic Mission, from the beginning laid great stress on the training of native priests. For this it first opened an Apostolic School[89] in 1903 at Ranchi for boys who desired to study for priesthood, and in 1915, a Major Seminary, called St. Albert's College, whose first alumni were ordained priests in 1917. This College soon developed into a large Regional Major Seminary catering to the needs of several neighbouring dioceses.

10. Humanitarian Services

The most successful of all the Christian Missions operating in Chotanagpur in the realm of conversion and Church organisation was the Roman Catholic Mission. From the very start, it vigorously adopted varied measures for the material welfare and advancement of the people among whom it worked, and achieved significant success. The Catholic missionaries rightly perceived that unless effective means were devised to improve the material condition of their converts, religion would have very little hold on their minds.[90]

Economic welfare of the people received early, active and continuous attention of the Roman Catholic Mission. It commenced its work in Chotanagpur at a time, when agrarian problems had assumed an acute and alarming form, particularly in Ranchi District, on account of the unscrupulous exploitation of the aboriginals--

Mundas, Oraons and Kharias, – by their 'alien' zamindars.[91] There were constant disputes between zamindars and tenants and occasionally, armed uprising of the latter.[92] The Catholic missionaries, especially Fr. Lievens and Fr. Hoffmann, took up the cause of the illiterate aboriginals. Referring to their services to the aboriginals, Fr. Grosjean, the Superior of the Bengal Mission, reported to the Jesuit Provincial of Belgium, thus: "For those two great missionaries, they (the aboriginals) owe in thousand not only the salvation of their souls but under God, the very preservation of their race."[93]

Fr. Lievens played the pioneer role in this matter.[94] He learnt the tribal languages and studied the local land laws and customs and the rights and duties of the zamindars. He vigorously and openly championed the cause of the aboriginals and fought their battles against zamindars and money-lenders in the court and outside.[95] He consulted lawyers and magistrates and taught the people how to win their cases in the law courts. He advised them to take receipts at the time of paying rents.[96] With the help of Fr. Lievens and some other Catholic missionaries, a large number of aboriginals, Christian and Non-Christian, could save their lands and rights from being usurped by the zamindars.

Another Jesuit missionary who did yeoman service to the aboriginals, specially the Mundas, in the agrarian domain, was Fr. John Baptist Hoffmann.[97] He was a German, and he started as a missionary in the Munda area in 1893. He was an eminent Mundari scholar, and he studied so thoroughly the tribal laws of succession and their agrarian system of ownership rights, that he became an acknowledged authority in the field. During the Survey and Settlement Operations of 1902, he rendered a memorable service to the cause of the Mundas by explaining most lucidly to the authorities the true nature and extent of their rights in Khuntkatti villages and lands.[98] The Amending Act, called the Bengal Act V of 1903, dealt chiefly with the rights of the Mundari Khuntkattidars or original clearers of the soil, as the treatment hitherto accorded to them was, in the words of the Select Committee, "one of the chief causes of the agitation which has long disturbed the people locally known as the Mundaris".[99] Fr. Hoffmann also contributed in the enactment of the Chotanagpur Landlords and Tenure Procedure Act of 1905.[100] He was closely associated by the Bengal Government while drafting the bill, which when passed, was known as the Chotanagpur Tenancy Act of 1908.[101] It may be said that it was Fr. Hoffmann who actually dratted the bill. The Chotanagpur Tenancy Act cut at the root of the land problem and restored to the tribes their rightful ownership of the land.

In 1908, Fr. Hoffmann started an industry[102] at Ranchi to train Munda and Oraon boys and other young men in the manufacture of tiles with cement and sand. The secret of the art of polishing, colouring and enameling tiles and making floral decorations on them were also taught. This industry was discontinued later on and it was carried on by individual masons who were trained there.

To enable the Catholic Christians to avoid money-lenders who gave loans on ruinous terms and to draw loans from their own banks, Fr. Hoffmann, on the pattern of the Reiffeisen Credit Co-operatives in Germany, started the Chotanagpur Catholic Co-operative Credit Society[103] at Ranchi in 1909. The Society was registered with the Government of Bengal on December 2, 1909.[104] It at once became popular. Within three years, the Society had 8630 members and a substantial capital of Rs. 48,000. A two-storied building was constructed at Ranchi for its Head office. In 1917, the Society had 17 circles, 400 rural units and a capital of Rs. 1,60,000. It was open to Catholic Christians only. It gave loans for purchasing cattle, buying and improving lands, building bands, digging tanks, sinking wells, buying seeds, repairing houses, paying school fees and fighting law-suits, etc.[105] The Society continued to function and grew despite occasiona l set-backs and difficulties. In 1947, it had 22,511 members and a working capital of Rs.16,10,930.15. It was opened to Non-Catholics also.[106]

Fr. Hoffmann also launched in 1914, a Catholic Co-operative Stores Society[107] to do away with the middleman in the production and consumption of agricultural goods for its members and also to train up the aboriginals in the art of marketing. This venture, however, did not succeed and, in 1921, it was discontinued. Fr. Grignard, while analysing the causes of its failure, wrote in an article entitled, *An experiment in Co-operation* that it was due to the carelessness of the managers and store-keepers, defective system of accounting, immobilization of capital and finally indifference of the share-holders.[108]

The Catholic Mission rendered laudable service during the famines of 1897, 1899 and 1908. With liberal aid from abroad and from within India, Chotanagpur Mission organised relief operations at several places and saved many lives from death from starvation.[109]

The Catholic Mission started the Catholic Labour Bureau[110] in 1918. It sent several Catholic aboriginals to the tea gardens in Assam and as labourers to the Andaman Islands. During the Second World War, it sent over 20,000 aboriginals to the labour corps all over the front. The bureau with a missionary as its director has continued function as an agency for providing employment to the Catholic Christians of Chotanagpur.

11. Empowerment through Education and Industrial Training

The greatest contribution of the Mission has been in the field of education. Some of the finest schools, whether for boys or for girls, in Chotanagpur, are run by the Catholic Mission.[111] Education of boys and also of girls, received early and active attention and support. Fr. Lievens and his companions realised that education was the most effective means for removing the main cause of exploitation of the tribals and their backwardness.[112] Schools were, therefore, set up in many Christian villages. From the beginning, there was not a single Mission station without having a Boarding School. It is said that the missionaries purchased lands in the villages where conversion was expected to take place. They built a house, a chapel and started a school almost in every village. In 1874, when the Mission station at Burudih was opened a group of nuns came and started a Convent School[113] which was soon closed down due to the outbreak of small-pox. It is said that there were no less than 30 schools by the year 1886.[114] The number of these Schools rose to 60 by October 1887.[115]

In 1887, Fr. Motet started a Lower Primary School[116] at Ranchi for the education of the children of the Catholic converts in Ranchi and its neighbourhood. It was then called St. Peter's School.[117] It was soon deemed necessary to admit into this School, boys from the Catholic Mission centres in the interior of the District of Ranchi with a view to training them to the posts as Catechists (Preachers) and School teachers. A large building was constructed for the School and it was renamed as St. John's School. It became Middle English School in 1903, and a High English School, in 1905.[118] It had been a school for Catholic boys only but from 1904, Non-Christian boys also were admitted as day-scholars. It was affiliated[119] to the Calcutta University in 1908, and, in that very year, one Munda boy successfully passed the Matriculation examination. The boarders paid a nominal fee for boarding, lodging and tuition.

The Mission gave much stress and attention to female education too. Attempts were made from the beginning to open separate schools for girls. In order to see to the education of girls, different congregations of Sisters, such as the Loretto Sisters, the Daughters at the Cross, the Daughters of St. Anne, and Ursuline Sisters were called in.[120] When the Mission station of Burudh was built in 1874, a group of nuns started a school for girls there.[121] This school was disbanded soon due to a severe attack of small-pox. In 1890, an Irish congregation of nuns called Loretto Nuns, then well-known in Calcutta for the great boarding house and Loretto School in Chowringhee Lane and the excellent orphanage at Entally, started the Catholic Girls' School at Ranchi.[122] In January 1903, the Ursuline Nuns from Belgium came and took charge of this School and the boarding house attached to it.[123] Such boarding schools were opened in other important Mission stations like Khunti, Rengari, Tongo, Noatoli and Mahuadanr.

By 1910, the Catholic Mission had besides St. John's' High School at Ranchi, no less than 140 Boys' Schools with 7,683 boys and 21 Girls' Schools with 4,760 girls.[124] Of the 21 Girls' Schools, four were big Convent Schools, each with a strong staff of European nuns and tribal Sisters. From 1911 onwards, one Father was appointed as Inspector of Catholic Schools.[125] The first man to be appointed was Fr. Van Hoeck. At the end of 1920, the Boys' Middle School known as St. Mary's Middle School, at Samtoli in Simdega, was raised to the High School standard. This became the second High School of the Mission in Chotanagpur.

In 1921, when Van Hoeck was transferred to Patna as its first Bishop, Fr. Oscar Sevrin succeeded him. In 1922 the Catholic

Mission had 519 schools with 12, 020 boys and girls.[126] The number of schools and scholars went on increasing. By 1930, the number of schools rose to 700.[127] In 1936, St. Ignatius Middle School at Gumla became a High School.

The world-wide economic depression in the 1930s adversely affected the schools and the members of the Catholic Church were requested to meet the expenses of their schools. When the Second World War broke out in 1939, the Mission was in great difficulty, and the number of schools went down.[128] At the end of the War in 1945, the situation improved and the number of schools rose again. During the War itself, the Catholic Mission planned to start a college at Ranchi. In 1944, St. Xavier's College[129] with Fr. Charles Saldanha, a Patna Jesuit as its first Principal, was started with 135 students at Ranchi. Fr. Saldanha remained there for a very short period and was succeeded by Fr. Schokaert. The College then taught up to the Intermediate Standard in Arts, Science and Commerce. In 1945, the Mission had five High Schools with 1,778 boys and three Girls' High Schools with 868 girls. In 1947, the Carmel Sisters started a Girls' College at Ranchi.[130]

The Catholic Mission laid great stress on vocational training also, to improve the economic condition of the Catholic converts in particular and of the people of Chotanagpar in general. It set up an Industrial School[131] at Ranchi in 1894. It was intended to turn out good carpenters and masons. This institution which did good work was discontinued after a few years when a more ambitious Industrial School was opened by Fr. Vandacle at Khunti, where weaving, dyeing, carpentry, iron works and silk worm-rearing were taught.[132] At the sudden death of Fr. Vandacle, Fr. De Staercke took charge of the school.[133] He made several important improvements in weaving, carpentry and iron-works departments. The silkworm-rearing industry became very profitable and it found favourable markets in England, France, Italy, Russia, Turkey and Japan.[134] Later on, however, it was closed down. Carpentry, weaving and agriculture schools were opened in many Mission stations. A Carpentry Training School was started by Fr. Bodson at Katkahi in 1921. Another Carpentry School was opened at Mandar in 1923. During the same year, Weaving Schools were opened at Katkahi, Torpa and Noatoli.

The Agriculture Schools at Samtoli and Noatoli were started by Fr. Cardon. The Khunti Technical School was started in 1939 with tailoring and weaving sections. Girls too were taught in weaving and agriculture.

The Mission started a Lace School at Ranchi in 1905.[135] This School was meant for Indian Catholic women living in the town of Ranchi and its neighbourhood. It is said that the laces made there were in great demand in Calcutta and even in far away Europe. In course of time, Lace Schools were started in other Mission stations like Khunti, Tongo and Rengari. In 1923, the Lace Schools at Ranchi, Khunti, Tongo and Rengari provided employment to 400 ladies. These Schools continued.

12. Medical Service

The Catholic Mission did not neglect medical service. Every missionary centre maintained a dispensary of its own.[136] In 1947, the Medical Mission Sisters[137] started a modern Hospital, known as the Holy Family Hospital at Mandar in Ranchi District. They started another hospital, known again as the Holy Family Hospital, at Kodarma in Hazaribagh District. The Sisters of the Holy Cross have been working in the Sadr Hospital at Hazaribagh since 1938. The Ursuline Sisters have been rendering help to the Sadr Hospital at Ranchi.

13. Contribution to Language and Literature

The contributions of the Roman Catholic missionaries to the spread of Hindi and to the development of the tribal languages and literature have been of considerable importance. When the missionaries first came to Chotanagpur, they adopted Hindi as a medium of their contact with the aboriginals, Hos, Mundas, Oraons and Kharias, and also as the medium of instruction in their schools. To be more effective in their missionary work among the tribal people, they studied and learnt their languages. Fr. Lievens, within a few months, learnt Mundari and Oraon.[138] Some of the missionaries wrote and published books and thus developed the tribal languages and enriched them with Christian literature.

The most outstanding work of the Catholic missionaries has been the *Encyclopaedia Mundarica*[139] written by Fr. Hoffmann. He was assisted by Fr. Van den Emelen, another eminent scholar of Mundari and some Munda elders. The 13-volume *Encyclopaedia Mundarica* is an excellent treatise on Mundari vocabulary and describes the customs and practices of the Munda tribe. It was published by the Government of Bihar during 1930-1941. This work was very highly praised by the Royal Asiatic Society of London. Fr. Hoffmann also wrote and published a *Mundari Grammar* (pp. 222) in 1903, and *A Mundari Grammar with Exercise* in 1907.[140] Fr. Hoffmann also published an article[141] "Mundari Poetry, Music and Dances" in the *Journal of the Asiatic Society of Bengal*, Vol. II. For the distinguished work and other humane services to the tribal people, the Government awarded Fr. Hoffmann the *Kaiser-i-Hind* medal in 1913. Just before his repatriation to Germany, be was given a 'Certificate of Honour' by the Government.[142]

Some other missionaries also wrote and published valuable books or articles on the customs, music and folklores of the tribal people of Chotanagpur. Frs. Grignard, Bleses, De Gryse and Bodson wrote and published grammars in the Oraon language. Fr. Grignard's *A Grammar of the Oraon Language* (pp. 311) and *An Oraon- English Dictionary* (pp. 687) were published in 1924.[143] A *Dictionary of the Kharia Language* (pp. 125) was published by Frs. Floor and Druart in 1934.[144] Fr. Dehon published an article "Customs of the Oraons" in the *Journal of the Asiatic Society of Bengal*, Vol. II, in 1906.[145] Fr. Nowrangi wrote a grammar on the Nagpuria Language. The Catholic Mission has been publishing a monthly journal called *Nishkalanka* in Hindi since 1922.

The Mission has a press of its own, called the Catholic Press, at Ranchi. It has gained for itself a good name for its excellent printing and its high standard of workmanship.[146]

14. Conclusion

Overall, the Catholic Mission in Chotanagpur, under the leadership of the Jesuits, made tremendous progress in terms of founding not only mission centres, churches and ecclesiastical institutions, but also educational, vocational and industrial institutes which catered to the

Christians and Non-Christians. The impact of the Mission work can be noted in various fields: social, cultural, religious, educational, economic, agrarian and political. The greatest transformation seems to be turning a largely agrarian Christian tribal society into a literate, bureaucratic society. Today, tribal Christians being employed in blue and white collar jobs are settled in many cities in India. In other words, yesterday's forest-dwelling tribals have become today's literate citizens of India's mainstream society, playing prominent roles in civil society.

Secondly, leadership in the Christian community has been completely transferred from foreigners to Indians, mostly tribals, which is a sign of great development of a marginalized tribal society till yesterday. Thirdly, missionaries have been accused of 'detribalising' the tribals in Chotanagpur. However, the ground reality is otherwise. The tribals who converted to Christianity have remained as tribals in everyway in their social and cultural life and have retained their nominal identity through their clan or surnames. Of course there have been changes in religion, practices, and beliefs which accord them their new religious identity. The tribals have integrated most of their indigenous customs, festivals and practices (which are not against the values of Christianity) into Christian life. In sum, the Christianisation of the tribals in late 19th and early 20th centuries, did not entail de-tribalisation, unlike in Goa during the Portuguese period of evangelization in the 16th century. Besides, tribal Christianity has added its identity to the already heterogenous Christianity in India. The tribal Christianity in Jharkhand is yet another varieity of Christianity with its distinct identity.

Endnotes and References

1 *Mission Belge du Bengale Occidental*, September, 1869, p. 4; Henry Josson (1921), *La Mission du Bengale Occidental*, Bruges (Brussels) Vol. I, p. 272; S. C. Roy (1912), *The Mundas and Their Country*, pp. 290-291; *A Short Historical Survey of the Catholic Church in Chotanagpur* (hereinafter, SHSCCC), 1st May, 1962 (typed unpublished MSS), Manresa House, Ranchi, p. 1.

2 *Mission Belge du Bengale Occidental*, September, 1869, p. 4.

3 "Stockman to Steins", Chaibasa, November 25, 1868, in *Mission Belge du Bengale Occidental*; "Stockman to General", Chaibasa, November 11, 1873; SHSCCC (1962), p. 1.
4 "Stockman to Steins", Chaibasa, November 25, 1868, in *Mission Belge du Bengale Occidental;* SHSCCC (1962) p. 1.
5 SHSCCC (1962), p. 1; Fidelis de Sa (1975), *Crisis in Chotanagpur,* p. 116.
6 de Sa (1975), p. 117.
7 Ibid.
8 *Mission Belge du Bengale Occidental,* September, 1869, p. 4; Henry Josson (1921), Vol.II, p. 399; Roy (1912), p. 291.
9 Josson (1921), Vol. I, pp. 401-402.
10 *Mission Belge du Bengale Occidental,* July 1874, p. 4. "Stockman to General", Chaibasa, November 11, 1873, 2b-1, 3.
11 Marlier A. (1929), *Een Jezuiet Missionaries, Pater Constant Lievens,* Louvain, p. 134; SHSCCC (1962), p. 1; Roy (1912), pp. 291-292.
12 "Report of Steins to General", December 7, 1876, in *Archivum Romanum Societatis Iesu Bengale,* 2b-1, 18.
13 SHSCCC (1962), p. 1; Roy (1912), p. 292; K. Sheetal (1939), *Chotanagpur ki Kalishya ka Brittant* (News about the Chotanagpur Church), p. 191.
14 *Mission Belge du Bengale Occidental,* January 1879, pp. 16-18; Josson (1921), Vol. I, p. 407.
15 Grosjean's printed statistics to General, 1881-1885 in *Archivum Romanum Societatis Iesu Bengale* 3-11, 18.
16 de Sa (1975), p. 120; Roy (1912), p. 292.
17 de Sa (1975), p. 120.
18 Josson (1921), Vol. I, p. 417; SHSCCC (1962), p. 1.
19 SHSCCC (1962), p. 1; Josson (1921), Vol. II, p. 130; Roy (1912), pp. 292-293; Sheetal (1939), p. 172.
20 de Sa (1975), p. 121.
21 Ibid., p. 121; V. Tucker, *The Catholic Church of Chotanagpur* (typed unpublished MSS), March 4, 1961, p. 1; Marlier (1929), p. 151.
22 J. B. Hoffmann, *Private Memoirs* in Jesuit Archives, Ranchi.
23 "Grosjean Memoir", in *Vermeire's Collection: Lievens does,* p. 24; V. Tucker (1961), p. 1.
24 "Lievens to Provincial", Torpa, November 22, 1887, in *Archivum Provinciae Belgicae Septentrionalis Societatis Iesu,* India, VI, 5.
25 J. B. Hoffmann (1923), *37 Jahre Missionar in Indian,* Innsbruck, p. 10.

26 Josson (1921), Vol. II, p. 135; SHSCCC (1962) p. 2.
27 "Grosjean Memoir", op. cit., p. 2.
28 "Lievens to Provincial", Torpa, November 22, 1887, in *Archivum Provinciae Belgicae Septentrionalis Societatis Iesu*, India, VI. 5.
29 de Sa (1975), p. 126.
30 Roy (1912), p. 306; Sheetal (1939), p. 173.
31 "Grosjean to General", Calcutta, September 28, 1886, in *Archivum Romanum Societatis Iesu Bengale* 3-11, 22.
32 Tucker (1961), March 4, p. 1; SHSCCC (1962), p. 2; Roy (1912), p. 306.
33 "Lievens to Provincial", Torpa, July 30, 1887, in *Lallemand,* Cahier, IV, p. 10.
34 Josson (1921), Vol. I, p. 454; Roy (1912), p. 293; Sheetal (1939), p. 172.
35 Tucker (1961), March 4, p. 1; SHSCCC (1962), p. 2; Josson (1921), Vol. II, pp. 149, 168-169, 188-189.
36 F. J. Bowen, *Father Constant Lievens, S.J.-The Apostle of Chotanagpur*, p. 111; Roy (1912), p. 293.
37 Quoted by de Sa (1975), p. 133.
38 "Gosjean to Provincial", Calcutta, June 30, 1888, in *Archivum Provinciae Belgicae Septentrionalis Societatis Iesu*, Grosjean, II
39 SHSCCC (1962), p. 2; Roy (1912), p. 293; de Sa (1975), p. 150.
40 de sa (1975), p. 151.
41 Josson (1921), Vol. II, pp. 188-189; Tucker(1961), March 4, p. 1; SHSCCC (1962), p. 2.
42 Roy (1912), p. 307; Tucker (1961), 4th March, p. 2; SHSCCC (1962), p. 3.
43 SHSCCC (1962), p. 2.
44 Ibid., p. 3.
45 Ibid; Tucker (1961), 4th March, p. 1.
46 SHSCCC (1962), p. 3.
47 Ibid., p. 3; Tucker (1961), March 4, p. 1.
48 Josson (1929), Vol. II, pp. 221, 226-227; SHSCCC (1962), p. 3.
49 Roy (1912), p. 307.
50 SHSCCC (1962), p. 3; Roy (1912): He says 71, 270.
51 SHSCCC (1962), p. 5.
52 Roy (1912), p. 307.
53 SHSCCC (1962), p. 5.
54 Roy (1912), p. 307.
55 Ibid.

56 Tucker, 4th March, 1961, p. 2; SHSCCC (1962), p. 6.
57 Josson (1921), Vol. II, p. 379.
58 Tucker (1961), 4th March, p. 2; SHSCCC (1962), p. 6.
59 *Newsreel,* September, 1958.
60 *Nishkalanka,* Vol. VII, No. 8, August 1927, p. 118.
61 *Nishkalanka,* Vol.VIII, No. 4, April 1928, p. 65.
62 *Nishkalanka,* Vol.VIII, No. 5, May, 1928.
63 *Nishkalanka,* Vol. XIII, No. 6, June, 1933, pp. 107-116; Tucker (1961), 4th March, p. 2.
64 Tucker (1961), p. 2.
65 Ibid; SHSCCC (1962), p. 6; *Nishkalanka,* Golden Jubilee Special Issues, April and May, 1935.
66 *Newsreel,* February, 1959; *Nishkalanka,* Golden Jubilee Special Issues, April & May, p. 35.
67 *Nishkalanka,* Golden Jubilee Special Issues, April & May, p. 35; Tucker (1961), 4th March, p. 3.
68 Henry Holsten, SJ (1920), *Inscriptions on Christian graves and memorial tablets in the Purnea District,* Bihar and Orissa, Patna, pp. 8 & 71; p. 1.
69 J. Portelli, S.J. (1960), *The Catholic Mission to the Santali land of the Districts of Purnea and Santal Parganas.*
70 Ibid., p. 1
71 Ibid., p. 2.
72 Ibid.
73 Ibid., p. 3.
74 Ibid.
75 Ibid.
76 Ibid., p. 4.
77 Ibid.
78 Ibid.
79 Monsignor Urban McGarry (1960), *The Catholic Mission in the Bhagalpur District and Adjacent Santal Areas,* p. 2.
80 Ibid.
81 Ibid.
82 Ibid., p. 3.
83 SHSCCC (1962) p. 6.
84 Ibid.
85 *Nishkalanka*, Vol. XXIII, No. 11, November, 1943, p. 149.
86 SHSCCC (1962) p. 6.
87 Private notes, Jesuit Archives, Ranchi.

88 SHSCCC (1962), p. 4; Tucker (1961), 4th March, p. 6.
89 Roy (1912), p. 313; SHSCCC (1962), p. 4.
90 Roy (1912), p. 316.
91 Ibid., p. 289; SHSCCC (1962), p. 2.
92 *Government Report on The Administration of Bengal under Sir Andrew Fraser K.C.S.I.*, pp. 60-64 (quoted in Roy (1912), p. 345.
93 *Life of Rev. Fr. John Baptist Hoffmann*, MSS, Manresa House, Ranchi, pp. 8 &18.
94 Josson (1921), Vol. II p. 135.
95 Tucker (1961), 4th March, p. 2.
96 *Newsreel*, No. 5, May-August, 1959.
97 Roy (1912), p. 344; Tucker (1961), p. 2; SHSCCC (1962), p. 4.
98 Roy (1912), p. 344.
99 Quoted in Roy (1912), p. 344.
100 Roy (1912), p. 344.
101 *Life of Rev Fr. John Baptist Hoffmann*, p. 17; SHSCCC (1962), p. 4.
102 Roy (1912), p. 317.
103 Ibid., p. 321; Josson (1921), Vol. II, p. 370; SHSCCC (1962), pp. 4-5.
104 Roy (1912), p. 321.
105 Tucker (1961), 4th March, p. 4.
106 SHSCCC (1962), p. 5.
107 Ibid; Tucker (1961), 4th March, p. 4.
108 *Catholic Herald*, Nov. 1922.
109 Josson, Vol. II, p. 221.
110 Tucker (1961), 4th March, pp. 4-5.
111 Ibid., p. 3.
112 SHSCCC (1962), p. 3.
113 Ibid., p. 1.
114 Josson (1921), Vol. II, p. 140; Van Der T. Schuerren (1922-25), *Belgian Mission of Bengal,* Vol.1, *Calcutta,* p. 9.
115 Schuerren (1922-25), p. 9.
116 Roy (1912), p. 310.
117 Josson (1921), Vol. II, p. 151.
118 Roy (1912), p. 310.
119 Ibid.
120 SHSCCC (1962), p. 4; Josson, Vol. II, p. 184.
121 SHSCCC (1962), p. 1.
122 Roy (1912), p. 314.
123 Ibid.

124 Ibid., p. 309.
125 SHSCCC (1962), p. 4.
126 *Nishkalanka,* Vol. II, No. 8, August 1922, p. 100.
127 Ibid., Vol. XI, No. 4, April 1931, p. 105.
128 Ibid., Vol. XX, No. 6, June 1940, p. 105.
129 Ibid., Vol. II, No. 8, July 1944, p. 104.
130 Ibid., Vol. XXVII, No. 7, July, 1947, p. 16.
131 Roy (1912), p. 317.
132 Ibid.
133 Ibid., p. 318.
134 Ibid., p. 319.
135 Ibid., p. 315.
136 SHSCCC (1962), p. 4.
137 Tucker (1961), 4th March, p. 4.
138 J. B. Hoffmann, *Private Memoirs.*
139 N. Kumar (1970), *DIstrict Gazetteer: Ranchi,* p. 505; Tucker (1961), 4th March, p. 5.
140 Kumar (1970), p. 506.
141 Ibid., p. 507.
142 Ibid.
143 Josson (1921), Vol. II, p. 369.
144 Kumar (1970), p. 507.
145 Ibid.
146 Tucker (1961), 4th March, p. 4.

Chapter 3

The Baptist Missionary Society in Bihar

1. The Beginnings in Bengal

One of the earliest Protestant Missions to begin work in Bihar was the Baptist Missionary Society (BMS), founded in 1792[1] in England, largely through the efforts of Dr. William Carey. The Society did not have much funds to start with but Dr. Carey was anxious to undertake Mission work anywhere in the world without funds from the Society. One Dr. John Thomas, who had become a missionary after renouncing his job as a surgeon in the English East India Company, persuaded him to work in Bengal. They boarded a Danish ship and landed in Calcutta on November 11, 1793, without a license from the directors of the English East India Company.[2]

The arrival of William Carey in 1793, opened a new chapter in the history of Christianity in India.[3] "With him", says Dr. Latourette, "begins a new era in Protestant Missions not only in India but also in the entire world."[4] The hostility of the English authorities in India to organize mission work on the one hand, and the patronage accorded by the Danes, on the other, forced Dr. Carey and his friends to make Serampore in Bengal, as the centre of their missionary activities.[5] On January 10, 1800, Serampore became the headquarters of the BMS in India, and from there, the Society commenced work in Bihar.[6]

2. Entry into Bihar

Soon after the establishment of the permanent head quarters, the BMS sent missionaries to Patna, Danapur, Monghyr and other places in Bihar. Although details are somewhat obscure, it would seem that Patna was actually the first station in North India to be founded by the BMS.[7] In January 1811, Mr. John Chamberlain and Mr. Peacock were sent out to Agra by river. On March 5, 1811, during the journey to Agra, Mr. Chamberlain wrote to Serampore that Mr. and Mrs. Moore were in a pleasant situation and Patna was an important station.[8] He further said, that Mr. and Mrs. Moore deserved help if that was possible. While returning to Serampore from Agra in September, 1812, he found Mr. Thompson at Patna and Mr. Rowe at Danapur. At the request of Mr. Thompson, he along with Mr. Rowe, visited and preached to his little congregation of Roman Catholics and a few Protestants.[9]

Mr. Thompson, mentioned by Mr. Chamberlain, was appointed to Patna in 1812.[10] He died in 1840. Others associated with the Mission work at Patna, during the early years, were Revs. Burton, Rose, Lawrence, Philips, Beddy and Start. Three leaves of a Church register dated 1832 show that the Church there was founded that year, during the pastorate of Rev. Beddy.[11] The membership included both Indians and Europeans, and the services were held in a building at Bankipur. There were converts from both Hindus and Muslims.[12]

Mr. Start[13] had come to Patna as chaplain in the English East India Company, and his wife was the niece of Mr. William Gurney, treasurer of the BMS. He joined the Mission in 1831, and in 1849, took charge of the work in Patna. Mr. Start was surprisingly successful in securing the services of a number of European evangelists and priests, mostly Baptists and Lutherans, often on a voluntary basis. In those days, very little stress was laid on denominationalism, at least at Patna. Amongst these workers were Rev. J. F. Ullmann, the famous hymn-writer, and translator, and Messrs. Kalberer and McCumby who later joined the BMS and carried on the work begun by Mr. Start. Rev. D. P. Broadway was appointed 1n 1857 and from 1866, until about in 1892, he remained in charge of the work at Patna.[14]

3. Mission Expansion

The BMS Mission gradually expanded to a few urban centres and villages. The centre at Monghyr was started by Mr. John Chamberlain, who settled there in February 1816,[15] and on April 20, baptized Captain and Mrs. Edwin Page in the Ganges. In December 1817, the first Indian convert, a Brahmin, Hingham Misser [Mishra],[16] was baptized. He was forced to give up his wife and children as they were not inclined to follow his new religion. He relinquished his home for embracing Christianity. On October 17, 1818, one Hari Das was baptized but he went away secretly on February 27, 1819. The first recorded Church meeting was held on June 7, 1819, having apparently been convened for the formation of a Church.[17] Nine Europeans and two Indians, who were present, signified their adherence to the fellowship. Mr. Edwin Page gladly agreed to be the Elder in the Church.

Mr. John Chamberlain died in December 1821 on his way to England. Mr. William Moore of Patna was appointed as pastor of the church at Monghyr.[18] By 1825, there were 34 names on the Church roll, 23 Europeans and 11 Indians.[19] The Church had been established on strict Baptist principles, but in 1826, it became "Free Communion", the whole of the European members consenting, the Indians not unanimous. To meet the situation, it was resolved to hold a strict Baptist Communion service on the first Sunday of each month and an open Communion service on the second Sunday. At first, the English and Hindustani services were held in the same church until, in 1863, the English congregation built a fine church,[20] costing Rs. 30,000, in the Fort, and the old building became the Hindustani Church. In 1882, the Indian Church of 35 members elected, for the first time, their own pastor, Nirvazi Misser [Mishra].[21] From the arrival of Rev. John Chamberlain down to recent times, the BMS ministered to both Indian and European communities. Rev. J. Parsons, who was stationed at Monghyr from 1841 to 1857,[22] opened up English Church service at Jamalpur also, on Thursday evenings. There was also a Sunday service, originally started by Rev. T. Evans, as a temperance effort.

The first formal extant record of Baptist Church work in Patna, after 1832, is the "Minutes of the Baptist Quarterly Conference of the Baptist Missionaries, Patna District, held in the Baptist Mission House, Bankipur, on Saturday, June 14, 1890".[23] Rev. D. P. Broadway and Rev. J. Stubbs of Bankipur, Rev. W. S. Mitchell of Monghyr, Rev. H. Patterson of Gulzarbagh, Patna, and Dr. W. Carey of Danapur were present. To this conference, Rev. Patterson reported that a sum of Rs.700 had been collected for the purpose of erecting a building to be used as a church and lecture hall. It was resolved that such a building be erected at a cost not exceeding Rs. 3,000. This was opened in March 1893.[24] The District Conference was dissolved in December 1891 and Station Committees substituted. From March 1892 to January 1919, there was, however, a District Committee of which all missionaries of Patna, Bankipur, Gaya and Monghyr were members and to which were referred all maters of administration including estimates of building schemes, the need for schools and other such matters.

In 1890, the District for which the Patna Station Committee was responsible, included Patna city, Gulzarbagh, Bankipur, Danapur and Khagaul. Arrah was the principal out-station. The aim of the missionaries was to preach the Gospel in every part of the District. Indeed in June 1892, Rev. Patterson undertook to prove that "there is not a street, or a *basti* or a corner of any importance from Danapur to the East end of Patna where Mr. Broadway has not preached".[25] In 1893, the Committee decided to make each of the seven Indian evangelists responsible for a ward. The scheme could not be successfully carried out due to reduction in staff.

4. Education, Health Care and Women Empowerment

Though there was lack of staff, Mrs. Broadway opened a day-school for girls in Bankipur and another at Khagaul, and began to teach women in their homes.[26] By 1889, there were 30 girls attending each of the schools, and 56 pupils in *zenanas*. The work increased until there were three schools (for Bengali-speaking girls) in Bankipur, Khagaul and Danapur as well as for nearly 200 pupils in zenanas.[27]

These were taught by three or four teachers and four or five Bible-women. In 1912, Miss Whittakar initiated a Bible-study School for women-workers, for whom bi-annual meetings were held. Its purpose was to gather together Hindi-speaking women from the Churches and Missions in Bihar for a few days of Bible study and fellowship. In 1914, Miss Whittakar[28] was transferred to Shimla and next year, Miss Tresham[29] retired after nearly thirty years of service at Bankipur. Their places were never filled permanently, and since 1932, no one was set apart for evangelistic work outside the Boarding School.

In 1898, Shiv Prakash Pande wrote to Mr. Alfred Baynes in London asking that a missionary be stationed at Arah, and a similar request was made to Rev. Patterson by an Indian doctor. After a careful consideration, it was perceived that "these matters seem to point to a leading of Divine Providence that we should station workers in Arrah, which is at present occupied by no other Mission, but has been worked regularly for many years by visits from Bankipur, Danapur and Patna".[30] Two Indian workers were stationed there under the supervision of the missionary at Danapur. These brethren must have done effective work, for in 1908, it was reported that 200 *Chamars* (one of the Dalit castes) were ready to become Christians and that four had been baptized.[31] In view of the promising nature of the work the question arose of whether it could be more thoroughly undertaken, but when it was ascertained that there was no likelihood of a Danapur missionary being available, it was decided with deep regret that, the American Methodist Mission, which had recently entered the area, should be, asked to take over the work.

In 1903, District work was opened at Jehanabad.[32] A gift was received from England in 1907 for the opening of a District dispensary and, at the end of the year, one was opened at Taregna, seventeen miles from Patna.[33] This led to the placing of an evangelist and his wife, to follow up the dispensary work and get into touch with the patients in their homes. A school for boys and another for girls were opened. The work at Jehanabad and Taregna had been steadily maintained in spite of the Swarajist Movement which greatly affected the Taregna Girls' School and teaching among zananas. Occurrences of cholera,[34] plague and small-pox, from time to time, disturbed the work, but by constant health care in stricken homes, the Mission workers won the affection of the people. Economic considerations held back some who were truly converted, but the standard of Christian character was set high and there occurred a few definite conversions, amongst them was a Hindu lad from one of the schools who also won over his wife. The New Testament was read in many homes at Jehanabad and Taregna.

During those years, plague was a familiar spectre, so that the services rendered by the Bankipur Dispensary[35](1904-1915) brought many opportunities of presenting the Gospel. During an epidemic, an Indian Government official met a missionary making her way amongst the stricken houses. She apologized for not shaking hands since her own were soiled from her work. Afterwards he said, "As I looked at her hands stained with the care of my stricken people, I felt that I was looking upon the hands of Jesus Christ."[36]

With the appointment of the Indian staff came the necessity of arranging for the education of the Christian families. An amount of Rs. 20 per month was sanctioned from London in a letter, dated November 19, 1886, the proviso being that it would be ostensibly and really a Christian school. Boys and girls were housed and taught together for several years, but it was difficult to arrange for their efficient care and discipline. It was not until 1898, when Rev. J. G. Dann took over the boys' school and Miss Angus took charge of the women's work in Patna, that the schools were really established.[37] Of the boys who passed from the Mission Middle School to High School and College, many won distinctions and secured high posts in the Government and other spheres. Later, under changed social conditions, the school ceased to serve the Christian community in the way it did, and in 1927-28, it was disbanded, arrangements for the education of the boys being made in other schools.[38]

The Girls' School grew from 5 pupils to 50 in a few years, until both the school and hostel became too small.[39]A Teachers' Training Class was opened in 1905 with 5 students.[40] In February 1919, the present buildings, later to be known as Angus Girls' School, were formally opened by the Governor of Bihar, under the Principalship of Miss Tuff.[41] Numbers grew until there were, in 1942, 148 children in the Middle School and 18 students in the Training Class. Of the latter, 12 were preparing for the senior and 6 for the Junior Vernacular

Certificate. The Senior Class was opened in 1938. Among the boarders were three college students and eleven high school students who attended outside classes.

The importance of reaching the large student population of Patna was recognized early and, in 1892, fortnightly lectures were given to English-speaking Indians. When Rev. A. E. Collier came to Bankipur in 1894, he began to hold Bible classes for college students.[42] Rev. J. I. Hasler also tried to carry on this work. He was an enthusiastic colporteur and sold scores of English New Testaments and sometimes full Bibles. He also made contacts with educated Indian gentlemen (both Hindus and Muslims) from time to time and they met in his house to pray and to discuss matters of religious experience and practice.[43] For a few years, the Y. M. C. A. (Young Men's Christian Association) had been conducting a student's hostel, but, in 1924, they had to withdraw their resident secretary, and Rev. R. Lund was asked to supervise it. In 1928, the Patna University authorities intimated that unless a resident warden was appointed, all financial assistance would be discontinued, and so, lest the opportunity be lost, it was resolved to utilize the old boys' school building and to invite Rev. H. Bridges to take charge.[44] There was an accommodation for 50 students: Hindus, Muslims and Christians living together. There, for ten years, by means of lectures, Bible study, games and friendship, Rev. Bridges endeavored to win students for Christ and had the joy of seeing many students baptized and received into the fellowship of the BMS Church.

By 1930, the congregation of the Baptist Church, situated in Bankipur, was largely composed of the people who had been brought up in other denominations, and it was felt that its witness would be strengthened if these people could take full share in its administration.[45] A constitution was, therefore, drawn up and accepted by the Church, which in 1932 became the Patna Union Christian Church. The services of the Church continued to be conducted by missionaries and evangelists with the help of laymen, until 1941 when, after much prayer and deliberation, Rev. Patras Bihari was called to the pastorate.[46]

After 1912, when Patna became the capital of Bihar, there was a large influx of people from other towns. Greatly helped by the Mission, the Christian community which settled at Gardanibagh obtained land and erected a Church, which was opened as a Union Church in 1931.[47] The Christian community in Khagaul also built a church, which was opened in 1932. This was also a Union Church.

During Rev. J. Parsons at Monghyr, work had been started at Jamalpur where Sunday service was originally begun by Rev. T. Evans. Regular services continued to be held there from 1886 until 1917. Then, under the leadership of Rev. J. W. Ginn, the Free Church community built a very fine church which was opened by the Agent of the East Indian Railway.[48] The Indianization of Railway and Government services, however, seriously affected the work at Jamalpur.

5. Work among Santals and Dalits

By 1926, three Boys' Schools, four Girls' Schools and four out-stations were maintained from Monghyr, while a Santali preacher was appointed for work in Santali villages. For some years, a High School was also maintained through the generosity of Mr. Herschell Dear, a Polish Jew.[49] Coming to India as a boy, Mr. Dear embraced Christianity, and later as a prosperous merchant, donated large sums to religious and charitable causes. The financial crisis of 1925-1926 resulted in the closing of schools, the out-stations and practically all the District work.[50] On the retirement of Miss Bion in 1932, the women's work too was closed. From that time, until 1934, the emphasis was on Church work, Indian and European. After the transfer of Rev. E. T. Stuart to Monghyr in 1935, District-work was again opened, though on a smaller scale. An intensive work was carried on amongst Chamars in 35 villages.[51]

The earthquake of 1934 laid in ruins practically the whole of Monghyr and did not spare Mission property. Thirteen Indian houses, two Mission houses and the Hindustani Church were destroyed, and the Monghyr English Baptist and Jamalpur Union churches were seriously damaged.[52] The necessary repair and reconstruction of Mission property was carried out soon. In case of Jamalpur Union Church, Rs. 4,000 was raised by subscription. The foundation-stone of the new Hindustani church was laid on May 18, 1936, the anniversary of the opening of the original church. In memory of the founder of the station, the church was named the Chamberlain Memorial Church.[53]

Monghyr had been outstanding amongst BMS stations in North India in the contribution it has made to vernacular literature.[54] Rev. John Chamberlain translated the New Testament and some parts of the Old Testament into Braj. He also made a new translation of the Hindi New Testament to replace the Serampore translation, which was already recognized by Rev. Carey as being unsatisfactory. He also composed hymns in Hindi and Bengali. In 1854, a further translation of the Hindi New Testament was undertaken by Rev. Parsons assisted by Mr. Christian, an indigo planter. The first copies of this were received from the Calcutta Mission Press in March 1868. This was the generally accepted version until 1921, when it was replaced by a version prepared by a committee of which Rev. Denn of Patna was the convener. Messrs John Parsons and John Christian also wrote hymns. The original *Geet Sangrah* (collection of hymns) was prepared by them, whilst Christian himself published *Satya Shatak*, a compilation of a hundred *bhajans*, which is still in circulation. There was also set up in Monghyr in 1879 a lithograph press for the printing of books in *Kaithi* script.[55]

Mission work was started in Gaya also, a famous place of pilgrimage. During the Hindu feast *Pitri Paksh mela*, held each year, about one lakh people assembled in Gaya. Messrs Kalberer, Start and McCumby of Patna were amongst those who made regular visits to this mela or fair, selling Gospels printed at the Serampore Press.[56]

In 1845, a property in the heart of Gaya was purchased, but it was not until 1857 that Rev. A. Frieff of Berlin became the first resident missionary.[57] It is said that he spoke the vernacular extremely well and usually carried some sweets in his pocket for children. It is evident that he established respect for the Gospel, and when Rev. Prem Chand succeeded him, he took over a well-developed work. Rev. Prem Chand also was held in great respect. At the request of the Government, he undertook an enquiry into the cultivation of opium. During these years, a small Church must have been growing, for in 1893 the members collected Rs.850 for the erection of a chapel. The present Church was built in 1908 under the direction of Rev. A. E. Collier.[58]

6. Collaboration with Regions Beyond Mission

In 1911, Rev. G. E. Hicks was lent to the BMS by the 'Regions Beyond Mission', a sister Mission society. In 1908, Mission work began at Tekari,[59] and, in 1910, Nawada [60]was opened as an out-station. Daudnagar was opened in 1923 and Aurangabad, in 1925. Limitations of staff and money, however, compelled the closing of all these except Nawada, where work amongst the Chamars continued steadily. In 1924, the staff reached the maximum strength of sixteen workers. With such a large staff, a great deal of touring could be undertaken, and usually six men went into camp for a period lasting from the close of the rains until Christmas and then again until the start of the hot weather. Along with this bazar-preaching was a constant form of witness. The volume of work may be judged by the fact that, in 1916, over 600 New Testaments and 12,000 Gospels were sold.[61] Gaya had been fortunate in having men with a distinct genius for work. Mathew Pande had the power to hold a bazar audience and clearly convey to people the Christian truth.

School work for the children of low-caste people, basket-makers, sweepers and others, was carried on extensively. Mr. Hicks greatly developed this, and to prevent it from becoming a dead end, arranged that the more alert boys should be sent to the Industrial School of the Regions Beyond Mission in Siwan. There, after completing the Middle School examination they were given a three years' course in carpentry.

In 1914, a committee of local gentlemen, wishing to commemorate the reign of King Edward VII, acquired a distillery and opened it as a small leper asylum. This was placed in charge of Mr. Hicks.[62] The erection of buildings worth at least Rs. 1,00,000 and the building up of the community life of 250 people was no mean task, but it had been a source of joy to all who had been connected with it. It offered a field for presenting the Gospel to people in desperate need, whilst a number of untainted children had been educated and trained in some useful employment.

Work among girls and women was opened at Tekari in 1885 by Mrs. Kirwan, and, in Gaya, in 1896, by Mrs. McLeod.[63] Tikari is only eighteen miles from Gaya, but in those days, no bridge spanned the river which divided them, and during rains, it was completely cut off. From 1891 until 1927, Miss Wince,[64] who succeeded her mother, lived there alone. In Gaya, Mrs. McLeod was succeeded by her daughter. At one time two schools for Hindi-speaking and one for Bengali-speaking girls were run. These were the first two schools of any kind for girls in Gaya. Later on, due to retrenchment, only one remained, which continued to be popular. Schools were also opened for low-caste children, and by 1915, there were three in Dom villages.[65] Alongside, institutional work was conducted among the zenanas.

Throughout the years of the 20th century, missionaries ministered also to the needs of the local Protestant European Community at Gaya. Services were held in the Railway Institute, attendances rising to a peak on Christmas and Easter days, but falling low during the hot weather. The children of the railway community offered a splendid opportunity for Sunday school work, and from the days of Mrs. Collier, a successful Sunday school had been maintained. The pastor, Rev. K. A. Josh,[66] was a local high-caste convert. He was definitely set apart for this office by the Church and sent to Bareilly for theological training largely at the expense of the Church. During the eight years of his ministry, a house for the Pastor was built at a cost of Rs. 200, a boundary wall erected around the new cemetery, the cost being met by a public subscription, and electricity installed in the Church building.

Since about 1940, all the BMS churches in Bihar were constituted under the 'Baptist Union' and its Baptist Union Councils which functioned at Gaya, Monghyr and Patna.[67]

7. Conclusion

Overall, the BMS had a conspicuous presence in Bihar not only because of its churches and schools, but also due to the membership of some Hindu elites. Because the missionaries were fewer in number, the BMS did not expand to many districts. However, wherever they worked they left a deep impression of Christianity. The BMS was the first Mission which converted the Dalits (Chamars) in central Bihar.

Endnotes and References

1 Rev. Philip John (1960), *Baptist Missionary Society in Bihar* (typed unpublished MSS), p. 1; Rev. M. A. Sherring (1884), *The History of the Protestant Missions in India from the Commencement in 1706 to 1881,* p. 53.
2 H. H. Dodwell (1932), *The Cambridge History of India,* Vol.VI, p. 98.
3 Haridas Bhattacharyya (1956), *The Cultural Heritage of India*, Vol. IV, p. 564.
4 D. S. Latourette, *A History of the Expansion of Christianity as quoted in the Cultural Heritage of India,* Vol. IV, p. 564.
5 Dodwell (1932), p. 99.
6 Philip John (1960), p. 1.
7 Rev. William Buyers (1848), *Recollections of Northern India*, pp. 200-201.
8 Philip John (1960), p. 1.
9 *Nineteenth Annual Report of the Calcutta Mission Society, 1839,* (printed in 1840), p. 36.
10 *Sixteenth Annual Report of the Calcutta Mission Society* (1836), p. 25.
11 Philip John (1960), p. 1.
12 Ibid.
13 Buyers (1848), pp. 202-203.
14 Philip John (1960), p. 2; *The Indian Report of Baptist Mission Society, North-West Bengal* (1892), p. 133.
15 *The Oriental Baptist,* Jan.-Dec. (1847), p. 212; Sherring (1884), p. 139; L. S. S. O' Malley, *Bihar and Orissa District Gazetteers: Monghyr* (1926), p. 62.
16 Philip John (1960), p. 2.
17 Ibid.
18 *The Oriental Baptist,* July (1847), p. 213.
19 Philip John (1960), p. 2.
20 Ibid.
21 Ibid., p. 3
22 *The Oriental Baptist,* July (1847), p. 215; *The Oriental Baptist,* Vol. XII (1858), p. 154; *Annual Report of the Calcutta Baptist Missionary Society for 1857,* (printed in 1858), p. 51.
23 Cited by Philip John (1960), p. 3.
24 Philip John (1960), p. 3.
25 *Thirty seventh Annual Report of the Calcutta Missionary Society*, p. 52.

26 *The Indian Report of the Baptist Mission Society: North India Report* (1888), p. 63, and (1889), p. 62.
27 Philip John (1960), p. 4.
28 *The Indian Report of the Baptist Mission Society: North India Report* (1914), p. 21.
29 Ibid., (1915), p. 9.
30 Cited by Philip John (1960), p. 4.
31 Philip John (1960), p. 4.
32 *The Indian Report of the Baptist Mission Society: North India Report* (1903), p. 14.
33 *The Indian Report of the Baptist Mission Society: North India's Report* (1904), p. 45.
34 *The Indian Report of the Baptist Mission Society: North India's Report* (1920), p. 137.
35 *The Indian Report of the Baptist Mission Society: North India's Report* (1901), p. 41; Rev. Philip John (1960), p. 5.
36 Cited by Philip John (1960), p. 5
37 Philip John (1960), p. 5.
38 Ibid., p. 6
39 Ibid.
40 Ibid.
41 *The Indian Report of the Baptist Mission Society- North India Report* (1916), pp. 12-13.
42 *The Indian Report of the Baptist Mission Society: Northern India and Orissa for 1901*, p. 11.
43 Philip John (1960), p. 6
44 Ibid.
45 *The Indian Report of the Baptist Mission Society Annual Report* (1930), p. 116.
46 *Minutes of the North-India Conference* (held at New Delhi, Feb. 28th – March 1st, 1932), p. 13.
47 Philip John (1960), p. 7.
48 Ibid.
49 Ibid.
50 Ibid.
51 Ibid., p. 8.
52 Ibid.
53 Ibid., p. 7.
54 Ibid.
55 Ibid.

56 *A Report of the Baptist Mission in India* (1854), pp. 49-50.
57 *Thirty seventh Annual Report of the Calcutta Missionary Society*; Philip John (1960), p. 9.
58 *The Indian Report of the Baptist Mission Society: North India Report for 1908*, p. 26, and for 1909, p. 196.
59 *The Indian Report of the Baptist Mission Society, North India Report for 1908*, p. 26.
60 Ibid (1909), p. 194.
61 Ibid (1916), p. 40-41.
62 Ibid., p. 46.
63 Philip John (1960), p. 10.
64 Ibid.
65 Ibid.
66 Ibid., p. 11.
67 Ibid.

Chapter 4

The Church Missionary Society in Bihar and Jharkhand

1. English Chaplaincy Service

The presence of English missionaries in "the Bay"[1] (of Bengal) region began with chaplaincy service by Rev. John Evans in 1678 to the English East India Company's employees. His duties included ministering to the workers in the nitre (salt) factory at Patna as well as to those at Balasore, Kasimbazar, Malda and Dacca. Land travel being impossible without an armed escort, it was necessary for him to make the journey to Patna by river which meant traveling up from Calcutta in one of the nitre barges in March or April and returning with the laden barges some eight months later. As time went on, it became possible to make the return journey to Patna from Calcutta in less than four months, and, as trade increased, small mounted parties came to make the journey in ten days, so that it was often possible for the Chaplain to visit Patna once in two years.

Later on, when the need arose for the Company to protect its servants, a force of European and Indian troops was posted in a newly-built cantonment at Danapur, 11 miles west of Patna, which was one of the places in that stretch of the Ganges where big merchants, Indians as well as Europeans, had built fortified warehouses and landing wharves. In course of time, the number of Europeans in Bihar increased.[2] They came as employees of the Company, indigo planters and zamindars, and later as Government officers and railway servants. To serve them a few churches were built and Chaplains were posted at various stations.[3] Of these, some were paid by the Indian Ecclesiastical Establishment (I.E.E.), some by the military, some by the railway administration, and others by funds raised within the Church itself. So far, no attempt was made to start missionary work any where in Bihar. The English East India Company was vehemently opposed to missionary activity in India.[4]

Towards the close of the eighteenth century, some Chaplains of the Company themselves led the way to missionary work in Bengal and Bihar.[5] Rev. David Brown was the Chaplain of the Old Mission Church in Calcutta for 25 years from 1787 to 1812. In the words of Canon Sandy, "the Old Mission Church, Calcutta, be regarded as the true birthplace of the Church Missionary Society, and the Rev. Brown as the true father of it".[6] Canon Sandy says that Brown, Grant and Udny met together to consult more definitely about a "Church Mission for Bengal and Bihar" and Brown drafted a scheme for it and sent it to England but it did not lead to any work being started in Bihar.[7] Rev. Charles Simeon in England joyfully responded to their invitation, which led them in a subsequent letter to write: "What we have now heard from you is sufficient to excite us to continue steadfast in prayer and the Lord's will be done, and the Gospel of his Grace be sent to the heathen of the East in Bengal and Bihar."[8] In 1799, the Church Missionary Society (CMS) was formed in England.

In May 1806, came Rev. Henry Martin[9] as the Chaplain of the East India Company in Calcutta. Before the end of the year, he was busily engaged in acquiring Persian, Sanskrit and other languages, in translating the *New Testament* into Hindustani and in conversing with all classes of people on the subject of Christianity. Proceeding to Danapur, he opened five schools for the instruction of Indians and translated portions of the *Book of Common Prayer* into Hindustani sufficient for public worship. [10]

2. Mission Initiated by the Society for the Propagation of the Gospel

In 1823, Bishop Reginald Heber[11] was consecrated at Lameth as Bishop of Calcutta. His Diocese included not only the whole of Indian sub-continent but various other countries including Ceylon and Australia.[12] In the following year, he toured northern India,[13] visiting Bhagalpur, Danapur, Buxar, Chunar and Benares, touching Rajmahal, where he met some Paharias from the neighbouring hills of Bhagalpur.

According to Dr. Eugene Stock, "the first man to call attention to the claims of the hill-tribes in Bihar upon the Church's sympathy seemed to have been Bishop Heber."[14] It was at his instance that the Society for the Propagation of the Gospel (SPG) sent, in 1826, Rev. T. Christian[15] to Bhagalpur to commence work among the Paharias. He could reside among them from December to March only and spent the remainder of the year in officiating at Bhagalpur and at Monghyr. He was also engaged in reducing the Paharia language to writing, compiling a vocabulary and endeavouring to translate portions of the Bible. Some children were entrusted to him for education. Two sons of a Paharia Chief and two other children were baptized. Rev. Christian won the confidence of the Paharias but he soon fell a victim of jungle fever and died on December 16, 1827. His wife also died soon. The Bishop of Calcutta had regarded the Mission "as the nucleus of future possible good on a more extended scale than any other district in India", but with the death of Rev. T. Christian, this hopeful prospect vanished and the work was not renewed.[16] In 1845, the Christ Church,[17] later on, the Pro-Cathedral of the Diocese at Bhagalpur, was dedicated. One of the leading lay members of the congregation there was the Commissioner, Mr. Drown, son of Rev. David Brown, to whom reference has already been made earlier.

3. Independent CMS Mission in Bihar

In 1848, the Chaplain of Bhagalpur, Rev. Vaux,[18] wrote to the Secretary of the CMS in Calcutta, pleading the need of Bihar, and especially for the Paharias and Santals, asking for a missionary to be sent there, and promising that the local congregation would provide a house with a school building, and pay for the expenses of a school. The CMS in England sent Rev. E. Droese,[19] a German missionary, who had been working in India, since 1842 with the Gossner Mission of Berlin, and had recently been ordained by Bishop Wilson of Calcutta, to Bhagalpur. The Society made it clear that it was opening this work at Bhagalpur purely on an experimental basis, and that it was not accepting financial responsibility for anything other than missionary's salary.

In April 1850, Rev. E. Droese and his wife landed at Narga through the Ganges,[20] where now stands the Bishop's compound. So well did the experiment succeed that Rev. Droese remained at Bhagalpur for 36 years before retiring to take up fresh work in Mussoorie where he died in 1891. Rev. Droese acquired some land at Champanagar, on the outskirts of Bhagalpur, which later on formed the Bishop's compound and by the end of 1853, built a bungalow. Next year, the St. Savior's Church at Champanagar was dedicated, and he founded a primary orphanage[21] Also, Mrs. Droese opened a school for girls. As early as in 1856, the CMS had accepted full responsibility for this work.[22]

4. CMS Mission to the Paharias and Santals

Before Rev. Droese reached Bhagalpur, a Sunday school was being conducted for the children of the Paharia soldiers belonging to the Corps of Hill Rangers, founded by Mr. Augustus Cleveland, Collector of Bhagalpur from 1780 to 1784, and stationed at the fort of Nathnagar.[23] Rev. Droese soon found that the Paharias were more responsive than the people of other castes he met. This led him to devote much of his time in the cold weather every year to itinerating in the hills where the Paharias lived, and, in a short time, he learnt their language and reduced it to writing.[24] He also opened a few schools but when the Santal Rebellion broke out in 1855, the pupils fled to Bhagalpur and were taken into the School at Champanagar.

Rev. Droese returned to Santal Parganas in 1856. He saw fearful signs of carnage which left a large number of children as orphans, many of whom he took to Champanagar. The new Deputy Commissioner of Santal Parganas, Mr. Georgo Yule,[25] encouraged him to open schools for Paharias and Santals, and obtained a Government grant for them. By 1859, when the CMS sent Rev. T. E. Hallet to Bhagalpur for evangelistic work among the Santals, there were twelve of these schools with 400 pupils, staff and students alike being all Non-Christians.[26] After a year, his health broke down and he died soon after he returned to England. He was succeeded by Rev. E. L. Puxley and from then onward, the CMS Bihar Mission and the CMS Santal Mission followed separate and largely independent courses.

Rev. E. L. Puxley began to live among the Santals in 1860.[27] An ex-cavalry officer, he had been designated to work in Lucknow, but an officer who had taken part in quelling the Santal Insurrection, persuaded him to take up work among the Santals instead. Permission was granted and he was introduced to the Deputy Commissioner of Santal Parganas, Mr. George Yule, who advised him to begin work at Hiranpur.[28] He opened a boarding school there, taking with him all the Santal students then attending Rev. Droese's School at Champanagar. He also started a Teachers' Training Class for some promising boys. When the railway construction bungalow at Taljhari,[29] 30 miles to the north, became vacant in 1863, Rev. Puxley bought them with his own money, and transferred the Boarding School at Hiranpur to Taljhari in 1864, the school at Hiranpur continuing as a day-school. The land on which the Mission buildings stood at Taljharl, was later handed over to the Mission as a free gift in appreciation of its work for the Santals.

Before he could start work at Taljhari, Rev. Puxley had to return to England on sick leave, and was succeeded by Rev. W. T. Storrs[30] from Lucknow. In 1864, he baptized the Mission's first two converts, both members of Puxley's Training Class - Ram Charan Das, a Hindu, who had lived among the Santals from infancy, and Bhim Hansdak, a pure Santal. Both, were subsequently ordained,

Ram Charan Das becoming a deacon in 1866 and a priest in 1878, and Bhim Hansdak, a deacon in 1878 and a priest in 1895.[31]

When Rev. Puxley returned to India, Rev. Storrs was invalided home. And when Rev. Storrs came back in 1866, Rev. Puxley had to retire altogether owing to ill-health. Work, however, went on, and in 1868, there were 400 Christians[32] scattered. Meanwhile, Rev. H. W. Shackell,[33] a brilliant Cambridge scholar, whom the CMS had originally sent to India to work among educated Hindus and Muslims, resolved to change his plans and devote himself to work among the Santals. He set up in 1868, at his own expense, the third Mission station at Pathra,[34] near Godda, some 45 miles to the west of Hiranpur and on the other side of the Rajmahal Hills. On January 6, 1869, Bishop Milman of Calcutta laid the foundation of the Epiphany Church at Taljhari and formally opened the Church in 1872.[35] Rev. Shackell was transferred to Benares after two or three years and was finally invalided home in 1873. By 1877, the CMS Santal Mission had about 1500 Christians.[36]

Despite losses from ill-health, the number of missionaries increased. Some of the missionaries remained and served for several years.[37] Rev. Alfred Stark spent 22 years, mostly among the Paharias; Rev. James Brown, 37 years; Rev. John Blaich, 31 years; Rev. F. T. Cole, 45 years and Rev. T. Lanman for 47 years, first as a missionary and then as the first Bishop of Bhagalpur.

The year 1878 marked a further advance in missionary work in Bihar. Two new Mission stations[38] were opened at Barharwa, nearly half-way between Hiranpur and Taljhari, and at Bhagaya, some 40 miles north of Pathra. At the same time, Rev. Storrs returned to the Mission for twelve months and prepared the first three Santals for Holy Orders.[39] They were ordained at Taljhari on St. Andrew's Day (November 30), 1878. Each of the five Mission stations was the centre of a Mission District with a missionary in charge of it. In 1888, the three Mission Districts of Hiranpur, Taljhari and Barharwa were amalgamated and the Management was entrusted to a Native Church Council with a missionary as its Chairman.[40] Its aims were self-support and self-extension. Rev. Cole became the first chairman of the Native Church Council. He remained in the post for over twenty years. The Godda (Pathra) and Bhagaya Districts continued to work under the direction and control of Missionary Superintendents.

In 1893, the Native Church Council accepted responsibility for the Santal colony[41] in Jalpaiguri District of Bengal, over 200 miles from Taljhari, with the co-operation of the Government as a reserve for Santal emigrants. Owing to rising costs, shortage of trained workers and other causes, the work outside Santal Parganas and the Santal colony was later closed down or handed over to other Christian Missions.

On April 12, 1899, the CMS in London celebrated its centenary,[42] and the Santal Church, sent a gift of Rs. 1,330 to the Society. The CMS Santal Mission had, in 1903: 4,310 Christians, 46 schools and 1,338 scholars of whom 1171 were boys and 167 were girls.[43] In 1904, a Jubilee of the Santal Insurrection or Rebellion, which had aroused Government and missionary interest in the Santals, was observed and to commemorate that event, the Christians at Barhait, where the Rebellion started, built a new and pucca church, with the help of the Native Christian Council and the Deputy Commissioner, Santal Parganas.[44] Rev. Puxley presented the western or main door of the new church. It was he who had opened the door of the Gospel to the Santals.[45]

In 1910, the Golden Jubilee[46] of the CMS Santal Mission was celebrated with great rejoicing. The Church of the Good Shepherd at Barharwa was built, as a memorial of the Jubilee. The number of Christians then was 4,775.[47] In 1912, the Bhagaya Mission District was also brought under the Native Church Council. In 1916, the Native Church Council was reconstituted as the Santal District Church Council and was made responsible for all the branches of the work of the Church throughout the whole area of the CMS Santal Mission including Godda District. One of the first acts of the new District Church Council was to elect committees for schools and for work among women. Lady missionaries like Miss K. M. W. Farler and Miss E. B Adams arrived to manage women's department. Miss Farler served for 42 years, and Miss Adams, for 40 years.[48]

5. CMS Mission at Patna

In 1859, Rev. J. J. Varnier,[49] then known as Father Felix, a Roman Catholic Chaplain at Allahabad, left the Catholic Church and, after spending six months at Bishop's College at Calcutta, was accepted as a missionary by the CMS and was sent to Patna, the capital of Bihar. He arrived on February 20, 1860. He received great assistance from Rev. W. C. Bromehead, the Chaplain of Danapur, and began work by establishing schools, preaching in the bazar, and carrying religious conversation in private circles of native society. In 1860, a second missionary was appointed to Patna, Rev. F. Pettinato,[50] but he did not remain long. During Rev. Varnier's absence in England on sick leave (1863-66), the Mission, entrusted to Rev. R. L. Bonnaud, Rev. W. M. Lethbridge and Rev. R. More, declined.[51] Rev. Varnier was gladly welcomed on his return by the people at Patna. In 1866, he exchanged visits with Keshub Chander Sen, the Brahmo Samaj leader, whom he regarded as an instrument of God for paving the way to the reception of Christianity.[52]

About 1863, a Mission school of the Society at Patna was transferred to Danapur[53] and, in 1867, Rev. J. J. Varnier and Rev. W. M. Lethbridge of Patna visited and held services at Danapur. They represented the need of a resident missionary and, later on, Rev. F. Orton, the Chaplain of Danapur secured Elahi Buksh, first as a Scripture Reader and afterwards, as Curate, for the Hindustani-speaking Indian Christians there.[54] When leaving on furlough, Rev. Orton proposed to place Mr. Baksh in connection with the Society, the greater part of his salary being provided by the European and Indian congregations. This was agreed in 1876, but within two years, Mr. Baksh died. The Society promised to continue its aid if a successor could be found, but its connection with Danapur does not appear to have been resumed until 1884. Since then, the native work was carried on by lay agency, generally under the supervision of the Chaplain.[55]

In 1882, the Church of England Zenana Missionary Society[56] (CEZMS) came to assist the CMS work at Bhagalpur. A German missionary, Miss Haitz, arrived with two Indian fellow-workers. From 1883 to 1887, this Mission engaged in medical work also, under the supervision of one Dr. Fanny Butler. In 1887, the CEZMS opened work at Jamalpur. The year 1890 saw the arrival of another stalwart of the Mission, Rev. J. A. Cullen.[57] During the first ten years of his service, he founded a leper home at Bhagalpur, established an out-station at Forbesganj in the north-east of Purnea District and also became Chaplain of Bhagalpur, which had hitherto been a separate post.

In 1897, a disastrous fire destroyed the bungalow at Champanagar compound and all records of Rev. Droese and other Mission papers were burnt.[58] The Fraser Hostel at Jamalpur was founded in 1904 for the benefit of the boys from Champanagar orphanage, employed in the East Indian Railway workshop there. Rev. Cullen had gone home on leave. He could not return to India due to the First World War. His place was taken by Rev. (later Canon) H. Perfect, who had been serving in the Mission since 1903.[59] He was the Chaplain of Purnea, and, when the Baptist Missionary Society relinquished its work in Purnea District in 1935, the CMS Bihar Mission accepted the responsibility of managing the work.

Within a few months, however, the CMS in London decided that during the next few years, it would withdraw all its support to the Bihar Mission except for its educational work. This decision brought to an end the evangelistic work of the CMS Bihar Mission in many places.[60]

6. All Bihar CMS Council

The idea of forming a separate diocese in Bihar had grown strong. In 1940,[61] Canon Lenman was appointed Archdeacon of Bhagalpur and given the responsibility of preparing for the inception of a new diocese in Bihar. The Santal District Church Council and the Bihar District Church Council (which managed the CMS Bihar Mission area with headquarters at Bhagalpur) were dissolved and an Archdeaconry Council was constituted to be the forerunner of the Council of the new diocese. On January 6, 1943, Archdeacon Lenman was consecrated as its first Bishop, and, nine days later, he was enthroned in the Christ Church at Bhagalpur.[62] Thus, the Diocese of Bhagalpur was born with the main object that the Santal Christians might have a Bishop who could give intimate pastoral care and supervision.

The early years of the new Diocese saw a big decrease in the number of missionaries among the Santals, particularly of men.[63] There was an I. E. E. Chaplain at Patna, a military Chaplain at Danapur, a railway Chaplain at Jamalpur and a diocesan Chaplain at Muzaffarpur, while a missionary priest also served as Chaplain of Bhagalpur.[64] The chaplains and missionaries ministered to small English-speaking congregations in a large number of other centres. The Government services becoming increasingly managed by Indians, the number of Europeans was waning. The grant of independence in 1947, led to a further sharp decrease in their numbers, withdrawal of the Chaplains at Danapur and Muzaffarpur and rapid increase of Indians as Church officials.[65]

The CMS Diocese of Bhagalpur, during the period under review, engaged itself, like other contemporary Christian Missions in Bihar, in various philanthropic activities like educational, medical, literary and others, and, in those fields, its achievements have been great and glorious. It was the first Christian Mission to work among the Paharias, the most backward hill-tribe of Bihar.

7. Ministry of Education

Education received early and special attention. Education of both boys and girls was encouraged. While requesting for a missionary, Rev. Vaux, the Chaplain of Bhagalpur, wrote to the Secretary of the CMS in Calcutta in 1848, that the local congregation would provide a house with a school building and pay for the expenses of a school.[66] Rev. Droese and his wife reached Bhagalpur in 1859. In 1854, Rev. Droese founded a primary school (first privately-managed school in Bhagalpur) at Champanagar.[67] The school had to be built up from nothing, for the first teachers employed in it were mostly very ignorant, knowing little except how to keep ordinary bazar accounts and to write notes in Kaithi script, and they had to be taught to read the printed characters themselves, before they could teach them to the children. This attempt met with a storm of protest from many parents and pupils. More than half of the pupils left the school, though many of them returned within a few weeks. In spite of much opposition, the school continued. Later it became a High English School and was affiliated to Calcutta University in 1887.[68]

This High School was called the CMS Boys' High School. Owing to certain difficulties, the High School classes were suspended for a time, but was re-affiliated in 1892.

Mrs. Droese started a girls' school at Champanagar.[69] She also had to face difficulties when Paharia girls from the families of the Paharia soldiers of the Corps of Hill Rangers stationed at the fort of Nathnagar were admitted to the school, pupils of other castes left the school.

Rev. Droese soon realised that the Paharias were more responsive than other castes. He, therefore, spent much of his time among them and opened a few Schools for them but when, in 1855, the Santal Rebellion broke out, the pupils fled to Bhagalpur and were admitted to the School at Nathnagar.[70] In 1856, Rev. Droese returned to Santal Parganas. The new Deputy Commissioner, Mr. George Yule, encouraged him to open new schools in the District, both for Paharias and Santals, and obtained Government grant for them.[71] In 1859, there were twelve of these schools in existence with 400 boys, staff and students being all Non-Christians.[72]

When the Church of England Zenana Missionary Society[73] (CEZMS) started work at Bhagalpur in 1882, Miss Haitz took charge of the CMS primary schools at Champanagar and Nathnagar. She soon opened a new primary school at Sahibgunj and Assanampur.[74] New primary schools were opened later at Bhagalpur but owing to the lack of men and money, only two of them survived. In 1890, a Bengali School[75] was started at Jamalpur and another school was set up there in 1892 when a missionary was stationed there. A primary school was started at Colgong [Kahalgaon] in 1899. The Christ Church Girls' School at Bhagalpur--the main institution founded by CEZMS--was raised to the High School standard in 1936, and was, for several years, in charge of Miss Tuhin Tarafdar, a neice of Bishop Tarafdar.[76]

In 1903, the CMS Boys' High School, under its Principal, Rev. H. M. Moore, was moved from Champanagar to the centre of Bhagalpnr town.[77] At that time, there were 41 students on the roll. In 1905, Rev. Moore started commercial classes in short-hand and type-writing and book keeping for the benefit of those students who were unable to go on to higher studies. Rev. Hoare was succeeded by

Rev. S. K. Tarafdar.[78] He was the real maker and builder of the CMS Boys' High School. During his Principalship (1909-1935), the High School acquired new and fine buildings and playgrounds, a large number of students and good reputation. In course of time, many new High Schools sprang up in the neighbourhood but the CMS Boys' High School continued to function as usual.

As stated above, the CMS Boys' High School was transferred from Champanagar to the centre of Bhagalpur town in 1903. Next year, Mrs. Perfect (wife of Rev. H. Perfect) opened a small school at Champanagar with seven little children. Two years later, Miss F. E. Orme,[79] arrived from England to take charge of the school. In 1909, it was raised to the Upper Primary Standard and, in 1912, to the Middle Vernacular Standard.[80] It was then decided to separate the girls from boys. The CMS took over the Christian Mission's orphanage at Deoghar and all girl students with Miss Orme were transferred from Champanagar to Deoghar.[81] The Boys' Middle School remained at Champanagar and continued to impart education.

The Boarding School for girls at Deoghar[82] had only 40 students at the start. Under the care of Miss Orme, the School, named as St. Mary's Girls' School, soon became a Middle English School. A Junior Training Class was started with three students, one of whom stood first in the whole of Bihar and Orissa.[83] In 1934, the Middle School was recognized as High School.[84] A Senior Teachers' Training Class[85] was opened there in 1941. For her outstanding service to the cause of education, Miss Orme was awarded both the Coronation medal and the *Kaiser-i-Hind* medal.[86]

With the arrival of Rev. Puxley, the CMS Santal Mission began and a regular attempt was made to set up schools in Santal Parganas. At the suggestion of Mr. George Yule, Rev. Puxley started Mission work at Hiranpur where he at once set up a Boarding School for boys, taking with him all the Santal boys of Rev. Droese's school at Champanagar.[87] He also started a Teachers' Training Class.[88] When he acquired the railway construction bungalow at Taljhari, he shifted, in 1864, the Boarding School there, leaving the School at Hiranpur to continue as a day-school. It was immediately recognized by the Government and was given a grant. This School received a fresh impetus in 1886, when the Boarding Schools at different centres in the District were all centralised at Taljhari with Rev. John Blaich as Principal.[89]

In 1910, the Boarding School at Taljhari was raised to the Middle English Standard.[90] It had a Bengali section and a Hindi section until 1907, when the latter was transferred to Pathra. In 1912, Hindi replaced Bengali as the medium of instruction used in the upper classes, Santali remaining medium in the lower classes. Attempts were made to make it a High School but due to financial difficulties, it could not be done. In 1929, it was named as St. John's School.[91] A Government Guru Training School under Mission control was attached to the School. Later it was closed down by the Government.

The CMS Santal Mission conducted a Middle School for girls at Barharwa. It was called St. Thomas Girls' Middle School.[92] This school was founded at Taljhari in 1876 by Mrs. Cole. It was moved to Barharwa three years later. It was raised to the Upper Primary Standard in 1890 and to Middle Vernacular Standard in 1906. In 1912, the medium of instruction in the upper classes was changed from Bengali to Hindi. Miss Adams was its Principal for many years.

At Pathra, the Mission founded and developed a boys' school and a girls' school. The origin of the boys' school may be traced back to the year 1827, when the Government founded a school at Bhagalpur for the sons of Paharias' servicemen in the corps of Hill rangers stationed there.[93] A few years later, when the Church Missionary Society started work at Bhagalpur, this school was handed over to the Mission. The Government continued to pay all the expenses of the Paharia boys. In 1857, the Corps of Hill Rangers was disbanded and this resulted in the decrease in the number of the Paharia boys in the school. In 1882, therefore, the Paharia boys were removed from the school and the "Hill Boys" Boarding School was opened for them at Bhagaya.[94] In 1891, it was moved to Pathra, making it a full-fledged school for Paharias and Santals.[95] In 1907, the Santal boys of Hindi section of the Taljhari School and who were from the Godda District, were transferred to Pathra. In the same year, the school was raised to the Middle Vernacular Standard, and, in 1914, to Middle English Standard,[96] naming it as St. Mark's Middle School.

There was a demand for a girls' school at Pathra. The girls' school at Barharwa was far away from the area. In 1915, Mrs. Lenman opened a small boarding school with 20 girls,[97] which was raised in 1920 to the Upper Primary Standard. Miss E. M. Grandy was in charge of the School for many years. In 1931, an industrial class was attached to the school. In 1939, the Lower Primary classes of the two Schools (boys and girls) at Pathra were combined.

On the eve of the Second World War, the CMS Santal Mission had some 40 village Primary Schools[98] serving as feeders to the Boarding Schools, but these were all closed down during or soon after the War, partly because the rise in the teachers' salaries made it impossible to finance so many schools with the available funds and partly because of the complete cessation of District Board grants to those schools.[99]

8. Medical Service

The CMS was not indifferent to medical service but definite steps towards it were taken only the 1880s. In this sphere, the CMS Santal Mission has the greatest contribution. During 1883-1887, the CMS Bihar Mission conducted medical work at Bhagalpur under the supervision of Dr. Fauny Butler.[100] In 1926, a retiring I.C.S. Judge,[101] wishing to make a parting gift to the Province in which he had served for the greater part of his career, offered to donate anonymously to the CMS, a sum of money sufficient to build and endow a twelve-bed hospital somewhere in Bihar. His offer was gratefully accepted and it was decided to locate the hospital at Hiranpur. Dr. H. C. Edmunds[102] was sent out to India to inaugurate the hospital in 1927. On December 5, 1929, the Mission Hospital was opened by Sir Hugh Stephenson, Governor of Bihar and Orissa, and dedicated by the Most Rev. Foss Westcott, Metropolitan of India.[103]

The Hospital quickly attracted patients of all castes and creeds. Despite financial difficulties, the number of beds was raised to forty. In 1937, a further gift from the original donor together with a grant from King George V Silver Jubilee Fund, made it possible to build a separate Women's Hospital and Nurses' Home and to increase the number of beds to sixty.[104] The new buildings were opened by Sir Maurice Hallet, Governor of Bihar in January, 1938, and dedicated by the Most Rev. Foss Westcott. After the Second World War, ten beds were added. The Hospital possessed two large operation theatres, one for general surgery and the other for eye surgery. Dr. Edmunds remained there for many years and was decorated with M.B.E. in 1946. His mother too looked after the patients and was awarded the *Kaiser-i-Hind* medal.[105] He was ably assisted by an Indian, Dr. S. K. Shaw, who joined the medical staff in 1930.

In addition to the Hospitals at Hiranpur, the Mission had dispensaries under Santal compounders in all main stations, but due to financial difficulties and the increasing facilities provided by the Government, all dispensaries except that at Taljhari, were closed down.[106]

The CMS made arrangements for the treatment of leprosy patients. When Rev. J. A. Cullen came in 1890, he founded a Leper Home[107] at Bhagalpur, which was, later on managed by the 'Mission to Lepers'. Medicines were distributed among the leprosy patients at Pathra and Barharwa and a Leprosy Clinic was established at Hiranpur.[108]

9. Contribution to Language and Literature

The CMS has contributed much towards the development of Paharia and Santali languages and literature. Rev. Droese frequently moved among the Paharias and within a short time, he learnt their languages and literature and rendered them in written form.[109] Rev. Puxley and other missionaries, male and female, working in Santal Parganas, learnt and patronized Santali language and literature. Rev. Puxley was the first missionary to reduce Santali to writing.[110] He published a valuable *Santali Dictionary*. He also translated the *Gospel of St. Mathew* in Santali. After him, other missionaries translated and published the four Gospels, the Acts, many Epistles, the Psalms, and a *Bible History* in Santali. The *Book of Common Prayer* and hymn books were printed and published in Santali.[111] Many schools books were also printed and published in Santali.

Canon Cole, after his retirement from the Chairmanship of the Native Church Council in 1909, spent the rest of his life in the

Divinity Training work and in the production of Bible commentaries and Christian literature.[112] He was responsible for the CMS version of the Santali *New Testament.* Rev. C. H. Koomar translated John Bunyan's *Pilgrim's Progress* into Santali.[113]

As seen above, the most significant mission work of the CMS in Bihar was its work among the Paharias and Santals. The CMS was one of the earliest missionary society to work among them. Their contribution to these communities is also characterized by the founding of educational institutions, health care eentres, especially leprosy clinics in remote areas. In areas of women empowerment, their service through the Zenana Mission cannot be ignored. Also, the CMS enriched Santali language and literature by creating Christian literature in it.

Endnotes and References

1 F. L. Taylor (1960), *History of the Church in the Diocese of Bhagalpur* (Typed Unpublished MSS), p. 1; Church Missionary Society (CMS), *Santal Mission* (hereinafter, *CMS Santal Mission, 1860-1960*), (1961), Introduction; Eyre Chatterton, *A History of the Church of England in India Since the Early Days of the East India Company* (1924), p. 57.

2 Taylor, p. 1

3 Ibid.

4 George Park Fisher (1887), *History of the Christian Church*, p. 590.

5 Eyre Chatterton (1924), p. 108.

6 Quoted by Eyre Chatterton (1924), p. 111.

7 Ibid., p. 111; M. A. Sherring (1884), *The History of the Protestant Missions in India from their commencement in 1706 to 1881*, p. 56.

8 Quoted by Sherring, pp. 56-57; C. F. Andrews (1908), *Handbook of English Church Expansion: North India*, p. 6.

9 Sherring, p. 73.

10 Sherring, p. 73.

11 Taylor, p. 2

12 Arthur Mathew, *Christianity and the Government of India* (1600-1920), p. 115.

13 Taylor, p. 2; Eyre Chatterton (1924), p. 132.

14 Quoted in *CMS, Santal Mission, 1860-1960.*

15 Taylor, p. 2; Sherring, p. 139; H. W. Tucker (1893), *Digest of the S. P. G. Records, 1701-1892*, pp. 490-491; Eyre Chatterton (1924), p. 132.
16 Tucker, p. 491; *CMS, Santal Mission, 1860-1960.*
17 Taylor, p. 2.
18 Taylor, pp. 2-3; *CMS, Santal Mission, 1860-1960*, p. 1.
19 *CMS, Santal Mission, 1860-1960*, p. 1; F. L. Taylor, p. 3.
20 Taylor, p. 3.
21 Ibid.
22 Ibid.
23 Ibid., p. 4; W. W. Hunter (1877), *Statistical Account of Santal Parganas*, Vol. XIV, p. 305.
24 Taylor, p. 4; Hunter (1877), Vol. XIV, p. 302; *CMS, Santal Mission, 1860-1960*, p. 1.
25 Taylor, p. 4; *CMS, Santal Mission, 1860-1960*, p. 1.
26 Ibid.
27 *CMS, Santal Mission, 1860-1960*, p. 2; Sherring, p. 155; Taylor, p. 13.
28 Taylor, p. 13; *CMS, Santal Mission, 1860-1960*, p. 2.
29 *CMS, Santal Mission, 1860-1960*, p. 2.
30 Taylor, p. 14; *CMS, Santal Mission, 1860-1960*, p. 2.
31 CMS, *Santal Mission, 1860-1960*, p. 2; Taylor, p. 14.
32 Taylor, p. 14; *CMS, Santal Mission, 1860-1960*, pp. 2-3.
33 *CMS, Santal Mission, 1860-1960*, p. 3; Taylor, p. 15.
34 *CMS, Santal Mission, 1860-1960*, p. 3; Taylor, p. 15.
35 *CMS, Santal Mission, 1860-1960*, p. 3; Taylor, p. 14; Sherring, p. 156.
36 Taylor, p. 15; *CMS, Santal Mission, 1860-1960*, p. 3.
37 Ibid.
38 Tayor, p. 15; *CMS, Santal Mission, 1860-1960*, p. 3.
39 Ibid.
40 Taylor, p. 15; *CMS, Santal Mission, 1860-1960*, pp. 3-4.
41 *CMS, Santal Mission, 1860-1960*, p. 4.
42 *CMS, Santal Mission, 1860-1960*, p. 5.
43 *Proceedings of the CMS (1903-1904) (Statistics of the Bengal Mission 1903*), p. 191.
44 Taylor, p. 17; *CMS, Santal Mission, 1860-1960*, p. 5.
45 Ibid.
46 Ibid.
47 Ibid.

48 Taylor, p. 19; *CMS, Santal Mission, 1860-1960*, p. 6.
49 *Annual Report of the Church Missionary Society (CMS) (1860*), p. 184; *Calcutta Diocesan Committee of the Society Report (1860)*, pp. 1&7; Tucker, p. 494.
50 *Annual Report of CM S (1860*), p. 130; Tucker, p. 494.
51 *Annual Report of CM S (1863*), p. 87; Tucker, p. 494.
52 *Annual Report of CM S (1866*), p. 117; Tucker, p. 494.
53 Tucker, p. 494; *Annual Report of CM S (1863-64*), pp. 95-96.
54 *Annual Report of CM S (1884*), p. 22; Tucker, p. 495.
55 *Annual Report of CM S (1884*), p. 22; Tucker, p. 495.
56 Taylor, p. 12.
57 Ibid., p. 4.
58 Ibid.
59 Ibid., p. 5.
60 Ibid.
61 Taylor, p. 28; *CMS, Santal Mission, 1860-1960,* p. 6.
62 *CMS, Santal Mission, 1860-1960*, p. 7; Taylor, p. 28.
63 Taylor, p. 28.
64 Ibid., p. 1.
65 Ibid.
66 Ibid., p. 3.
67 Ibid.
68 Ibid., p. 6.
69 Taylor, p. 3.
70 *CMS, Santal Mission, 1860-1960*, p. 2; Taylor, p. 4.
71 Taylor, p. 4; CMS, *Santal Mission, 1860-1960,* p. 1.
72 *CMS, Santal Mission, 1860-1960*, p. 2; Taylor, p. 4.
73 Taylor, p. 12.
74 Ibid., p. 13.
75 Ibid.
76 Ibid.
77 Ibid., pp. 5-6.
78 Ibid., p. 6.
79 Ibid., p. 10.
80 Ibid.
81 Ibid.
82 Ibid., p. 11.
83 Ibid.
84 Ibid.
85 Ibid.

86 Ibid.
87 Ibid., p. 13; *CMS, Santal Mission, 1860-1960*, p. 2.
88 *CMS, Santal Mission, 1860-1960*, p. 2; Taylor, p. 14.
89 Taylor, p. 20; *CMS, Santal Mission, 1860-1960*, p. 9.
90 *CMS, Santal Mission, 1860-1960*, p. 9.
91 Ibid; Taylor, p. 21.
92 Taylor, p. 21; *CMS, Santal Mission, 1860-1960*, p. 10.
93 *CMS, Santal Mission, 1860-1960*, p. 11; Taylor., p. 23.
94 Taylor, p. 23; *CMS, Santal Mission, 1860-1960*, p. 11.
95 Ibid.
96 *CMS, Santal Mission, 1860-1960*, p. 11.
97 Ibid., p. 12.
98 Taylor, p. 20; *CMS, Santal Mission, 1860-1960*, p. 8-9.
99 Taylor, p. 20.
100 Ibid., p. 13.
101 *CMS, Santal Mission, 1860-1960*, p. 13.
102 Taylor, p. 26; *CMS, Santal Mission, 1860-1960*, p. 13
103 Ibid.
104 Ibid.
105 Taylor, p. 27.
106 Ibid., p. 28.
107 Ibid., p. 4.
108 Ibid., p. 28.
109 Hunter (1877), p. 302; Taylor, p. 4.
110 Taylor, p. 14; *CMS, Santal Mission, 1860-1960*, p. 2.
111 Taylor, pp. 18-19.
112 Ibid., p. 18; *CMS, Santal Mission, 1860-1960*, p. 6
113 Taylor, p. 18.

Chapter 5

The Gossner Evangelical Lutheran Mission in Bihar and Jharkhand

1. Early Beginnings in Bihar

The earliest Christian missionaries to reach Jharkhand (Chotanagpur) were Germans, and the first Christian Mission to start missionary work there was the Gossner Evangelical Lutheran Mission (GELM), commonly known as the Gossner or German Mission,[1] that arrived at Ranchi in November 1845 from Berlin in Germany. But the early beginning of the GELM was in the plains of Bihar under the Mission called the Ganges Valley Mission. The credit for sending out missionaries to Bihar goes to Rev. J. E. Gossner (1773-1858). He was a scholarly Bavarian Priest, who, on being excommunicated from the Roman Catholic Church on account of his liberal approach, joined the Evangelical Lutheran Church and devoted the latter part of his life in founding Missions in different parts of the world.[2] On December 12, 1836, he established in Berlin the Gossner Mission and sent out missionaries to different countries including India.

His missionaries to India, sent out in 1838, landed in Calcutta and were conducted to Patna by one Rev. W. Start,[3] an Englishman and originally a clergyman of the Church of England, and now a wealthy self-supporting missionary. They began work at Patna but soon afterwards, they had to close it down for want of funds. Undaunted by this failure, Rev. Gossner sent out another batch of missionaries to India in 1840, who went the same way as the first Gossner missionaries, this time with greater success. This Mission, later known as the Ganges Valley Mission, succeeded in establishing stations at Ghazipur, Buxar, Chapra, Muriaro, Muzaffarpur, Suratpur, Darbhanga and other places and made some conversions.[4] In 1890, there were four foreign missionaries and 600 Christians connected with the Mission.[5] The First World War forced it to close down its work. The Christians there joined other Christian Missions and its property was sold.[6]

In July 1844, Rev. Gossner sent out from Berlin, four German missionaries, namely Rev. Emile Schatz (leader), Rev. August Brandt, Rev. Friedrich Batsch and Rev. Theodore Janke, to India.[7] Two distinct opinions have been expressed on the location of their work. It is certain that it was not Chotanagpur. Some writers are of the view that Rev. Gossner sent them to India without definitely indicating the field of their labour.[8] Others say that they had a definite instruction from Rev. Gossner that "they should go to work among the Karens of Burma. If that was not possible, then they were to go to do mission work with Rev. Prochnow around the town of Kotgarh in the Himalayan Valley."[9] This seems to be the correct view. This has been maintained by the Gossner Church in Chotanagpur and Assam.[10]

Rev. Gossner's attention to mission work in Burma was roused by a German lady,[11] whose husband, Helter, a physician of considerable scientific attainments, was killed by the Karens during 1842-43, at the town of Mergui in southern Burma. His widow appealed to Rev. Gossner to send missionaries to work among the killers of her husband and offered her residence and lands at Mergui on favourable terms for a mission station. In response to her appeal, Rev. Gossner sent out those four missionaries to work among the Karens of Burma.[12] The missionaries reached Calcutta on December

13, 1844, and stayed with Dr. John Haeberlin,[13] a German Lutheran Priest and Secretary of the British and Foreign Bible Society in Calcutta, in connection with the Church Missionary Society of London. They could not proceed to Burma as the American Baptist Mission was already there. They also could not go towards Shimla in the Himalayan region due to the apprehension of an Anglo-Sikh hostility. For certain reasons, their plan to go to Tibet also failed.

2. Beginnings in Jharkhand

While living in Calcutta in a state of uncertainty and anxiety, they came across some aboriginals of Chotanagpur,[14] who were working there as coolies. Due to the oppression of the zamindars, many aboriginals migrated from Chotanagpur to Assam and Bengal. It was in Calcutta that the interest of the missionaries was aroused in the aboriginals of Chotanagpur. They were impressed by their simple and merry life and at once made enquiries about them and their country. They began to think seriously of going to Chotanagpur.[15] Some of the British officers at Ranchi, like Commissioner Major Ouseley and Deputy Commissioner Captain Hennyngton, were interested in starting missionary work among the aboriginals of Chotanagpur. When Major Ouseley and Captain Hennyngton heard that four German missionaries had arrived in Calcutta and were in search of a suitable field, they insisted that the latter should come to Ranchi and work among the Mundas and Oraons of Chotanagpur. Captain Hennyngton wrote to Dr. Haeberlin to direct the four missionaries to Chotanagpur. The missionaries finally decided to go to Chotanagpur.

They left Calcutta for Ranchi on February 25, 1845.[16] They traveled on bullock carts or on foot. Dr. Haeberlin accompanied them up to Bankura. Leaving them with one Dr. Check at Purulia, Dr. Heaberlin went to Ranchi and made necessary arrangements with the Government officers at Ranchi about the opening of missionary work. He then returned to Bankura and told the missionaries about the arrangements made for them at Ranchi and also about the people they were going to. The four missionaries left Bankura on October 15, and traveling via Purulia and Sille, they reached Ranchi on November 2, 1845.[17] They were received by Commissioner Ouseley.

The *Annual Report of the Chotanagpur Mission* (Anglican Mission) for the year 1895 says that on November 4, they pitched their tents in a mango grove near Hatma, a little village, near Ranchi and, on November 11, they held their first Christian worship on the land obtained for their Mission work.[18] On December 1, 1845, they laid the foundation of the first station of the Gossner Mission at Ranchi and named it "Bethesda" or the House of Grace.[19] The historic spot at which they pitched their tents is marked by a memorial cross inscribed with the names of the tour pioneer missionaries.

3. First Conversions

The field that spread out before them was by no means easy and encouraging.[20] There was a socio-economic crisis in Chotanagpur, and particularly, in Ranchi District. The aboriginals were very much agitated due to the aggressions of landlords on their tenancy rights and also to the introduction, in 1834, of the British administration in Chotanagpur. They were most unhappy and helpless. The missionaries preached in the markets and neighbouring villages. A few orphans,[21] rescued by a magistrate during famine, were entrusted to their care. They were baptized in 1846.[22] On August 2, 1846, one of the pioneer missionaries, Rev. Janke, died and was buried at Ranchi.[23] Fresh missionaries arrived. During 1845-50, Rev. Gossner sent 19 men and 2 women missionaries to Chotanagpur.[24] Branch stations were opened at Domba (1846), Lohardaga (1848) and Govindpur[25] (1850).

In spite of their best efforts, the missionaries could not make any conversion outside for about four and a half years. Tired and discouraged, they wrote to Rev. Gossner that the people would not be converted and that they should be permitted to go to another area and work.[26] Little did they realise that their labours were not in vain. Rev. Gossner, however asked them to stay on and continue the work. Their labour was soon rewarded. On June 9, 1850,[27] four Oraons, Nabin, Kesho, Bandhu and Ghuran, were baptized with their families at Ranchi by the head of the Mission, Rev. Schatz. It is said that there were altogether 11 adults. On October 26, 1851,[28] two Mundas; Sadho and Mangta, were baptized with their families by Rev. Schatz at Ranchi. On November 18, 1851, the foundation-stone of a large and imposing church was laid at Ranchi.[29] Then there were only 40 baptized Christians. The Church was built by a lay missionary, Mr. A. Hertzog. On the 24th December, 1855, the Church was consecrated and called the Christ Church.[30]

On the next day, (Christmas Day) 40 Bengalis,[31] including Paulus Nemo of village Illo-Jargo, were baptized. Soon after consecration, the Gossner Mission had more than 400 baptized members and about 800 inquirers.[32]

The conversions, once begun, went on increasing rapidly. As already stated, the aboriginals were in a State of acute disturbance and helplessness. Many of them turned, for protection and peace, to the religion of the rulers which the missionaries preached. The missionaries also openly helped their converts in redressing their agrarian grievances. In 1853, a branch station was opened at Singhani in the Hazaribagh District to work among the Santals.

Referring to the annual conversions Dr. Joseph Mullens says: "In that year (1850), they baptized eleven adults; in 1851, twenty-seven; in 1852, thirty-eight; in 1854, sixty-five; in 1856, ninety-six. Before the Mutiny, they had baptized 420 adults of whom 180 were communicants and their native Christian community consisted of more than 800 adults, young and old, living in more than sixty villages."[33] By April 1857, the Gossner Mission had 900 Christians and 2000 inquirers.[34]

The tendency of the aboriginals of Ranchi District to become Christians and seek the help of missionaries was resented by the landlords who, as *Gossner Mission Reports* indicate, held consultations to devise ways to prevent the spread of Christianity, and, if possible, oust the Christians and Christian missionaries from Chotanagpur.[35]

4. Political Uprising and Persecution of Christians

The First War of Independence (the Uprising of 1857, or called the 'Sepoy Mutiny') offered them the wished-for opportunity. There were signs of unrest among the Indian soldiers at Hazaribagh and Doranda cantonments. On July 31, 1857, the uprising in Chotanagpur began at Hazaribagh.[36] The Government officers at Ranchi had already advised the missionaries to evacuate Ranchi. The missionaries were most reluctant to leave their converts. On July 31, they assembled all the converts then present at Ranchi, explained how things stood, bade them farewell and let them and the school children retire to villages. Next day, they hurriedly left Ranchi with their wives and children and fled on foot towards Calcutta. With great difficulty, they reached Raniganj, the nearest railway station to Calcutta. From there, they reached Calcutta by train on August 17. Thus, ended the first period of the Gossner Mission in Chotanagpur.[37]

Commissioner Dalton and other European officers at Ranchi fled to Bagodar on the Grand Trunk Road. The rebels at their arrival at Ranchi attacked the court, plundered the treasury and broke open the jail. On the way to Doranda, they tried to destroy the Christ Church. Four cannons were placed before the building. Of the four cannon balls that were fired on it, only one hit the tower, without doing any damage. At Doranda, the rebels were joined by some local zamindars of whom the most prominent were Thakur Bishwanath Sahi of Barkagarh and Pandey Ganpat Rai of Bhownro, who seized the opportunity to enrich themselves and suppress the Christians as well as Christianity in the District. In the circumstances, the Christians of Ranchi District had to suffer terrible persecution and hardship. [38] Their properties were plundered and confiscated. Those who were found were brutally beaten and ill-treated. The Christ Church and the bungalows in the Mission Compound at Ranchi were plundered. A Christian village called Peabhusharan was completely destroyed. A group of Christians hid themselves in an island near Dumbargari on the Karo river. Many died of starvation. Practically every convert in the District suffered. All remained loyal in spite of their suffering.

5. Restoration of Peace and Rapid Expansion of the Mission

On October 2, 1857, the rebels were completely defeated at Chatra in the District of Hazaribagh and the uprising at Ranchi and Hazaribagh practically came to an end. Two of the German missionaries, Rev. A. Brandt and Rev. F. Bohn, came back to Ranchi on October 4. The rest returned early next year. After the restoration of peace, the Christians came out from their hiding places and returned to their villages. They met the missionaries at Ranchi. The reunion was pathetic. The missionaries wept when they saw the destruction of their properties and heard of the terrible persecution their followers had suffered in their absence.

Soon afterwards, the Gossner Mission had to taste another misfortune. On March 30, 1858,[39] Rev. Gossner, who was 84, died. Before his death, he wanted to hand over his Mission in Chotanagpur to the Church Missionary Society[40] in London, but when the latter declined, he committed the Mission to the German people. A committee, known as Home Board or the Curatorium,[41] was set up to manage its affairs in future.

The next ten years were a period of rapid expansion[42] for the Gossner Mission. During the uprising of 1857, the native Christian community was broken up, but their dispersion over the District seems to have given a considerable impulse to Christianity, and the number of converts rapidly increased after the restoration of order. The landlords also, apparently afraid of what they had done, ceased to molest the people for a while. Commissioner Dalton (1857-1875) was a friend of the Christians and missionaries. People came in crowds to the missionaries to be baptized. On the Christmas Day, 1858, about 1500 Christians came to Ranchi for worship and more than 150 families desired baptism. They were followed by 60 families on January 1, 1859. The number of baptized Christians in 1860 was 1700.[43] In 1863, the number rose to 3401.[44] After 1860, the number of Christians increased at an average of 1225 per year for the next seven years. Branch stations were opened at Purulia (1863) in Manbhum District and at Chaibasa (1865) and Porahat (1867) in Singhbhum District. In 1867, the number of Christians was 10,274.[45]

6. Organizational Crisis and Split (1861-68)

Then occurred the unfortunate split in the Gossner Mission in Chotanagpur. The relation between the Curatorium and the missionaries was not happy from the beginning. At the transfer of the Mission from the personal care of Rev. Gossner to the management of the Curatorium, the previous connection that existed between Rev. Gossner and the missionaries in Chotanagpur was broken. The connection between the Curatorium and the missionaries assumed more of a business character. So as early as 1861, dissension[46] began between the Curatorium and the missionaries. During the year, Rev. Emile Schatz, who had been the head of the Mission in Chotanagpur from the very start, retired and returned to Germany, and the general superintendence and chief control of the Mission devolved on Rev. F. Batsch, who had been one of the four pioneer missionaries. The Curatorium had, in the Gangetic valley, other Missions, entirely independent of the Mission in Chotanagpur, which was headed by Rev. Sternberg in 1861. The Curatorium wanted to unite the several Missions and make Rev. Sternberg the head of all, superseding Rev. F. Batsch, one of the original founders of the Gossner Mission in Chotanagpur. The Ranchi missionaries, in a body, protested against this decision. The Curatorium was annoyed and requested them to quit the Gossner Mission.

The misunderstanding was, however removed and Rev. F. Batsch was appointed as the head of the Mission in Chotanagpur.[47] However, lack of sympathy continued between Berlin and Ranchi. This manifested in various ways and ultimately, in 1864, there came a crisis. The salaries of the missionaries fell into arrears for five months due to the failure of remittance from Berlin. At such a time, Bishop Cotton, the Metropolitan of India in Calcutta, visited Ranchi in April 1864. On Sunday, April 23, he attended the Hindi service in the Christ Church, at which 143 persons were baptized. On hearing about the serious financial difficulty, the Bishop, on May 4, wrote to the Curatorium strongly pleading on behalf of the missionaries.[48] He also suggested that if the Curatorium could not send speedy and liberal help, then, according to the dying wish of Rev. Gossner, his work should be carried on by the Church Missionary Society in communion with the Church of England. A committee, known as the Calcutta Auxiliary Committee, was set up in Calcutta to raise funds for the Gossner Mission in Chotanagpur. The Committee sent Rs. 3,000 in 1864 and Rs.11,000 in 1865.[49]

As the number of Christians had increased, the necessity for a training school for Indian priests and catechists had become increasingly apparent. In January 1866, the first stone of a Theological Seminary was laid by Commissioner Dalton. The missionaries begged the Curatorium for educated missionaries to train Indian priests and to take more active part in the general education work of the Mission. In response to their urgent appeal, the Curatorium sent out several young missionaries, mostly university graduates, between 1865 and 1867, to work in the Theological Seminary and the schools of the Mission. The most prominent of them was Rev. A. Nottrott, who, later on, became the head of the Mission. A serious conflict soon arose between the senior and the younger missionaries. The latter complained to the Curatorium against the senior missionaries, particularly Rev. F. Batsch and Mr. A. Hertzog, of malversation, neglect of Mission duties and misuse of Mission funds.[50] The Curatorium sent out its secretary, Rev. Hermann Ansorge, to investigate the charges and to introduce, a new constitution in the Mission in Chotanagpur.

Rev. Ansorge reached Ranchi at the end of September 1868 and called a conference of all the missionaries at Ranchi on November 18, 1868.[51] The differences between the two groups of missionaries could not be solved. Rev. Ansorge then tried to introduce the new constitution, according to which, instead of one missionary as the head of the Mission, there would be a Central Committee, called *Vorstand*, of three persons. However, Rev. F. Batsch and six other missionaries vehemently opposed the new constitution and arrangement, and appealed to the Curatorium against Rev. Ansorge's decision and withdrew from the Gossner Mission before hearing from it.[52]

The action of Rev. Ansorge[53] and the Curatorium continued to be a subject of criticism in certain quarters. Critics hold that Rev. F. Batsch and his followers, who had labored so much for the establishment and strengthening of the Gossner Mission in Chotanagpur, could not be accused of misuse of funds and negligence of duties. Being the only pioneer missionary left on the field, Rev. F. Batsch should have been allowed to continue as the head of the Mission work in Chotanagpur. By their unwise and unjust action, Rev. Ansorge and the Curatorium forced the six senior missionaries--the builders of the Mission--to quit the Gossner Mission and join the Anglican Mission. Supporters of the action hold that since 1861 there had been a series of serious conflicts between the Curatorium and the senior missionaries and also between senior and younger missionaries.[54] Very often, Rev. F. Batsch and his friends showed an attitude of insubordination. Unity and discipline were the two essentials in any organisation. For the smooth working of the Mission and for the proper management of the rapidly increasing missionary work, the situation required a change in the existing system of administration of the GEL Mission in Chotanagpur. Doubtless there were mistakes and misunderstandings on both sides.[55] The crisis assumed an all-India as well as an international form, and, in my opinion, some powerful external forces were trying to encourage and hasten the split. The dispute was purely personal and organizational and no doctrinal issues were involved in it.[56]

The unfortunate dispute which caused the split soon after the conference at Ranchi, affected not only the missionaries but their converts as well, who were completely bewildered at the whole affair. The total number of the baptized Christians up to November 1868 was about 11,108.[57] The senior missionaries, especially Rev. F. Betsch, had tremendous personal influence over them. The converts were attached more to the person of the missionaries who converted them, than to the religion of Christianity. Many of the elders and teachers who were at Ranchi, met every night at the residence of one Mr. William Luthor Daud Singh and discussed their future, when the dispute between the senior missionaries and the Curatorium was taking a serious turn and the senior missionaries were thinking of withdrawing completely from the Gossner Mission.[58] Most of them decided to adhere to the senior missionaries.[59] They sought the advice of Commissioner Dalton. When they told him that they would side with the senior missionaries, he promised that he would also never abandon Rev. F. Batsch and his colleagues.[60] They returned and told Rev. F. Batsch about it. Rev. F. Batsch and his colleagues were very much pleased and elated. Commissioner Dalton at once called a meeting of the English officials at Ranchi and Doranda at his residence where a decision was made to support the seceding missionaries and their convert-followers with all their means.[61]

In the last week of November 1868,[62] the seceded missionaries moved out of the Gossner Mission compound at Ranchi with their personal belongings and took shelter in the bungalow and the attached small houses of the Survey Department on the eastern border of the Mission Compound. Most of the teachers and all school children at Ranchi and a considerable number of converts joined them. It was not possible to ascertain the exact number of the converts who followed them as their loyalty to either party was not very clear. By March 1, 1869, the reply of the Curatorium reached Ranchi. It upheld Rev. Ansorge's action, accused the seceded missionaries of insubordination and decreed that from November 22, 1868 - the day of their refusal and appeal – they were to be regarded as seceders.[63]

7. Split in GEL Mission: the Birth of the Anglican Church

It is said that Rev. F. Batsch and his colleagues first approached the Church Missionary Society[64] with a request to accept them as its missionaries, but it refused and advised them to obey the orders of the Curatorium. Then they approached the Anglican Bishop Robert Milman,[65] the Metropolitan of India in Calcutta. Bishop Milman came to Ranchi on March 16, 1869. The followers of the seceded missionaries, some hundreds in number, with their teachers, preachers and elders at their head, submitted a petition[66] to him in Hindi to receive them, according to the dying wish of Rev. Gossner, into the Anglican Church. The "Ranchi Committee" also requested the Bishop to admit the seceded missionaries and their followers to the Anglican Church.[67] The Bishop agreed and went back to Calcutta. He returned to Ranchi on April 16, 1869, and, next day, he formally admitted the seceded missionaries and 624 of their converts, men and women then present at Ranchi, into the Anglican Church.[68] The new congregation was placed under the care and control of the Society for the Propagation of the Gospel (SPG). The split was complete; it led to the establishment of a new Christian Mission in Chotanagpur.

The action of Bishop Milman, admitting the Lutheran missionaries and converts of the Gossner Mission into the Anglican fold, became a subject-matter of great controversy[69] in India and outside. This event was flashed in the Indian and German Press. *The Englishman*,[70] a Calcutta newspaper, took up the defence of the new group and criticized the Gossner Mission and the Lutherans. *The Church Gazette*,[71] the organ of the Anglican Bishop of Calcutta, criticized Rev. Ansorge and the Lutherans. On the other hand, *The Friend of India*[72] supported the young missionaries and criticized

Bishop Milman. In Germany, the matter became a national problem. It is true that Bishop Milman personally visited Ranchi and studied the whole situation before he decided to admit the Lutheran missionaries and the converts into the Anglican Church. It is also true that in those days, there were several cases of Church-changing in India, and missionaries too frequently changed their Missions. Whatever might have been the reasons and circumstances, the action of Bishop Milman in admitting the missionaries and a considerable number of the converts of the Gossner Mission to the Anglican Church was a turning point in the history of the GEL Mission and gave birth to the Anglican Mission in Chotanagpur.[73]

8. Resurgent Growth of GEL Mission

The schism of 1868-69, though sad and disastrous, did not dishearten the Gossner missionaries.[74] The Curatorium vigorously supported the faithful missionaries. On May 16, 1869, Rev. Ansorge ordained the first Indian Priest, Paulus Nemo[75] of the Illo-Jargo in Manbhum District. The number of Christians at the end of 1871 was 14,107.[76] This number rose to 16,916 in 1872.[77] At the end of 1873, the Mission had eight stations and 19,172 Christians.[78] Other stations founded in the Ranchi District were Chainpur (1892), Khutitoly (1895), Gumla (1895), Kinkel (1899), Amlessa (1901) and Koronjo (1903). Outside the District, Chakradharpur (1893), Rajgangpur (1900), Karimati (1902) and Jharsugda (1904) became Mission stations.[79] Also, many of the Christians of the Gossner Mission, however, either joined the Catholic Mission that entered Chotanagpur in 1869 or reverted to their aboriginal religion during the Sardar Agitation (1879-1890), when the Gossner missionaries did not offer help, as they did before, to the aboriginals who were fighting for their rights on their ancestral lands against the claims of landlords.[80] Due to the ignorance of the British officers about the peculiarity of the land tenure laws and customs, the aboriginals, Christian and Non-Christian, passed through a period of agony and helplessness. Yet, the Gossner Mission continued to expand. In 1881, it had 31,780 Christians.[81]

In 1895, the Gossner Mission completed its fiftieth year and its Golden Jubilee[82] was celebrated on Saturday, November 9, at Ranchi.

Commissioner Grimley unveiled the Jubilee Memorial Cross erected with the names of the four pioneer missionaries inscribed. The Metropolitan of India was also present on the occasion and gave his greetings and message. The second monument of the Jubilee was the completion of the translation of the New Testament into Mundari by Rev. A. Nottrott. In 1895, the Gossner Mission had 13 stations and about 40,000 Christians scattered in 1200 villages.[83]

After 1895, the missionary activity was carried on particularly in the neighboring Native States[84] of Gangpur, Jashpur, Bamra and Bonai, where new stations were founded. Attention was given to Assam also, to which many Christian aboriginals of Chotanagpur had migrated for their livelihood. By 1913, the Mission had 96,543 Christians, of whom 73,000 belonged to Ranchi District.

9. World War Crisis and Organizational Rearrangement

The outbreak of the First World War in 1914 at once created another great and dangerous crisis in the Gossner Mission. The Mission was a German Mission. All aid from Germany was stopped. All German missionaries, 34 in number, were interned in July 1915, and then in November, repatriated to Germany.[85] There was gloom throughout the Gossner Church. The German missionaries expected to return soon, and therefore, while departing, they made certain temporary arrangements. They requested the Anglican Bishop of Chotanagpur, Rt. Rev. Foss Westcott[86] to take the Church and its schools under his care. According to the Chotanagpur Diocesan Report of January 1916, the Gossner Mission had 89,000 baptized Christians and 10,600 inquirers, who were looked after by 34 missionaries, assisted by 43 Indian priests and 377 catechists or preachers.

For the internal administration of the Church, a Central Committee[87] was formed in place of Vorstand, with Rev. Hanukh Dato Lakra as Chairman and Rev. Anandmasih Soy as Secretary. The War did not end as early as was expected and the Central Committee continued to function. After some time, Mr. Peter Hurad became the Secretary and Mr. Nirmal Soy, the Treasurer, while Rev. H. D. Lakra continued to be the Chairman of the Central Committee. Bishop Westcott managed the schools with Government grants and the subsidy from the Society for the Propagation of the Gospel. In

1917, the Bishop proposed a plan to unite the Gossner and Anglican Missions after the War but the Central Committee rejected the plan.[88]

The First World War ended in November 1918. The Government of India made it clear that the German missionaries would not be permitted to return to Chotanagpur and the Gossner Mission property there, being enemy property, was confiscated.[89] At this time, a definite proposal came from the Anglican Mission of Chotanagpur for a Church Union but this time also, the Central Committee rejected the proposal.[90] The Central Committee represented to the Government, giving reasons that the Gossner Mission property in Chotanagpur and Assam could not be taken as enemy property.

The National Missionary Council, the official organisation of the Protestant Christian Missions working in India, met during the end of 1918.[91] There it was reported that 97,000 Christians of the Gossner Church were ready to join the Anglican Mission. It was opposed by Mr. Peter Hurad, who represented the Gossner Church. He was supported by Dr. John Aberly of the American Lutheran Mission in Guntur. A Commission of Enquiry[92] with Dr. S. K. Dutta as Chairman was appointed to visit Chotanagpur and ascertain the views of the members of the Gossner Church about their future. The Commission reached Ranchi in March 1919. It completed the enquiry and requested the Central Committee to call a *Mahasabha* or General Conference of the Church at Ranchi in July, 1919.

On July 4, 1919, the Government of India wrote to Government of Bihar and Orissa that it had agreed to release the property of the Gossner Mission in Chotanagpur and Assam to an institution or Mission which functioned in Chotanagpur.[93] It made it quite clear that the property could not be given to any Mission, majority of whose members were other than Englishmen and whose expanses were borne by them. Obviously, the order was meant to prevent the American Lutheran Missions to come to the aid of the Gossner Church.

Amidst heavy odds and heavy rains, 79 delegates and the members of the Central Committee met in a Mahasabha at Ranchi from July 8 to July 10, 1919.[94] The members of the Commission of Enquiry had also come. The problem before the delegates was really very great and delicate. On July 10, 1919, a draft for the Declaration of Autonomy, prepared by the Central Committee, was presented to the Commission of Enquiry at the Christ Church, where the Mahasabha was being held. The draft declaration was unanimously passed by the Mahasabha, signed by all the members of the Central Committee and 79 delegates and then handed over to the Commission of Enquiry. The decision was momentous and historical. The Gossner Mission in Chotanagpur and Assam came to an end and Autonomous Gossner Church began.[95]

10. Autonomous Gossner Church: German Assistance Again

Soon after the Declaration of Autonomy, Rev. C. A. Rupley of the American Lutheran Mission at Guntur came to Ranchi for the help of the newly-born Gossner Church. On August 18, 1919,[96] the Central Committee passed a resolution expressing deepest gratitude to Bishop Westcott for his valuable advice and aid during War. The National Missionary Council met at Hazaribagh on October 19, 1919, and set up an Advisory Board[97] with Dr. S. K. Dutta as Chairman and Rev. Rupley as Secretary. Rev. Rupley became also the Secretary of the Board of Trustees[98] of the Gossner Church property with the Commissioner of the Chotanagpur Division as the ex-officio Chairman.

Along with Mr. Nirmal Soy, Rev. Rupley prepared a constitution for the administration of the Gossner Church. It was adopted by the Mahasabha on November 23, 1920, and was registered with the Government on July 30, 1921.[99] The Gossner Church became a legally constituted body recognised by the National Missionary Council of India and the Government. The Central Committee was replaced by the Church Council according to the new Constitution.[100] Rev. Hanukh Dato Lakra, Mr. Peter Hurad and Mr. Nirmal Soy were respectively elected by the Mahasabha as the first President, Secretary and Treasurer of the Autonomous Gossner Church.

The Gossner Church declared autonomy but soon it realised how difficult it was to maintain it. Gradually, there developed a desire in the Church to invite the German missionaries.[101] An agreement was signed between the Home Board in Berlin and the Gossner

Church, and, in 1927, two German missionaries, Rev. A. John and Rev. H. Prehn, reached Ranchi.[102] The Advisory Board was dissolved in 1928 and the American missionaries departed from Ranchi.

A new period began in the Gossner Church. The Home Board sent missionaries, old and new, and also annual subsidy. Due to the world-wide economic depression, the subsidy was stopped from 1930. Bitter misunderstanding, dissension and financial distress began in the Church. In 1938, Rev. J. Stosch, Director of the Gossner Mission Society in Germany, was invited and elected President of the Church.[103] He succeeded to a great extent in easing the situation. Troubles continued to appear here and there but the Church grew in strength and number under his able guidance.

11. Second World War and Formation of Native Administration

In September 1939, the Second World War broke out, and all the German missionaries were interned. On March 2, 1942, the Deputy Commissioner of Ranchi requisitioned almost all the buildings and grounds of the Gossner Church compound at Ranchi to accommodate the military personnel.[104] The Mahasabha elected Rev. Joel Lakra,[105] M.A., B.D., S.T.M., President of the Church in place of Rev. J. Stosch. While the War went on, serious cases of dispute occurred in the Church.

The Second World War came to an end in 1945. The presence of regular internal quarrels and disturbances created a necessity for revising the Constitution of the Church. In 1946, the Church invited Rev. (Dr.) J. Boy Strock, another American Lutheran, to work in the Church and help it in revising the Constitution. A Commission of 35 members, with Rev. Roy Strock as Chairman, was formed to revise the Constitution.[106] On August 15, 1947, India became independent. At the end of the year the Gossner Church had 1,69,474 baptized numbers and 2,357 inquirers.[107]

12. Impact of GEL Church on Society

The Gossner Mission or Church did not confine itself to conversion only. It rendered significant service in various spheres--agrarian, social, educational medical, literary, etc., -- to the people among whom it worked. The Gossner Mission was the first Christian Mission to enter the hilly and forest land of Chotanagpur excluding Santal Parganas. The missionaries had to work against heavy odds. Some died due to unfavourable climate.[108] They championed the cause of the oppressed and illiterate aboriginals, Mundas and Oraons, against their alien zamindars in agrarian disputes, spread education by setting up schools both for boys and girls, built hospitals, the most famous being the Leper Asylum at Purulia, set up a printing press and published religious and educational books in Hindi, Mundari, Oraon and other languages. The Church's contribution in some key areas may be noted here.

12.1 Agrarian Crisis and Mission's Assistance

At the time when the Gossner Mission started at Ranchi, there was much agrarian unrest,[109] in Chotanagpur, particularly in Ranchi District. This was a reaction to the exploitation of the aboriginals, Mundas and Oraons, by the zamindars. These zamindars were from outside and had been allowed to settle down in Chotanagpur by the Maharaja of Chotanagpur. Gradually, they began to exploit the tribals through money lending, business, duplicity in forcing the tribals to mortgage their lands, and appropriating tribal lands. The gullible tribals were being reduced to slavery in their own lands. In their frustration and perplexity, many aboriginals turned to the missionaries and to the religion of the British rulers for protection and peace. From their conversion to Christianity and contact with missionaries, the illiterate and oppressed aboriginals gained a more resolute spirit and greater moral courage to protect their rights and lands.[110] The missionaries also gave them every possible help in their legal struggle in the courts against the zamindars, and, now and then, drew the attention of the Bengal Government to the gravity of the situation in the Ranchi District.[111]

With a view to legal and authorized settlement of the title to Bhuinhari lands, the Bengal Council passed the Chotanagpur Tenures Act in July 1869. The operations under the Act continued till 1890. The Act, however, failed to give satisfaction to the aboriginals, and the Gossner missionaries forwarded a memorial to the Bengal

Government complaining against the way in which the Indian Special Commissioners had been conducting the operations, and prayed for their replacement by British officers.[112] Memorials, signed by many Christian aboriginals were forwarded to the Governor-General in 1881, to the Secretary of State for India in 1882 and to Bengal Government in 1886. A representation signed by three members of the *Vorstand* was presented to Queen Victoria.[113] During the Survey and Settlement (1902-1910) of the Munda country, Rev. A. Nottrott and other missionaries gave valuable advice to the Mundas and other tribes about the settlement operations and helped them in maintaining their rights over their lands. As noted in Chapter 2, the Catholic Mission was also assisting the tribals in their legal struggles. The Jesuit missionary Fr. John Baptist Hoffmann literally drafted a definitive and comprehensive Chotanagpur Tenancy Act which was accepted and passed by the Government in 1908. This Act gave legal protection to the tribals from land alienation and agrarian oppression.

The Gossner Mission started a Co-operative Bank under Rev. E. Muller in September 1907 for the benefit of its Christians.[114] It was developed by Rev. Wagner and its branches were opened in all the stations in the Division. The scheme, however, failed after the departure of the German missionaries from the field in 1915.

12.2 Educational Service

Education was indeed, from the very beginning, and remained throughout, one of the main commitments of the Gossner Mission. The German missionaries were pioneers in the field of education for both males and females, in Chotanagpur. The first Christian Mission School[115] was started at Ranchi by this Mission in 1846. The first students were orphans, about 20 in number, who had been rescued during famine and put under the care of the missionaries by a magistrate. The parents were at first reluctant to send their children to this School fearing that the missionaries would make them Christians. Apart from giving free education, the missionaries gave one anna per week to each student as a measure of encouragement. Holsten says that in 1852 the school had 28 boys and 14 girls. On December 1, 1852, a separate school[116] for girls, later known as the Bethesda School, was opened at Ranchi. Both were Boarding Schools. The Uprising of 1857 forced the school children to flee to villages and forests.[117]

After the restoration of peace, the Mission reorganized the schools at Ranchi and opened schools at Purulia, Chaibasa and at a few stations in villages. All the expenses were borne by the Mission. In 1863, the Government of India granted Rs. 50 per month.[118] A Normal Training School was started at Ranchi for male youth from among the Christian aboriginals to prepare themselves to become qualified teachers.[119] A Theological Seminary whose foundation had been laid in 1865, was established at Ranchi in 1867, to prepare persons for priesthood.[120]

At the split in the Gossner Mission in November 1868, most of the teachers and students joined the Anglican Mission.[121] According to the report of the Director of Public Instruction for 1872-73, the Mission had a seminary, three boarding schools and one village school.[122] In October 1874, Lord Northbrook, the Viceroy of India, visited the Boarding School (boys) at Ranchi, granted Rs. 50 for prizes and presented a portrait of Queen Victoria to the School.[123] According to the statistics of the Mission for 1874, there were Boarding Schools at Ranchi, Purulia and Chaibasa, with 209 boys and 64 girls, and several village schools having 956 Christian and 358 Non-Christian pupils.[124] In 1881, the Mission had 74 schools with 1515 students.[125] The Boys' Boarding Upper Primary School at Ranchi was raised to the Middle Vernacular Standard in 1884. Besides the Middle School at Ranchi, there were, in 1895, eight urban Upper Primary Schools with 320 boys and girls and 80 village Primary Schools with 1605 boys and 145 girls.[126] The Middle School became a High School in 1896.[127] In 1907, a Training School for girls was also opened at Ranchi.[128]

The outbreak of the First World War was most unfortunate for the Gossner Mission and its schools. All German missionaries were repatriated. Before their departure from Ranchi in July 1915, they requested Bishop Westcott of the Anglican Mission to manage the Schools.[129] The Bishop agreed, raised emergency staff, collected money and managed the schools. According to the *Annual Report of the Chotanagpur Mission* for 1916, the Gossner Mission had then 36

Boarding Schools, 240 village Primary Schools and 13 Kindergartens with about 9,000 pupils. In 1919, when the Anglican support was withdrawn, there was much disappointment all over the Church Schools. Several of them had to be closed down for want of funds. There was a proposal to close down the Gossner High School too.[130]

Situation improved with the formation of the Advisory Board in October 1919. In 1921, the Gossner Church had one High School, 6 Middle Schools and 208 Primary Schools with 4,764 boys and 1,483 girls.[131] In the same year Rev. I. Cannaday became the Secretary of the Advisory Board. The Bethesda Girls' Upper Primary School at Ranchi was raised in 1921 to the Middle Standard.[132] The Advisory Board annually set apart a considerable amount for the education of the young men of the Church in colleges to prepare educated leaders.[133] In 1923, Mr. Joel Lakra, a young Oraon graduate in Arts of the Calcutta University, was sent by the Church Council to study Theology at Chicago in U.S.A. He returned in 1927 with the M.A., B.D. and S.T.M. degrees. He was the first member of the Church to study abroad.[134] Mr. Dhan Masih Panna became the first aboriginal graduate and also first aboriginal magistrate in Jharkhand.

When the Advisory Board was dissolved in 1928, and the German missionaries returned, the whole burden of managing the schools fell upon the Church Council. It appointed an officer, known as the Head Supervisor of Lutheran Schools for the management of the Middle and Primary Schools. Mr. Nirmal Soy held the post for many years. In 1932, 96 Primary Schools were handed over to the Ranchi District Board for financial reasons. In 1939, the Gossner Church had one High School, 6 Middle Schools and 160 Primary Schools. Due to the military occupation of the Church compound at Ranchi in 1942, the Gossner High School, the Seminary and the Bethesda Girls' Middle School were shifted elsewhere.[135] The Middle School at Takarma became a High School in 1945.[136] Two years later (1947), the Bethesda Girls' Middle School too was recognized by Bihar Government as High School.[137]

As during the management of the Advisory Board, the Lutheran Federation of India also allotted a good amount of money annually to help the boys and girls of the Church in their college studies. This scheme was discontinued when Government scholarship was made available to all aboriginal students reading in colleges.

The Gossner Mission had a Lace School for many years. In 1905, Rev. A. Nottrott sent two aboriginal Christian girls to Kalimpong to learn lace-work. The Government granted Rs. 200 towards their training. On their return, in 1906, the German Mission Lace School was opened at Ranchi.[138] It was closed down, later on, for financial stringency.

12.3 Medical Service

The Gossner missionaries preached, taught and healed too. Two of the early missionaries, Rev. Konrad and Rev. Lohar, were doctors.[139] In 1882, Rev. F. Hahn started a leper asylum at Lohardaga.[140] In 1887, another leper asylum was founded at Purulia by Rev. Uffmann.[141] When he died, Rev. Hahn took charge of the same. He was awarded a gold medal by the Bengal Government in recognition of his services to the suffering humanity.[142] Both, the asylums got financial support from the Edinburgh Society for Lepers in the East. The Asylum at Lohardaga was discontinued. During the First World War, the Leper Asylum at Purulia was taken over by the Church Missionary Society. It used to accommodate 1000 patients.

Besides the Elizabeth Hospital founded at Ranchi January 13, 1892,[143] small dispensaries were opened at Lohardaga, Govindpur, Takarma and other principal stations. In 1908, 4,220 cases were treated at the Ranchi Hospital and 1,918 cases at Lohardaga Dispensary.[144] Some students were sent for training in medicine at the Agra Medical School, and most of them returned qualified for medical work in the Mission.

The First World War proved disastrous for medical institutions.[145] Only the Elizabeth Hospital and the dispensaries at Govindpur and Takarma survived. Later on, the Elizabeth Hospital and the Mission Dispensary at Govindpur were closed down for want of men and money.

12.4 Mission's Contribution to Language and Literature

The German missionaries did pioneering work in the study of tribal languages and in the promotion of tribal literature. The early missionaries used Hindi for communication and for liturgical purposes but later on, and especially after 1868, much stress was laid on the study and use of tribal languages in congregational work. A new missionary had to pass at least one of the tribal language examinations. Two missionaries, Rev. (Dr.) A. Nottrott and Rev. Hahn, played a prominent role in enriching tribal languages. When Rev. Hahn enriched the Oraon language, Rev. Nottrott enriched Mundari with their literary contributions.

It is said that one of the early missionaries, Rev. Henry Batsch, used to preach in Oraon language. As early as 1868, Rev. Hahn[146] had prepared the *Kurukh (Oraon) Grammar* and a small *Kurukh Dictionary*, which were published in 1900 and 1903, respectively. Rev. Hahn later on translated Biblical stories in the Oraon language. Rev. Flex's *Oraon Grammar* and *Oraon Dictionary* were very popular.[147] Rev. Nottrott was an outstanding Mundari scholar. He got the first *Mundari Primer* and *Mundari Hymn-book* printed at Benares in 1871.[148] In 1881, he published the first *Mundari Grammar* in the German language to assist the new German missionaries coming to Chotanagpur.[149] This book was, later on, translated into English by Rev. Wagner. Rev. Nottrott practically devoted the best part of life in the translation of the Bible into Mundari. The Mundari translation of the New Testament was published and presented to the Gossner Mission during the Golden Jubilee celebrations in 1895.[150] The whole Bible was published by the British and Foreign Bible Society, Calcutta, in 1911.[151] The University of Leipzig in Germany conferred on Rev. Nottrott the Honorary Doctorate degree in Mundari language. Rev. Eidnes developed the Nagpuria language. In 1911, he wrote and published an article in Nagpuria on drinking.

Not only tribal literature, but Hindi literature too received encouragement. A stone lithographic press was set up by the Mission at Ranchi in 1873.[152] A fortnightly official journal in Hindi, known as *Gharbandhu* (Home-relative),[153] was started in Hindi. A printing press was set up in 1882 and numerous books and booklets in Hindi, Mundari and Oraon languages were printed and published from this press.[154]

For some years after the departure of the German missionaries in 1915, the publication work remained neglected due to financial difficulty. Later on, it was resumed and prayer books and hymn books in Mundari, Oraon and Kharia languages were written and published. The Church Council commissioned Rev. U. E. Kujur and Rev. Samuel Bage to translate the New Testament into Oraon and Kharia languages, respectively.[155]

13. Conclusion

The Gossner Mission was the first Christian Mission to enter Chotanagpur, at a time when the worst oppression of the tribal people was going on. The missionaries and their religion gave the latter hope and security. They enhanced their sense of self-respect both as individuals and as a race.[156] They widened their outlook and opened out new avenues of employment and usefulness. Overall, the Mission mediated their socio-economic, occupational and educational transformation. As a result, tribals have risen from being an oppressed and diffident community to an upwardly mobile and confident community which can take leadership in its hands. What is particularly noted in the history of the GEL Mission is that crises became stepping stones to further development. While one crisis facilitated the emergence of another Church (Anglican Church: see Chapter 6), another crisis facilitated the formation of the Autonomous GEL Church.

Endnotes and References

1 W. W. Hunter (1877), *A Statistical Account of Bengal,* Vol. XVI, p. 423; S. C. Roy (1912), *The Mundas and their Country,* p. 227; K. Sheetal (1939), *Chotanagpur ki Kalishya ka Brittant* (News about Chotanagpur Church) pp. 8-9; C. H. Swavely (1952), *The Lutheran Enterprise in India,* p. 51; E. Wueste (1967), *Chotanagpur ki Masihi Mandil Ka Itihas* (History of the Chotanagpur Christian Church),1845-1890, 4th edition, p. 7; M. G. Hallet (1917), *Bihar & Orissa District Gazetteers: Ranchi,* p. 39.

2 Eyre Chatterton (1901), *The Story of Fifty Years' Mission work in Chotanagpur,* pp. 2-3; Hunter (1877), Vol. XVI p. 423, K. Sheetal (1939), pp. 2-3; C. F. Andrews (1908), *Handbook of English Church Expansion: North India,* pp. 35-36; *History of Christianity in India with*

its prospects, Madras (1895), p. 53; H. W. Tucker (1893), *Digest of the S. P. G. Record,* p. 495; Swavely (1952), p. 49.

3 William Buyers (1848), *Recollections of Northern India,* p. 202; Swavely (1952), p. 49.

4 Sherring (1884), *The History of Protestant Missions in India,* p. 140; Buyers (1848), pp. 202-203; L. S. S. O'Malley (1907), *Bengal District Gazetteer: Muzaffarpur,* p. 32; *Imperial Gazetteer of India,* Vol. II: *Bengal,* (1909), p. 79; Swavely (1952), p. 49.

5 *History of Christianity in India* (1895), p. 61.

6 Swavely (1952), p. 49.

7 J. Cave-Browne (1870), *The Chotanagpur Mission,* p. 1; Chatterton (1901), p. 4; *Historical Sketches, No. II – Chota Nagpore,* 1896, p. 25; A. Nottrott (1874), *The Gossner Mission unter den kols;* D. Walter Holsten (1949), *Johannes Evangelista Gossner, Glaube and Gemeinde,* p. 235; Swavely, (1952), p. 49; *Chota Nag pore Mission,* Quarterly Paper No. 1, February (1874), p. 4.

8 Hunter (1877), Vol. XVI, p. 423; Tucker (1893), p. 495; Andrews (1908), p. 36; Joseph Mullens (1863), *A Brief Review of Ten Years' Missionary Labour in India Between 1852 to 1861,* p. 4; Eyre Chatterton (1901), p. 4-5; Swavely (1952), p. 49.

9 Waeste (1967), p. 3; Sheetal (1939), p. 5; Seeberg (1969), *Gossner Evangelical Lutheran Church: Chotanagpur Aur Assam ka Itihas (History of Chotanagpur and Assam), 1919-1969,* p. 2; *Panjika* (Church Annual Calendar), 1975, p. 3.

10 Ibid., p. 1; Wueste (1967), pp. 2-3., Sheetal (1939), p. 4; Chatterton (1901), p. 3; *Historical Sketches, II- Chota Nagpore* (1896), p. 25.

11 Ibid., p. 1; Wueste (1967), pp. 2-3; Sheetal (1939), p. 4; Chatterton (1901), p. 3; *Historical Sketches, II- Chota Nagpore* (1896), p. 25.

12 Wueste (1967), p. 3; Sheetal (1939), p. 5; *Gossner Pariwar* (Gossner Family)(1969), p. 1.

13 *Gossner Pariwar* (Gossner Family)(1969), p. 2; Sheetal (1939), p. 5; Wueste (1967), p. 4.

14 Hunter (1877), Vol. XVI, p. 423; Chatterton (1901), p. 5; Roy (1912), p. 227; Sheetal (1939), pp. 6-7; Andrews (1908), p. 36; Nottrott (1874), p. 171; *Chota Nagpore Mission:* Quarterly Paper No. 1, February (1874), p. 4; *Gossner Pariwar* (1969), p. 2; Tucker (1893), p. 495; Mullens (1863), p. 40; Seeberg (1969), p. 2.

15 Wueste (1967), pp. 5-6; *Gossner Pariwar* (1969), p. 2; Sheetal (1939), p. 7; Swavely (1952), p. 50; S. K. Patro & B. H. Mather, *The Anglican Church in Chota Nagpore, 1869-1969,* p. 1.

16 Sheetal (1939), pp. 7-8; Nottrott (1874), p. 173; Wueste (1967), p. 6; Swavely (1952), p. 50; Swavely (1952), p. 50; *Gossner Pariwar*, (1969), pp. 2-3.
17 Swavely (1952), p. 51; Roy (1912), p. 227; Sheetal (1939), pp. 8-9; Wueste (1967), p. 7.
18 *Annual Report of the Chotanagpur Mission* (1895), pp. 3, 15.
19 Nottrott (1874), p. 174; Wueste (1967), p. 7; Sheetal (1939), p. 9; *Gossner Pariwar* (1969), p. 3.
20 Chatterton (1901), p. 21.
21 Chatterton (1901), p. 21; Cave-Browne (1870), p. 10. Tucker (1893), p. 496; Sheetal (1939), p. 10.
22 Sheetal (1939), pp. 10 & 21.
23 Ibid., p. 11.
24 Ibid., p. 13; Swavely (1952), p. 52; Wueste (1967), p. 9.
25 Sheetal (1939), pp. 11-12; Wueste (1967), pp. 10-11; Roy (1912), p. 228.
26 *Die Biene auf dem Missionsfelde* (monthly publication of the Mission in Berlin) 1862, p. 51; Wueste (1967), pp. 14-15; Sheetal (1939), pp. 15-16; Swavely (1952), p. 51, Chatterton (1901), pp. 22-23.
27 *History of Christianity in India* (1895), p. 53; Hunter (1877), Vol. XVI, p. 424; Sheetal (1939), p. 18; Wueste (1967), p. 17; Roy (1912), p. 228; Swavely (1952), p. 52.
28 Roy (1912), p. 228; Sheetal (1939), pp. 21-22; Swavely (1952), p. 52; Wueste (1967), p. 17; Seeberg (1969), p. 3.
29 Seeberg, p. 3; Swavely (1952), p. 53; Roy (1912), p. 228; Wueste (1967), pp. 20-21; Sheetal (1939), p. 22.
30 Hunter (1877), Vol. XVI, p. 424; Roy (1912), p. 228; Wueste (1967), p. 20; Sheetal (1939), p. 22; Swavely (1952), p. 53.
31 Seeberg (1969), p. 3; *Gossner Pariwar* (1969), p. 8.
32 Sheetal (1939), pp. 22-23; Roy (1912), pp. 228-230; *Die. Biene auf dem Missionsfelde* (1856), pp. 65-67.
33 Mullens (1863), p. 41; Walter Holsten (1949), p. 246.
34 Roy (1912), (Quoted from the *Mission Report*), p. 230; Wueste (1967), p. 23, *Gossner Pariwar* (1969), pp. 9-10.
35 Sheetal (1939), p. 26; Wueste (1967), pp. 25-26.
36 Chatterton (1901), pp. 26-28; Roy (1912), pp. 230-231; Sheetal (1939), pp. 29-30; Wueste (1967), pp. 29-31; Swavely (1952), p. 54.
37 Chatterton (1901), p. 28.
38 Ibid., p. 32; Roy (1912), (Quoted from *Mission Report*), p. 231; Sheetal (1939), pp. 33-34; Wueste (1967), p. 33-35; Mullens (1863), pp. 41-42; Swavely (1952), p. 54.

39 Sheetal (1939), p. 47; Wueste (1967), p. 37; Swavely (1952) p. 55.

40 Hunter (1877), Vol. XVI, p. 424; Cave-Browne (1874), p. 212; Tucker (1893), p. 496; Andrews (1908), p. 40; Chatterton (1901), pp. 33-34.

41 Chatterton (1901), p. 35; Hunter (1877), Vol. XVI, p. 424; Sheetal, (1939), p. 46; Wueste (1967), pp. 38-39.

42 Hunter (1877), Vol. XVI; p. 424; Roy (1912), (Quoted from *Mission Report*), pp. 238-239; Sheetal (1939), p. 47.

43 Roy (1912), (Quoted from *Mission Report*), p. 240.

44 Sherring (1884), p. 146.

45 Roy (1912), Quoted from *Mission Report*, p. 240; Sheetal (1939), p. 48; Wueste (1967), p. 43; *Die Biene auf dem Missionsfelde* 1868, p. 34.

46 Walter Holsten (1949), p. 240; Cave-Browne (1870), p. 32; Wueste (1967), pp. 45-46; Sherring (1884), p. 152.

47 Cave-Browne (1870), p. 86; Wueste (1967), p. 47.

48 Cave-Browne (1870), p. 33; Nottrott (1874), p. 212; Chatterton (1901), p. 41; Walter Holsten (1949), pp. 240-245; Sheetal (1939), pp. 56-57; Wueste (1967), p. 40.

49 Chatterton (1901), p. 42; Sheetal (1939), p. 57.

50 Chatterton (1901), pp. 44-45; Sheetal (1939), p. 60; Walter Holstan (1949), p. 258; Mrs. Murray Mitchell (1871), *A Missionary's Wife among the Wild Tribes of South Bengal*, pp. 48-49.

51 Cave-Browne (1870), pp. 50-51; Chatterton (1901), pp. 45-47; Sheetal (1939), pp. 60-62; Wueste (1967), pp. 48-49.

52 Cave-Browne (1870), p. 60; Hunter (1877), Vol. XVI, p. 425; Chatterton (1901), p. 47; Sheetal (1939), p. 62; Wueste (1967), p. 49.

53 Cave-Browne (1870), p. 55; Sherring (1884), p. 152; Chatterton (1901), pp. 45-46; Sheetal (1939), pp. 61-62.

54 Swavely (1952), pp. 55-56; Wueste (1967), pp. 49-50; Seeberg (1969), pp. 6-7.

55 Chatterton (1901), p. 46.

56 *Gossner Pariwar* (1969), 1845-1969, p. 11.

57 *Chota Nagpore Mission:* Quarterly Report No. 1, February (1874), p. 4; Hunter (1877), Vol. XVI, p. 424.

58 Sheetal (1939), p. 63.

59 Ibid.

60 Ibid., pp. 63-64.

61 Ibid., p. 65.

62 Ibid., pp. 65-66; Hunter (1877), Vol. XVI p. 423; Tucker (1893), p. 496.

63 Cave-Browne (1870), p. 60; Hunter (1877), Vol. XVI, p. 425; Chatterton (1901), p. 47; Roy (1912), p. 246; Sheetal (1939), p. 62; Wueste (1967), p. 49.
64 Wueste, p. 50; Swavely (1952), p. 56.
65 Swavely, p. 56; Hunter (1877), Vol. XVI, p. 423; Tucker (1893), p. 496; Chatterton (1901), p. 47.
66 *Historical Sketches* (1896), No. II, *Chota Nagpore*, p. 6; Chatterton (1901), p. 48; Sheetal (1939), p. 69.
67 Sheetal (1939), p. 70; Chatterton (1901), p. 48.
68 Chatterton (1901), pp. 52-54; Hunter (1877), Vol. XVI p. 425; Tucker (1893), p. 496; Sheetal (1939), pp. 74-75.
69 Walter Holsten (1919), p. 262; Cave-Browne (1870), p. 77.
70 *Die Biene auf dam Missionsfelde* (1869), p. 86.
71 Ibid., (1870), p. 79.
72 *The Friend of India,* May 27, 1869.
73 Seeberg (1969), p. 7; Swavely (1952), p. 56.
74 Swavely (1952), p. 57; Seeberg (1969), pp. 7-8.
75 Seeberg (1969), p. 13; Wuaste (1967), p. 51; *Annual Report of the Gossner Mission* (1869), p. 34; Swavely (1952), p. 57.
76 Sherring (l884), (Quoted from Mission Statistics) p. 153.
77 Hunter (1877), Vol. XVI, p. 434.
78 Ibid.
79 Roy (1912), pp. 256-257.
80 Swavely (1962), pp. 57-58.
81 Sherring (1834), (Quoted from) Mission Statistics), p. 160.
82 *Annual Report of Chotanagpur Mission* (1895), pp. 3-4; Swavely, (1952), p. 58.
83 Swavely, (1952), p. 59.
84 Ibid.
85 *Chotanagpur Diocesan Report*, January, 1916, p. 2; Swavely (1952), p. 60; *Gossner Pariwar* (1969), p. 14; Seeberg (1969), p. 19.
86 Seeberg (1969), p. 19; *Chotanagpur Diocesan Report*, January, 1916, pp. 2-4; Swavely (1952), p. 60.
87 Swavely (1952), p. 61.
88 *Gharbandhu* (official monthly newspaper of the Gossner Mission), July 15, 1919, p. 3; *Gossner Pariwar* (1969), p. 15.
89 Swavely (1952), p. 61.
90 Ibid.
91 Ibid., p. 62.

92 Swavely (1952), pp. 62-63; *Gossner Pariwar* (1969), p. 15; Seeberg, (1969), p. 23.
93 *Gharbandhu*, August 15, 1919; Swavely (1952), p. 62; *Gossner Pariwar* (1969), p. 16; Seeberg, (1969), p. 26.
94 Walter Holsten (1949), p. 376; Swavely (1952), p. 64; *Gossner Pariwar* (1969), pp. 16-17.
95 *Gharbandhu,* August 15, 1919, pp. 125-126; Swavely (1952), p. 64.
96 *Gossner Pariwar* (1969), p. 18; Seeberg (1969), p. 31.
97 Swavely (1952), p. 64.
98 Swavely (1952), p. 64; Walter Holsten, (1949), p. 377.
99 Swavely (1952), p. 65; Seeberg (1969), pp. 33-34.
100 Seeberg (1969), pp. 33-34.
101 Ibid., p. 37; Swavely (1952), p. 67.
102 Swavely (1952), p. 67.
103 Ibid., p. 69; Seeberg (1969), p. 50.
104 Swavely (1952), pp. 71-72; Seeberg (1969), p. 51.
105 Swavely (1952), p. 72.
106 Swavely (1952), pp. 78-79; Seeberg (1969), p. 58.
107 *Panjika* (Register), (1963)
108 Wueste (1967), pp. 10&14; Sheetal (1939), p. 12; *Gossner Pariwar* (1969), p. 4.
109 Roy (1912), p. 226; S. C. Roy, *Bihar & Orissa Research Society Journal,* Vol. XVII, p. 361; Chatterton (1901), p. 20.
110 Hunter (1877), pp. 441-443; Roy (1912), p. 440 (Quoted from *Mission Report*).
111 Sheetal (1939), p. 53.
112 Roy (1912), p. 284.
113 Ibid., p. 277.
114 Roy (1912), p. 256.
115 Sheetal (1939), p. 10; Chatterton (1901), p. 22; Walter Holsten (1949), p. 243; Nottrott (1874), p. 176.
116 *Panjika* (1975), p. 26; Wueste (1967), p. 12; *Ranchi District Gazetteer* (1970), p. 471.
117 Roy (1912), quoted from *Mission Report*, p. 231; Wueste (1967), p. 33; Sheetal (1939), p. 29.
118 Letter written by Mr. Wyllie, Under Secretary to the Government of India, Home Department, No. 4372, dated 11.7.1863.
119 Roy (1912), p. 253.
120 Ibid.
121 Sheetal (1939), p. 66.

122 Hunter (1877), Vol. XVI (Quoted from Director of Public Instruction's Report), p. 438.
123 *Annual Report of the Gossner Mission: 1874*, pp. 43-44.
124 Hunter (1877), Vol. XVI, p. 440
125 Sherring (1884), p. 160.
126 Swavely (1952), p. 59.
127 Roy (1912), p. 250.
128 Ibid., p. 153.
129 *Annual Report of the Chotanagpur Mission* (1916), p. 2; Swavely (1952), p. 60.
130 Ibid.
131 Typed report of the Church Council for the revision of the Ranchi District Gazetteer.
132 *Ranchi District Gazetteer* (1970), p. 471.
133 Swavely (1952), p. 65.
134 Ibid., p. 66.
135 Swavely (1952), pp. 71-72.
136 *Panjika* (1976), p. 24.
137 *Ranchi District Gazetteer* (1970), p. 471.
138 Roy (1912), p. 253.
139 Sheetal (1939), p. 14.
140 Roy (1912), p. 256.
141 Ibid.
142 Ibid.
143 Walker Holsten (1949), p. 331; Roy (1912), p. 255.
144 Roy (1912), p. 255.
145 Seeberg, (1969), pp. 81-82.
146 *Ranchi District Gazetteer* (1970), p. 506.
147 Walter Holsten (1949), p. 304.
148 Roy (1912), p. 248.
149 Ibid., pp. 248-250.
150 Swavely (1952), p. 135; Roy (1912), p. 255.
151 Roy (1912), p. 255; *Panjika* (1975), p. 14.
152 S. C. Roy (1912), pp. 253-254.
153 Ibid., p. 255.
154 Ibid., p. 254.
155 Swavely (1952), p. 80.
156 Article on "The Effects on the Aborigines of Chotanagpur of their contact with Western civilization", *Bihar and Orissa Research Society Journal*, Vol. XVII, pp. 381- 386; W. W. Hunter (1877), Vol. XVI, pp. 440-441.

Chapter 6

The Anglican Mission/Society for the Propagation of the Gospel Mission in Jharkhand

1. Introduction

The Anglican Mission to Chotanagpur (Jharkhand), or simply called the 'Chotanagpur Mission' (Anglican)[1] had a unique and unusual start: first it began with the support of the Society for the Propagation of the Gospel based in England and secondly it emerged out of the crisis in the Gossner Evangelical Lutheran Mission (GELM) in Chotanagpur.[2] Being closely connected with the British Colonial authority in India, this Mission came along with the British rulers some of whom were evangelistically inclined and the Mission sort of belonged to the Colonial rulers. Unlike other missionary societies, it did not make an entry into the native population, but was asked to shoulder responsibility for an already established Gossner Mission in Chotanagpur. That is to say, the Anglican Mission to Chotanagpur actually entered into other men's labours and started at once with full possession of thousands of Christians belonging to the GELM, founded in 1845. In the words of Rt. Rev. Eric J. Trapp, Secretary of the United Society for the Propagation of the Gospel in London, "the circumstances of that beginning were most unusual".[3]

2. Early Beginnings: Chaplaincy Service

The Mission began with chaplaincy service in Hazaribagh. The grant of the Dewani (revenue authority) of Bengal, Bihar and Orissa by the Mughal Emperor, Shah Alam II, to the British East India Company on August 12, 1765, led to the establishment of British authority over Chotanagpur too. British military, civil officers and soldiers, mostly Anglican Christians, were stationed at Hazaribagh, Ranchi and other administrative centres in Chotanagpur. An English military chaplain was posted at Hazaribagh for their spiritual care. In 1842, the Government built a church, called the St. Stephen's Church[4]–the first church in Chotanagpur–capable of accommodating 400 persons, at Hazaribagh, for their worship.

Some of the British officers were interested in missionary activities and they tried to invite Christian missionaries to work among the aboriginals of Chotanagpur, and, in fact, it was their interest and encouragement that facilitated the establishment and stability of the Christian Missions in Chotanagpur.[5]

Already in 1840, Major Ralph Ouseley, the Agent of the Governor General in the South-West Frontier Agency, took the lead in the matter. At the suggestion of his Assistant, Lieutenant Samuel Richard Tickell, he wrote to Bishop Wilson in Calcutta, urgently requesting him to send missionaries to Kolhan area centred round Chaibasa.[6] Bishop Wilson forwarded the request to the Society for the Propagation of the Gospel (SPG) in London. The Society agreed but as no English missionary was forthcoming, the opportunity for founding an Anglican Mission in Chotanagpur then was lost.[7]

3. Anglican Mission Emerges from Gossner Mission Split

However, the Anglican Mission was destined to begin in Chotanagpur in the most unusual and dramatic way. As noted in Chapter 5, it arose out of the unfortunate split[8] that occurred in November 1868 in the GELM in Chotanagpur. The founder of the Gossner Mission,

Rev. Johannes Evangelista Gossner of Berlin in Germany, died on March 30, 1858, leaving the management of his Mission in the hands of a committee called the Curatorium in Berlin.[9] In fact, he had earlier requested the Church Missionary Society of London to adopt the Mission, but was rejected by the latter. Three years after his death, in 1861, Rev. Emile Schatz, who had been the head of the Mission work in Chotanagpur from the very start, retired and returned to Germany. His place was taken over by Rev. F. Batsch, the only pioneer missionary left in the field.

Soon after the departure of Rev. Schatz, conflicts began between the Curatorium and the missionaries in Chotanagpur.[10] The missionaries were put to great financial difficulty. Such was the situation, when in April 1864, Anglican Bishop Cotton, the Metropolitan of India in Calcutta, visited Ranchi. This was the first contact of the Gossner Mission with an Anglican Bishop. [11] The Bishop was very much impressed with the missionary activities and he strongly appealed to the Curatorium for more funds. He also suggested that if the Curatorium was unable to send speedy and liberal help, then according to the last wish of Rev. Gossner, the Mission work in Chotanagpur should be carried on by the Church Missionary Society, in communion with the Church of England.[12]

In response to an appeal made by the missionaries at Ranchi, the Curatorium sent out, between 1865 and 1867, some young missionaries, mostly university graduates, to Chotanagpur. Soon there arose a bitter conflict between the senior and the younger missionaries. The latter complained to the Curatorium against the former, of malversation, neglect of Mission duties and misuse of Mission funds.[13] The Curatorium sent out its Secretary, Rev. Hermann Ansorge[14] to investigate the charges and to enforce a new constitution for the better management of the Mission work in Chotanagpur. There was to be a committee of three missionaries, called the *Vorstand*, instead of one missionary as the head of the Mission work in Chotanagpur. Rev. Ansorge called a meeting of the missionaries at Ranchi on November 18, 1868.[15] Without giving any judgment on the spot, Rev. Ansorge strongly appealed to the missionaries to forget the past and to sign the new Constitution.[16] Out of the 14 missionaries, eight complied but Rev. F. Batsch, Rev.

Henry Batsch, Rev. F. Bohn, Mr. A. Hertzog, Rev. J. Pohlenz and Mr. F. Krueger refused to sign. They opposed the Constitution as unjust and appealed, on November 22, 1868, to the Curatorium against the actions of Rev. Ansorge and they withdrew from the Gossner Mission before hearing from it.[17]

The rupture was complete and after some days, in the last week of November 1868, the seceding missionaries moved out of the Gossner Mission compound at Ranchi with their property and took shelter in the bungalow and the attached small houses of the officers and workers of the Survey Department on the eastern border of the Mission compound.[18] They at once sent an appeal, backed by all the influential English civilians at Ranchi, to Bishop Robert Milman, the Metropolitan of India in Calcutta, to receive them into the Anglican Church.[19]

The division was not confined to missionaries alone. It profoundly affected their converts too. The senior missionaries and especially Rev. F. Batsch, being one of the four pioneer missionaries, had great influence over them.[20] At Ranchi, all the students in the two Boarding Schools, all teachers and most of the preachers joined them in the new place.[21] The principal places or villages where the converts of the Gossner Mission followed the seceded missionaries were Ranchi, Itki, Kachabari, Bargari, Phate-yatoli, Saparom, Duru, Takra, Birhu, Maranghada. Murhu, Dorma, Tapkara, Ramtolya, Romchu, Digri, Soeko, Kender, Beterkera, Kajra and Jeypore in the Ranchi District, Singhani and Dumar in Hazaribagh District and Chaibasa in Singhbhum District.[22] About the number of these converts, different writers have given different figures.[23] In the then circumstances, the exact number could not be ascertained and given. In my opinion, a majority remained with the Gossner Mission.

The seceded missionaries had no funds and no accommodation to support and shelter themselves and their followers, particularly school children and teachers of Ranchi, in their new place. As expected and led by Commissioner Edward Tuite Dalton, the English officials and residents at Ranchi and Doranda at once formed a committee, known as the "Ranchi Committee"[24] to support the seceded missionaries and their followers during the time their appeal to Berlin was pending. The "Ranchi Committee" appealed to the Curatorium[25] on November 30, 1868, to redress the genuine grievances of the senior missionaries.[26] It also warned the Curatorium that the approval of Rev. Ansorge's action would be disastrous to the Gossner Mission in Chotanagpur. While forwarding the appeal, the Calcutta Auxiliary Committee wrote to the Curatorium to withhold judgment till it received a detailed report which was dispatched to Berlin quickly. The reply of the Curatorium reached Ranchi by March 1, 1869. It upheld Rev. Ansorge's decision and action, accused the seceded missionaries of insubordination and dismissed them from the Gossner Mission service from November 22, 1868, - the day of the refusal and appeal.[27]

Bishop Milman had been informed of the unhappy state of affairs in the Gossner Mission long before the actual split, by the English officials at Ranchi.[28] Soon after the split, the seceded missionaries and the English officials at Ranchi had appealed to him to act immediately and to receive the seceded missionaries and their followers into the Anglican Mission.[29] He waited for the final reply of the Curatorium, and, in the mean time, he consulted the Calcutta Secretary of the Church Missionary Society, if the latter would be willing to adopt the seceded German missionaries and their followers. When it declined,[30] the Bishop consulted the Society for the Propagation of the Gospel (SPG) which agreed to adopt and finance the new Mission work in Chotanagpur.[31]

Bishop Milman arrived at Ranchi on March 16, 1869, and stayed with Commissioner Dalton.[32] There the converts, who followed the seceded missionaries, some hundreds in number, with elders, preachers and teachers, met him and submitted a petition in Hindi to him to receive them, according to the last wish of Rev. Gossner, into the Anglican Mission.[33] The Ranchi Committee also submitted a strongly worded memorial urging him to admit the seceded missionaries and their followers to the Anglican Mission.[34] The Bishop acceded to their request. He then returned to Calcutta, promising to come back to Ranchi about the middle of April to receive them formally into the Anglican Church.[35]

On April 16, 1869, Bishop Milman arrived at Ranchi[36] along with Rev. J. Cave-Browne, the officiating Secretary of the SPG, Rev. C. E. Driberg, a senior SPG missionary in the Calcutta Diocese, Rev.

F. W. Robberds, the Chaplain of Hazaribagh and Rev. M. R. Burges, his domestic Chaplain. Early in the morning, on Saturday, April 17, 1869, the Bishop and his companions entered the temporary church that had been erected of wooden posts, straw and palm leaf and he confirmed 624 Christians, men and women. On Sunday, April 18, he ordained Rev. F. Batsch, Rev. H. Batsch and Rev. F. Bohn first as deacons, and soon afterwards as priests, and also a Preacher Wilhelm Luther Daud Singh, as deacon. Then there was the celebration of Holy Communion at which 650 persons communicated. On Monday, April 19, 41 inquirers were baptized.

The ordination of the Lutheran Pastors and the admission of the converts into the Anglican Church were both unusual and controversial.[37] This event became a much debated issue in India, England and Germany as the media highlighted it. While some strongly supported, others vehemently criticized Bishop Milman. Whatever might be the opinion, the relation between the two Missions, old and new, was bitter, sad and painful and continued to be so for some years.

Before he left Ranchi for Calcutta towards the end of April 1869, Bishop Milman set up a local committee consisting of three pastor-missionaries and three civilians, with Commissioner Dalton as Chairman to manage the newly-founded Mission.[38] This was commonly known as the Anglican or the SPG Mission. The name "Chotanagpur Mission" originally referred to the German Mission, was adopted after the schism of 1869 by the new Mission working under the Society for the Propagation of the Gospel in London. One member Rev. J. Pohlenz soon rejoined the Gossner Mission at Ranchi after being pardoned by the Curatorium.[39]

What was the actual number of the Christians who joined the newly formed Anglican Mission? It is not certain as documents give differing numbers. In November 1868, just before the split, the total number of the baptized Christians in the Gossner Mission was about 11,108.[40] According to Mr. W. W. Hunter, no accurate returns of the number of baptized converts were available for the first year (1869-70) in which the Anglican Mission was at work.[41] The first *Annual Report* of the Mission (1869-70) says that the number of its Christians was 6000. According to Rev. Eyre Chatterton and Rev. K.

Sheetal, the number in 1870 was 5,773. The second *Annual Report* of the Mission for the year 1870-71 also says that the number of Christians with the Mission was 5,773.

4. Organization and Consolidation

The new Anglican 'Chotanagpur Mission' urgently needed organization and consolidation. At the request of the newly-ordained missionaries and with the consent of Bishop Milman, the SPG invited Rev. Jabez Cornelius Whitley, a clergy of the Anglican Mission near Delhi, to superintend the newly constituted Mission and to "comfort and sustain the German clergy."[42] He arrived with his wife and two children on Sunday, June 21, 1869, and formally took charge of the Mission, to the delight of its missionaries and converts.

The converts, owing allegiance to the new Mission, were scattered in more than 300 Christian and partially Christian villages. Rev. Whitley divided the whole congregation into 35 circles, each having 10 to 15 villages.[43] They were placed in charge of catechists or preachers who were commissioned in a special service on October 24, 1869.[44] He visited all the circles. With the help of the supporters of the Mission, enough money was raised in twelve months to build small churches in nearly all the 35 circles.[45]

Bishop Milman came to Ranchi for the third time in 1870. A meeting of the missionaries and English residents at Ranchi and Doranda was held at the residence of Commissioner Dalton where a decision was made to raise funds for building a suitable and permanent church at Ranchi.[46] Its foundation was laid on September 12, 1870,[47] by Commissioner Dalton. The plan was designed by Col. Rowlatt, the Judicial Commissioner of Chotanagpur.[48] The church was built by Mr. A. Hertzog, who was the builder of the Gossner Mission Church at Ranchi.

On February 24, 1872, Bishop Milman came to Ranchi again and ordained Deacon Wilhelm Luther Daud Singh, a priest. He became the first Indian priest of the Anglican Church in Chotanagpur.[49] The Secretary of the SPG in Calcutta, Rev. F. R. Valliangs, joined the permanent staff of the Mission. On March 8, 1873, Bishop Milman consecrated the new church which was called St. Paul's Cathedral.[50] Next day, in the same church, the first five aboriginals, undergoing theological training since March, 1870, at Ranchi, were ordained deacons.[51] They were immediately sent out on mission: Masihdas Kachachap to Itki, Marcus Hembo to Maranghada, Prabhusahay Bodra to Murhu, Zakaria Carol to Tapkara and Athnasius Tuti to Ramtolyo, all in Ranchi District.

5. Mission Expansion

The years between 1870 and 1880 were most fruitful in the missionary effort in Chotanagpur. At the end of his first year at Ranchi, Rev. Whitley wrote that Christianity was spreading spontaneously.[52] According to the *Mission Report* for the year April 1870 to March 1871, there were 5,773 baptized members and 924 inquirers in the Church.[53] Of these, 5,411 belonged to Ranchi District, 184 to Singhbhum District and 178 to Hazaribagh District. At the end of 1871, Rev. H. Batsch retired and returned to Germany due to ill-health.

The friends at the Mission expressed a desire to have information about its work at shorter intervals. It was, therefore, decided to print a *Quarterly Paper* for circulation among the friends and supporters of the Mission. The first *Quarterly Report* was lithographed and issued in February 1874. By March 1874, the Mission had 6,960 baptized Christians and 1,338 inquirers.[54] On September 30, 1874, the number of the baptized Christians rose to 7,496.[55] In October of the same year, the Viceroy of India, Lord Northbrook,[56] came to Ranchi and visited both the Missions. He was very much impressed with the evangelistic and educational works of the Anglican Mission in Chotanagpur.

Bishop Milman visited Ranchi for the last time in February 1875 and ordained Messrs. F. Krueger, Harcus Hembo, Prabhusahay Bodra, Zakaria Carol, Athnasius Tuti and Masihdas Kachchap Priests.[57] In the same year, Col. Dalton, who had been the Commissioner of Chotanagpur since 1857, retired and returned to England. Next year in 1876, Bishop Milman the founder of the Anglican Mission in Chotanagpur, died at Rawalpindi.[58] He was succeeded by Bishop Johnson.

Bishop Johnson visited Chotanagpur in November, 1877. On the way, he ordained Rev. Oscar Flex a Priest at Hazaribagh. Rev.

Flex[59] had belonged to the Gossner Mission and was stationed at Singhani. In 1878 a Theological Class[60] was opened at Ranchi with eight students. In May of the same year, Rev. Whitley began the publication of the *Chotanagpur Dut Patrika*,[61] a lithographed monthly newspaper in Hindi. In 1880, the number of Christians of the Mission rose to 10,679.[62] Rev. Oscar Flex and Mr. A. Hertzog retired from missionary service. Mr. Hertzog served as a lay missionary in Chotanagpur for thirty years. He was a great builder. His greatest and lasting monuments are the two huge churches at Ranchi. In 1881, Rev. Whitley visited the Anglican Christians of Chotanagpur, who were working as coolies in the tea-gardens of Cachar in Assam.[63]

The Mission staff was strengthened with the arrival of Mr. A. Logsdail (1882), Mr. D. J. Flynn (1883) and Mr. F. C. Boyd (1883) from England.[64] The "Sardar War" and the arrival of the Roman Catholic Mission at Ranchi greatly affected the Mission. Many of its Christians reverted to their original religion or joined the Catholic Mission.[65] In March 1884, Rev. F. Batsch and his wife retired and returned to Germany. Rev. Batsch had worked as a missionary in Chotanagpur for forty years.[66] He lived for 22 years more and died in January, 1907.

In 1885, a petition signed by all the priests and deacons in the Mission was submitted to Bishop Johnson, the Anglican Metropolitan of India, for his recommendation for the appointment of a bishop for Chotanagpur.[67] In 1887, Rev. F. Bohn retired and retuned to Germany where he died. Rev. Bohn had come to Ranchi on the Christmas Eve, 1851, when he found only 52 baptized people in addition to 13 orphans.[68]

6. Anglican Chotanagpur Diocese

In 1890, Chotanagpur, previously attached to Bengal Diocese, was made a separate Diocese and Rev. J. C. Whitley was consecrated as the first Bishop of Chotanagpur on March 23, 1890, in the St. Paul's Cathedral, Ranchi, by Metropolitan Johnson, assisted by the Bishops of Bombay and Lahore.[69] On September 30, 1890, the Mission had 12,519 baptized members and 567 inquirers.[70]

Thus from 1890, the Anglican Mission in Chotanagpur started a new era. It had now a Bishop of its own. A Synod of all clergy, both

Indian and European was set up.[71] While Rev. F. Krueger retired and returned to Germany in 1891, new missionaries joined the Mission staff between 1890 and 1900. Two lady missionaries (honorary) Miss Whipham and Miss Ingle, arrived and Zenana Mission work (for women) began in Chotanagpur.[72] Miss Whipham took up zenana work and Miss Ingle, hospital work.

7. Collaboration with Dublin University Mission

In response to Bishop Whitley's appeal in 1891, the Dublin University Mission[73] from Ireland came to work in his Diocese and took over charge of the Mission work in the District of Hazaribagh on March 8, 1892. On September 30, 1892, the number of the Christian community was 13,081.[74] On September 30, 1897, the number rose to 13,859.[75] Next year, Bishop Whitley visited the Chotanagpuri Christians working in the tea-gardens of Darjeeling and Assam.[76] The Birsa Uprising (1899-1900) caused some excitement and confusion in the Mission field, particularly in Murhu and Ranchi circles. On September 30, 1900, the Anglican Mission had 14,972 baptized members, 1017 inquirers, 11 European missionaries and 15 Indian priests.[77] The principal Mission stations were Ranchi, Chaibasa, Maranghada, Itki, Ramtolya, Murhu, Kachabari, Bargari, Duru, Tapkara, Dorma, Takra, Katbari, Phateyatoli, Jeypore, Saparom and Pithoria.[78] Hazaribagh was the centre of the Dublin University Mission.

In 1901, the Dublin University Mission was asked by Bishop Whitley to extend its work to Ranchi District also. The Dublin workers served through medical and educational institutions.[79] However, in 1908, the Dublin University Mission had to withdraw its workers from Ranchi.[80] Mission work was extended to Manbhum District with Purulia as headquarters. In 1902, Rev. W. Daud Singh of Chaibasa was awarded a Certificate of Honour[81] in the Coronation Durbar organized by the Colonial administration at Ranchi. Two years later, on October 17, 1904, Bishop Whitley died of heart failure at Darjeeling.[82] He served the Anglican Mission in Chotanagpur, for more than 35 years. On September 30, 1904, the Mission had 17,028 baptized members and 885 inquirers.[83]

Bishop Whitley was succeeded by his nephew, Rev. Foss Westcott, M. A., from Kanpur. He joined on November 30, 1905, and remained in the post till July 20, 1919. During his regime several important developments and events took place.[84] Many new missionaries, men and women, arrived. The most prominent was Rev. (Dr.) K. W. S. Kennedy who was stationed at Murhu. A new Mission District known as Gangpur District was formed in 1911.[85] The first elected Diocesan Council was held at Ranchi in April 1913.[86] The Gangpur District was renamed as Manoharpur District when Manoharpur was selected as its headquarters. The number of the Anglican community in 1914 rose to 20, 028.[87]

8. Support to Gossner Mission

When the First World War broke out, the Anglican Mission had to come to the rescue of the Gossner Mission in Chotanagpur.[88] All supplies from Germany were stopped. Bishop Westcott tried to raise funds for the maintenance of the German missionaries. In July 1915, these were interned, and, later on, sent back to Germany. At the time of leaving Ranchi, they left the Gossner Mission and its schools under Bishop Westcott's care and support.[89] While the Church was managed by a Council of local leaders, the schools were supervised and financed by the Bishop. The Government agreed to continue the financial aid given to them. The Bishop promised not to receive any Lutheran into the Anglican Church during War. When the War ended in 1918, a scheme was put forward by the Anglican Mission for the union[90] of these two Missions in Chotanagpur. It was rejected by the leaders of the Gossner Church. Subsequently, the *Mahasabha* of the Gossner Church declared autonomy on July 10, 1919,[91] and with this the Anglican supervision of and support to the Gossner Mission ended on October 28, 1919.

9. Further Expansion

Bishop Westcott became the Metropolitan[92] of India in 1919 and Rev. Alex Wood succeeded him as the Bishop of Chotanagpur. He was consecrated on December 6. 1919, at Ranchi.[93] The consecration coincided with the celebration of the Golden Jubilee of the Anglican Mission in Chotanagpur.[94] In 1919, the Anglican Mission had 19

European missionaries, 26 Indian clergy, 139 Preachers, 10 Bible women, 27 churches, 134 Chapels, 31 Stations, 22,171 baptized Christians and 814 inquirers.[95]

In January 1920, a new station was opened at Kamdara in the Ranchi District and the Sisterhood of St. Deny's started work in Chotanagpur.[96] In 1925, Bishop Wood framed a new Constitution which was approved in the special session of the Diocesan Council.[97] He invited Rev. G. N. L. Hall, a brilliant Cambridge scholar, to work in Chotanagpur. Early in May 1926, Bishop Wood was transferred as Bishop of Nagpur, and, in his place, Rev. (Dr.) K. W. S. Kennedy, D.D., M. B., a great Mundari scholar, became the fourth Bishop of Chotanagpur.[98] He was consecrated on December 12, 1926, in St. Paul's Cathedral, Ranchi. A new Mission station was founded at Lohardaga in Ranchi District.

In April 1928, the Anglican Church in Chotanagpur became a part of the Provincial Autonomous Church of India, Burma and Ceylon within the world-wide 'Anglican Communion'.[99] Rev. E. H., Whitley was appointed the first Archdeacon of the Diocese of Chotanagpur. He was awarded the *Kaiser-i-Hind* gold medal by the Government. At the end of 1930, the Mission had 31,600 baptized Christians.[100] The whole Anglican Church in Chotanagpur was divided into 9 Districts: Ranchi, Chaibasa, Murhu, Itki, Manoharpur, Kamdara, Dhanbad, Jamshedpur and Lohardaga.

In 1936, Bishop Kennedy was succeeded by Bishop G. N. L. Hall.[101] When the Second World War broke out in 1939, there was much disturbance in the normal work of the Mission. In 1940, the Diocese at Chotanagpur completed fifty years[102] and on November 2 & 3, the Golden Jubilee of the Diocese was celebrated at Ranchi. The Metropolitan of India, Rev. (Dr.) Foss Westcott and Bishop Hardy of Nagpur participated.[103]

The number of Christians in the Diocese of Chotanagpur had risen from 13,000 in 1890 to 40,000 in 1940. In 1942, the School and many other buildings of the Mission compound at Ranchi were requisitioned by the Government for keeping military personnel.[104] On August 15, 1947, India became independent. The Diocese of Chotanagpur was not much affected by the winding up of the Indian

Ecclesiastical Establishment, as was the case elsewhere.[105] There were many native missionary personnel to manage the Church.

10. Impact of the Anglican Mission

The activities of the Mission were not merely evangelistic and pastoral, though they had been the primary aims. Educational, medical, literary and other allied and welfare activities also received great attention.

10.1 Education Service

Side by side with the growth of the Church, there was from the beginning, the growth of education as an essential part of the Church development. During the split in the Gossner Mission in November 1868, all the school children, boys and girls, in the two Boarding Schools at Ranchi, followed the seceding missionaries along with their teachers.[106] This was followed at Singhani, Chaibasa and some other places in the interior. The seceded missionaries had to arrange for the education of these children as early as possible.

With the assistance of the English civil and military officers and friends, the missionaries at once set up a Boarding School at Ranchi.[107] The number of students was about 100. There were separate rooms for boys and girls to live but they studied together. Messrs. W. L. Daud Singh, Dayadham, Nathan Tirkey, Puran Prasad, Amus and Antony Dhan were appointed teachers.[108] In April 1869, when Anglican Mission officially began in Chotanagpur, there were altogether 13 schools, all Primary, in the Mission; one Boarding School at Ranchi and 12 Village Schools. There were 60 boys and 40 girls at Ranchi and 219 students in the Village Schools.[109] At the end of 1869, the Mission had altogether 394 scholars. At Ranchi there was a difficulty in keeping all school children who were actually admitted. The village children, quite unaccustomed to restrictions, often felt the discipline of the school irksome, and many of them, specially girls, ran off to their houses after a few months.[110]

On February 19, 1870, Mr. Roger Dutt, a student of Bishop's College, Calcutta, arrived to take charge of the Boarding School at Ranchi.[111] He had been sent by Bishop Milman. He found 12 teachers at Ranchi. He soon opened a Training School for them.[112]

All the boarders were free. The subjects that were taught were English, Arithmetic, Geography, Hindi, Bible and singing. During the year April 1870 to March 1871, ten more Village Schools were opened.[113] Thus, there were now altogether 23 Lower Primary Schools. In the Ranchi Boarding School alone, there were 106 boys and 54 girls. The number of day-scholars was 45. There were altogether 567 scholars in the Ranchi and Village Schools.[114] Of the Village Schools, two were at Singhani and Sitagarh in the District of Hazaribagh and two were at Chaibasa and Katbari in the District of Singhbum. A separate house was built in 1871 on the north of the Church Road for the residence of the girls reading in the Ranchi Boarding School.[115]

During the year April 1873 to March 1874, the Mission had 591 scholars, 418 boys and 173 girls.[116] On October 29, 1874, Lord Northbrook,[117] the then Viceroy of India, visited the Boarding School at Ranchi and granted a sum of Rs. 50/- together with a portrait of Queen Victoria. From January 1877, the boys and girls of the Ranchi Boarding School began to sit in separate classrooms.[118] With the efforts of Mr. Roger Dutt, the Boys' Boarding School, called St. Paul's School, which began under a pipal tree (now remaining as a landmark of the past) near the Cathedral, attained Middle Standard in 1881.[119] Next year, seven boys were sent up for the first time for the Middle Standard Examination. All seven passed, six in the first division and one in the second.[120] There was a Training School then known as Normal School at Ranchi.

In 1885, a separate school for girls was opened at Ranchi. It was also then known as St. Paul's School.[121] It later developed as St. Margaret's Girls' High School.[122] In 1887, the number of pupils in the Mission's schools rose to 1058. There were 919 boys and 139 girls. Three years later, in 1890, the number of boys rose to 1032 and that of girls, to 295. In 1892, Mr. P. K. Nundy was the Head Master of the Boys' Middle School and Mrs. Nundy, Head Mistress of the Upper Primary Girls' School at Ranchi.[123] That year, there were 1072 boys, and 308 girls in the various schools of the Mission.[124] On September 30, 1895, the total number of pupils was 2,116. Among them were 680 boys and 21 girls, who were Non-Christians.[125] In the same year, Mrs. O' Connor, after consulting Bishop Whitley, started a Blind School at Ranchi,[126] where she taught reading in Braille-type and basket-making. She was assisted in her work by Miss Whitley who continued the work after her retirement. This institution gradually developed into a great philanthropic agency in the service of the blind men and women.

In 1897, the Upper Primary Boys' and Girls' School at Chaibasa was raised to the Middle English Standard.[127] Separate arrangement was made for the education of the girls reading there.[128] In 1898, an Industrial School was set up where students were taught carpentry, weaving, wood-carving and stone-work. Two Primary Schools, one for boys and other for girls, were started at Pithoria Mission station.[129] In 1900, the Mission had altogether 2,641 pupils, of whom 804 boys and 50 girls 130 were Non-Christians.[130] The Schools at Ranchi and Chaibasa were conducted very efficiently and many scholars annually received Government scholarship. [131]

In 1901, a school for girls and another for boys were opened at Chutiya adjoining Ranchi, among Hindus and Muslims.[132] In that year, there were 16 male and 5 female students in the Blind School at Ranchi. Of them, 7 men and one woman were Non-Christians.[133] There were 18 students in the Industrial School at Chaibasa in 1902.[134] A Training School for males, known as St. Paul's Teachers' Training School, was opened at Ranchi in 1904.[135] On September 30, 1904, there were altogether 3,058 pupils in the various schools of the Mission. Of these 1,002 boys and 147 girls were Non-Christians.[136] In 1907, the Upper Primary School for boys at Murhu became a Middle English School. Next year, in 1908, under Miss A. F. Roe, St. Pauls' Girls' School at Ranchi was recognised as Middle English School.[137]

In the same year (1908), St. Paul's Middle English School for boys became a High School[138] and it presented the first six candidates for the Calcutta University Entrance Examination in March, 1909, in which all passed, two in the first division. Canon Cosgrave became its Principal in 1909. In June 1909, a Training School for females was started at Ranchi by Miss Beatty with 16 students.[139] A Lace School was also opened at Ranchi with 20 girls.[140] On September 30, 1910, there were altogether 118 schools in the Mission. Of these, 45 were for boys, 10 for girls, and the rest were for both.[141]

In 1911, Miss Knott set up a Boarding School for girls at Murhu. Two schools for girls were started in 1913 at Doranda among Non-Christians, one for Hindi-speaking and the other for Bengali-speaking children.[142] The Bengali Boys' School at Doranda became a Middle English School in1915. During the year, the Mission had 155 schools, 80 for boys, 23 for girls and 52 for both.[143] The total number of pupils was 5,381. Of these, 2,066 boys and 391 girls were Non-Christians.

On February 17, 1919, St. Paul's Girls' Middle School at Ranchi was recognized by Government as a High School and the Metropolitan Foss Westcott laid the foundation of a new building for the High School on St. Margaret's Eve.[144] The School was renamed as St. Margaret's Girls' High School. In that year, there were 89 students in the Lace School and 46 students, blind and crippled, in the Blind School. By the end of 1922, there were two schools, a Middle English School for boys and an Upper Primary School for girls, each with a hostel attached, in each District headquarter with the exception of Manoharpur.[145]

On March 1923, a school for European and Anglo-Indian girls, named Bishop Westcott School, was opened at Namkum.[146] In 1924, the Blind School moved into the newly-built buildings in the Cathedral compound with workshop, class-rooms, show-room and office. There were then 59 inmates. The Lace School that year had 52 students.

In 1925,[147] the Mission had 150 schools of which 27 were for girls and 13 were Night Schools. The total number of pupils was 5,360. In February 1927, a school for European and Anglo-Indian boys was started at Namkum. Some Indian boys and girls were also admitted into those schools. In 1930,[148] the Mission conducted 144 schools, having 6,751 students. There were 24 schools for girls and 18 Night Schools. Among the students, 2388 boys and 520 girls were Non-Christians. On July 20, 1935, St. Margaret's Girls' High School celebrated its Golden Jubilee.[149] In the beginning of 1936, Lady Linlithgow, wife of the then Viceroy, Lord Linlithgow, visited the High School.[150] The Lace School made very good sales in 1938. An Endowment Fund was created for the Blind School. In 1942, the School buildings at Ranchi were occupied by the military personnel, causing much disturbance to education work at Ranchi.[151] For some time, St. Margaret's Girls' High School was shifted to Hazaribagh and St. Paul's High School to Zila School buildings at Ranchi, during the War.

10.2 Medical Service

Medical work of the Mission started after 1874[152] when sufficient funds and personnel were available due to the efforts of Rev. F. R. Vallings and the ladies of Ranchi, who raised a fund for building a Mission Hospital (built by Mr. A. Hertzog) in 1874. Medicines were dispensed by Rev. F. Bohn with the assistance of a compounder named Johan.[153] They managed the Hospital till 1882. Rev. A. Logsdail carried on the work with Johan from 1883 to 1886.[154] In 1890, Miss Ingle took charge of the Hospital, assisted by Johan.[155] When Rev. A. Logsdail took charge of the Mission work at Chaibasa, he opened a dispensary at his residence and tried to collect money for a hospital. The Hospital building was completed in the beginning of 1893.[156] From its opening till September 30, 1893, 453 cases were treated.[157] In the hospital at Ranchi, from March to December 1894, 55 in-patients and 10,891 out-patients were treated.[158] During the year ending September 30, 1897, 78 in-patients and about 6,113 out-patients were treated at the Hospital in Ranchi.[159] Up to 1900, there was no qualified doctor either at Ranchi or at Chaibasa.

In 1904, Rev. (Dr.) K. W. S. Kennedy,[160] one of the pioneers of the Dublin University Mission at Hazaribagh, joined the Anglican Mission and carried on the work in the Hospital at Ranchi up to October. Then at the close of 1904, he was sent to Murhu, where he at once started a dispensary on April 5, 1905. In the same year, a hospital called St. Luke's Hospital was built there. Within nine months of its start, 6,070 out-patients and 25 in-patients were treated,[161] besides 49 major operations. Miss Poole replaced Miss Ingle at the Ranchi Hospital, which was later on placed in charge of Dr. Arit Kachchap. [162] In 1910, 50 in-patients and 4,763 out-patients were treated there.[163]

In 1911, Rev. O. W. Stallard was posted at Itki. His wife was a Doctor.[164] The erection of a hospital there was immediately started and completed in 1912. It consisted of a dispensary, four tiny wards and an operation room.[165] This hospital was later on called St. Deny's Hospital. Dr. A. T. Williams arrived at Murhu to assist Rev. (Dr.) Kennedy.[166] Early in 1917, Dr. Williams went to France in command of a Labour Company recruited in Chotanagpur. Dr. Kennedy built another hospital at Kamdara. It was dedicated in 1921 by the Metropolitan and was named Epiphany Hospital.[167] On June 11, 1922, on St. Barnabas' Day, the Hospital at Ranchi was re-named St. Barnabas' Hospital.[168] In January 1925, Sisters Rachel and Alethe of the Community of St. Deny's arrived at Manoharpur to start a hospital.[169] In 1926, Dr. Peter Kachchap, son of Dr. Arit Kachchap, joined St. Barnabas' Hospital. The total number of patients there that year was 15,000. The hospital at Manoharpur, called St. Francis' Hospital, was completed in 1927. Sister Rachel was in charge of it.[170]

In 1929, Dr. Helen Synge was at Kamdara, Miss Imrie at Itki, Dr. K. E. D. Dauncey at Murhu and Sister Rachel at Manoharpur.[171] On September 24, 1931, a new operation theatre was opened at St. Barnabas' Hospital by Lady Stephenson, wife of the then Governor of Bihar and Orissa, Sir Ganesh Dutt Singh, Minister of Local Self-Government and the Inspector-General of Civil Hospitals were present on the occasion.[172] In February 1939, Dr. Arit Kachchap retired after over forty years of devoted and faithful service to the Mission and St. Barnabas' Hospital.[173] Dr. Arit Kachchap was invested with *Kaiser-i-Hind* medal, merited by his long and honourable service at St. Barnabs' Hospital, Ranchi. A Leper Clinic was opened at Manoharpur in November 1939 by Sister Lucie, assisted in the work by Johan who had a special training in the treatment of leprosy.[174]

The Anglican Mission managed the Leper Asylum at Purulia. It had been started by a Gossner Mission missionary, Mr. Heinrich Uffmann, in 1887.[175] In 1915, the Gossner Mission authorities handed over the Asylum to the Church Missionary Society and Rev. E. Cannon became the first CMS missionary superintendent. In 1921, Rev. E. B. Sharpe took charge of the Asylum. It developed rapidly and in 1932, there was accommodation for 750 lepers. In 1938, it completed 50 years. During these years, 13,000 leprosy patients found shelter and friendship there.[176] Mr. Kristo Kumar Dutt was awarded the *Kaiser-i-Hind* for his long and honourable service as the Care-taker of the Leper Asylum at Purulia. Rev. Sharpe also served the institution for many years. It has become one of the biggest of its kind in India.

10.3 Contribution to Literature and Language

The Anglican Mission in Chotanagpur did much for the development of literature, particularly in aboriginal languages. Bishop Whitley started a newspaper in Hindi called the *Chotanagpur Dut Patrika* in 1878.[177] In 1874, the Mission began to publish a *Quarterly Paper* in English.[178] It was later known as the *Chotanagpur Diocesan Paper.* Bishop Whitley was a great scholar of Hindi and Mundari.[179] He translated many hymns (church songs) from English to Hindi. He wrote a *Mundari Grammar* and translated the New Testament and a portion of the *Book of Common Prayer* in Mundari. His son, Rev. E. H. Whitley, wrote and published an excellent little grammar in the colloquial language, Sadri. Rev. (Dr.) K. W. S. Kennedy was a renowned scholar of Mundari.[180] Along with Rev. (Dr.) A. Nottrott of the Gossner Mission, he revised the Mundari Bible. He also translated the *Prayer Book* in Mundari. Rev. W. L. Daud Singh and Rev. Abraham Bodra translated the *Prayer Book* into the Ho language.[181] The Mission has a bookshop of its own at Ranchi.

10.4 Other Philanthropic Activities

Like other Christian Missions, the Anglican Mission engaged itself in other philanthropic activities for the social and economic uplift of the people particularly the tribals of Chotanagpur. Its schools and hospitals were open to all, Christians and Non-Christians, Tribals and Non-tribals. It had an orphanage[182] at Ranchi for many years. It had been started and maintained for several years by Miss Ingle, out of her own funds. Co-operative Banks had been opened chiefly among the Oraons.[183] These Co-operative Banks were really Agricultural Banks set up primarily to help the farmers who were hit by famines and to save them from the hands of money lenders.[184] During famines of 1897 and 1900 the Mission rendered valuable service to the people by organising relief works at several places in Ranchi and Singbhum Districts.[185]

When Rev. E. B. Whitley was nominated to the Legislative Council of Bihar and Orissa he tried to represent the aboriginals of Chotanagpur in the civil administration. Miss Whipham was awarded the *Kaiser-i-Hind* medal in recognition of her service to the cause of education.[186] Rev. E. B. Sharpe was also awarded the same in 1928 for his distinguished service to the Leper Asylum at Purulia.

The Anglican Mission laid great stress on the development of games, particularly, football and hockey in schools.[187] More than once, the Ranchi Anglican Mission Aboriginal Boys' Hockey Team, patronised by Bishop Whitley, won Hockey Challenge Cup at Ranchi and Calcutta,[188] and the Beighton Cup too. It was Canon Cosgrave, who took Mr. Jaipal Singh, a Munda young man of village Takra in the District of Ranchi, and a student of St. Paul's High School, Ranchi, to England where he obtained an M. A. degree from Oxford. Mr. Jaipal Singh was the first captain of the Indian Olympic Hockey Team that won the World Championship in hockey at Amsterdam in Holland in 1928.

11. Conclusion

One of the prominent Christian Missions in Jharkhand, the Anglican Mission has made its mark felt in Jharkhand thanks to its educational, medical and other philanthropic services to the people of Jharkhand. The Mission's services, as noted above, have been available to all, irrespective of caste or creed, but preferentially to the tribal converts. The most signal contribution of this Mission seems to be its medical service to the leprosy patients. Assessing the mediating engagement of the European missionaries one can say that it has produced a) much socio-economic and religious transformation of the converts, and b) fostered native/tribal leadership to carry on the work begun by the foreign missionaries. The latter achievement has facilitated the transformation of the Mission itself into an autonomous Church. Also, one can observe the emergence of Christian tribal leadership in the general society of Jharkhand: in civil administration, in politics, in bureaucratic responsibilities, etc. Overall, though the Anglican Church is not numerically very strong, its leadership in civil society seems to be significant.

Endnotes and References

1 Though belonging to different denominations, each European Mission which entered Chotanagpur simply called its Mission, 'Chotanagpur Mission'. Therefore, this common title can be confusing unless its denominational identity is known.

2 *Historical Sketches: Missionary Series, No. II, Chota Nagpore* (1896), p. 26.

3 *Chotanagpur me Anglikan Kalisiya ki Shatvarshiya Jayanti* (Centenary of the Anglican Church in Chotanagpur), *1869-1969* (hereinafter, *Anglican Church Centenary*), (1969): Message of centenary greetings by Rt. Rev. Eric J. Trapp.

4 Eyre Chatterton, (1901), *A story of fifty year's of Mission work in Chotanagpur*, London. p. 162.

5 S. K. Patro & B. H. Mather, (1969), *The Anglican Church in Chotanagpur*, p. 1.

6 Ibid., pp. 1-2; H. H. Tucker, *Digest of the S. P. G. Records from 1701 to 1892*, (1893), p. 496.

7 Patro & Mather, (1969), p. 2.

8 7 W. W. Hunter, (1877), *The Statistical Account of Bengal: Vol. XVI, Hazaribagh and Lohardaga Districts,* London, p. 427; M. A. Sherring, (1884), *The History of the Protestant Missions in India,* London, p. 152; Chatterton, (1901), p. 51; *Chotanagpur Mission Quarterly Paper*, No. 1, February 1874, p. 4; Kushalmay Sheetal, (1939), *Chotanagpur Ki Kalishya Ka Brittant* (Newsletter of the Chotanagpur Church), Allahabad, pp. 60-62; E. Wueste, (1967), *Chotanagpur Ki Masihi Mandli ka Itihas* (History of the Chotanagpur Christian community), *1845-1870,* 4th edition, pp. 49-50; C. H. Swavely, (1952), *The Lutheran Enterprise in India*, p. 56.

9 *Annual Report Chotanagpur Mission* (hereinafter, ARCM) *(1869-70)*; *Chotanagpur Mission Quarterly Paper,* No. 1, February 1874, p. 4; Hunter (1877), p. 424; Wueste, (1967), 4th edition, p. 39; Sheetal, (1939), pp. 46-47.

10 Wueste, (1967), pp. 45-46; Swavely, (1952), p. 55.

11 ARCM *(1869-70)*, pp. 1-8; Tucker, (1893), p. 496; Chatterton, (1901), pp. 40-41; Sheetal, (1939), p. 55; Wueste, (1967), p. 40.

12 J. Cave-Browne, (1870), *The Chotanagpur Mission,* p. 33; ARCM *(1869-1870)*, pp. 1-8; Tucker, (1893), p. 496; Wueste, (1967), p. 40; Sheetal, (1939), pp. 56-57; A. Nottrott, (1874), *The Gossner Mission unter den Kols*, p. 212; D. Walter Holsten, (1949), *Johaness Evangelista Gossner: Gla1be and Gemeinde*, pp. 240-245.

13 Chatterton, (1901), pp. 44-45; Sheetal, (1939), p. 60; Murray Mitchell, (1871), *A Missionary's Wife among the Wild Tribes of South Bengal*, pp. 48-49; Walter D. Holsten, (1949), *Joahnnes Evangelista Gossner*, Glalube & Gemeinde, Gottingen, p. 258; E. Wueste, (1967), pp. 45-46.

14 Cave-Browne, (1870), p. 50; Hunter (1877), p. 424; Wueste, (1967), p. 48; Sheetal, (1939, p. 60; Patro & Mather, (1069), p. 2.

15 Wueste, (1967), p. 48; Sheetal, (1939), p. 60; Chatterton, (1901), p. 45; Cave-Browne, (1870), p. 50; Holsten, (1949), p. 258; Hunter, (1877), p. 424.

16 Wueste, (1967), p. 49; Chatterton, (1901), p. 46; Sheetal, (1939), p. 62; Holsten, (1949), p. 258.

17 Hunter, (1877), p. 425; Cave-Browne, (1870), p. 60; Sheetal, (1939), p. 62.

18 Tucker, (1893), p. 496; Sheetal, (1939), pp. 65-66; Hunter, (1877), p. 423; *Chotanagpur Mission Quarterly Paper*, No. I, February 1874, pp. 4-5.

19 Chatterton, (1901), p. 47; Wueste, (1967), p. 50; Hunter, (1877), p. 423; Swavely, (1952), p. 56.

20 Swavely, (1952), p. 56.

21 Sheetal, (1939), p. 66; Wueste, (1967), p. 50.

22 Sheetal, (1939), pp. 67-68.

23 Note the differing numbers in various sources. Cave-Browne, (1870), p. 53: "Seven thousand"; Chatterton, (1901), p. 48: "Six or seven thousand'; Sheetal, (1939), p. 68: "About seven thousand"; Tucker, (1893), p. 496: "Seven thousand"; Andrews, (1908), *Handbook of English Church Expansion, North India,* London, p. 42: "About seven thousand"; Wueste, (1967), p. 50: "About six or seven hundred"; Holsten, (1949), p. 260: "3000 to Anglicans and 7000 remained Lutheran"; *Die Biena auf dem–Missionsfelde* (A monthly publication of the Mission in Berlin), 1869, p. 260: "Majority remained Lutherans".

24 Sheetal, (1939), p. 65.

25 The appeals and other relevant papers have been published under the name "Ranchi Pamphlet".

26 Cava-Browne, (1870), p. 44; *The Englishman*, June 15, 1869; Mitchell, pp. 64-65; *Historical Sketches: Missionary Series*, Vol. II, Chotanagpur, (1896), p. 6.

27 J. Cave-Browne, (1870), p. 60; Chatterton, (1901), p. 47; S. C. Roy, (1912), *The Mundas and their Country*, p. 246; Wueste, (1967), p. 49; Sheetal, (1939), p. 62; Hunter, (1877), p. 425.

28 Sheetal, (1939), p. 65.
29 Ibid ; Tucker, (1893), p. 496.
30 ARCM, *(1869-70)*, pp. 1-8; Tucker, (1893), p. 496; Chatterton, (1901), p. 49; Sheetal, (1939), pp. 70-71.
31 Hunter, (1877), p. 425; Chatterton, (1901), p. 47; Sheetal, (1939), p. 69.
32 Ibid.
33 Sheetal, (1939), p. 69; Chatterton, (1901), p. 48.
34 Chatterton, (1901), p. 48; Sheetal, (1939), p. 70.
35 Sheetal, (1939), p. 71; Chatterton, (1901), p. 49.
36 ARCM, (1869-1870), pp. 1-8; *Chotanagpur Mission Quarterly Paper* No. I, February 1874, pp. 5-6; Hunter, (1877), p. 425; Chatterton, (1901), pp. 52-55; Sheetal, (1939), pp. 72-77; Swavely, (1952), p. 56; Wueste, (1967), p. 50; Tucker, (1893), p. 496; Patro & B. R. Mather, (1969), p. 4; Roy, (1912), pp. 246-247.
37 Letter from the Lutherans of Berlin to Bishop Milman on April 21, 1869; Editor's comments in *Friends of India*, dated May 7 and June 17, 1869; Cave-Browne, (1870), p. 95; Swavely, (1952), p. 56; Chatterton, (1901), p. 60; Sherring, (1884), p. 152; Sheetal, (1939), pp. 77-78; Hunter, (1877), p. 425; Holsten, (1949), p. 262.
38 Chatterton, (1901), p. 59; Sheetal, (1939), pp. 79-80.
39 Sheetal, (1939), p. 88; Chatterton, (1901), p. 65; Wueste, (1967), p. 50.
40 Hunter, (1877), p. 422; *Chotanagpur Mission Quarterly Paper* No. 1, February 1874, p. 4.
41 Hunter, (1877), p. 426; ARCM, *(1869-70)*, p. 6; Chatterton, (1901), p. 85; Sheetal, (1939), p. 147; Roy, (1912), p. 266: 5,733 baptized persons.
42 Tucker, (1893), p. 496; Sheetal, (1939), pp. 81-83; Roy, (1912), p. 248; Chatterton, (1901), p. 62; Andrews, (1908), p. 42.
43 Andrews, (1908), p. 65; Tucker, (1893), p. 497; Hunter, (1877), p. 480; Sheetal, (1939), p. 88.
44 Hunter, (1877), p. 480; Sheetal, (1939), p. 88; Chatterton, (1901), p. 66; Patro & Mather, (1969), p. 5.
45 Chatterton, (1901), p. 66; Patro & Mather, (1969), p. 5.
46 Sheetal, (1939), pp. 93-94; Chatterton, (1901), pp. 71-72.
47 ARCM, *(1870-1871)*, p. 12; Chatterton, (1901), p. 72; Sheetal, (1939), p. 97.
48 Sheetal, (1939), p. 97; Chatterton, (1901), p. 72; ARCM, (1870-71), pp. 11-12.

49 *Chotanagpur Mission Quarterly Paper,* No. 1, February 1874, p. 6; Chatterton, (1901), p. 75; Sheetal, (1939), p. 113.
50 Hunter, (1877), p. 428; *Chotanagpur Mission Quarterly Paper,* No. I, February 1874, p. 6; Chatterton, (1901), p. 75; Sheetal, (1939), pp. 121-122.
51 Hunter, (1877), p. 430; Tucker, (1893), p. 498; *Chotanagpur Mission Quarterly Paper,* No. I, February 1874, p. 6; Chatterton, (1901), p. 75; Sheetal, (1939), pp. 122-123; Roy, (1912), p. 258; Andrews, (1908), p. 43.
52 Quoted in Chatterton, (1901), p. 67.
53 ARCM, *(1870-71),* p. 33; Hunter, (1877), p. 426.
54 ARCM, *(1873-74),* p. 33.
55 *Chotanagpur Mission Quarterly Paper,* No. 3, November 1874, p. 2.
56 Sheetal, (1939), pp. 129-130; Chatterton, (1901), pp. 80-81.
57 Tucker, (1893), p. 498; Chatterton, (1901). p. 83; Sheetal, (1939), p. 133.
58 Chatterton, (1901), p. 84; Sheetal, (1939), p. 138.
59 Chatterton, (1901), p. 169; Sheetal, (1939), p. l41.
60 Sheetal, (1939), p. 141.
61 Ibid., p. 142.
62 Ibid., p. 147; Chatterton, (1901), p. 85.
63 Chatterton, (1901), p. l03; Sheetal, (1939), p. 170.
64 Chatterton, (1901), p. 96.
65 Ibid., p. 101; Sheetal, (1939), p. 173.
66 Tucker, (1893), p. 499; Chatterton, (1901), p. 97; Sheetal, (1939), pp. 157-159.
67 ARCM, (1885), p. 50; Chatterton, (1901), p. l08; Sheetal, (1939, p. 174; Tucker, (1893), p. 499.
68 ARCM, *(1904),* p. 26; Sheetal, (1939), pp. 168-169.
69 ARCM, *(1890),* p. l; Tucker, (1893), p. 499; Chatterton, (1901), pp. 113-114; Andrews, (1908), p. 44; ARCM, *(1904),* p. 27.
70 Chatterton, (1901), pp. 113-114: He says 12,890; Roy, (1912), p. 268: He says 12, 500; Sheetal, (1939), p. 174.
71 *Annual Report Dublin University Mission* (1892-93), p. 8; Chatterton, (1901), p. l23; Patro & Mather, (1969), p. 9.
72 Patro & Mather, (1969), p. 10; Chatterton, (1901), p. 124.
73 Chatterton, (1901), p. 124; Tucker, (1893), pp. 499-500; Roy, (1912), p. 267; Patro & Mather, (1969), p. 10.
74 ARCM, (1891-92), p. 21.
75 ARCM, *(1896-97),* p. 36.

76 Chatterton, (1901), pp. 139-140; ARCM, (1898), pp. 11-14.
77 ARCM, (1900), p. 45.
78 Ibid.
79 ARCM, (1901), p. 4; *Annual Report of Dublin University Mission,* (1901), p. 10.
80 *Annual Report of Dublin University Mission,* (1908), p. 11.
81 ARCM, (1902), p. 26.
82 ARCM, (1904), p. 4.
83 Ibid., p. 75.
84 Patro & Mather, (1969), p. 12.
85 ARCM, (1911), p. 5.
86 ARCM, *(1913),* p. 3.
87 ARCM, *(1914),* p. 44.
88 *Chotanagpur Diocesan Report,* January 1916, p. 2; Patro & Mather, (1969), p. 12.
89 Swavely, (1952), p. 60; Patro & Mather, (1969), p. 12; Seeberg (1969), p. 19; *Chotanagpur Diocesan Report,* January 1916, pp. 3-4.
90 Swavely, (1952), p. 61.
91 Ibid., p. 64; *Gharbandhu* (Home Relative), August 15, 1919, pp. 125-126.
92 *Annual Report of Chotanagpur Mission,* (1919), p. iv, 3; *Annual Report of Dublin University Mission,* (1919), p. 7.
93 Patro & Mather, (1969), p. 12; *Anglican Church Centenary,* (1969), p. 9.
94 Patro & Mather, (1969), pp. 12-13.
95 ARCM, (1919), p. 50.
96 Patro & Mather, (1969), p. 13.
97 Ibid.
98 Ibid., p. 14; *Chotanagpur Diocesan Paper,* January 1927, p. l.
99 Patro & Mather, (1969), p. 15.
100 *Chotanagpur Diocesan Paper,* July, l930, pp. l0-20.
101 Ibid., October, 1936, p. 1.
102 Patro & Mather, (1969), p. 14.
103 *Chotanagpur Diocesan Paper,* July 1940, pp. 10-20.
104 Patro & Mather, (1969), p. 16.
105 Ibid.
106 Sheetal, (1939), p. 66.
107 Ibid., p. 67.
108 Ibid., p. 68.
109 ARCM, (1870-71), p. 21.

110 ARCM, (1870-71), pp. 18-19.

111 *Chotanagpur Mission Quarterly Paper*, No.I, February 1874, p. 6; MSS letter from Whitley to Cave-Browne, dated 25th March, 1870; Sheetal, (1939), p. 92.

112 ARCM, (1870-71), p. 18; Sheetal, (1939), p. 92.

113 ARCM, (1870-71), p. 21.

114 Ibid.

115 Sheetal, (1939), p. 104.

116 ARCM, (1873-74), p. 33.

117 *Chotanagpur Mission Quarterly Paper,* No. 3, November 1874, p. 9; Sheetal, (1939), p. 130.

118 Sheetal, (1939), p. 138.

119 ARCM, (1882), p. 4; Sheetal, (1939), p. 152.

120 ARCM, (1882), p. 5.

121 ARCM, (1904), p. 21; *Anglican Church Centenary,* 1969, p. 42.

122 *Anglican Church Centenary,* 1969, p. 42.

123 ARCM, (1892), p. 8.

124 Ibid., p. 21.

125 Ibid., (1895), p. 35.

126 Ibid., p. 5; Chatterton (1901), p. 137; Roy, (1912), p. 264.

127 ARCM, (1897), p. 6.

128 ARCM, (1898), p. 5; ARCM, (1901), pp. 14-15.

129 ARCM, (1898) pp. 18-19.

130 ARCM, (1900), p. 45.

131 Ibid., pp. 812.

132 ARCM, (1901), p. 21.

133 ARCM, (1901), p. 24.

134 ARCM, (1902), p. 15.

135 *Anglican Church Centenary,* 1969, p. 42.

136 ARCM, (1904), p. 75.

137 *Anglican Church Centenary,* 1969, p. 42.

138 ARCM, (1909), p. 11.

139 Ibid., p. 9.

140 ARCM, (1909), p. 11; Roy, (1912), p. 261.

141 ARCM, (1910): Statistics.

142 ARCM, (1914), p. 12.

143 *Chotanagpur Diocesan Report*, January 1916, p. 10.

144 *Anglican Church Centenary,* 1969, p. 42; N. Kumar, *Bihar District Gazetteers: Ranchi* p. 468.

145 ARCM, (1922), p. 13.

146 ARCM, (1923), p. 15.
147 ARCM, (1925), p. 8
148 ARCM, (1930), p. 25.
149 Patro & Mather, (1969), p. 15.
150 Ibid.
151 Ibid., p. 16.
152 ARCM, (1873-74), p. 15.
153 *Chotanagpur Mission Quarterly Paper,* No. 3, November 1874, pp. 8-9; Sheetal, (1939), p. 128.
154 Sheetal, (1939), p. 128.
155 Ibid.
156 ARCM, (1893), p. 18.
157 Ibid.
158 ARCM, (1895), p. 7.
159 Ibid.
160 ARCM, (1904), p. 18; *Anglican Church Centenary,* 1969, p. 47.
161 ARCM, (1906), p. 17.
162 Sheetal, (1939), p. 128.
163 ARCM, (1910), p. 10.
164 ARCM, (1911), p. 22.
165 ARCM, (1912), p. 30.
166 Ibid., p. 19.
167 *Anglican Church Centenary,* (1969), p. 40.
168 Ibid., p. 31.
169 Ibid.
170 ARCM, (1929).
171 ARCM, (1931), p. 8.
172 *Chotanagpur Diocesan Report* No.70, April 1939, p. 7.
173 *Chotanagpur Diocesan Paper* September 1941.
174 Roy, (1912), p. 256.
175 *Chotanagpur. Diocesan Paper*, September 1941, p. 9.
176 Sheetal, (1939), p. 142.
177 *Chotanagpur Mission Quarterly Paper,* No. I, February 1874; Roy, (1912), p. 265.
178 ARCM, (1904), p. 7, Paper No. 7.
179 Patro & Mather, (1969) p. 14.
180 *Annual Report of Chotanagpur Mission,*(1902), p. 25.
181 Roy, (1912), p. 265; ARCM, (1899), p. 29
182 Roy, (1912), p. 265.
183 *Annual Report of Chotanagpur Mission*, (1902), pp. 32-33.

184 ARCM, (1900), pp. 19-24.
185 *Chotanagpur Diocesan Paper,* No. 24, October 1927, p. 10.
186 ARCM, (1901), p. 13; ARCM, (1902), p. 11; Roy, (1912), p. 263.
187 Roy, (1912), pp. 263-264.

Chapter 7

The Santal Mission of the Northern Churches in Jharkhand

1. First Period: From Individual Efforts to Indian Home Mission

The Santal Mission of the Northern Churches, "the largest Santal Christian Mission"[1] in India, was founded in the District of Santal Parganas in Jharkhand by Mr. Hans Peter Boerresen, a 40-year-old Danish engineer, and Mr. Lars Olsen Skrefstud, a 26-year-old Norwegian missionary.[2] They came to India originally to work in the Gossner Mission in Chotanagpur. While staying in Berlin, they became great friends and offered themselves to the Gossner Mission in Chotanagpur on condition that they would be permitted to live and work together. For certain reasons, they could not come out to India together. Mr. Skrefsrud was sent out by the Gossner Mission Society in November 1863 to Purulia in the District of Manbhum, where he arrived before Christmas. Mr. and Mrs. Boerresen and the bride of Mr. Skrefsrud reached Purulia in April 1865.[3]

The two friends lived and worked at Purulia for six months. The Gossner Mission authorities at Ranchi did not allow them to work together and in November 1865, they left the Gossner Missionary Society and also that part of the country to work together elsewhere.[4]

They had no European connections, no friends and no helpers.[5] When they left the Gossner Mission, they wrote to the authorities of the Danish Missionary Society, asking to be taken into their service; but the Society regretted that they were unable to accede to their wishes.[6] They had no means of their own, and were, therefore, in great difficulty. At such a critical time, certain Bengali Christians came to their rescue, gave them shelter by placing a furnished villa at their disposal, some seven miles from Calcutta, and supplied all their needs.[7] They met the Secretary of the Bible Society in Calcutta, who advised and encouraged them to work among the Santals of Bihar.[8]

While making enquiries on the feasibility of starting mission work among the Santals, they came into contact with an ex-military Baptist missionary, Rev. Edward C. Johnson, who had been stationed at Suri in the Birbhum District of Bengal. Rev. Johnson was also anxious to start mission work among the Santals and had built for himself a mud-hut at Belbuni, a Santal village, in Santal Parganas. There in that mud-hut, the three missionaries met about Christmas 1866[9] and decided to start a Mission to the Santals with Indian support. The new Mission was called the "Indian Home Mission to the Santals".

2. Second Period: Founding of the Benagaria Mission, 1867

Soon after this decision, Messrs. Boerresen and Skrefsrud and their families temporarily settled at Suri. They looked for a suitable place for their future work. They found one on April 7, 1867, near Benagaria in Santal Parganas. They raised a heap of stones in an open field, held a short service with a hymn and prayer and called the place "Ebenezer"[10] (hitherto hath the Lord helped us). When the missionaries proceeded to the spot in the middle of May 1867, they found that the field with the heap of stones was not exactly suitable for the end in view and so, they moved a few hundred yards to the south, where now stands the Benagaria station. They visited Meher

Chand Roy, the landlord of the place, who lived at Moluti, four miles off. The landlord came to the spot with the headman of Benagaria on May 23, 1867, and on the same day, the land to build a Mission station was secured.[11]

After the rains, all the three missionaries, along with one Hezekiah Das, a school teacher, arrived there on September 26, 1867.[12] They erected two temporary sheds of branches and straw, one for themselves to live and the other for Hezekiah Das to live and conduct a school.[13] The foundations of the various houses to be built were laid within a year, the houses in the compound were built and the missionaries entered into them in the rainy season of 1868.[14]

3. Inter-denominational Mission: Baptist Support, Lutheran Character

The Mission began as an international and inter-denominational body. Rev. Johnson was an Englishman and a Baptist; Mr. Boerresen was a Dane and a Lutheran; Mr. Skrefsrud was a Norwegian and a Lutheran. They carried on the mission work unitedly. They were supported by the Baptist Missionary Society and many friends in India. On February 10, 1869, Rev. Johnson was badly mauled by a tiger at a village called Amehua, and he withdrew permanently from the newly organised Mission.[15] Henceforth, Messrs. Boerresen and Skrefsrud, both Lutherans, became the leaders and managers of the Mission. The Baptist Missionary Society continued to give a monthly contribution even after the withdrawal of Rev. Johnson. Persons belonging to various nationalities and denomnations in India also extended their help but the Mission field in Santal Parganas became increasingly Lutheran in character.

The Mission obtained its first converts on the Easter Day, March 28, 1869, when three Santal young men from the newly established school, Siram, Jogot and Raghu, were baptized by Mr. Skrefsrud, at Ebenezer in the presence of a large gathering.[16] By that time, Mr. Skretsrud had mastered the language of the Santals. The number of Christians increased to 15 by end of 1869.[17] In 1870, Mrs. Skretsrud died of heat fever and was buried at Benagaria. She was the first missionary to die on the Mission field. A piece of land was acquired in 1871 at Dudhiani, 50 miles west of Benagaria, for building another Mission station. Mr. Edward Cornelius, who joined the Mission staff in August 1869, worked there for a couple of years until he left the Mission in 1872.

In the year 1874, there occurred a terrible famine in Bengal.[18] The Government of Bengal placed Mr. Boerrosen (Mr. Skretsrud was on furlough) in charge of some relief work at Nankar. Thousands of people were enabled to pull through until crops eased the situation. The special correspondent of the *Times of London*, who visited Bonsgaria, was very much impressed with the management of relief works. He wrote a vivid article to the *Times* telling of what he had seen. This article did very much to tell the people in England that there was a Santal Mission.[19] During the year, 1592 persons were baptized.[20] The Christians belonged to 144 villages. On April 9, 1876, Siram Soren and Surju Murmu were ordained priests at Benagaria by Rev. Wenge[21] of Calcutta, for their proper spiritual care and supervision. Messrs. Boerresen and Skrefsrud were not ordained then. By the close of the year 1876, the number of the baptized Christians rose to 2,246.[22]

4. Multi-lateral Support from Abroad

The period of Indian support lasted ten years (1867-1877).[23] The arrangement about the finance of the Mission was not at all satisfactory. Mr. Boerresen made regular fund collection tours starting from Calcutta and visiting Benares, Allahabad and other important towns in Northern India.[24] The mission work, therefore, suffered due to lack of funds. The two pioneers, therefore, tried their best to obtain, during their respective furloughs, recognition and aid from various countries of Europe. On May, 16, 1876, Mr. Boerresen left India with the definite purpose of seeking a new arrangement about financial support. The Baptist Missionary Society, which had been giving a monthly contribution to the Mission, did not favour this idea, and demanded a written statement from Mr. Boerresan that the Baptist Missionary Society was to inherit the work when the pioneers were no more or could no more manage the affairs of the growing work of the Mission. This Mr. Boerresen refused and the connection with the Baptist Missionary Society ended in 1877.[25] Mr. Boerresen, however, succeeded in getting recognition and support in Scotland, England, Denmark and Norway, where supporting committees were set up. [26] Mr. Boerresen was ordained in Denmark in 1877.[27]

5. Second Period: Independent Santal Christian Church, 1880

The second period of the Mission began in 1878. The formation of the supporting committees in England, Scotland, Denmark, Norway, and later on, in the United States of America and Sweden, gave the Mission a much stronger foundation financially and there was a rapid expansion of work.[28] All supporting committees had direct communication with the pioneers at Benagaria. New stations were founded at Dumas and Asanbani (1879), Chondorpura and Mohulpahari (1880). In 1880, the founders of the Mission executed 8 Deeds of Trust, to safeguard the Mission and its properties, giving all the Mission properties, present and future, to four persons, Messrs. Boerresen and Skretsrud and the two friends of the Mission, Mr. T. T. Allen, who had retired from Indian Civil Service as Legal Remembrancer to the Government of Bengal, and Mr. Robert Allen, Barrister-at-Law. This arrangement was to continue till the Santal Christian Church established by the Mission took upon itself the whole responsibility of managing its affairs and needed no foreign aid.[29]

During his second furlough (1881-83), Mr. Skrefsrud visited Norway, Sweden and Denmark and strengthened the missionary cause in those countries. On the 26th July, 1882, he was ordained in Norway.[30] Mission stations were established at Haripur, Sapedoha, Simoldohi and Banga in 1883, at Karikador in 1884, at Chandpur in 1885, at Gadiapani in 1887, at Baromasia and Majdiha in 1890 and at Kakjol in 1896, all in the District of Santal Parganas in Jharkhand.[31]

6. Santal Christian Colony in Assam and North Bengal

Mission work was extended to Assam and North Bengal.[32] To help the new Santal Christians who wanted to emigrate to Assam and Bengal for their livelihood, Rev. Skrefsrud and seven Santal headmen left

Benagaria in September 1880 and selected Guma Duar in Goalpara District of Assam for their settlement.[33] It was then a forest waste land measuring about 25 square miles. With the approval of the Government of India, permission was given by the local Government to make a Christian settlement there. After one month of the return of Rev. Skrefsrud and his party, Rev. Boerresen and 15 Santals went there, cleared the forest, erected six temporary huts and returned. The first batch of settlers, consisting of 42 Christian families reached there on February 8, 1881.[34] Thus a Santal Christian colony was started in Assam. More Christian Santals joined them. Pastor Siram Soren was posted there for their care and guidance. The Mission acquired the Mornai and Tamai Tea Gardens, which were adjacent to the Santal Christian colony from the original planters in 1890.[35] The Santal Christians at Gums Duar came into contact with the native community of Boros. The first Boro family was baptized on January 8, 1888.[36] In 1900, the Mission started work at Chatai in Dinajpur in North Bengal.

The Mission celebrated the 25 years' Jubilee in 1892 at Benagaria. During 1867-92, 6256 Non-Christians were admitted to the Church by baptism and 936 children of 37 Christian parents were baptized.[37] On June 2, 1901, one Jalpa Soren was ordained as pastor for the Mission work in Dinajpur in North Bengal. This ordination was the last act of Rev. Hans Peter Boerresen (commonly known as Papa Saheb); he died at Benagaria on September 23, 1901.[38]

The Mission acquired a *zamindari* in 1901 in Nanksr when Rev. Skrufsrud purchased the same from Mr. R. Allen, formerly one of the trustees of the Mission.[39] An independent German missionary, Mr. Albert Haegert (at one time in the Mission from January 1873 to March 1875) had built three Mission stations at Kaerabani, Dhorampur and Maharo, all in the District of Santal Parganas. At his death in 1904, they were purchased by Rev. Skrefsrud from his heirs on payment of Rs.60, 000.[40] On January 24, 1909, Rev. Skrefsrud became a victim of a serious stroke and he died at Benagaria on December 11, 1910.[41] Thus, disappeared the last of the pioneer missionaries, Rev. Skrefsrud (commonly known as Kerap Sabeb) from the Mission work. With his death, the second period of the Mission came to a close.

7. Third Period: Formation of the Santal Mission of the Northern Churches

The third period of the Mission began in 1911. Before his death, Rev. Skrefsrad signed a legal document with his left hand giving authority to Rev. P. O. Bedding, who had been in the service of the Mission since January 1890, to carry on the work. With the passing away of both the founders, there arose a necessity for a new arrangement regarding the management of the Mission work. The representatives of the supporting committees in Denmark, Norway and the United States met at Oslo in Norway in 1910 and framed a new constitution, with a new name "**The Santal Mission of the Northern Churches**".[42] While all the property on the Mission field and the legal authority remained with the Trust Body, administrative boards known as 'Home Boards' were set up in Denmark, Norway and the United States. They were to send man and money to the Mission field. A provision was made for an annual conference of the missionaries on the Mission field.

The new arrangement enabled the Mission to expand its work in different directions.[43] The first missionary conference was held on the field in 1911. In a few years' time, many new missionaries arrived, new Mission stations were founded, the old Mission stations and buildings were rebuilt and much needed institutions like schools, leper colonies and hospitals were opened. Koroya became a station in 1911. Work was carried on vigorously among the Boros in Assam. In 1911, the first Boro pastor, Ratia Boro, was ordained.[44] New stations at Gaorang, Thajobari and Bongaegaon were founded among the Boros; Narainpur and Nimasarai stations were built to work among the Bengalis of Santal Parganas and Bengal; Joema and Haraputa stations were built for the growing Santal work in Assam. The churches at Dumka, Kaerabani, Maharo, Chanderpura and Basetkundi were built and consecrated during the period.[45]

8. Pulling through Two World Wars

The outbreak of the First World War in 1914 greatly disturbed the work of the Mission. In 1917, it completed fifty years, and the Golden Jubilee was celebrated in the midst of the War on September 26 all over the Mission area.[46] The number of Christians of the Mission on September 30, 1917, was 20,281.[47] Since the commencement (1867-1917), up to September 30, 1917, in all 24,038 persons were baptized by the Mission according to the statistics given in the annual reports.[48]

Even through there were many difficulties during the World War (1914-1918) and afterwards, the Mission not only continued its work steadily but also constantly extended it. In 1923, Rev. P. O. Bodding retired and was succeeded by Rev. Rasmus Rosenlund, a Dane, who had joined the Mission staff in 1910 and who guided the affairs of the Mission till August 1940 (except in 1925-27 and 1933-34 when he was away on furlough) .

The Second World War (1939-1945) saw Denmark and Norway occupied by the Nazi forces, and the Mission was cut off from 4/5th of its regular support.[49] The Home Board in the United States could not shoulder alone the great burden. During the crisis, generous help was received through the Federation of the Evangelical Lutheran Churches in India, from the Lutheran World Federation, from the Norwegian Government in exile in London, from remote places like Iceland, the Facroe Islands and New Zealand, and from the Norwegian sailors on the high seas.[50] The Santal congregations of the Church of Scotland Mission sent contributions. The Tea Gardens in Assam yielded a good income. In 1940, there were on the field 10 American, 10 Danish and 31 Norwegian missionaries.[51] The total number of Christians in the Mission in 1941 was 25,695 of which 9,537 belonged to the District of Santal Parganas.[52]

In 1947, India became independent. The division of the country into Indian Union and Pakistan affected the Mission field. The areas in the Rajshahi, Malda and Dinajpur Districts in North Bengal, went over to East Pakistan (presently, Bangladesh).[53] The secretaries (Hallen, Dixen and Thorman) of the three Home Boards in Norway, Denmark and the United States respectively visited the Mission field. According to the *Annual Report* (1947), the Mission had over 100 missionaries, 52 Indian priests and 28,703 Christians of whom 9,840 belonged to the District of Santal Parganas in Jharkhand.

9. Impact of the Mission

During the period from 1867 to 1947, the Santal Mission of the Northern Churches, originally known as the 'Indian Home Mission to the Santals', engaged not only in evangelism and conversion but also did admirable and lasting service for the educational, medical, literary, social and economic progress of the people among whom it had worked. Its greatest achievement has been in the field of literature.

9.1 Educational Service

The Mission laid great stress on education from the very start. It commenced work among an entirely illiterate population. Its emphasis on education was, therefore, quite natural. It is on record that when the three pioneer missionaries started work at Benagaria on September 26, 1867, they erected, on the very first day, two temporary sheds, one for themselves to live in, and the other for Hezekiah Das whom they brought with them from Suri, to live and conduct a school.[54] The beginning was very primitive. A few boys, rather young men, began to attend the school in the shed out of curiosity. Siram Soren was one of the few who first attended. Hezekiah was a Bengali and, therefore, the medium of instruction was Bengali.[55] A separate school for girls also was set up by Mrs. Boerresen. As the early Santal girls of the locality were constantly running away for fear, Mrs. Boorresen, in 1870, got three or four orphan Santal Christian girls from the Baptist Mission in Midnapur in Orissa to have them as a nucleus.[56] Thus, began the Girls' School at Benagaria. In the early years, Mr. Bunckholdt, a young Norwegian teacher, and Mr. Hustan, originally an English indigo planter six miles away, worked in the schools at Benagaria. In 1886, a Swede, Dr. E. Heuman, took charge of the Boys' School. It was raised to the Middle Vernacular Standard, with two years' additional course in English.[57] The Girls' School too was rebuilt. The girls there did not leave until they were married.[58] Besides these two schools at Benagaria, there were several village schools and in many places, evening schools. The medium of instruction continued to be Bengali until 1911 when the new Province of Bihar and Orissa was created and the schools were asked by the local Government to change over the mediam of instruction to Hindi.[59]

Mrs. Boerresen continued to work in the Girls' School up to an advanced age. In 1903, Mr. J. J. Ofstad took charge of the Boys' School. Both the schools worked well at Banagaria upto about 1905 when due to the infection of various diseases, the Boys' School was transferred to Karikador, and then to Kaerabani in 1911.[60] There the existing fine school buildings were planned and erected by Mr. Ofstad. The Girls' School too was shifted to Maharo, near Dumka, during 1910-13.[61] Thus, both the schools started at Benagaria in 1867 ceased to exist.

A Training School was started along with the Boys' School to train Village School teachers. Such a Training School was opened for girls too, and was attached to the Girls' School.[62] At the suggestion of the Deputy Commissioner[63] of Santal Parganas, Industrial Schools were started in connection with the Schools at Kaerabani (boys) and Maharo (girls). The boys were taught carpentry and the girls, sewing, embroidery and lace-making. The running cost of the Industrial Schools was shared half-half by the Government and the Mission. Two girls were sent by the Mission to the Scottish Industrial Mission at Kalimpong for training in lace-making.[64] Another Industrial School was set up at Benagaria. The different schools of the Mission received aid from the Government. In 1916, a Divinity School was started at Benagaria to impart theological instruction. The first head of this institution was Rev. R. W. Steinthal. Schools were opened in Assam and Bengal also. Due to the language difficulty the Mission had to open separate boarding schools for boys and girls, for Santals, for Boros and for Bengalis.[65]

In course of time, the Boys Middle School at Kaera-bani was raised to a High School, and the Girls' school at Maharo, to a Middle School. According to the *Annual Report* of 1941, the Mission had 40 village schools, 11 station schools, 5 Middle, Training and High Schools with 120 teachers and 2304 pupils in the District of Santal Parganas; 32 village schools, 4 station schools and 3 Middle, Training and High Schools with 60 teachers and 1195 pupils in Assam; 26 village schools, 3 station schools and 2 Middle and Training schools with 61 teachers and 1202 pupils in Bengal. In 1947,[66] the Mission had altogether 117 schools, 212 teachers and 3938 pupils. The Benagaria Industrial School continued. There were 15 students in the weaving section, 13 students in the carpentry section and 4 staff during 1947.

9.2 Medical Service

The early missionaries had no specific medical knowledge. No serious attempt was made in the beginning to have a medical staff. The first dispensary of the Mission was opened at Benagaria in 1874 (famine year), and a Santal who had been previously trained by a European doctor was put in charge.[67] In 1902, a Danish doctor, Mr. Johansen, arrived at Banagaria but he returned to Denmark after a few months.

As years passed, there was a strong feeling for having medical missionaries.[68] The European staff was increasing and it was desirable to have qualified doctors on the spot in cases of need. Besides, among the Santals there was a strong belief in superstitions, evil spirits and witches. They had their own medicines, some very valuable, but they relied more on sorcery and sacrifice. There was a need for qualified doctors to work among such people. An appeal was, therefore, sent in 1912 to the Home Boards for the same.

In response to the appeal, the Home Board in Denmark sent out Dr. B. B. Bogh and Dr. (Miss) Christine Larson in the autumn of 1915.[69] Dr. Bogh was stationed at Benagaria, and Dr. Larson, at Dumka. Money was collected and sent particularly from Denmark for building a hospital and for purchasing surgical instruments and other essentials for a doctor's craft and the comfort of the patients. In 1916, Dr. Bogh started the Benagaria Christian Hospital by rebuilding the emptied Girls' School.[70] Between the 1st January and the 30th September 1916, 31 in-patients, and 2379 out-patients were treated and 160 operations were performed in this hospital.[71] A younger brother of Dr. Bogh came in 1919. He had been sent out for Assam. While staying with his brother at Benagaria, he saw some lepers who came to the missionaries for alms. He remained in the Santal Parganas and started a leper colony at Saldoha.[72] The Government contributed liberally both towards the buildings and the running expenditure. The Colony developed and there was an accommodation for 350 inmates. The Mission started another Leper

Colony in 1939 at Santipara in Assam. A dispensary was opened at Benagaria. In 1946, Dr. K. Hagen, an American, joined the Benagaria Christian Hospital. In 1947, 16,010 out-patients and 872 in-patients were treated and 155 operations were performed there.[73] At Saldoha, more than 600 lepers were treated as in-door and out-door patients,[74] during the year. There were weaving and carpentry workshops for giving useful training to the patients.

9.3 Language and Literary Contributions

The most significant contribution of the Mission was in the field of Santali language and literature. The Santals will ever remain grateful particularly to Messrs. Skrefsrud and Bodding for their memorable works towards the development of their language and literature. The works of these two missionaries have lifted the whole Santal tribe out of the unknown dark in such a way that something of inspiration and admiration is noticeable in the new generation of Santals.[75] Due to their efforts, the Santali language has become a medium of instruction in Primary Schools and also a subject up to the Matriculation Standard in Santal Parganas and some of its neighbouring areas. Several books and booklets have been written and published in Santali, in Roman script.

The Santals had no written literature up to the time of the arrival of the missionaries among them. Very few of the Santals had learnt to read and write, but then not Santali, but Bengali. The Santali language was very imperfectly known by outsiders. The Mission's first missionaries made use of Bengali, but this was only so long as they had not acquired sufficient mastery of the Santali language. The "Indian Home Mission to the Santals" had a definite purpose; it sought to bring the Gospel to the downtrodden tribe. To reach the people, it was necessary to use their language. Mr. Skrefsrud possessed exceptional linguistic gifts. He at once began to learn Santali, and in 1873, he wrote a *Santali grammar.*[76] His famous book, *The Traditions and Institutions of the Santals* was published in Santali in 1887.[77] He began to write it in 1870. He took down in Santali the words of a Santal sage or guru embodying the traditions and institutions of the Santals. He requested the sage to instruct a Santal chief and himself in all the inner lore of the tribe. This book is the most authoritative book on the traditions, customs and institutions of the Santals. It was reprinted in 1916 with a few additions. The book was translated into English by Rev. P. O. Bodding and was published during the Second World War by the Ethnographical Museum at Oslo in Norway.[78] The English version was constantly asked for by Government officers as well as pleaders who had to deal with the Santals not knowing their language sufficiently to reach the original. Mr. Skretsrud had also begun to compile a *Santali Dictionary* primarily to find out the words suitable for translating the Bible in the language of the people. He passed on the work in 1890 to Rev. Bodding. Mr. Skretsrud also translated into Santali several school books, Bible stories, hymns and songs, mostly from Bengali.[79] He edited the Mission's *Hymn Book.* He spent much time in translating parts of the Bible into Santali. During 1890-93, he translated and saw printed the first three Gospels, and also translated in the rough, the fourth Gospel.

Rev. P. O. Bodding continued and developed the work begun by Mr. Skrefsrud. He wrote *A Santali Grammar for Beginners* and the *Materials for a Santali Grammar.*[80] He completed the compilation of the *Santali Dictionary.* It was published in five volumes (with 3406 pages) in 1932, 1934, 1935, and 1936. The funds for the publication were provided by the Norwegian Academy of Science and it was printed at Oslo.[81] Rev. Bodding became more famous for his collections of Santal implements, coins and folklore. He furnished the Ethnological Museum at Oslo with probably the richest collections of Santal implements that can be found anywhere. When he left India in 1934, he had with him more than 3000 stone-age stones. His collection of coins is also found at Oslo.[82] The Asiatic Society of Bengal has published his *Studies in Santal Medicine and connected Folklore* and *How the Santals live.* His main collection of folklore, however, has been pub1ished in several volumes by the Institute for Comparative Cultural Research at Oslo.[83] Rev. Bodding completed the translation of the Bible into Santali in 1903. It was published in 1914.[84] Many other missionaries of the Mission had also enriched the Santali language and literature. Rev. J. Gausdal has written the history of the Mission in Santali. Being encouraged by the missionaries, some Santal Christians like N. Jacobo Soren, connected with the Mission have written poems, hymns and books in the Santali language. The

Mission had a weekly paper called the *Pera Hor* (The Guest) in Santali. More than 1700 copies were issued per week from the Mission Press at Benagaria.[85]

The Mission also contributed to the Boro or Mech language and literature. Mr. Skrefsrud studied the Boro language and wrote a short grammar, a small vocabulary and reading books on it.[86] He wrote some religious books also. His work was continued by Pastor Dabarn who wrote a *Primer, Church Service Book* and *Hymn Book*.[87] Rev. A. Kristiansen translated the New Testament into Boro in 1938.[88] A new periodical in Boro language, *Phunni Hathorkhi* (The Morning Star) was published from 1947.

The Mission had its own printing Press at Benagaria.[89] The Earliest press was set up in 1879 with the help of some Scottish friends. A new and Larger press was installed in 1886. The Mission set up a fairly Larger press in 1890. It has so far printed and published thousands of books and booklets in the Santali and other languages.

9.4 Social and Economic Service

The Mission has done a good deal for the social and economic welfare and uplift of the people particularly of the Santals among whom it has been working since 1867. The Mission lifted the whole Santal tribe out of the unknown dark: it has, in fact, 'discovered' the Santals and gave them place and honour in the wider society. The District of Santal Parganas was full of licensed liquor shops when the pioneer missionaries arrived. Mr. Skrafsrud started an agitation to get these shops abolished and managed to secure a great number of Santals to sign a petition for their abolition.[90] It was perhaps not so easy, but Mr. Skrefsrud got the Santal women to cooperate, and their influence over their husbands carried the day and most of the liquor shops were abolished.

The Santals of the District of Santal Parganas were very much oppressed by money lenders and landlords. Mr. Skrafsrud mixed freely with the Santals, learnt their language and institutions and soon understood their problems. He collected materials to prove the illegalities of the landlords. In 1871,[91] he and Mr. Boarresen went to Calcutta and put the matter before the then Lieutenant Governor, Sir George Campbell. It resulted in an investigation being held, which showed that the complaints were amply justified. The Government passed laws for the protection of the lands and rights of the poor and illiterate Santals. In times of famine (like that of 1874), the Mission managed relief works and saved many from starvation-deaths. The Mission founded a colony in Assam for the settlement of Santal emigrants. Industrial Schools were set up, with the co-operation of the Government, at Kaerabani, Maharo and Benagaria to provide more avenues of employment.

The Mission maintained an orphanage at Koroya in the District of Santal Parganas.[92] In 1947 it had 19 children. One of the girls, Punta Baske, passed her Middle Vernacular Examination at the end of the year.

10. Conclusion

As has been noted above, the Santal Mission of the Northern Churches was begun by individual missionaries who had terrific vision, will-power and commitment because of which the Mission survived many odds and travails. The Mission was remotely supported by many well-wishers and benefactors. The Mission made a deep impact on the lives of the Santals, especially the leprosy patients. Also, it made signal contribution to developing Santali language and literature, besides somewhat enriching the language of the Boros. The literary masterpieces of Skrefsrud and Bodding stand as lasting contribution to the Santals.

Endnotes and References

1 J. M. Macphail, *Andrew Campbell, Missionary to the Santals*, p. 12.

2 *Fiftieth Annual Report of the Santal Mission of the Nothern Churches* (SMNC), *1916-1917*, (1917), p. 2; C. H. Swavely (1952), *The Lutheran Enterprise in India,* p. 106; L. S. S. O'Malley (1910), *Bihar District Gazetteers: Santal Parganas,* p. 85; J. Gausdal (1953), *Ebeneser Evangelikal Lutheran Church (in Santali),* p. 16; M. A. Sherring (1884), *The History of Protestant Missions in India.* p. 155; Campbell, D. D., p. 12; E. Wueste (1967), *Chotanagpur ki Masihi Mandli ka Itihas* (A History of the Christian community of Chotanagpur), (1845-1890), 4th edition, p. 43.

3 *Fiftieth Annual Report*, SMNC, (1917), p. 2; *Seventy-fifth Annual Report* SMNC (portion of the *Twenty-fifth Annual Report* reproduced), p. 4.

4 *Fiftieth Annual Report*, SMNC, (1917), p. 2; Gausdal (1953), p. 16; Swavely (1952), p. 106; *Seventy-fifth Annual Report*, SMNC, (1941), p. 5 (reproduced from *Twenty-fifth Annual Report,* 1892); Wueste (1967), p. 43.

5 *Seventy-fifth Annual Report*, SMNC, (1941): *Twenty-fifth Annual Report* reproduced), p. 5.

6 *Fifteenth Annual Report*, SMNC, (1917), p. 4.

7 *Seventy-fifth Annual Report,* SMNC (1941) (portion of *Twenty-fifth Annual Report* reproduced), p. 5; Wavely (1952), p. 106.

8 Wavely (1952), p. 106.

9 Gausdal (1953), p. 15; Swavely (1952), p. 107; *Fiftieth Annual Report*, SMNC, (1917), p. 3; Sherring (1884), p. 157; O' Malley (1910), p. 85.

10 *Fiftieth Annual Report*, SMNC, (1917), p. 4; Gausdal, (1953), p. 16; *Seventy-fifth Annual Report,* SMNC, (1941) (reproduced from *Twenty-fifth Annual Report*), p. 6.

11 Gausdal (1953), p. 17; *Seventy-fifth Annual Report*, SMNC, (1941) (portion of *Twenty-fifth Annual Report* reproduced), p. 6.

12 Swavely (1952), p. 115; Gausdal (1953), p. 17; *Fiftieth Annual Report*, SMNC, (1917), p. 4.

13 Gausdal (1953), p. 17; Swavely (1952), p. 115; *Fiftieth Annual Report*, SMNC, (1917), p. 10.

14 *Seventy-fifty Annual Report,* SMNC, (1941) (portion reproduced from *Twenty-fifth Annual Report*), p. 7; Gausdal (1953), p. 17.

15 Gausdal (1953), pp. 17-18; Swavely (1952), p. 108.

16 *Fiftieth Annual Report*, SMNC, (1917), p. 11; Swavely (1952), p. 111; Gausdal (1953), p. 18; *Seventy-fifth Annual Report,* SMNC, (1941) (portion of *Twenty-fifth Annual Report* reproduced), p. 7.

17 Gausdal (1953), p. 18.

18 Ibid., p. 21.

19 *Fiftieth Annual Report*, SMNC, (1917), p. 17.

20 Ibid., p. 17; Gausdal (1953), p. 21; Swavely (1952), p. 111.

21 Swavely (1952), p. 111; Gausdal (1953), p. 22.

22 Gausdal (1953), p. 87; *Seventy-fifth Annual Report*, SMNC, (1941), p. 8.

23 Swavely (1952), p. 108; *Seventy-fifth Annual Report*, SMNC, (1941), p. 8.

24 Swavely (1952), p. 108; Gausdal (1953), p. 19.
25 Gausdal (1953), p. 22; Swavely (1952), p. 108.
26 *Fiftieth Annual Report*, SMNC, (1917), p. 6; *Seventy-fifth Annual Report*, SMNC, (1941), p. 8.
27 Swavely, (1952), p. 108; *Fiftieth Annual Report*, SMNC, (1917), p. 6; Gausdal, (1953), p. 23.
28 Swavely, (1952), p. 109; *Seventy-fifth Annual Report*, SMNC, (1941), p. 8.
29 *Fiftieth Annual Report*, SMNC, (1917), p. 7.
30 Swavely (1952), p. 109; Gausdal (1953), p. 23.
31 *Fiftieth Annual Report*, SMNC, (1917), pp. 67-89.
32 Gausdal, (1953) pp. 25-26; *Fiftieth Annual Report*, SMNC, (1917), pp. 23-24; Swavely (1952), p. 112.
33 Gausdal (1953), p. 25; Swavely (1952), p. 112.
34 *Fiftieth Annual Report*, SMNC, (1917), p. 24; Gausdal (1953), p. 26.
35 Gausdal (1953), p. 26; *Seventy-fifth Annual Report,* SMNC, (1941), p. 8.
36 Swavely (1952), p. 113.
37 *Seventy-fifth Annual Report*, SMNC, (1941), p. 95.
38 *Fiftieth Annual Report*, SMNC, (1917), p. 49; Gausdal (1953), p. 36; Swavely (1952), p. 110.
39 *Fiftieth Annual Report*, SMNC, (1917), p. 47.
40 Gausdal (1953), p. 37; *Fiftieth Annual Report*, SMNC, (1917), p. 29; O' Malley (1910), p. 85.
41 Gausdal (1953), p. 38; *Fiftieth Annual Report*, SMNC, (1917), p. 50.
42 Swavely (1952), p. 110; Gausdal (1953), p. 29; *Seventy-fifth Annual Report*, SMNC, (1941), p. 9.
43 *Seventy-fifth Annual Report*, SMNC, (1941), p. 9; Swavely (1952) p. 110; Gausdal (1953), pp. 40-41.
44 *Fiftieth Annual Report*, SMNC, (1917), p. 93.
45 Gausdal (1953), p. 40; *Seventy-fifth Annual Report*, SMNC, (1941), p. 9.
46 *Fiftieth Annual Report*, SMNC, (1917), pp. 62-65.
47 Ibid., p. 118.
48 Ibid.
49 Swavely (1952), p. 122.
50 Ibid.
51 Ibid., p. 110.
52 *Annual Returns*, SMNC, (1941).
53 *81st Annual Report*, SMNC, (1947), p. 36.

54 Swavely (1952), p. 115; Gausdal (1953), p. 17.
55 Swavely (1952), p. 116.
56 *Fiftieth Annual Report*, SMNC, (1917), p. 36; Swavely (1952), p. 116; Gausdal (1953), p. 20.
57 *Fiftieth Annual Report,* S.M.N.C., (1917), pp. 34-35.
58 Ibid., p. 36.
59 Swavely (1952), p. 116; *Fiftieth Annual Report*, SMNC, (1917), p. 55.
60 Swavely (1952), p. 116; *Fiftieth Annual Report*, SMNC, (1917), p. 35.
61 *Fiftieth Annual Report*, SMNC, (1917), p. 37; Swavely (1952), p. 116.
62 *Fiftieth Annual Report*, SMNC, (1917), p. 37.
63 Swavely, (1952), p. 110; *Fiftieth Annual Report*, SMNC, (1917), p. 38.
64 *Fiftieth Annual Report*, SMNC, (1917), p. 38.
65 Swavely (1952), p. 117.
66 *81st Annual Report*, SMNC, (1947).
67 *Fiftieth Annual Report*, SMNC, (1917), p. 41.
68 Ibid., p. 42.
69 Ibid., p. 43.
70 Swavely (1952), p. 119.2
71 *Fiftieth Annual Report*, SMNC, (1917), p. 112.
72 Swavely (1952), pp. 119-120.
73 *81st Annual Report*, SMNC, (1947), p. 28.
74 Ibid., p. 22.
75 Swavely (1952), p. 121.
76 Ibid., p. 117.
77 *Fiftieth Annual Report*, SMNC, (1917), p. 33; Swavely (1952), p. 120.
78 Swavely (1952), p. 120.
79 *Fiftieth Annual Report*, SMNC, (1917), pp. 115-116.
80 Swavely (1952), p. 121.
81 Ibid., p. 121; Roy Choudhury (1965), *Gazetteer of India, Bihar: Santal Parganas* p. 165.
82 Swavely (1952), p. 121.
83 Ibid.
84 *Fiftieth Annual Report*, SMNC, (1917), p. 116.
85 Swavely (1952), p. 121.
86 *Fiftieth Annual Report*, SMNC, (1917), pp. 116-117.

87 Ibid., p. 117.
88 Swavely (1952), p. 121.
89 *Fiftieth Annual Report*, SMNC, (1917), pp. 40-41.
90 Ibid., pp. 13-14.
91 Ibid., p. 13.
92 Swavely (1952), p. 126; *81st Annual Report*, SMNC, (1947), p. 19.

Chapter 8

The Santal Mission of the United Free Church of Scotland in Bihar and Jharkhand

1. The Beginnings at Pachamba (Hazaribagh District)

The Santal Mission of the United Free Church of Scotland has been one of the oldest Christian Missions in Jharkhand, working among the Santals, not in their stronghold in the Santal Parganas, where the Church Missionary Society (CMS), the Santal Mission of the Northern Churches and other Christian Missions occupy the field, but in their scattered villages lying to its south and west in the Districts of Hazaribagh, Manbhum in Jharkhand and Monghyr, in Bihar.[1]

The desirability of founding a Mission to the Santals in connection with the Free Church of Scotland seems to have been first suggested by the famous Scottish missionary, Dr. Alexander Duff, and Dr. Murray Mitchell, acting Principal of the Duff Institution in Calcutta, and was associated with the former in carrying the idea into execution.[2] Dr. Alexander Duff, spent most of the cold season of 1861-62 on tour among the Kols in Chotanagpur, accompanying Commissioner Colonel Dalton. Part of the cold season of 1862-63 was spent among the Santals in the hilly region between Chotanagpur and Rajmahal on the Ganges, making enquiries with a view to establishing a Mission among them.[3] The Free Church had several generous friends in Calcutta who were prepared to support a Mission to the Santals in Jharkhand.[4] Later, with the object of finding a suitable site for a Mission station, Dr. Mitchell also made a tour of the area in the cold season of 1868-69.[5]

The Santal Mission was begun in 1869 as "a new off-shoot from the Bengal Mission". Its first *Annual Report* of 1870, says that towards the end of 1869, the Free Church Mission of Scotland in Calcutta sent Mr. Vernieux, an Anglo-Indian gentleman, who had formerly been an agent of the Bible Society in Calcutta and who had made a tour of enquiry among the Santal villages lying in the neighbourhood of the East Indian Railway beyond Raniganj, and as a result of his report, Pachamba, about three miles from Giridih in the District of Hazaribagh, was finally fixed upon as the headquarters of the Santal work.[6]

Mr. Vernieux commenced work at Pachamba about the end of 1869.[7] Assisted by a Bengali and a Santal Christian, he opened a school there and carried on the work till the arrival of the first European missionary, Rev. (Dr.) Archibald Templeton, M. D. at Pachamba on the 15th December, 1871.[8] He assumed charge of the new Mission, and Mr. Vernieux's connection with it ceased a few months afterwards.[9] In 1872, Dr. Templeton was joined by Mr. Andrew Campbell,[10] a stone-mason by trade, not as a member of the Mission staff, but as a manager at an agricultural bank which was financed by Dr. Templeton's brother in Glasgow, with the object of bringing relief to the poor Santals by delivering them from the clutches of money-lenders. From the first, however, Mr. Campbell took a keen and practical interest in all the works at the Mission. He immediately built the first Free Church Mission Hospital at Pachamba with eight beds,[11] and, thus began medical work too. The number of students in schools increased. The Mission obtained its first converts when five young men, including Joseph Sido, from the

Boarding School at Pachamba were baptized by Rev. Templeton in 1874.[12]

Next year (1875), Dr. James A. Dyer joined the Mission staff as a medical missionary, and Mr. J. Ewen, as an evangelist.[13] At the end of the year, the Mission had 20 baptized Christians.[14] In 1876, Mr. Ewen joined the Baptist Mission and Rev. (Dr.) Templeton retired and returned to Scotland due to illness. Mr. W. H. Stevenson,[15] a certificated teacher, arrived in 1877 to take charge of the educational activities of the Mission. The number of converts at the end of the year rose to 48.[16] In 1878, Mr. Campbell was appointed a member of the Mission as a lay evangelist and the Santal Mission at Pachamba was made practically independent of the Bengal Mission, and, for the first time, it issued a report of its own.[17]

2. Mission Expansion

For some time, a scheme of extension had been under consideration.[18] The Foreign Mission Committee in Scotland at its meeting in 1878 sanctioned the opening of two new stations, one in Chakai area in Monghyr and the other in Govindpur area in Manbhum.[19] In the beginning of 1879, there were three European missionaries at Pachamba: Mr. Campbell, Dr. Dyer and Mr. Stevenson. In March 1879, Dr. Dyer secured a lease of seven acres of land for a station at Bamdah, a small Santal village in the District of Monghyr, thirty miles to the north of Pachamba.[20] While Dr. Dyer tried in the north Mr. Campbell, packing his things on bullock carts and accompanied by a few Santal Christians, left Pachamba and moved towards south-east and founded, in the same year in April, a new station at Pokhuria in Tundi thana in the Govindpur subdivision of the District of Manbhum,[21] about thirty miles southeast of Pachamba. He obtained a lease of the whole village without difficulty, for it was said to be haunted.[22] Thus by 1880, the Santal Mission carried on work in three Districts Hazaribagh, Monghyr and Manbhum.[23] Work was done in three languages, Santali, Hindi and Bengali. There was a proposal to set up a fourth station in the Gawan area of the District of Hazaribagh. Outstations ware opened at Patror and Palgunj which were connected to Pachamba.

Till 1880, there was no ordained minister in the Mission. In 1881, Mr. Campbell was ordained in Calcutta.[24] An outstation was opened at Jamdiha, four miles from Pokhuria, where land was purchased and four Christian families were settled. In 1883, the station at Bamdah obtained its first convert when one Matla Chandrae Hembrom,[25] eldest son of the village chief, was baptized with his wife and child. In 1885, a Christian village was planted at Baritand, connected to Pachamba.[26] Dr. Dyer was ordained in 1886, and Mr. Stevenson, in 1887. Miss Sprot, the first lady missionary of the Mission, joined in 1887.[27] Next year (1888), Rev. Stevenson died of cholera[28] while trying to save others, who had fallen victims of cholera, and Rev. (Dr.) Dyer took charge of the work at Pachamba. During the year, the devoted zeal of a Santal girl,[29] who had been baptized in the school at Pokhuria, induced about 200 Santals of her village Kolhor or Chetan Toondee to take baptizm at the hands of Rev. Campbell at a time. The first church of the Mission was built by Rev. Campbell at Pokhuria and was opened in 1888.[30] In 1889, Dr. J. M. Macphail came and was stationed at Bamdah as the first resident missionary.[31] In 1890, the total number of baptized members of the Mission since its commencement was 674.[32]

The Santal Mission completed its twenty-fifth year in 1894. During the year, 36 persons were baptized, making a total of 850 since the beginning of the Mission.[33] There was a severe famine in 1896-97. All the three stations in Bihar dispensed relief on a large scale.[34] Help came from Scotland, England, America and other parts of India. Food kitchens were opened for the infirm, the aged and children. Work was provided for able-bodied men and women. Several roads and tanks were constructed. For his services during the famine, Rev. Campbell received thanks and *Kaiser-i-Hind* medal from the Government. In 1900, the number of Christians in the Mission rose to 1308, and the new Church at Bamdah was consecrated.[35] In 1903, the University of St. Andrews in Scotland conferred on Rev. Campbell the degree of Doctor of Divinity in recognition of his services.[36]

In 1904, the Home Committee sent out Dr. James Kitchin to strengthen the missionary staff. He founded the fourth station in 1908 at Tisri[37] in the Gawan thana of the District of Hazaribagh, some forty miles north-west of Pachamba. The idea of establishing a fourth station expressed in 1880 was at last fulfilled. In 1910, the number of converts was 1607.

3. Steady Growth

The *Mission Report*[38] of 1915 says that there were then four principal stations in the Santal country: Pachamba, Bamdah, Pokhuria and Tisri, each under a European missionary. There were seven out-stations under Santal workers. The Christian community numbered 1898. In 1916, Joseph Sido, the first convert of the Mission, and one of the best Santal preachers (evangelists), died at Pokhuria. On July 8, 1919, Rev. A. Campbell[39] also died there after a long and faithful service of 47 years. During the period, he had only two brief furloughs in Scotland. He rendered a distinguished service, not only to the Mission at Pokhuria and the people around, but also to various bodies like the Manbham District Board, the Bihar Missionary Council, the Calcutta British and Foreign Bible Society, the Patna University and the Bihar and Orissa Legislative Council. He was an Honorary Magistrate for many years. On of his most valuable works is the *Santali Dictionary* of 706 pages and more than 20,000 words. He was succeeded by Rev. William Hamilton, M. A., who arrived at Pokhuria in 1920. The Christian community now numbered 1737.

In 1921, another pioneer missionary, Rev. (Dr.) James A. Dyer,[40] retired after forty-six years of devoted and faithful service, and was succeeded at Pachamba by Dr. William Dempster who arrived in October of the same year. The work of the Mission actually began about the end of 1869 but the first missionary, Rev. (Dr.) Archibald Templeton, arrived at Pachamba on December 15, 1871, and, therefore, it was considered appropriate that the fiftieth anniversary of that date should be regarded as the Jubilee of the Mission. On December 15, 1921, the Mission celebrated the Golden Jubilee[41] at Pachamba amidst huge Santal gatherings. In 1923, two pioneer missionaries of the Mission, Rev. Templeton and Rev. (Dr.) Dyer died in their retirement.[42] In November of the same year, a young missionary, Dr. Arthur F. Smith came and was sent to Bamdah to assist Dr. J. M. Macphail.[43] In 1924, the first convert of the Mission at

Bamdah, Matla Chandrae Hembrom, was appointed an unordained pastor.[44]

In 1925, Dr. Ronald M. Macphail, son of Dr. J. M. Macphail, returned to his birth-place after an interval of twenty years.[45] Both the missionaries, father and son, worked at Bamdah. The Mission established friendly relations with the Santal Mission of Northern Churches, the American Baptist Mission and the American Methodist Mission which were also working among the Santals in Bihar and cooperated with them in preparing and publishing religious books in Santali and in advancing Santali language and literature.[46]

On June 15, 1939, the last of the three pioneer missionaries of the Mission, Dr. James M. Macphail, died[47] after forty years of faithful and fruitful service, and was buried at Bamdah where he worked through out his stay there. In the same year, the Mission was given a new name. Uptil now, it was known as the "Santal Mission of the United Free Church of Scotland". Now, it was called the "**Santal Mission of the Church of Scotland**".[48] In 1930, Dr. D. W. Tayler arrived. The number of converts in the four stations of Bihar was 1862. In 1933, Dr. William Dempster returned to Scotland, and his work in the Pachamba Hospital was carried on by one Dr. Alexander Paul. Early in 1934, the *Kaiser-i-Hind* medal was awarded to Dr. James Kitchin of Tisri in recognition of his services to the suffering humanity. The Mission became a member[49] of the Santal Christian Council that was formed in 1935 by nine Christian Missions working among the Santals in Bihar and Orissa. In November, Rev. Donald Davidson arrived and took charge of the Mission work at Pachamba. Uptil now, the missionary there had been a medical man. Since then, the missionary-superintendent used to be an ordained minister with high educational qualifications. In 1939, Rev. Robert Waddell arrived. In 1947, the Mission had four European missionaries, each in charge of a station, four Indian priests, seven evangelists, twenty-eight elders, 2571 converts and eleven out- stations.[50]

4. Medical Service

Besides preaching, the Santal Mission of the Church of Scotland actively engaged itself in medical, educational, literary and various other philanthropic activities. In medical sphere, its achievements have been most marvellous. Of the four pioneer missionaries, three were medical men, and uptil 1934, the missionary-superintendent of the Mission was a doctor. Of the four stations, Pokhuria alone had no hospital. The hospital at Bamdah was famous in northern India for eye surgery. The first hospital was opened at Pachamba in 1871[51] by Rev. (Dr.) Archipald Templeton, M. D., soon after his arrival. The hospital had eight beds[52] and was built by Mr. A. Campbell who was originally a stone-mason by trade. In 1875, Dr. Dyer came and joined the new hospital. He was often on tour and treated patients in camps also. In 1879, Mr. Campbell founded a station at Pokhuria and soon set up a dispensary there. Medical work there was carried on by an Indian Christian doctor who had been previously under Dr. Dyer at Pachamba.[53] When he left the station in 1884, Mr. Campbell had to attend to the sick himself, not only in the Mission, but in the District for several miles around Bamdah which had a centre of medical work when Dr. J. M. Macphail was posted there in 1889 as the first resident missionary.[54] Both Dr. Dyer and Dr. Macphail were skilful in eye surgery. Dr. Macphail had to pay Rs. 5 to a patient to convince him before he was allowed to do his first cataract operation.[55] In 1891, 9830 cases were treated at Pachamba and 2433 cases at Bamdah.[56] A hospital was built at Bamdah and was officially opened in 1894.[57] By 1894, when the Mission completed twenty-five years, at least 1,00,000 patients were attended to and several hundreds received back their eye sight.[58]

In 1895, all the three stations carried on medical work regularly. Over 12,000 patients[59] were treated in 1900 at the different dispensaries and hospitals connected with the Mission. In 1908, Dr. Kitchin set up a new station at Tisri[60] where mica owners had opened a dispensary and a small hospital. They had been closed due to depression in mica trade. Dr. Kitchin reached there and carried on the dispensary and hospital. During 1908, 11,967 patients were treated in the hospitals and dispensaries of the Mission. In 1915, about 25,000 new patients were treated.[61] The Monghyr District Board decided to give a monthly grant of Rs.50 to the Bamdah Hospital. A new hospital and a new dispensary were opened at Tisri in 1916. The Government of Bihar contributed Rs. 1, 000 towards the cost of the buildings.[62] In 1921, nearly 20,000 patients were treated in the dispensaries and hospitals of the Mission.

In 1925, there were 4,227 eye operations and 978 general operations in the three hospitals.[63] At Bamdah, Dr. J. M. Macphail and Mrs. (Dr.) Macphail were joined by their son, Dr. Ronald M. Macphail.[64] During the rains, Sir Ganesh Dutt Singh,[65] the Minister for Local Self-Government of Bihar, visited the Hospital at Pachamba, highly appreciated its work and granted Rs. 1,000 towards the building of a new dispensary and dressing rooms in memory of Dr. Dyer. He also granted Rs.500 for providing comfort to the patients. He wrote in the inspection report that it was the type of hospital required to give medical relief to the masses of India and being run on the lines of the ancient Hindu Village Hospital, it suited to the mode of life of the village people. In 1934, the number of patients, treated at Pachamba, Bamdah and Tisri was 24,107. More than 4,000 eye operations were performed. At Bamdah alone, 3,854 eye operations took place. The statistics of 1947 say that there were three hospitals, one dispensary, three European doctors, one Indian doctor, eighteen medical assistants, 19,512 hospital patients and 7,886 operations.[66]

5. Educational Service

Education too received much attention and encouragement from the Mission. Almost from the very beginning, it specialised in education, particularly of girls. In fact, the Mission was a pioneer in the subject in the area in which it has been working.

Soon after his arrival, the first missionary of the Mission, Mr. Vernleux, opened a school at Pachamba about the end of 1869.[67] He was assisted by one Bengali and one Santali Christian. Education, however, was quite a new thing amongst the Santals, and very few indeed cared to take advantage of it. According to the *Mission Report* for 1872,[68] the schools were three in number: a Boarding School for boys at Pachamba and two village schools. The number of pupils was 35.

In 1873, a Boarding School for girls was opened with six students on the rolls at Pachamba.[69] Funds for the school were provided by Women's Foreign Mission in Scotland. According to the

Annual Report for 1873, the Mission had a Boarding School for boys at Pachamba with 32 students, a Boarding School for girls with six students and five village schools, with 50 students and eight male and one female teachers.[70] In1875, the Boys' Boarding School had 44 pupils, the Girls' Boarding School, 23 pupils and the Village Schools, 79 pupils.[71] In the *Annual Report* for 1876,[72] the Boys' Boarding School at Pachamba had been called as Boys' Training School and it was for the purpose of training teachers for the village schools. All the boys there read Hindi and Santali, while to a few of the more advanced scholars, instruction was given also in English. That year, the Mission had two Boarding Schools at Pachamba and nine schools in villages. The Sub-Inspector of School examined the Boys' School, and expressed much satisfaction with the progress made. Next year (1877), Mr. W. H. Stevenson, a certificated teacher, arrived and took charge of the educational operation of the Mission.[73]

In 1879, the Mission had one Boys' Boarding School and one Girls' Boarding School at Pachamba and only five village schools. There were altogether 87 boys and 29 girls.[74] Mr. Campbell opened a school at Pokhuria. The disturbances among the Santals in 1880-81, forced the Government[75] to pay more attention towards them and to make efforts to enlighten them by means of education. A grant at Rs. 600 was made for the Schools in Tundi Thana and all the schools were placed under the Mission at Pokhuria. When the grant from Scotland was reduced in 1882, the Mission school at Pokhuria was closed down.[76] In the following year, the Government handed over to the care of the Mission at Pachamba[77] all the village schools for Santals in the District of Hazaribagh. The Government paid the salary of the teachers and the Mission supplied Christian Santals as Circle Inspectors. In 1884, the School at Pokhuria was reopened and a school was opened at Bamdah. A separate school for Christian girls with 13 names on the roll was opened in 1885 at Pokhuria.[78] In 1887, Miss E. Sprat came and took charge of the Girls' School at Pachamba.[79] Next year, Mr. Stevenson died of cholera while trying to save others attacked by cholera, and the Mission lost an able educationist.[80]

From the outset, the Mission aimed at training its own teachers.[81] There was a Training School for boys at Pachamba in connection with the Boys' Boarding School. Mr. Campbell was very much interested in .introducing new industries or improving those already in existence among the Santals and he started an Industrial School at Pokhuria soon after the foundation of the Mission.[82] Students were taught carpentry, masonry, iron-work, gardening, printing and silk-worm rearing. In 1889, there ware two Training Schools for boys, one at Pachamba and the other at Pokhuria, with 130 students, one Industrial School at Pokhuria with 18 pupils, 47 schools for boys and 7 schools for girls with 871 boys and 143 girls.[83]

When the Mission completed its twenty-fifth year (1894), there were 33 schools for boys, 7 for girls and 11 for both.[84] By that year, as the *Annual Report*[85] says, the Mission, as an educational agency, brought to its schools over 1,200 Santal children. In 1900, the Mission had 59 schools for boys, 6 for girls, and 8 for both with 1167 boy students and 276 girl students.[86]

In 1905, the number of schools rose to 91. During 1913-14, the Manbhum District Board sanctioned the opening of 40 new schools for aboriginals and Mr. Campbell was authorised to open and conduct those schools.[87] In 1915, there were 150 (according to *Hazaribagh Gazetteer* (1917), 152 schools with 2765 students.[88] The number of girl students was 414. In 1927, the Boys' School at Pokhuria was raised to the Middle Vernacular Standard. Next year, the Girls' School at Pachamba too was raised to that standard. Nevertheless, the Mission had to close down many village schools in the District of Hazaribagh when the District Board of Hazaribagh reduced the grant it was giving to those schools. On account of financial stringency, many schools had to be closed down and most of the Girls' Primary Schools were united with Boys' Primary Schools. In 1932, there were only 65 schools and 1323 pupils. Since then, there was rise and fall of schools and students. In 1937, there were 48 schools for boys, 3 for girls and 36 for both. There were 1531 boys and 205 girls.[89] In 1947, the Mission had 50 schools and 1469 pupils.[90]

6. Contribution to Santali Language and Literature

The Mission has contributed greatly towards the development of Santali language and literature. First, Mission work was conducted mostly in Santali, which facilitated the mastery of the language by the missionaries. The early missionaries did pioneering work in Santali literature too. Rev. Campbell was a great Santali scholar.[91] He was a prolific hymn-writer, and also produced a series of Santali School Books. He translated many English works like *The Story of Joseph* and *Peep of Day* into Santali. He wrote and published in English a book on *Santal Folklore*. A monthly paper in Santali, *The Dharwak* (the name given to the branch of a tree that is circulated among the Santal villages as a signal that the people are being summoned to a big hunt) was printed and published by him for some years. The Bible was translated into Santali, and the printing was done at the Pokhuria Press under Rev. Campbell's immediate supervision. His most substantial literary monument, however, has been the *Santali Dictionary*, an invaluable work of 706 pages and over 20,000 words, compiled in 1902. Rev. W. E. White and other colleagues cooperated with him in compiling the same. Rev. Campbell set up a printing press[92] in 1890 at Pokhuria where printing was done in English, Hindi, Bengali and Santali. Dr. R. M. Macphail of Bamdah wrote a *Santali Grammar*. With the efforts of the Santal Christian Council, of which the Santal Mission of Scotland has been an important and active member, the Patna University recognised Santali as one of the Matriculation subjects from 1940.[93]

7. Socio-economic and Humanitarian Service

Dr. Campbell was untiring in his efforts[94] to improve the material and economic conditions in which people lived. He taught the people trades that served as alternatives or auxiliaries to farming. At Pokhuria, he used to teach cultivation of castor oil, brick-making, brick-laying, carpentry, printing, iron-work, silk culture, book-binding, lace making and weaving of cotton cloth. He formed an Agricultural Bank at Pokhuria to help the Santals but it could not continue for long. The Mission also tried to render economic help to the people around. During the terrible famine of 1896-97,[95] all the three existing stations in Bihar dispensed relief on a large scale. At Pokhuria, about 5000 persons depended on Rev. Campbell for their daily bread. The Mission saved many lives from death and starvation.

8. Conclusion

As noted above, the Santal Mission of the Church of Scotland (SMCS) began as the Bible says, as 'a small mustard tree, but grew into a big tree giving protection to many birds'. A small band of dedicated pioneers built up SMCS in a small territory which expanded to four villages mainly. The Mission's first undertaking was school and then hospital not church or residence of missionaries. These came up gradually. The Mission's signal contribution to the Santals was eye care and eye surgery in those localities which did not have sufficient health care infrasture. The second most significant contribution was enriching Santali language and literature, creating valuable Christian literature in Santali. Some of the valuable books in Santali were written by the missionaries of this Mission.

Endnotes and References

1 *Annual Report of the Santal Mission of the Free Church of Scotland* (hereinafter, *Annual Report SMFCS*) (1894), pp. 3-4.

2 J. M. Macphail (n. d.), *Andrew Campbell, Missionary to the Santals* (hereinafter, *Campbell*), p. 12; Lister, E. (1917), *Bihar and Orissa District Gazetteer: Hazaribagh*, p. 82.

3 J. M. Macphail (n. d.), *Campbell,* p. 12; J. M. Macphail (1904), *Missions of the United Free Church of Scotland* (hereinafter, MUFCS), p. 34; R. M. Macphail (n. d.), *The Santal Mission*, Pachamba, p. 12; George Smith, *Life of Alexander Duff* (1879), Vol. II, p. 429.

4 George Smith, *Life of Alexander Duff* (1879), p. 429; J. M. Macphail, *Campbell,* p. 12; J. M. Macphail, MUFCS, p. 34; R. M. Macphail, *The Santal Mission*, p. 12.

5 J. M., Macphail, *Campbell,* pp. 12-13; J. M. Macphail, MUFCS, p. 34.

6 *Annual Report SMFCS* (1870), p. 2; *Annual Report SMFCS* (1894), pp. 2 & 7; Murray Mitchell, (1871), *A Missionary's Wife among the Wild Tribes of South Bengal*, London, p. 70; R. M. Macphail, *The Santal Mission*, p. 14; J. M. Macphail, *Campbell,* p. 13; Lister (1917), *District Gazetteer: Hazaribagh*, p. 82.

7 *Annual Report SMFCS,* 1894, pp. 3 & 7; W. W. Hunter (1877), *The Statistical Account of Bengal*, Vol. XVI, p. 85.

8 *Annual Report SMFCS,* 1878, p. 6; *Annual Report SMFCS,* 1894, p. 7; J. M. Macphail, *Campbell,* p. 13.

9 *Annual Report SMFCS,* 1878, p. 6.

10 J. M. Macphail, *Campbell,* p. 13; R. M. Macphail, *The Santal Mission,* p. 14; *Annual Report SMFCS,* 1894, p. 7.

11 J. M. Macphail, *Campbell,* p. 14; *Annual Report SMFCS,* 1894, p. 7.

12 *Annual Report SMFCS,* 1874, pp. 7 & 23; J. M. Macphail, MUFCS (1904), p. 35; J. M. Macphail, *Campbell,* p. 18.

13 J. M. Macphail, *Campbell,* p. 14; *Annual Report SMFCS,* 1878, pp. 7-8.

14 *Annual Report SMFCS,* 1878, p. 8.

15 Ibid; *Annual Report SMFCS,* 1894, p. 7; J. M. Macphail, *Campbell,* p. 14.

16 *Annual Report SMFCS,* 1878, p. 9.

17 *Annual Report SMFCS,* 1894, p. 7; *Annual Report SMFCS,* 1878, p. 1.

18 J. M. Macphail, *Campbell,* p. 14; Lister (1917), p. 83.

19 *Annual Report SMFCS,* 1879, p. 26.

20 *Annual Report* SMFCS, 1879, p. 24; *Annual Report* SMFCS, 1894, p. 8; Lister (1917), p. 83; L. S. S. O'Malley (1926), *Bihar and Orissa District Gazetteers: Monghyr* (Revised edition), Patna, p. 62.

21 J. M. Macphail, *Campbell,* pp. 14-15; *Annual Report SMFCS,*1879, pp. 26-27; *Annual Report SMFCS,* 1894, p. 8; Lister (1917), p. 83.

22 J. M. Macphail, *Campbell,* p. 18; J. M. Macphail, MUFCS, 1904, p. 58; *Annual Report SMFCS,* 1881, p. 23; R. M. Macphail, *The Santal Mission,* p. 15; *Annual Report SMFCS,* 1881, pp. 23-24.

23 *Annual Report SMFCS,* 1894, p. 8; Lister (1917, p. 83.

24 J. M. Macphail, *Campbell,* p. 19; Lister (1917), p. 83.

25 *Annual Report SMFCS,* 1883, pp. 20-21.

26 *Annual Report SMFCS,* 1894, p. 9

27 *Annual Report SMFCS,* 1887, p. 4; *Annual Report SMFCS,* 1894, p. 9.

28 *Annual Report SMFCS,* 1894, p. 10.

29 Ibid., p. 9.

30 Ibid., p. 10; J. M. Machpail, *Campbell,* p. 21.

31 *Annual Report SMFCS,*1894, p. 10; R. M. Macphail, *The Santal Mission,* R. M. p. 16; *Bamdah Christian Hospital* (1970), p. 2.

32 *Annual Report SMFCS,* 1890, pp. 4 & 35.

33 *Annual Report SMFCS,* 1894, p. 39.

34 *Annual Report SMFCS,* 1897, pp. 3-8, 28-29; J. M. Macphail, *Campbell,* pp. 26-27.
35 *Annual Report SMFCS,* 1900, p. 3
36 J. M. Macphail, *Campbell,* pp. 26-27; R. M. Macphail, *The Santal Mission,* p. 15.
37 *Annual Report SMFCS,* 1908, pp. 32-33; R. M. Macphail, *The Santal Mission,* p. 116.
38 *Annual Report SMFCS,* 1915, pp. 3-4.
39 J. M. Macphail, *Campbell,* pp. 28-31; *Annual Report SMFCS,* 1924, pp. 18-19.
40 *Annual Report SMFCS,* 1922, p. 4.
41 *Annual Report SMFCS,* 1921, pp. 3-4.
42 *Annual Report SMFCS,* 1923, p. 3.
43 Ibid., p. 4.
44 *Annual Report SMFCS,* 1924, p. 41.
45 *Annual Report SMFCS,* 1925, pp. 3 & 19.
46 *Annual Report SMFCS,* 1925, p. 4; *Annual Report SMFCS,* 1926, pp. 4-5.
47 *Annual Report SMFCS,* 1929, p. 3; *Bamdah Christian Hospital,* 1970, p. 4.
48 *Annual Report SMFCS,* 1929, pp. 3-4.
49 R. M. Macphail, *The Santal Mission,* p. 23.
50 *Annual Report SMFCS*: Mission Statistics, 1947, p. 31.
51 *Annual Report SMFCS,* 1878, p. 7.
52 *Annual Report SMFCS,* 1894, p. 7; J. M. Macphail, *Campbell,* p. 14.
53 J. M. Macphail, *Campbell,* p. 20; *Annual Report SMFCS,* 1894, p. 18.
54 *Annual Report SMFCS,* 1894, p. 10; R. M. Macphail, *The Santal Mission,* p. 16.
55 *Bamdah Christian Hospital,* 1970, p. 3; *Sight for the Blind, The Story of Bamdah Hospital,* (n. d.), Bamdah, Santal Parganas, p. 1.
56 Annual Report, 1891, pp. 11 &16.
57 O' Malley (1926), *District Gazetteer: Monghyr,* p. 62. Sight for the Blind, *The Story of Bamdah Hospital,* p. 2.
58 *Annual Report SMFCS,* 1894, p. 32.
59 *Annual Report SMFCS,* 1900, p. 4.
60 *Annual Report SMFCS,* 1908, pp. 3 & 30.
61 Lister (1917), p. 84; *Annual Report SMFCS,* 1915, p. 4; *Annual Report SMFCS,* 1926, p. 5.
62 *Annual Report SMFCS,* 1912-1913, p. 32.
63 *Annual Report SMFCS,* 1925: Statistics.

64 Ibid., pp. 3 & 19.
65 Ibid., p. 11.
66 *Annual Report SMFCS,* 1934, p. 4.
67 *Annual Report SMFCS,* 1878, p. 6; *Annual Report SMFCS,* 1894, p. 7.
68 *Annual Report SMFCS,* 1878, pp. 6-7; Lister, 1917, p. 82.
69 *Annual Report SMFCS,* 1878, p. 7.
70 *Annual Report SMFCS,* 1878, p. 7
71 Ibid.
72 *Annual Report SMFCS,* 1876, p. 23.
73 *Annual Report SMFCS,* 1878, p. 8.
74 *Annual Report SMFCS:* Statistics of the Mission for the year 1879.
75 *Annual Report SMFCS,* 1894, p. 9; J. M. Macphail, *Campbell,* p. 19.
76 J. M. Macphail, *Campbell,* p. 9.
77 *Annual Report SMFCS,* 1883, pp. 4 & 11; *Annual Report SMFCS,* 1894, p. 9.
78 J. M. Macphail, *Campbell,* p. 20.
79 *Annual Report SMFCS,* 1894, p. 9.
80 Ibid., p. 10; J. M. Macphail, *Campbell,* p. 14.
81 *Annual Report SMFCS,* 1894, p. 21.
82 Ibid., pp. 30-31; J. M. Macphail, *Campbell,* pp. 28-29.
83 *Annual Report SMFCS,* 1889, pp. 15 & 19.
84 *Annual Report SMFCS,* 1894, p. 39.
85 Ibid., p. 33.
86 *Annual Report SMFCS,* 1900, p. 27.
87 *Annual Report SMFCS,* 1913-14.
88 *Annual Report SMFCS,* 1915, p. 4.
89 *Annual Report SMFCS,* 1937, p. 20.
90 R. M. Macphail, p. 31.
91 Ibid., p. 15; J. M. Macphail, *Campbell,* pp. 23-25; *Annual Report SMFCS,* 1894, p. 31.
92 *Annual Report SMFCS,* 1894, p. 31.
93 *Annual Report SMFCS,* 1937, p. 2.
94 J. M. Macphail, *Campbell,* p. 28; *Annual Report SMFCS,* 1894, p. 30.
95 *Annual Report SMFCS,* 1897, pp. 3-8, 28-29; J. M. Macphail, *Campbell,* pp. 26-27.

Chapter 9

The Dublin University Mission in Jharkhand

1. The Founding of the Mission

The Dublin University Mission (DUM) in Chotanagpur (Jharkhand) began when the first group of DUM missionaries arrived at Hazaribagh on March 8, 1892. But, the formation of DUM had begun two years earlier, in October 1890, at Dublin, Ireland, by a group of zealous members of the Trinity College in Dublin. They approached Rev. R. D. O. Martin, the organising Secretary of the Committee of the Dublin University Auxiliary to the Society for the Propagation of the Gospel (SPG) in England, with a request for work in a mission field under that Society and in connection with the Dublin University.[1] They were responding to a circular sent to all the graduates of the Dublin University in December the previous year.

The Dublin University Committee proposed to the Standing Committee of the SPG that the new Mission should look to the Society for a portion of the money required, and to the University for the supply of men, and the balance necessary for their support. It was further proposed that the members of the Mission should all be graduates of the Dublin University and they should lead a community life, receiving no salary apart from a small sum of Rs. 300 per annum for personal expenses.[2]

The Standing Committee expressed its thankful readiness to accept the Dublin University community for work in Chotanagpur, subject to the approval of the Bishop. [3] Soon after his consecration in March 1890, Bishop J. C. Whitley of Chotanagpur made a special appeal to England for a community of men to work in his Diocese.[4] The Society had also recently made a special grant of £ 400 a year for the opening of fresh work in the newly-formed Diocese of Chotanagpur.[5] The Society immediately communicated the offer to Bishop Whitley who, in his letter from Ranchi on December 6, 1890, to Rev. H. W. Tucker, Secretary of the Standing Committee of the SPG in London, gladly welcomed the offer and promised to assign the Mission a special district.[6]

The first member of the Dublin University Mission to Chotanagpur, Rev. Eyre Chatterton, M.A., B.D. Head of the Mission, Rev. C. W. Darling, M.A., Rev. (Dr.) K. W. S. Kennedy, B.A., M.B., B.CH., Rev. J. A. Murray, B.A., Rev. G. F. Hamilton, B.A., and Miss Frances Hassard, a nurse, sailed from London on December 10, 1891, and reached Ranchi on January 22, 1892.[7] Bishop Whitley gave them a very hearty welcome. He had already decided to locate the new Mission at Hazaribagh. There the Dublin missionaries reached on a "push-push" (name of a conveyance) on March 8, 1892.[8] They immediately occupied the remains of the old military hospital buildings and their compound, which Bishop Whitley had obtained for the Mission from the Bengal Government on an annual rental of Rs. 3 only.[9]

2. Pitching the Tent at Hazaribagh and Vicinity

The Dublin missionaries found Hazaribagh the most backward of all the Mission stations in the Diocese of Chotanagpur.[10] The Bishop had put them in charge of the Anglican Congregation in the District of Hazaribagh.[11] The number of Christians in the District was then very small. The Anglican Christians were mostly at Hazaribagh,

Sitagarh, Dumar and Giridih. The congregation at Hazaribagh consisted mainly of Europeans and Anglo-Indians. They were either Government officials or pensioners. There was only one Indian Christian family consisting of the sexton of the old military Church, his wife and two children. The Military church, known as the St. Stephen's Church,[12] was built in 1842 for the European Regiment stationed at Hazaribagh. The Anglican Christians at Sitagarh and Dumar were aboriginals, and those of Giridih were Europeans. Bishop Whitley appointed Rev. Chatterton chaplain to the English residents.[13] Rev. Murray took charge of the Sitagarh congregation from the start (1892) and Rev. Kennedy took charge of the Dumar congregation from 1894.[14]

More missionaries, men and women, arrived at intervals during the next eight years. In August 1900, Rev. Chatterton resigned as he became the Bishop of Nagpur.[15] In his place, Rev. (Dr.) J. G. F. Hearn, M.D., was elected head of the Mission by the Brotherhood at Hazaribagh. At the invitation of Bishop Whitley, the Dublin missionaries began to serve the educational and medical institutions of the Anglican Mission at Ranchi.[16] Between 1900 and 1914, 15 men and 17 women missionaries arrived. Among them were Rev. S. L. Thompson (1901), Rev. J. C. Forrester (1907), Fr. (Miss) C. F. O'Meara (1908), Rev. F. H. W. Kerr (1913) and Rev. H. G. S. Kennedy (1914). In 1904, Rev. (Dr.) K. W. S. Kennedy and Rev. G. F. Hamilton, two of the original members of the Mission resigned.[17] In 1908, the Dublin Mission withdrew its missionaries from Ranchi.[18] In January 1912, Rev. (Dr.) Hearn resigned and Rev. J. C. Forrester[19] was elected Head of the Mission. In April 1912, the first lady missionary, Miss Frances Hassard, died[20] at Hazaribagh, and, according to her wish, she was buried among the people she loved and served.

3. Celebrating 'Coming of Age' (21 Years), 1913

In March 1913, the Dublin Mission completed twenty-one years of service in Chotanagpur and organised the 'Coming of age'[21] celebrations at Hazaribagh from the 1st to 7th December. Rt. Rev. Copleston, the Metropolitan of India, Sir Charles Bayley, the Lieutenant-Government of Bihar and Orissa, Lady Bayley, Rt. Rev.

Eyre Chatterton, Bishop of Nagpur, and Rt. Rev. Foss Westcott, Bishop of Chotanagpur, participated. On 2nd December, a new Christian village called Hearnganj after Dr. Hearn was inaugurated by Bishop Chatterton.[22]

In July 1915, the German missionaries of the Gossner Mission in Chotanagpur were interned[23] and the Dublin Mission was asked by Bishop Westcott to superintend the work of that Mission in the District of Hazaribagh. In 1920, Rev. Forrester resigned and Rev. H. G. S. Kennedy became the Head of the Mission. Between 1920 and 1930, many new missionaries came. Mr. A. F. Markham, an Englishman, joined the Mission staff in 1923.[24] In 1926, Rev. Kennedy resigned and was succeeded by Rev. A. O. Hardy as the Head of the Mission. More new missionaries arrived between 1931 and 1940. In 1935, Rev. Hardy[25] resigned and Rev. G. C. P. Stevenson became the Head of the Mission.[26]

4. Golden Jubilee Celebration, 1942

The Dublin University Committee in Ireland, in 1938, decided to publish the history of the Mission on the occasion of the Golden Jubilee of its formation in Ireland in 1940 and asked Rt. Rev. (Dr.) K. W. S. Kennedy, one of the original members of the Mission and formerly Bishop of Chotanagpur, to undertake the task.[27] The book entitled *Fifty Years in Chotanagpur* was published in 1939. In connection with the celebration, a 'thanksgiving service'[28] was held on Sunday, June 8, 1941, in the St. Patrick's Cathedral, Dublin. The special preacher was Rt. Rev. Eyre Chatterton, the first head of the Mission. Rt. Rev. (Dr.) K. W. S. Kennedy and Rev. G. F. Hamilton, two other original members of the Mission, were also present.

The Mission completed fifty years' service at Hazaribagh in 1942 and the Golden Jubilee[29] was celebrated in March. The Metropolitan of India was present on the occasion. In 1944, Miss (Dr.) M. Scott, M.B., came.[30] In 1946, Rev. F. R. Willis became the Head of the Mission.[31] After India achieved independence, the number of missionaries coming to join the Mission staff gradually declined.

5. Impact of the Mission

The Dublin University Mission, from the very start, engaged in four principal activities: evangelistic, pastoral, medical and educational. Its greatest contributions have been in the fields of education and Medicine. Most of the Mission staff were educationists, doctors and nurses. The main areas of services may be noted below.

5.1 Evangelistic Activities

The Dublin missionaries gave much importance to evangelism from the beginning. The first missionaries, at their arrival at Hazaribagh in March 1892, had no knowledge of the local language, Hindi or the local dialects. They, therefore, started learning Hindi. Some Hindi pundits from the local Government High School were engaged.[32] Then they engaged permanently one Pundit Lakshmi Narayan Tripathi, a high-caste Brahmin from Benares.[33] After sometime, the missionaries passed their first examination in Hindi and began preaching in market, melas and villages. They made extensive tours in the interior of the District and spent several days under canvas in villages.[34] They visited Mandu, Ramgarh, Gola, Chatra, Hunterganj, Ichak, Bagodar and other places.[35] The Indian preachers who often accompanied them were Bihari, Brojonath Bhattacharya and Mathew Brown.[36] They moved about in the Hazaribagh town too. Public lectures were delivered to the educated gentlemen of the town in the Keshab Hall.[37]

They were discontinued after sometime for want of response. The Lady Associates like Miss Hassard, Miss Richardson, Miss Beale and Miss Wickham regularly visited the women of the town and the neighbouring villages. The Mission hospitals, dispensaries and schools were important evangelistic agencies. A library was started in the Mission bungalow to enable missionaries and others to acquire more theological and general knowledge.[38]

It was felt necessary to open a centre among the Santals of the Damodar Valley in the District of Hazaribagh. Peterbar was selected in 1895 but soon it was found that Chitarpur would be better for an out-station.[39] Chitarpur was finally selected in 1899 and construction work was started.[40] The progress of conversion was very slow. In

1900, the number of Christians connected with the Mission was only 384.[41] In 1910, the number rose to 683.[42] In 1947, the number was about 2,000. Most of the Christians were of the Munda, Oraon and Santal tribes.

5.2 Pastoral Service at Expanded Missions

Soon after their arrival at Hazaribagh, the Dublin missionaries had to undertake pastoral duties. There were Anglican Christians (Indians and Europeans), at and in the District of Hazaribagh. The Indian Christians were at Sitagarh and Dumar and the European Christians were mostly at Hazaribagh, Giridih and Koderma. Bishop Whitley was the Chaplain of the Station Church at Hazaribagh. Later, Rev. Eyre Chatterton[43] was appointed by Bishop Whitley the Chaplain of the Station Church at Hazaribagh. Until the opening of the branch station at Chitarpur, all the missionaries lived at Hazaribagh and carried on pastoral work. For some years, the pastoral work was done by missionaries alone.

In 1899, a training class for preparing Indian preachers was opened.[44] In 1901, Rev. Hamilton and Rev. C. F. White were posted at Chitarpur.[45] Four new congregations were founded at Chitarpur, Peterbar, Turukdiha and Potmo. The Mission now realised the necessity of having Indian priests. In 1905, Prabhu Dan Raven and William Tirkey were ordained deacons.[46] They were ordained priests in 1908.[47] Mr. P. L. Singh was ordained priest in 1910.[48] In 1915, the German missionaries of the Gossner Mission in Chotanagpur were interned[49] and Bishop Foss Westcott asked the Dublin Mission to manage the Gossner Mission work in the District of Hazaribagh. In 1923, Gabriel Hemrom, who had been trained in the Bishop's College, Calcutta, was ordained priest.[50] In 1924, the Indian congregations were at Hazaribagh, Sitagarh, Dumar, Turukdiha, Chitarpur, Peterbar, Ramgarh, Ichak, Koderma, Sirka, Potamdaga, Potma, Gomia, Bermo, Bhurkunda, Giridih and Bokaro; the European congregations were at Hazaribagh, Giridih, Koderma, Ramgarh and Bokaro.[51] Emmanuel Soy, who was also trained in the Bishop's College, Calcutta, was ordained priest in 1925. By 1947, new Indian congregations were organised at Jobla, Kundru, Kothi and Chatra.[52]

5.3 Educational Service

The Dublin Mission laid great stress on the spread of education from the beginning. It was natural as all the men missionaries were graduates. Soon after their arrival at Hazaribagh, the Dublin missionaries decided to start a Christian Boarding School,[53] just as other Missions at Ranchi had, and appealed to their friends in Ireland to undertake the support of children. They also decided to start a school for the children of English and Anglo-Indian residents[54] of Hazaribagh. The Loretto Sisters of the Roman Catholic Mission had been running such a school there. They, however, closed it down about six months after the arrival of the Dublin missionaries.[55] An appeal was sent to Ireland for a lady teacher.[56] One Miss Kathleen Smith arrived and started a Girls' School for the European and Anglo-Indian children at Hazaribagh in March 1893.[57]

A village school was already at Sitagarh.[58] It was looked after by Rev. (Dr.) Kennedy who set up a Boys' School at Dumar,[59] in place of a German Mission school which had been closed down recently. A decision was made to start teacher training class to prepare teachers.[60] Miss Smith left in October 1893 and early in 1894 Miss Dyer again opened the European Girls' School with eleven students. A school for Bengali girls, was opened at Hazaribagh in 1895 under Miss Beale.[61] On April 15, 1895, a High School for boys, known as Dublin University Mission School,[62] was opened against heavy odds, at Hazaribagh with Rev. C. W. Darling as Principal and Rev. P. L. Singh as Head Master. It had seven students and seven teachers. Rev. Hamilton set up a school in 1897 for the Hindu and Muslim boys of Hazaribagh town. It became popular and was later on known as Hamilton Free School.[63]

The Dublin University Mission is more known for its College. The credit for establishing the first Degree College in Chotanagpur and one of the oldest colleges in Bihar goes to it. In those days, it was unthinkable to start a college at a place like Hazaribagh. The Dublin Mission attempted and succeeded. Early in 1899, the Mission started a college,[64] then known as Dublin University Mission College, and affiliated to Calcutta University. It taught up to first Arts Standard. There were 8 (according to Rev. Eyre Chatterton, 12) students in the first year, and 14 (according to Rev. Eyre Chatterton, 13) students in the second year.[65] Most of the second year students had failed three or four times in other colleges. In the words of Mr. Pedlar, the then Director of Public Instruction, they were the insoluble residues of other colleges.[66] The teaching staff consisted of Rev. J. A. Murray, the Principal who taught English and Logic, Mr. C. N. De, who taught Mathematics and Science, Rev. P. L. Singh who taught History and Mr. B. D. S. Choudhary who taught Indian languages. The classes were held in a rent-free bungalow attached to the Post Office. A donation of Rs. 300 was given by Raja Ram Narayan Singh of the Ramgarh Estate.[67] The University results of the first batch of those 'unpromising' students were nothing short of a miracle, for eight out of fourteen (according to Rev. Chatterton, the number was 9 out of 13) passed very creditably the First Arts Examination in 1900.[68] It was very encouraging, as the average in other Indian colleges seldom rose above 25 percent. The High School was now called the Dublin University Mission Collegiate School.[69]

More schools were set up at Hazaribagh and outside. A Girls' School was started at Chitarpur in 1901. Next year (1902), Miss White started three girls' schools, one in Mehtartoli, the other at Chamartoli and the third at Matwariall in Hazaribagh town.[70] The Hamilton Free School was raised to the Upper Standard. In 1903, two night schools[71] were opened in neighbouring villages. Every school of the Mission received a small monthly grant from the Government.[72]

In 1904, the Dublin University Mission College was raised to B.A. Standard with Rev. S. L. Thompson as Principal.[73] The Mission faced acute financial difficulty. At such time, the Lt. Governor of Bengal, Sir Andrew Fraser[74] visited Hazaribagh, and inspected the medical and educational institutions of the Mission. He was very much impressed, and he generously offered Rs. 15,000 if a similar sum would be raised by the public. In a short time, this was raised. The Government granted Rs.250 per month on condition that the College would be a residential College.[75] The Mission had to make necessary changes as students from different parts of Bengal were "pouring in".[76] In 1904, the number of students in the College was 86; 44 resided in the two hostels arranged by the Mission.[77]

In 1905, the High School had 222 students. The College was renamed as St. Columba's College in 1906.[78] In 1907, Sir Andrew Fraser laid the foundation of the new College building.[79] Next year (1908), Rev. P. L. Singh was appointed Principal of St. Columba's Collegiate High School (Dublin Mission Collegiate School was so renamed). In November of the same year, the College entered into possession of its own permanent buildings.[80] In 1910, the Mission had 25 Primary Schools with 602 students.[81] The Hamilton Upper Primary School with 170 boys was the largest Primary School in the District of Hazaribagh.[82]

In 1915, Rev. S.L. Thompson succeeded by Rev. F. H. W. Kerr[83] as Principal of St. Columba's College. In the Matriculation Examination, 8 out of 9 students passed from the Mission High School, all in the first division.[84] There were 204 students in the College in 1916. One student, Beni Simlai,[85] who graduated in 1915, was baptized. Eighteen were sent up from the Mission High School for the Matriculation Examination and all passed, ten in the first division and the rest in the second division.[86] In 1917, when Patna University was established, the St. Columba's College was transferred to it and the new Science Block was opened on November 3, 1917 by Sir Edward Gait, the Lt. Governor of Bihar and Orissa.[87]

On January 6, 1920, a separate school was opened for the Christian girls at Hazaribagh. It was named as St. Kiran's Girls' School.[88] The Non-Co-operation Movement and the rise in the cost of living led to the reduction of the number of students in St. Columba's College and St. Columba's Collegiate High School. In 1920, Rev. P. L. Singh,[89] Principal of the High School since 1908, was awarded the *Kaiser-i-Hind* medal by the Indian Government and in 1921, he was nominated as member to the Legislative Council of Bihar and Orissa. Intermediate Science classes were started in 1923 in St. Columba's College. In 1924, the College had 175 students and the High School, 208 students.[90] There were, in addition, nine day schools for boys, four night schools for boys and ten schools for girls in the Mission. The Hazaribagh District Board raised its annual grant to the Primary Schools of the Mission to Rs. 5000 per annum.[91] In November 1925, Mahatma Gandhi visited St. Columba's College and addressed the staff and students in the Whitley Hall on social service.[92] During the year, the Hindi Girls' School at Hazaribagh was raised to the Upper Primary Standard and a student of St. Columba's Collegiate High School, Devi Das Chatterjee, got second place in the Patna University at the Matriculation Examination. In 1926, the Dublin Mission had one college with 231 students, one High School with 230 boys, twelve day schools for boys, nine schools for girls and eight night schools for boys.[93] The St. Kiran's Girls' School at Hassardgunj was raised to the Middle English Standard from January 1, 1929.[94] In January, 1930, Mr. A. F. Markham[95] became the Principal of St. Columba's College.

In 1931, two members of the Lindsay Commission on Christian Higher Education in India visited the College and suggested that the College should be shifted to Ranchi but the Mission did not agree.[96] In January 1932, Rev. P. L. Singh retired from the Principalship of St. Columba's Collegiate High School after a long and devoted service of over thirty years.[97] Next year, the Bengali Girls' School, renamed as St. Brigid's School, was raised to the Middle English Standard.[98] The economic depression and the reduction of grants from the Ramgarh Estate hit hard the educational institutions of the Mission in 1937.[99] During the year, the Mission had a College with 240 students, a High School having 430 students, sixteen day Schools for boys, seven day schools for girls and two night schools for boys.

In October 1939, all grants from the Ramgarh Estate were withdrawn. In 1945, the Dublin Mission had one College with 335 students, one High School with 300 boys, one Upper Primary School for boys, twelve day schools for boys, nine day schools for girls and five night schools for boys.[100] In 1946, B. Sc. classes were started in St. Columba's College.[101] Next year (1947), St. Brigid's Middle School for Bengali girls was closed down as another school for Bengali girls was started at Hazaribagh town. A decision was made to raise St. Kiran's Girls' Middle English School to a High School. The Mission had then one College with 335 students, one High School with 300 students, one Upper Primary School with 145 boys, eleven day schools for boys, five night schools for boys, one Middle English School for girls, and six day schools for girls.[102]

5.4 Medical Service

One special feature of the Dublin Mission from the beginning was its strong medical staff.[103] Soon after they arrived at Hazaribagh, Rev. (Dr.) Kennedy and Miss Hassard began medical work with the aid of interpreters.[104] The old Military Hospital buildings, where they stayed, were admirably suited for various purposes. For two months, they treated the patients at the bungalow or in the neighbouring markets and villages. On May 6, 1892, a dispensary and a hospital for men were started.[105] The first in-patient of the new hospital was Bickna, a coolie, who had been employed in repairing the Mission buildings.[106] Shortly afterwards, a female dispensary and a hospital were opened under the care of Miss Hassard. In November 1892, another nurse, Miss Richardson, came to join her friend Miss Hassard.[107] In April 1893, Dr. J. G. F. Hearn came and strengthened the medical staff. Over 150 patients were admitted to the Mission Hospital up to 30th September, 1893.[108]

In 1897, dispensary work was started at Ichak and Peterbar.[109] Dr. Arit Kachchap visited Ichak twice a week on market days. Dr. Komal Tirkey took charge of the Dispensary at Peterbar.[110] During 1897, 15,536 out-patients and 323 patients were treated in the hospital and dispensaries at Hazaribagh, Peterbar and Ichak.[111] In 1899, Chitarpur was selected for a branch station and a Hospital and a dispensary Doctor.[112] Dr. Komal Tirkey was transferred to Chitarpur from Peterbar. In 1904, the first medical missionary, was started in 1900 with Rev. (Dr.) Kennedy as the first doctor.

In 1906, the first missionary Lady Doctor of the Mission, Miss Eva J. Jellet arrived.[113] Efforts were immediately made to build a female hospital to be called St. Columba's Zenana Hospital. The foundation-stone was laid by Lady Fraser, the wife of the Lt. Governor of Bengal, Sir Andrew Fraser, on November 7, 1907.[114] In 1909, another lady doctor, Miss C. E. O' Meara arrived.[115] In 1910, 722 in-patients and 22, 676 out-patients were treated in the hospitals and dispensaries of the Mission. Dr. Hearn and Miss Hassard died in 1912.[116] The construction of the Hospital building was complete in 1913 and was opened by Sir Charles Bayley, the Lt. Governor of Bihar and Orissa, on Saturday, the 6th December, 1913.[117] It had an accommodation for 40 in-patients. A private ward was available for richer Indian patients. For the lack of a male doctor, the male hospital was closed down in 1913.[118] For the first time, three Indian nurses, Mokta, Jaikumari and Tabitha were appointed at the female hospital.

The newly-built female hospital at once became very popular. The Government granted Rs. 4,000 per year.[119] In 1916, 925 in-patients and 25,695 out-patients were treated in the Hospital and dispensaries of the Mission.[120] The Commissioner of Chotanagpur granted Rs. 7, 000 in 1919 for the erection of a new out-patients' Dispensary in St. Columba's Zenana Hospital. In 1920, Miss Mabel Graham came. From that year, for nearly 20 years, the medical and educational institutions of the Mission received annual grants (about Rs.18,00) from the Ramgarh Estate.[121] In 1922, Dr. (Miss) O' Meara fell ill and died at her post on August 5.[122] Miss Mabel Graham extended and strengthened the Training School for nurses. In 1923, the Ramgarh Estate[123] donated Rs. 40,000 for building a Nurses' Home in St. Columba's Zenana Hospital. The Hazaribagh District Board approved a recurring grant of Rs. 1,000 per annum for the Hospital. The Mission Dispensary at Ichak was transferred in 1925 to a new building erected by the Ramgarh Estate and leased to the Mission for 15 years. Next year, the Ramgarh Estate donated Rs. 1,500 to St. Columba's Zenana Hospital and the new Nurses' Home was opened by the Rani of Padma (formerly Ramgarh).[124]

In 1929, 765 in-patients and 23,379 out-patients were treated in the hospitals and dispensaries of the Mission at Hazaribagh, Peterbar, Ramgarh and Ichak.[125] In 1932, the new bungalow for the residence of doctors and nursing sisters of St. Columba's Zenana Hospital was completed. The Ramgarh Estate contributed Rs.13,102 towards its construction.[126] A TB Ward was attached to the Hospital. The Inspector General of Civil Hospitals visited the Hospital on October 11, 1934. He was very much impressed with its efficiency. He wrote, "The whole institution is well organized and run with the greatest efficiency, and it was a pleasure to see the care and devoted attention bestowed on the patients...The hospital is well staffed, and an important feature is the nursing arrangements...The patients in this institution are lucky in this respect as well as in every other way".[127] In 1935, the Hospital statistics showed in patients 1,272; out patients 2,396; operations 467.[128]

In 1937, the boy Raja of Ramgarh attained majority and the Court of Wards ceased. There began a reduction of grants received from the Ramgarh Estate. The dispensaries at Ichak and Ramgarh were closed down. In 1938, all grants to medical work from the Ramgarh Estate were stopped.[129] Next year, Dr. (Miss) Binodini Porh, a tribal Christian lady, joined the St. Columba's Zenana Hospital. In 1941, Miss Mabel Graham was awarded the *Kaiser-i-Hind* medal for her service to the nursing profession.[130] Dr. (Miss) Margaret Scott joined the medical staff in 1944. In 1947, the St. Columba's Zenana Hospital had 96 beds and facilities of training 26 'B' grade nurses.[131]

5.5 Humanitarian and Industrial Service

The Dublin Mission had an orphanage, a Lace School, an Industrial School, a Carpentry School and a Printing Press. There was a terrible famine in 1897 and the Government handed over to the Mission certain orphan children. Miss Hassard took charge of them. An orphanage as started in 1898 with 33 boys and 14 girls,[132] looked after by Miss A. Roe and Miss M. Martin. The number of orphans gradually increased. During the First World War, the orphanage was taken to Singhani. It was shifted to Hassardgunj in1924. Later on, it ceased to exist as an orphanage. The Mission set up a Lace School[133] at Sitagarh for the Christian girls there. Later on, it was shifted to Singhani and ultimately to Hassardgunj. A Carpenters' Class was started at Hazaribagh in 1899 with Rev. F. F. White as its superintendent.[134] It existed for several years and a number of young men got training in carpentry. An Industrial School, rather a Weaving School was set up at Chitarpur in 1909,[135] but was closed down in January 1915. Also, a Printing Press[136] was established by Rev. J. C. Forrester, at Hazaribagh in 1916, but was, however, closed down in July, 1923.

6. Conclusion

The Dublin University Mission (DUM) in Jharkhand had the distinction of founding in 1899, the first Christian College (St.

Columba's College) at Hazaribagh, in Bihar and Jharkhand (which was part of undivided Bihar till 2000). As noted earlier, the College was an expansion of the Dublin University Mission School at Hazaribagh. The DUM laid great stress on higher education, as it took birth and was groomed in a university campus at Dublin, Ireland. The Mission conducted schools not only in cities, but also in villages. Definitely, education was the major ministry of this Mission. Equally significant was its contribution in health care, particularly through its famous hospital, St. Columba's Zenana Hosptial at Hazaribagh. Unlike Catholic Missions which did not have regular grants from the Colonial Government, both these institutions had enjoyed the patronage of the Colonial Government and also of the local Raja of Ramgarh.

Though the DUM did engage in evangelistic works, it did not gain many converts as some other Christian Missions did. The Mission also engaged in humanitarian work such as famine relief and orphan care. The DUM founded institutions to impart industrial training in carpentry, weaving, printing, etc., to enable the people to become self-sufficient. It seems that the Mission could not continue much of its work due to over-dependence on European personnel on the one hand, and negligence in recruiting and training Indian successors, on the other.

Endnotes and References

1 First *Annual Report Dublin University Mission* (hereinafter, ARDUM), 1890, p. A-2; Second ARDUM, 1891, p. A-2; *Historical Sketches, Missionary Series No. II, Chota Nagpore* (1896), p. 18; Eyre Chatterton (1901), *A Story of Fifty Year's of Mission Work in Chotanagpur*, London, p. 156; Lister, E. (1917), *Bihar & Orissa District Gazetteers: Hazaribagh*, p. 78.

2 First ARDUM, 1890, p. A-2; Second ARDUM, 1891, p. A-2; Eyre Chatterton (1901), pp. 156 & 158: By-laws of the Mission as inserted in all the ARDUM.

3 First ARDUM, 1890, p. A-3; Second ARDUM, 1891, p. A-4., Eyre Chatterton (1901) pp. 156; *Historical Sketches, Missionary Series No. II, Chota Nagpore*, p. 18.

4 First ARDUM, 1890, p. 9; H. W. Tucker (1894), *Digest of the S.P.G. Records from 1701 to 1892-1894,* p. 499; Eyre Chatterton, 1901, p. 157.
5 First ARDUM, 1890, p. A-3; Second ARDUM, 1891, p. A-4; Eyre Chatterton (1901), pp. 157-158.
6 First ARDUM, 1890, p. 6; Second ARDUM, 1891, p. 4.
7 First ARDUM, 1890, pp. 6, 8; H. W. Tucker (1894), p. 500; C. F. Pascoe, *Two Hundred years of S.P.G. Mission 1701 to 1900, (1901),* London, p. 500; Eyre Chatterton (1901), pp. 124 & 159-160; Lister (1917), p. 78; H. W. Tucker (1894), p. 500.
8 ARDUM, 1892, p. 5; Eyre Chatterton (1901), p. 169; S. C. Roy (1912), *The Mundas and Their Country,* Calcutta, p. 267; Lister (1917), p. 78; S. K. Patro & B. H Mather (1969), *The Anglican Church in Chotanagpur,* 1869-1969, Ranchi, p. 10.
9 Eyre Chatterton (1901), p. 164; Lister (1917), p. 78.
10 Second ARDUM, 1891, p. 17.
11 Ibid., p. 16; ARDUM, 1892, p. 6.
12 Eyre Chatterton (1901), p. 162.
13 ARDUM, 1892, p. 6.
14 Eyre Chatterton (1901), p. 175.
15 ARDUM, 1900, p. 10; Lister (1917), p. 78.
16 ARDUM, 1901, p. 11.
17 ARDUM, 1904, p. 11.
18 ARDUM, 1908, p. 11.
19 ARDUM, 1912, pp. 1 & 41.
20 Ibid.
21 ARDUM, 1913, p. 7; ARDUM, 1915, pp. 4 & 37-38.
22 *Annual Reports of the Chotanagpur Mission,* 1915, p. 37.
23 *Chotanagpur Diocesan Report,* January 1916, p. 2.
24 ARDUM, 1923, p. 17.
25 ARDUM, 1935, p. 16.
26 ARDUM, 1935, pp. 16-17.
27 ARDUM, 1938, p. 17.
28 ARDUM, 1941, p. 10.
29 ARDUM, 1942, pp. 8-9.
30 ARDUM, 1944, p. 13.
31 ARDUM, 1946, p. 7; *St. Columba's College Diamond Jubilee Souvenir Magazine, 1899-1959,* (1959), p. 38.
32 Eyre Chatterton (1901), pp. 169-170.
33 Ibid., p. 170.

34 ARDUM, 1893, p. 7; Eyre Chatterton (1901), pp. 195-196.
35 ARDUM, 1894, pp. 15-20; ARDUM, 1895, pp. 18-19.
36 Eyre Chatterton (1901), p. 172.
37 ARDUM, 1893, p. 11; ARDUM, 1894, p. 13.
38 ARDUM, 1896, p. 8.
39 ARDUM, 1895, p. 9.
40 ARDUM, 1899, pp. 13, 26.
41 ARDUM, 1900, p. 18.
42 ARDUM, 1910, p. 25.
43 Eyre Chatterton (1901), p. 173; ARDUM, 1892, p. 6.
44 ARDUM, 1899, pp. 26-27.
45 ARDUM, 1901, p. 15.
46 ARDUM, 1905, p. 31.
47 ARDUM, 1908, p. 23.
48 ARDUM, 1910, p. 24.
49 *Chotanagpur Diocesan Report*, January 1916, pp. 2-4.
50 ARDUM, 1923, p. 23.
51 ARDUM, 1924, p. 19.
52 ARDUM, 1948, p. 11.
53 ARDUM, 1892, p. 8.
54 Ibid., p. 9.
55 Eyre Chatterton (1901), p. 180; ARDUM, 1892, p. 9.
56 ARDUM, 1892, p. 9.
57 ARDUM, 1893, p. 26; Eyre Chatterton (1901), p. 180.
58 ARDUM, 1893, p. 10.
59 Ibid.
60 Ibid.
61 ARDUM, 1895, pp. 16 & 44.
62 ARDUM, 1895, pp. 14-15; ARDUM, 1896, p. 22; Eyre Chatterton (1901), p. 185.
63 ARDUM, 1898, pp. 12 & 18.
64 Eyre Chatterton (1901), p. 188; Lister (1917), p. 78.
65 ARDUM, 1904, p. 35.
66 ARDUM, 1900, p. 30; *St. Columba's College Diamond Jubilee Souvenir, 1899-1959,* (1959), p. 14.
67 Lister (1917), p. 79.
68 ARDUM, 1904, p. 35; Eyre Chatterton (1901), p. 188; Lister (1917), p. 79.
69 ARDUM, 1900, p. 23.
70 ARDUM, 1903, p. 24.

71 ARDUM, 1903, pp. 24-25.
72 Ibid., p. 25; Lister (1917), p. 81.
73 ARDUM, 1904, p. 36; ARDUM, 1905-1906, p. 12; Eyre Chatterton (1901), p. 79.
74 ARDUM, 1904, p. 36.
75 Ibid., p. 36; ARDUM, 1904-1905, p. 13.
76 ARDUM, 1904, p. 36.
77 ARDUM, 1904-1905, p. 36.
78 ARDUM, 1906, p. 24.
79 Lister (1917), p. 80.
80 Ibid., p. 80.
81 ARDUM, 1910, p. 29.
82 Ibid.
83 *Chotanagpur Diocesan Report*, January 1916, p. 40; *St. Columba's College Diamond Jubilee Souvenir, 1899-1959*, (1959), p. 15.
84 *Chotanagpur Diocesan Report*, January 1916, p. 40.
85 *Chotanagpur Diocesan Report*, 1917, p. 29.
86 *Chotanagpur Diocesan Report*, July 1916, p. 39.
87 *Chotanagpur Diocesan Report*, 1917, p. 28.
88 ARDUM, 1920, p. 24.
89 ARDUM, 1921, p. 8.
90 ARDUM, 1924, p. 19.
91 Ibid., p. 27.
92 ARDUM, 1925, p. 27.
93 ARDUM, 1925, pp. 19-22.
94 ARDUM, 1929, p. 56.
95 ARDUM, 1930, p. 36.
96 ARDUM, 1931, pp. 31-32.
97 ARDUM, 1932, p. 25.
98 ARDUM, 1933, p. 30.
99 ARDUM, 1937, pp. 12-13, 25.
100 ARDUM, 1945, pp. 11-13.
101 ARDUM, 1946, p. 15.
102 ARDUM, 1947, pp. 11-13, 19.
103 ARDUM, 1892, p. 6; Eyre Chatterton (1901), p. 193.
104 ARDUM, 1892, p. 6.
105 First ARDUM, 1894, p. 14; Eyre Chatterton (1901), p. 171.
106 Eyre Chatterton (1901), p. 171.
107 Lister (1917), p. 79.
108 First ARDUM, 1894, p. 15.

109 ARDUM, 1897, p. 20.
110 Ibid.
111 Ibid., pp. 21-22.
112 *St. Columba's College Diamond Jubilee Souvenir Magazine, 1899-1959,* p. 40.
113 ARDUM, 1906, p. 35.
114 ARDUM, 1907, p. 33.
115 ARDUM, 1909, p. 19.
116 *Chotanagpur Diocesan Report,* October 1912, p. 41.
117 Lister, 1917, p. 79.
118 Ibid.
119 Ibid.
120 ARDUM, 1916, p. 32.
121 *St. Columba's College Diamond Jubilee Souvenir Magazine, 1898-1959,* p. 40.
122 ARDUM, 1922, p. 24.
123 ARDUM, 1923, p. 34.
124 ARDUM, 1926, p. 33.
125 ARDUM, 1929, pp. 45-46.
126 ARDUM, 1932, p. 49.
127 ARDUM, 1934, p. 41.
128 ARDUM, 1935, p. 37.
129 *St. Columba's College Diamond Jubilee Souvenir Magazine, 1899-1959,* p. 40.
130 Ibid; *Chotanagpur Diocesan Report,* May 1941, pp. 1-2.
131 ARDUM, 1947, p. 13.
132 ARDUM, 1899, pp. 12-13.
133 ARDUM, 1903, p. 56.
134 ARDUM, 1899, p. 12.
135 ARDUM, 1908, pp. 56-57.
136 Lister (1917), p. 80; *Chotanagpur Diocesan Report,* July 1916, p. 40; ARDUM, 1919, p. 18.

Chapter 10

Other Christian Missions in Bihar and Jharkhand

Besides the Churches mentioned in the previous chapters, there are a few more Churches which engaged in missionary activity in both Bihar and Jharkhand. Some of these worked only in one of the two States, while others worked in both States. These Missions arrived later in the 19th century or early 20th century. In this Chapter we shall have a brief overview of these Missions. I have listed them in chronological sequence as can be noted from the founding year (within brackets) in the titles.

1. The Fellowship of Christian Assemblies Mission in Jharkhand and Bihar (1880)

The Fellowship of Christian Assemblies Mission was founded in Bihar at about 1880, when a Swedish seaman, Mr. E. Cornelius,[1] who had been converted on board a ship, left his ship in Calcutta, and realising that God was calling him, came to Jamtara in the District of

Santal Parganas and commenced work there. After about ten years, he was joined by other missionaries from the United Kingdom.

From Jamtara, the work was extended to two other areas of Santal Parganas and also to the District of Bhagalpur. The principal centres of the Mission were Jamtara, Mihijam, Karmataur and Subbonpur in Santal Parganas and Charkafather, in the District of Bhagalpur.[2]

The type of work carried on by the missionaries included schools, dispensaries, orphanages for boys and girls and leper clinics. The Mission conducted dispensaries at Buduhi, Jamtara, Mihijam and Bhaga.[3] The total number of Christians with the Mission was about 330.

In course of time, due to shortage of men and money, much of the work had to be curtailed. Eventually, the Mission handed over all its Primary Schools, except that of Mihijam, to the Government.

2. The Methodist Church in Jharkhand and Bihar (1884)

The Methodist Church that commenced work elsewhere in India in 1856,[4] has been one of the prominent Protestant Christian Missions of Bihar and Jharkhand. It started missionary work in 1884 at Pakur[5] in the District of Santal Parganas (Jharkhand), when one Mr. E. McLeod Smith was the Sub-Divisional Officer there. He was an earnest Christian and he used to gather his servants together for a religious service on Sundays. A muslim clerk Shahoo Munshi,[6] of village Sangrampur, was a regular attendant. He was attracted to Christianity and he desired baptizm. Bishop J. M. Thoburn of Calcutta sent Rev. W. A. Thomas to administer the rite. With the efforts of Shahoo Munshi, some more people of the place embraced Christianity.

This growing group was supervised for two years by Rev. J. P. Meik[7] from Calcutta (under the Bengal Methodist Conference). Mr. S. N. Das and other workers made longer visits, sold and distributed religious literature. Soon a little school was opened, eight persons were baptized, and a small house with two rooms was built for a teacher at Sangrampur. In 1886, Rev. E. S. Busby was appointed to Pakur. Nineteen persons, all Muslims,[8] were baptized during the year. At the end of the year, two small schools, one for boys and another for girls, were founded. The number of pupils was 40. The movement at Sangrampur was significant not only in opening a new station, but because it was perhaps the largest group movement[9] among Muslims in Bihar.

In 1888,[10] the headquarters of the Government at Pakur were transferred, and the Methodist Church purchased the whole site, 21 acres, with the old buildings. The Bengali boys' and girls' orphanages were moved to this place from Calcutta. In 1891, the number of converts rose to 130, most of whom were Muslims.[11] Santals, Muslims and Bengalis studied together. In 1897, the old Mission buildings were badly damaged by an earthquake. Next year, Miss Alma Jacobson came to assist Mrs. Meik in conducting women's work.

2.1 Santal Response

By 1916, the number of Santal converts increased so as to outnumber others.[12] Their tribal and social customs differed and Hindi had been recognised as their official language. Therefore, in the year 1924-1925, the Santal children were removed from the Bengali Schools and put in their own.[13] Further, Miss Mildred Pierce felt the need of a separate school for the Santals where their school life would be linked with their simple village life and so she laid the foundation for it. Later on, the Women's Foreign Missionary Society (WFMS) bought the main portion of the Pakur Mission property from the Board of Missions and there established a Santal school. In four years, the number of girls doubled and that of the boys trebled.[14] The Santal School was co-educational. Built much like a village, the School was called 'Jidato'[15] which means "village of persistent advance". Their church was also known by that name. Along with 'book learning', the students learnt occupations such as poultry-keeping, carpentry, fruit-farming, gardening and growing field crops. The School, later on, became a High School. The little school at Sangrampur was continued. A new school building was dedicated by Bishop Rookey in 1941.[16] The Bengali Girls' Boarding School at Pakur, managed by the Women's Foreign Missionary Society, was called Alma Jacobson-Keventer School. Later,[17] it became a co-educational Middle School.

2.2 Medical Service

Henry Swan says that a dispensary[18] was opened at Pakur sometime before 1898. In 1913, the medical work there was carried on by Miss Hilda Swan assisted by a nurse and a retired assistant surgeon. The work was expanded by Miss Marnie Reilley.[19] In 1919, there were 235 in-patients and 13,825 out-patients.[20] Next year, a sick ward was built for maternity cases. Miss Alley was in charge of it. In summer of 1923, Bishop Fisher of Calcutta transferred the Edith Jackson Memorial Dispensary from Calcutta to Pakur and also donated the sum needed to pay off the debt incurred in building a sick ward.[21] Ever since, the Memorial Hospital continued to render much-needed service. Medical work was conducted at Resra and Raghunathpur in Bihar. Dr. (Mrs.) Ilahi Baksh was at Rosra and, Dr. (Mrs.) E. Sukh, at Raghunathpur. Both the centres did very well.

2.3 Mission Expansion in Bihar

An attempt was made by Bishop Hurst in 1885 to start Mission work in the Tirhut Division in Bihar under the Methodist Lucknow Conference.[22] At his suggestion, Dr. Day of Syracuse University sent out Rev. and Mrs. Henry Jackson, formerly to North India.[23] They were appointed to Muzaffarpur in 1888. They pioneered in this new field by preaching to English congregation in the town and in Samastipur, and by bazar preaching and touring.[24] Mrs. Jackson, though not a physician, opened a dispensary and with the help of an Indian assistant, was able to treat an average of more than fifty persons a day. In 1902, Rev. Jackson was succeeded by Rev. W. P. Byers, and later by Rev. J. O. Denning in 1903. Baptizms were few but an attitude of friendliness had been won, even in places like Bettiah, where there was at first strong opposition. A small girls' school was opened at Chapra.[25] Owing to the illness of their sons, Rev. Denning and his wife had to go back to America in 1904 and Mr. and Mrs. W. D. Beal took charge of the developing work.

Rev. J. O. Denning and his wife returned from America in 1906. Along with them, came two young missionaries, Herman J. Schutz (Sheets) and Fred M. Perill, and one Miss Grace Bills (later Mrs. Sheets), for the Women's Foreign Missionary Society.[26] Work was spread to Dumraon where a preacher was stationed.[27] Rev. J. A. Ilahi Baksh took some of his Christians from Rasra to Dumraon.

In 1907, Arrah was included in the area known as Methodist Tirhut District under the Lucknow Conference,[28] with the centre at Muzaffarpur. Mr. A. L.[29] Grey, an independent missionary, had opened work there in1904. When financial support fell off, Mr. Gray asked Bishop Robinson to include his work in that of the Methodist Church. Adjustments were mutually agreed to. Mr. and Mrs. Grey were devoted missionaries and they brought with them property, a small orphanage and a small band of workers. At Rev. Denning's suggestion, they worked in Dumraon among the Chamars with encouraging success.[30] At the end of 1911, there had been 1,200 conversions.[31] Mr. Grey was transferred at this time and Rev. Parrill was put in charge of the Arah circle. Converts at this area were severely persecuted. In 1917, the Ballia-Arah District was supervised by Rev. Sheets.[32]

In 1919, Arah was made a separate Mission District and was placed under Rev. J. W. Pickett.[33] Miss Hyneman was the first District Evangelist. Rev. Pickett was succeeded by Rev. M. C. Singh as District Superintendent in 1926. He was followed by Rev. G. M. Massey. The Buxar District[34] was next formed in 1923, by Bishop Fisher, and placed under Rev. Emmanuel Sukh, M.L.C., as District Superintendent. The number of Christians increased steadily.

With the help of a gift of Rs. 500, given to Rev. Pickett by a visiting missionary lady, a school for girls[35] was opened at Arah in 1918. Its future seemed uncertain until 1921 when it was taken over by the Women's Foreign Missionary Society. Rev. Pickett purchased the Solano Estate, one-third for the Women's Foreign Missionary Society and two-thirds for the Mission Board. There the Sawtelle Memorial Girls' School was opened by Miss Edna Abbott, its first Principal.[36] The school made rapid progress under Miss Hyneman and Miss Tirsgaard.[37] A boys' school was started from the little orphanage opened by Mr. and Mrs. Grey.[38] Many of the boys were from neighbouring villages. In 1926, there were 54 boys in the hostel with Miss Richmond as its Superintendent.[39] The Sawtelle Memorial Girls' School became a co-educational Institution of Middle School Standard.

A new form of village service was planned and implemented at Buxar. It was a Brides' School.[40] It was successfully managed by Miss Mabel Sheldon and Miss Frances Paul. There young brides were trained to be good wives.[41]

Until 1926, Dhanbad was a circle in the Asansol District of the Bengal Conference. That year, the number of Methodists at Dhanbad and the places around was 564.[42] For a long time, this coal field circle was in the care of Rev. Benjamin A. Mott.[43]

During the period under review, the Methodist Church in Bihar had three Districts and about twenty Mission stations. The three Districts were Pakur, Tirhut and Arah. While the first was under Bengal Conference, the other two were under the Lucknow Conference. The Mission possessed a considerable number of Muslim Christians.

3. The Zenana Bible and Medical Mission in Bihar (1890)

The Zenana Bible and Medical Mission, later on called the Bible and Medical Missionary Fellowship, started its work in Bihar in 1890.[44] It is said that in 1884, one Mr. Robert Johnson asked the Zenana Bible and Medical Mission in England to open a medical Mission at Patna and promised £150 a year towards its cost. He died in 1887, but his widow continued the subscription and looked forward to and prayed every Wednesday, for the realization of their plan to found a medical Mission at Patna. In 1889, Dr. Grace Mackinnon offered her services.[45] In 1890, Dr. Mackinnon and Sister Gregory started medical work at Nuranibagh in the old Patna City. During 1890 and 1891, it seems that most of the work must have been among out-patients, though in 1892, it is mentioned that there was one bed available for a patient who could not attend daily. That year, there were altogether 11 in-patients and 7,670 out-patients.

In 1892, Dr. Mackinnon obtained land at Tripolia[46] about a quarter of a mile away, for building a hospital. In 1893, the Duchess of Teck, mother of Queen Mary, consented that the hospital be named after her, and, in the same year, the foundation stone was laid by the Lieutenant Governor of Bengal, Sir Anthony Macdonnell.[47] Dr. Mackinnon worked at Nuranibagh and also supervised the construction of the hospital building. There were 3 beds for in-patients at Nuranibagh and 10,817 out-patients. In 1895, Miss Derridan was appointed as the Assistant Lady Doctor.

In 1906, Dr. Stillwell joined the staff of the Duchess of Teck Hospital at Tripolia. She remained in service for 31 years. She started training nurses, midwives and compounders. Her reputation as a gyneacological surgeon was wide-spread. She was awarded, in 1925, the *Kaiser-i-Hind* medal for her long and devoted service to the sick.[48]

Besides doing hospital work, the pioneers treated patients in camps or in their houses. Dr. Mackinnon, helped by Dr. Mayne from Benares, conducted a camp for plague patients. In 1905, there were 6720 out-patients, 351 in-patients and 151 operation cases in the Hospital. The Hospital treated 8093 out-patients and 369 in-patients and performed 379 operations. The doctors visited 29,816 patients.[49] A Maternity Block was opened in 1917.[50] In 1920, the Hospital had 9,254 out-patients, 39,523 out patient attendances, 735 in-patients, 754 operations and 105 midwifery cases.

3.1 Expansion of Medical Service and Training

Further improvements were made in the Hospital in 1924, as the Countess of Dufferin Fund allocated Rs. 2,500 for the installation of electricity. In 1927, the Red Cross Society donated Rs. 8,000 for a tube well and a motor pump.[51]

With the help of Rs. 5,000 from the Government, Rs. 5000 from the Local Self-Government and funds from the local and the Zenana Bible and Medical Mission, four new private wards for paying patients were added in 1929. That year, the Hospital had 10,119 out-patients, 40,273 outpatient attendances, 1361 in-patients, 686 operations and 289 midwifery cases.[52] In 1931, Dr. M. W. Anderson joined the medical staff. With Rs. 5,000 from the Red Cross Society and Rs. 8,000 from the Zenana Bible and Medical Mission, new quarters for the Indian staff were constructed. In 1938, a Babies' ward with an accommodation for 28 cots was built.[53] This was erected as a memorial to Sister Symons, who died as a result of a riding accident. In 1939, the Hospital had 6,837 out-patients 38,852 out-patient attendances, 1,816 in-patients, 557 operations and 651 midwifery cases.[54]

The medical service of the Hospital was for women and children and the major part of its work was midwifery and gyneacology. The number of beds rose to 108. For about 20 years, a dispensary was held twice a week in Patna City, where the average daily attendance was 201.[55] This had to be closed down in 1929 owing to shortage of staff, opening of other Child Welfare Centres and the increasing transportation facilities which made it possible for patients to get their treatment elsewhere. In 1937, village dispensaries were started in various centres.

The Duchess of Teck Hospital had Training Schools for compounders and nurses.[56] In 1919, the Training School for compounders was recognised by the Government of Bihar. Miss Dwyer was the first trainee to pass the examination at Darbhanga. In 1938, Miss Cranston stood first in the Province in that examination. The first nurse to complete her training in general nursing was Miss Paulina Titus in 1916. The nurses and midwives formally took the examination of the North India Board of Mission Hospitals but from 1938 they took that of the Bihar Medical Examination Board.

The Second World War (1939-1945) brought increasing difficulties due to shortage of staff, A.R.P. (Air Raid Precaution) obligations, rising prices, shortage of food and drugs, and a fall in income.[57] In spite of these difficulties, the Hospital carried on its work. When workers were held up at home and new workers were not available, valuable help was received for short periods, from Dr. Harbord, Dr. Hodge, Dr. Fox, Dr. Yong, Sister Durston, Sister Burrows and many other friends from outside the Mission.[58] In 1942, after the riots, the village dispensary work had to be entirely closed down. One of these was re-opened in October 1946.

In 1920, a microscope was given to the Hospital as a gift to be used in the laboratory. In 1944, one of the compounders, Miss Reven, completed a Laboratory Technician's Course and came out first in the all-India examination. Many of the doctors and sisters working in the Hospital served various outside bodies or institutions.[59] In 1915, one of the Doctors became the Medical Officer to the Girls' Schools at Patna. Sister Fleming, Sister Robertson and Sister Bottom acted as Registrars of the Bihar Nurses' Registration Council. According to the statistics of the Hospital, there were, in 1945, 7,154 out-patients, 1,844 in-patients, 594 operations and 571 midwifery cases attended.[60]

The Zenana Bible and Medical Mission continued its philanthropic activity even after Independence, many lady doctors and Sisters came and served the Mission for many years. Among them, the most notable were Dr. Stillwell (31 years), Dr. Gupta (30 years) and Miss Emery (24 years).[61]

4. The Seventh-day Adventist Mission in Jharkhand (1898)

The Seventh-day Adventist Mission from the United States of America, with its India headquarters at Calcutta, opened a centre in Jharkhand in 1898, at Karmatanr,[62] in the District of Santal Parganas. The Mission began when its orphanage cum school at Calcutta was transferred to this place with Elder F. W. Brown in charge.

Elder Brown, the founder of the station, soon died. However, the work was carried on by Elder Spicer. Later on, a nurse, Miss S. E. Whiteis came to Karmatanr and served the sick for some years.[63] In 1902, an English School was started there by Miss Thekla Black and Miss Anna Orr, in connection with the orphanage there.

In December 1904, the Mission Printing Press was shifted from Calcutta to Karmatanr, and, Mr. J. C. Little was appointed in-charge and also the editor of a missionary newsletter, the *Oriental Watchman*. Though the English school there was transferred to Calcutta, another school (Middle English School) was founded at Karmatanr. By 1912, it had 50 boys in its rolls. The Mission also ran five village schools with about 150 boys and girls.[64] Boys and girls had separate Schools from 1917.

In 1900, Mr. W. A. Barlow, an English missionary, joined the Mission, and opened a station at Simultala,[65] about 30 miles north-west of Karmatanr. In 1903, he opened a school with 15 Santal boys. The object was to train workers and teachers who would start other schools among their own people. They were taught Hindi, Santali, Bible, Arithmetic, Reading and Spelling. After sometime, this School was closed down and another was started at a village called Babumahal, about ten miles from Simultala, by Rev. L. J. Burgess in 1905, with only two students in the beginning.[66] In 1912, the number of students rose to 23. Village schools were opened in some of the neighbouring villages. Two Night Schools were conducted for adults. A handloom was installed and weaving became one of the industries of the students. About 1908, Mr. R. H. Leech and his wife started a station at Jagadishpur at a distance of 21 miles from Karmatanr. But this station was abandoned after a few years.

Prior to 1919, there was a feeling that the school set up for Bengali boys in Calcutta should be transferred to a more suitable place where it could serve better as a central training institution for the students from Bengal, Bihar, Orissa and Assam. Accordingly, a house at Marobadi[67] at Ranchi was taken on rent and the Bengali School was moved to Ranchi, on November 25, 1919, under the supervision of Rev. L. J. Burgess and his wife. It was re-located in 1925 in a new building at Bargain, four miles north-west of Ranchi town.

The Mission opened a branch at Khunti in 1929. Ten years later, in 1939, Mr. C. J. Jensen opened a school, which served four aboriginal tribes--Mundas, Oranons, Kharias and Santals.[68] Mr. Jensen spent his own money to build and maintain the school. The Mission took charge of the School from Mr. Jensen in 1940. Different kinds of industries like bottling of tomato juice and peanut butter industry were set up to support the school.

In 1937, the Mission authorities decided to unite the schools at Ranchi, Karmatanr and Babumahal. The United School was located at Karmatanr and this was known as the Bihar Mission High School.[69] Initially, there were 77 boys and 31 girls in the Boarding and 15 boys and 10 girls as day scholars. Pastor N. G. Mookerjee was the Principal. The School was renamed, in 1940, as Robinson Memorial High School in honour of Elder D. A. Robinson, who had been in charge of the Mission work in India, with Calcutta as its headquarters, when Karmatanr was selected for Mission work in 1898.[70]

During World War II, the peanut butter industry established there, was developed. In 1944, the School supplied every week more than one-half ton of this product to the American army. Another profitable source of income was the Mission Printing Press, where students learned a trade, and at the same time, earned a major portion of their fees.

The Mission carried on medical work too, though on a small scale.[71] It maintained a small dispensary at Karmatanr. In 1947, Dr. R. U. Shearer opened a small dispensary and clinic on the property where the Bihar Mission High School was located at Ranchi.

5. The British Churches of Christ Mission in Jharkhand (1909)

Mr. Paul Singh, an Indian evangelist, opened the work of the British Churches of Christ Mission[72] in the District of Palamau, early in 1909, by establishing a small church at Daltonganj, the headquarters of the District. His guide was an English Christian, R. H. Parker. When Mr. Parker returned to England, he made an appeal to the Churches in his country to send a missionary to go to Palamau to work with Paul Singh. The appeal was answered not from England but from Australia from where Mr. and Mrs. Percy Pittman came in 1909[73] and remained in charge of the field until 1914. During their stay in Palamau, they erected a bungalow and a school building at Daltonganj. By 1912, two out-stations were founded at Garhwa and Laterhar in the same District.[74] In 1914, when the London Missionary Society relinquished its charge of the station at Dudhi in Uttar Pradesh, Mr. and Mrs. Pittman left Daltonganj to reside at Dudhi.

The first major venture in the field of education was the establishment of a small school at Daltonganj in 1914.[75] This later developed into a Middle English School for girls under Miss Eveline Bednock who added a hostel and an orphanage. In early 1930s, the Mission decided to enter the area to the south of Daltonganj, extending through Nawadih, Nawa Bhandaria to Baragar.[76] Mr. Penry Pryce and his Indian colleagues made frequent visits to the tribal people of that area, whom they found in a state of extreme poverty, oppressed by landlords and without educational and medical facilities. Mr. and Mrs. Pryce settled at Nawa Bhandaria.

Other missionaries arrived at Nawa Bhandaria[77] and launched a programme of adult literacy at about 13 centres in around Bhadaria. During times of scarcity, the Mission conducted relief programmes supported by Government agencies. From time to time, special medical facilities were also provided.

6. The Brethren in Christ Mission in Bihar (1914)

The Brethren in Christ Mission began its missionary work in Bihar, with Rev. and Mrs. Henry Smith and Miss Effice Rohrer who arrived in January, 1914[78] at Madhubani, then in the District of Darbhanga. Though Rev. Smith selected a site there to establish a Mission station, he could not buy land there because of its high price. He then turned his attention towards Madhepura and Supaul sub-divisions of the then District of North Bhagalpur.

On May 2, 1914, Rev. Smith and his party moved into a rented bungalow in Saur Bazar, eight miles south-east of Saharsa Junction. The bungalow belonged to Mr. H. D. Christian, a domiciled European living about four miles west of Saharsa. However, Rev. Smith decided to settle in Madhepura town.[79] So an old railway bungalow at Madhepura was taken on rent, and, after proper repairs, was made their centre on January 12, 1915 when the missionary party moved in from Saur Bazar.

Work had begun but the Mission had no permanent site of its own yet. Rev. Smith purchased a piece of land at Saharsa[80] and began the construction of a small bungalow. Early in 1916, another couple and one single lady missionary arrived to augment the missionary staff. From its beginning in Saur Bazaar, then in Madhepura and Saharsa, and later in Supaul, medical work was the main part of the Mission programme. In August 1917, the first convert, a Mohammedan young man was baptized.[81]

In October 1917, the Rohrer family took up residence at Supaul and next year, land was purchased for a station.[82] In the same year, additional land was purchased at Saharsa. Next year, two new missionary parties arrived.

In 1918, a school for boys was started in Saharsa but was closed down in 1927. The same year, 1918, the care of destitute widows and children was done around Saharsa. By 1920, three Mission stations had been founded and twelve missionaries had come to the field.[83] In April 1924, the leader of the Mission, Rev. Henry Smith, died of small-pox, at the age of 36 years.

The first church building was dedicated in Saharsa in 1925.[84] Another was dedicated in Supaul in 1931. Within the next few years, new workers came to the field. An orphanage for girls was opened in Saharsa and also a home for widows. The orphanage for boys in Supaul continued from 1918 to 1940 when it was moved to Barjora. The dispensary at Saharsa and Supaul ministered daily to many patients.

In 1927, the English Baptist Society withdrew from the Begusarai sub-division, and its work there was given over to the Brethren in Christ Mission.[85] The earthquake of January 1934, did considerable damage to the Mission property at Saharsa and Supaul. Besides, in 1934, the mighty Kosi river brought devastation to that area. The river came within one hundred yards of the Mission compound. Again in 1938, the flooding waters of the Kosi river compelled the Mission authorities to evacuate from Supaul.[86] Earlier in 1924, another terrible flood by Kosi had forced the closure of their Mission at Madhepura. Madhepura Mission station was rebuilt and opened in 1939. Next year (1940), a new station was opened at Barjora,[87] 20 miles east of Supaul. The orphanage for boys at Supaul was moved to Barjora and a village school was founded there. A church was dedicated there in 1947.

The Silver Jubilee of the Mission was celebrated with a three-day convention in Saharsa in the spring of 1939.[88] During the first twenty-five years, 19 missionaries had come to the field. One hundred and fifty-one persons had been baptized and the Christian community in Saharsa and Supaul numbered about 200.

The Quit India Movement in 1942 brought trial and suffering to the missionaries. Being foreigners, they were in great danger. Besides, the District was virtually an island in August that year, being cut off by flood waters from outside. After several weeks, the military arrived and, early in September, the entire missionary staffs were evacuated to Monghyr Fort, where they were kept until allowed to return to their stations in December, 1942.[89]

During the World War II years, the personnel and work were at a minimum. In 1945, when the Baptist Missionary Society felt unable to send workers to their field at Monghyr, the Brethren missionaries took it up. This resulted in the expansion of their work which was also possible because of the arrival of new missionaries. In 1946, a missionary couple was assigned to Monghyr. In co-operation with the Mennonite Central Committee, a Relief Dispensary was opened at Barjora early in 1947.

As early as 1939, the evangelistic workers of the Mission at Madhepura had contacted the Santals in the east of the District but not until 1943 was the possibility of work among them realised. From that time, the work among the tribal people went on. In April 1945, the first Santal[90] was baptized in his own village, eleven miles east of Madhepura. His witness brought his own sister who continued to witness and bring others. The first baptized young man died of tuberculosis only a few months after his baptizm. The first out-station for work among the Santals, along with a school, were opened at Khanawa in the District of Purnea in 1947.

7. The Assembly of God Mission in Bihar and Jharkhand (1914)

The Assembly of God (AG) Mission came from the United States of America and started work in 1914, when Miss E. Baugh and her co-worker arrived at Chapra in the District of Saran.[91] Miss S. Coxe and Mrs. Schoonmaker continued the work started by Miss Baugh.

In 1918, Miss M. Flint and Miss J. Krikland started mission work at Bettiah[92] in the District of Champaran. Land was acquired and a girls' school was opened. In 1928, Miss Hilda Wagenknecht took charge of the work there. She was assisted by Miss Mary E. Wagner, Miss Verona Rich, Miss Marion Midgett and Miss Francis Ivy. The girls' school at Chapra was raised to the Middle English Standard.

In 1922, the AG Mission purchased a property at Laheriasarai in the District of Darbhanga, and Rev. and Mrs. D. S. Mahaffey started work there. They were succeeded by Rev. and Mrs. J. J. Mueller, who opened a girls' school there. Mission work was extended to Samastipur in the same District.[93]

At about 1927, the AG Mission expanded its work to Jharkhand when Rev. and Mrs. D. S. Mahaffey settled at Chutupalu[94] in the District of Ranchi and built a small bungalow. It was a very backward area just on the border of Ranchi and Hazaribagh Districts with no school and no dispensary within the radious of six miles. In 1933, Rev. and Mrs. McClay took charge of the work there. Next year,

Mrs. McClay gathered a few children on the verandah of the Mission bungalow and began teaching them which, in 1935, became a primary school. A small dispensary too was conducted. The Mission there had six Christian families.

From Chutupalu, the work was extended to a village called Mutta in Ranchi District, where a Day School and a Night School were opened. In 1938, Rev. and Mrs. Mahaffey moved to Ramgarh, where land was purchased and a church was built. The congregation was made up of the Christians of many denominations. From Ramgarh, work was extended to Barka Khana, an important railway junction.

In 1942, Rev. and Mrs. M. C. Somaiya started work at Jamshedpur.[95] Four years later, in 1946, Rev. and Mrs. W. G. Long arrived at Gomoh and took charge of the English-speaking congregation in the Railway Church there.

8. Conclusion

In this chapter, we have seen that there were attempts to establish Missions by smaller but enthusiastic missionary societies as well as individuals from abroad. Three of the seven societies had opened their centres in both Jharkhand and Bihar. Two limited themselves to Bihar, and two, to Jharkhand.

One may also note that these Mission groups established their centres generally in such cities or villages which were hitherto untouched by any other Mission societies. Also, these missionary societies had to face tremendous difficulties, both personnel and financial crunch. Nevertheless, they built up small Christian communities in isolated locales which gave witness to the Gospel of Christ.

Endnotes and References

1 W. Crawford (1960), *The Fellowship of Christian Assemblies Mission,* p. 1.
2 Ibid.
3 Ibid.
4 John N. Hollister (1956), *The Centenary of the Methodist Church in Southern Asia*, p. 1.
5 Ibid., p. 186.
6 Ibid.
7 John N. Hollister (1956), p. 186; L. S. S. O'Malley (1910), *Bihar District Gazetteers: Santal Parganas*, (Revised 1938), p. 85.
8 John N. Hollister (1956), p. 186.
9 Ibid., L.S.S.O'Malley (1910) (Revised 1938), p. 86.
10 John N. Hollister (1956), p. 186.
11 Ibid.
12 Ibid., p. 319.
13 *Minutes of the Bengal Women's Conference*, 1929, Calcutta, p. 37; *Santal Parganas Gazetteer*, 1953, p. 117.
14 *Minutes of the Bengal Women's Conference*, 1929, p. 37.
15 John N. Hollister (1956), p. 320; L. S. S. O' Malley (1910), (Revised 1938), p. 86.
16 *Minutes of the Bengal Conference*, 1941, p. 35.
17 John N. Hollister (1956), p. 320.
18 Ibid.
19 *Minutes of the Bengal Women's Conference*, 1913, p. 40.
20 John N. Hollister (1956), p. 320.
21 *Minutes of Bengal Women's Conference*, 1924, as quoted by Dr. John N. Hollister (1956), p. 321.
22 John N. Hollister (1956), p. 187.
23 *North Western Christian Advocate*, March 27, 1912, p. 10.
24 John N. Hollister (1956), p. 187.
25 Ibid.
26 Ibid., p. 324.
27 Ibid.
28 Ibid.
29 Ibid.
30 Ibid.
31 Ibid.
32 Ibid., p. 325.
33 Ibid.

34 Ibid.
35 Ibid.
36 Ibid.
37 *Visions and Victories in Hindustan*, Methodist Publishing House, Madras, India, 1931.
38 John N. Hollister (1956), p. 325.
39 *Visions and Victories in Hindustan* (1931), p. 703.
40 John N. Hollister (1956), p. 325.
41 *Minutes of the Lucknow Conference*, 1921, p. 36; *Minutes of the Lucknow Conference*,1922, p. 33.
42 *Minutes of the Bengal Conference*, 1954, p. 32.
43 John N. Hollister (1956), p. 323.
44 *Golden Jubilee, 1895-1945: Zenana Bible Medical Mission*, The Union Press, Patna, 1945, p. 1.
45 Ibid., pp. 1-2.
46 Ibid., p. 2.
47 Ibid.
48 Ibid., p. 3.
49 Ibid., p. 12.
50 Ibid., p. 6.
51 Ibid. pp. 4-5.
52 Ibid., p. 13.
53 Ibid., p. 6.
54 Ibid., p. 13
55 Ibid. , p. 7.
56 Ibid., p. 3.
57 Ibid., p. 5.
58 Ibid., p. 5.
59 Ibid., pp. 8-9.
60 Ibid., p. 13.
61 Ibid., p. 1.
62 R. N. Dass (1960), *A Brief History of the Seventh-Day Adventists work in Bihar*, p. 1.
63 Ibid.
64 Ibid. p. 2.
65 Ibid., p. 4.
66 Ibid., p. 4.
67 Ibid. p. 7.
68 Ibid., p. 5.
69 Ibid., p. 3.

70 Ibid., p. 3.
71 Ibid. p. 7.
72 Keith Skillicorn (1960), *History of British Churches of Christ Mission in Palamau, Bihar,* p. 1.
73 Ibid.
74 Ibid., pp. 1-2.
75 Ibid., p. 2.
76 Ibid.
77 Ibid.
78 Anon, *History of the Brethren in Christ Mission in Bihar*, p. 1.
79 Ibid.
80 Ibid., p. 2.
81 Ibid.
82 Ibid., p. 3.
83 Ibid..
84 Ibid.
85 Ibid., p. 4.
86 Ibid.
87 Ibid., pp. 4-6.
88 Ibid., p. 5.
89 Ibid.
90 Ibid., p. 8.
91 M. C. Somaiya (1960), *The Assembly of God Mission,* Jamshedpur, p. 1.
92 Ibid.
93 Ibid.
94 Ibid.
95 Ibid., p.2.

Summary and Conclusion

1. Introduction

It is generally perceived that Christian missionary work in Bihar and Bengal, for that matter, in entire north India, began with British Colonial rule in Bengal in 1765. But the fact is otherwise: Christian missionaries of the Catholic Church had begun work in Bengal in early 16th century under the patronage of the Portuguese. In North India, they opened a centre at Agra in 1580, at the invitation of Emperor Akbar.

Similarly, the history of Christianity in undivided Bihar (which included Jharkhand) begins in early 17th century, prior to the British period. The Mughal Governor of Patna, Nawab Mukharrab Khan invited Catholic Jesuit priests from Bengal to his capital at Patna in 1620 to found a church there. Though this Mission was short-lived, Christian presence in Bihar definitively started in 1706 when the Capuchin missionaries from Italy set up a Mission centre at Patna.

Secondly, the spread of Christianity cannot be attributed to any patronage of the British, because the British Colonial traders were least interested in religion and had not permitted missionaries in their enclaves, unlike the Portuguese colonialists who supported Christian missionary activities in their enclaves elsewhere in India. After acquiring the right of revenue administration of Bengal Province in 1765, following their success over the Mughal forces at the Battle of

Buxar (1764) in Bihar, the British East India Company Government permitted only some chaplains who occasionally visited the European officers, military persons, and traders in Bengal and Bihar. Later in early 19th century, the British administration permitted missionaries which led to the arrival of missionaries of many Protestant Missions in eastern India, including Bihar and Jharkhand. The British being Protestants did support certain Protestant Missions though there was no official policy of patronage or favour to any religion. However, it may be noted that the Catholic Missions were not beneficiaries of the British rulers though some individual officers might have supported them.

Thus, from 17th to 20th centuries, a few Catholic and Protestant missionary societies came and set up Mission centres in various cities and villages, and established Christian communities in undivided Bihar. The story of these Christian Missions recounted in the previous 10 chapters covers the period up to Indian Independence. In this chapter, we take a brief re-look of the summary of this narrative. A short description of each Mission, with the year of its founding in brackets on the subtitle, is given below keeping the chronological sequence and denominational identities.

2. The Catholic Mission in Bihar (1620, 1703)

The earliest Christian Mission in Bihar was the Roman Catholic Mission led by Jesuit missionaries. In the reign of Jahangir (1605-1627), a Portuguese Jesuit missionary, Fr. Simon Figuieredo S.J. arrived at Patna in 1620 from Chandernagore in Bengal, at the invitation of Nawab Mukharrab Khan, the Mughal Viceroy of Bihar. Though the Nawab gave permission to preach in Patna, which was then a flourishing trading town with quite a few European Christian traders, the Jesuit missionaries encountered much hostility from the Muslim gentry, and were forced to close down the Mission in 1621. Thereafter, Jesuit missionaries from Bengal or Agra only visited Patna occasionally.

The next phase of the Christian Mission in Bihar begins only in 1703, when Franciscan missionaries of the Capuchin Order were deputed by the pope to the newly constituted Mission territory of Tibet and the surrounding areas. Traveling from Italy to India by sea, they landed at Chandernagar in Bengal, proceeded to Patna by the Ganges and then proceeded to Lhasa, capital of Tibet, via Bettiah and Kathmandu. Their first Mission centre in Bihar, established at Patna City in 1706, was only a transit house for the traveling missionaries from Chandernagar to Lhasa. In 1713, they built there the first church in Bihar now known as the Padre ki Haveli Church in the Old city of Patna (now called Patna City or Patna Sabib). During the next 60 years, the Capuchins had set up Mission centres in Tibet and Nepal but were forced to close down in 1745 and 1769 respectively. In the meantime, invited by the King of Bettiah, north Bihar, they opened a Mission centre in 1745 at Bettiah and built a church there in 1750. To the small native Catholic community, known as the *Bettiah Christians*, were added some 72 Nepali converts who were sent out from Nepal in 1769 and were settled in Chuhari village north of Bettiah town. Eventually they became part of the Bettiah Christian community.

Adding another Mission centre at Bhagalpur in 1779, the Capuchin Mission had four centres in Bihar till 1845 when Patna was created a Vicariate with a bishop to administer. During the period of its first bishop, Bishop Anastasius Hartmann, the Mission expanded to several cities in Bihar. A few religious Sisters also came to work in the Mission, in the field of education, health care and in other humanitarian works. In 1866, Patna Vicariate was created a diocese with headquarters at Allahabad.

In 1892, the northern section of Bihar was made the Bettiah Prefecture, and was given to the management of the Austrian Capuchins, who for the next 25 years, founded several Mission centres in north Bihar. However, during the First World War, the Austrian missionaries were interned by the British and so the Mission was orphaned, with only eight native diocesan Priests to serve the Church. During this crisis period Jesuit missionaries from America came to help out and so in 1919, a new diocese (Patna Diocese) was created in Bihar including Nepal, under the charge of a new Bishop Louis Van Hoeck, a Belgian Jesuit, of the Ranchi Mission. Bishop Van Hoeck emphasized founding of educational institutions in every Mission centre and founded an indigenous Religious Congregation, called the Sisters of the Sacred Heart, to carry out Mission work in rural areas.

In 1925 Jesuit missionaries from Patna began to evangelize the Santals of Bhagalpur District. In 1928, Fr. James Creane S.J. expanded the Santal Mission to other centres such as Baromasia, Poreya Hat, Gajhi, Harimorha and Narainpur in Santal Parganas District in present-day Jharkhand. Meanwhile, there was a Santal Mission in Purnea District begun in late 19th century, by the Jesuit missionaries of Bengal. Gradually many Mission centres along with educational and public utility institutions were established by the Mission there.

In 1928, when Bishop Van Hoeck was transferred to Ranchi, which was newly made a diocese, an American Jesuit of the Patna Mission, Bishop Bernard Sullivan succeeded. During his period of leadership many more Mission centres were opened in different districts and schools, in most of them. The period also witnessed mass response from the Dalits to the preaching of the missionaries. There was a mass conversion movement in the next three decades during which time a large number of Chamars and other Dalit castes converted to Christianity.

Increase in Church membership naturally entailed establishment of Church institutions such as schools, hospitals, dispensaries, orphanages, etc. For health care work, the Sisters of the Medical Mission from America arrived in 1939 and started the Holy Family Hospital in Patna City. In 1940, the Apostolic Carmel Sisters from Mangalore, opened the Patna Women's College for women's higher education. The Diocese was running nearly 10 schools till the time of Independence.

In 1938 the Bhagalpur section of Patna Diocese with a lot of Santal converts was handed over to the American Franciscan missionaries of the Third Order Regular (TOR Fathers). The American Fathers as well as their Indian members expanded the Santal Mission further which saw tremendous growth in the number of Christians, churches, and institutions.

In June 1947, Rt. Rev. Augustine F. Wildermuth succeeded Bishop Sullivan, at Patna. He invited the Sisters of Charity of Nazereth from the USA to found the Nazereth Hospital at Mokama, east of Patna. By the end of the decade the Diocese achieved great fame for its fine schools, college and hospitals, thanks to the Sisters of many missionary societies.

3. The Catholic Mission in Jharkhand (1868)

The Catholic Mission in Chotanagpur proved to be the biggest and most well-organised Christian Mission in Jharkhand. It commenced its work through the Bengal Mission, headquartered at Calcutta, that had been constituted and placed under the charge of the Belgian Jesuits in 1859. The first Jesuit missionary to enter Chotanagpur was Fr. Stockman, in 1868.

At the instance of Bishop Steins of Calcutta, Fr. Stockman, then at Midnapur in West Bengal, set out for Chaibasa in Chotanagpur to explore the possibility of starting a Mission station for the tribals whom he had met at Midnapur. Fr. Stockman reached Chaibasa on November 24, 1868, studied the situation, went back and came again on July 10, 1869 to found a Mission station there.

The Gossner Mission was already there and the Anglican Mission had just begun at Chaibasa. Fr. Stockman worked entirely among the Hos and the Mundas. Though the response of these tribals to preaching was slow, a few Mundas converted in 1873. From Chaibasa, missionary activity moved towards Ranchi. Other missionaries came and new stations were founded in Ranchi District but the progress of conversion was slow.

With the arrival of a young Jesuit missionary, Fr. Constant Lievens, popularly called 'Libin Saheb', in March 1885, the Catholic Mission to Chotanagpur witnessed rapid and remarkable expansion, and there began a mass-conversion movement. He studied the people and their problems as to help them in their difficulties. The agrarian unrest was at its peak, and, after 1868, the Gossner and Anglican missionaries were lukewarm in their support to the aboriginals in their struggle against zamindars. At such a critical time, Fr. Lievens adopted a new policy for the expansion of the Catholic Mission. He studied the local languages and the land tenure laws and openly and bravely championed the cause of the aboriginals against the unscrupulous exploitation of zamindars. The result was immediate and tremendous. People came to him in crowds to seek his help and to be baptized. Many Lutherans and Anglicans also joined the Catholic

Church. Before his premature death in 1893, the membership in the Catholic Church had risen to 77,000.

Many new stations were founded in Ranchi District. The expansion moved towards the District of Palamau and the Native States of Jashpur and Gangpur. In 1928, Ranchi was made a separate Diocese with Mgr. Louis Van Hoeck as its first Bishop. The Jesuits invited societies of Sisters (Loreto and Ursuline nuns) to work in the Mission. A native society of Sisters (Daughters of St. Ann) was also founded at Ranchi in 1903. These nuns helped expand church work especially among women through education and health care. Inspite of the difficulties in men and money the Catholic Church went on expanding and had some 3,56,903 members in 1947.

The expansion of the Catholic Church in Chotanagpur was the most striking and rare achievement of the Jesuit Fathers, led by Fr. Lievens. Many persons, anxious to be Christians to get assistance, were baptized perhaps without proper instruction. Besides, many Christians of the Gossner and Anglican Missions also joined the Catholic Mission, not necessarily due to any religious conviction, but to get liberation from the oppression of landlords and money-lenders.

Fr. Lievens and some Jesuit missionaries were so enthusiastic about giving help to their converts against the zamindars that some of the local British officers apprehended disturbances in Ranchi District and blamed the Jesuit missionaries for this. The Lieutenant Governor of Bengal, Sir Bayley visited Ranchi and personally saw the things, and his enquiry exposed the baselesness of the charges against the Jesuit missionaries. Any way, there were several cases of judicial conflict between the Jesuit missionaries and British Government officials during November 1889 to March 1890.

Even if the converts were not properly instructed before baptism, it must be admitted that the Mission succeeded splendidly in serving the cause of the illiterate and helpless aboriginal Mundas, Oraons and Kharias against the cruel exploitation by their landlords. The names of Fr. Lievens and Fr. John Baptist Hoffmann would go down in History as the great champions of the rights of the aboriginals of Chotanagpur against the ignorance and apathy of the British officials on the one hand, and the unjust claims and exploitation of the landlords, on the other. In a way, they saved the tribal population from being broken and reduced to poverty and serfdom.

The early Jesuit missionaries realised rightly that education was the best means for removing the main cause of exploitation of the tribals and their backwardness. The Mission, therefore, founded and maintained many Primary, Middle and High Schools, both for boys and girls, all over its area and thus contributed greatly towards the progress of education in Chotanagpur. The best schools in Chotanagpur belonged to the Catholic Mission. It started a College, the St. Xavier's College, in 1944. The Mission conducted many fine and efficient dispensaries and hospitals. The Catholic Bank at Ranchi and the Industrial Schools in various places were for the economic welfare of the people. Many Jesuit Fathers like Hoffmann, Grignard, Smet, Dehon, Bleses, Druart, Floor and others enriched the Mundari, Oraon and Kharia languages and literature. The contribution of Belgian Jesuit Fr. Camile Bulcke to the enrichment of Hindi is a signal missionary contribution to Hindi language. The Mission possessed a modern printing press at Ranchi.

The Fathers, Brothers, and Sisters, Foreign and Indian, belonging to different organisations working in the Catholic Church in Chotanagpur, have abundantly shown the way to live and die in the service of God and Humanity.

4. The Baptist Missionary Society in Bihar (1800)

The Baptist Missionary Society, founded in 1792 in England, began missionary work in Bihar from Serampore in Bengal. In January 1800, Dr. Willaim Carey and his friends made Serampore the headquarters of the Baptist Missionary Society in India. Soon after, the Society sent missionaries to Patna, Danapur, Monghyr and some other places on the Gangetic region. They worked among the upper class Hindus and Muslims.

From the beginning of the 20th century, they started work among the Dalits, like the Chamars, the Doms, Musahars, etc. Mission centres were opened at Gaya, Jahanabad, Nawadah, Tekari, Daudnagar and Aurangabad. Schools and dispensaries were founded at Patna and other centres. Work was also done among women and students at Patna. In 1940, all the churches of the Baptist

Missionary Society in Bihar were organised on a "Union" basis. The Baptist Missionary Society in Bihar contributed greatly towards the development of vernacular literature, like Braj, Hindi and Bengali. Its lithograph press at Monghyr (set up in 1879) printed and published books in Kaithi script.

5. The Church Missionary Society in Bihar and Jharkhand (1826)

At the suggestion of Bishop Heber of Calcutta, the Society for the Propagation of the Gospel (SPG) sent, in 1826, Rev. T. Christian to Bhagalpur to work among the Paharias. He died in 1827 and the work lapsed. In 1850, Rev. E. Droese, a German missionary came to Bhagalpur and worked there for 36 years. He began the Church Missionary Society (CMS) centre at Bhagalpur. He worked among the Paharias and the Santals too. When Rev. E. L. Puxley came, in 1860, to work among the Santals, the CMS Bihar Mission and the CMS Santal Mission followed separate and largely independent courses. The CMS Bihar Mission became a diocese (Diocese of Bhagalpur) in 1943, with Archdeacon Lenman as the first Bishop.

The CMS Bihar Mission with headquarters at Bhagalpur achieved very little in the field of evangelism and conversion but it established and maintained some very efficient and popular schools, like the CMS Boy's High School and the Christ Church Girls' High School, both at Bhagalpur, and St. Mary's Girls' High School with Junior and Senior Training classes, at Deoghar. Rev. Droese enriched the Paharia language by giving it a script.

The CMS Santal Mission was more successful both in conversion and social service. Its headquarters was at Hiranpur in the Pathra sub-division of the District of Santal Parganas. Other stations were Pathra, Barharwa, Taljhari and Bhagya. The CMS Santal Mission conducted several Middle and Primary Schools for boys and girls and thus encouraged and expanded education. It made Santali the medium of instruction in lower classes. The Mission founded two hospitals at Hiranpur, one for men and another for women, and made arrangements for the treatment of leprosy patients at Pathra, Barharwa and Hiranpur. The missionaries, men and women, learnt Santali, and some of them, like Rev. Puxley and Rev. Cole, wrote and published books in Santali and thus developed Santali language and literature.

6. The Gossner Evangelical Lutheran Mission in Bihar and Jharkhand (1840)

The Gossner Evangelical Lutheran Mission (GELM) began work in Bihar in 1840 and founded some Mission centres under its 'Ganges Valley Mission'. But, the Mission was not a success in Bihar. Its great success was in Jharkhand. In November 1845, four German missionaries, sent by Rev. Gossner, sought to evangelise the aboriginals in Jharkhand. They preached but for about four and a half years, nobody joined their Mission. Disappointed, they wanted to go elsewhere but stayed on at the insistence of Rev. Gossner. On June 9, 1850 some tribals responded to their preaching and received baptism.

Thereafter, the number of converts increased steadily because they found that the missionaries had come to help them in their agrarian problems. They were oppressed and exploited by the non-tribal landlords and money lenders. There was much unrest among the aboriginals of Ranchi District. Their socio-economic life and religious belief were rudely shaken. In their perplexity, many turned to the missionaries as a means of achieving liberation from oppression.

During the 'Sepoy Mutiny' (First War of Independence, 1857), the missionaries were suspected by the people and some attacked their Church: they were angered by the British rulers. Leaving the converts in the lurch the missionaries left for Calcutta to save their lives, but came back when the trouble was over. There arose some organizational problems in the next decade. On March 30, 1858, Rev. Gossner died and a committee, known as Home Board or Curatorium was set up in Berlin to manage his Mission. In November 1868, there occurred a split in the Gossner Mission at Ranchi, and six missionaries, mostly seniors, led by Rev. F. Batsch, left the Gossner Mission and, on April 17, 1869, joined the Anglican Mission along with a considerable number of converts.

The Gossner Mission, however, expanded rapidly. On the occasion of the Golden Jubilee in 1895, the Mission had 13 stations and 40,000 Christians scattered in 1,200 villages. At the outbreak of the first World War all the German missionaries were interned in July 1915 and later repatriated to Germany. Before they left Ranchi, they committed the Gossner Church to the care of the Anglican Bishop of Chotanagpur, Rt. Rev. Foss Westcott. When the War ended, the Government of India did not allow the German missionaries to return, and, on July 10, 1919, the *Mahasabha* or General Conference of Gossner Mission declared autonomy from foreign connection. Thus, in 1919, the Gossner Mission came to an end and the Gossner Church began: to be governed by Indian officers and a written Constitution.

The Gossner Church, in spite of financial and internal difficulties, went on growing in the ensuing period. In 1947, the Gossner Church had 1,69,474 baptized Christians and 2357 inquirers.

The Gossner Mission set up the first Christian schools, both for boys and girls, at several places in Chotanagpur and outside and encouraged and spread education. It set up dispensaries, hospitals and asylums for the sick. It rendered the oral tribal languages (Mundari, Oraon, Kharia and Ho) to written languages by giving scripts and printed and published books in those languages. The Mission set up the first printing press of Chotanagpur at Ranchi.

The Gossner Church since 1919, not only preached and made large-scale conversions, but also rendered splendid service to the people, especially the aboriginals of Chotanagpur, in various spheres: agrarian, social, educational, medical, literary, etc., during the one hundred years of its work till 1947. The early missionaries had to labour against many adverse circumstances. The aboriginals of Chotanagpur, among whom they began their work, were regarded as savages and outcasts by their fellow Indians and British officials. The Gossner Mission adopted them and raised their status both as individuals and as a race. It took up their just grievances against their landlords. The Christian converts got rid of the abject feeling of utter helplessness and imbibed a feeling of confidence and a spirit of independence and self-help.

There is no denying the fact that conversion took place mostly among the aboriginals, who had practically nothing to lose except their two century-old extortions and despondency, for a better mode of life. The Christian aboriginals of the Church got opportunity as well as encouragement to free themselves from the fetters of ignorance, economic degradation, moral despair and weakness of will, engendered by two centuries of oppression and repression by zamindars and money-lenders and culpable neglect by their advanced fellow men and the ruling Britishers.

There are some who accuse the missionaries that through conversion they created a new class or tribe of Christian aboriginals, thereby breaking the tribal unity. This is not true. The Christian and Non-Christian aboriginals continued to live together. The tribal feeling was, and continued to be, too strong to be broken by conversion. The different tribes, Munda, Oraon, Kharia and Ho, remained intact. The Mission schools and hospitals benefited both the Christian and Non-Christian aboriginals.

7. The Anglican or S. P. G. Mission in Jharkhand (1842/1868)

The Anglican Mission did not begin afresh. It got an established Mission or community of coverts in the very start. On November 22, 1868, six German missionaries led by Rev. F. Batsch, along with a considerable number of Lutheran converts, withdrew from the Gossner Mission, and were admitted in the Anglican Mission on April 17, 1869. They were placed under the care of the Society for the Propagation of the Gospel. Being Anglican, the new Mission had the full support of the English officials at Ranchi and Doranda.

On June 29, 1869, Rev. J. C. Whitley, an English clergyman, took charge of the Mission. As the number of converts increased, it was elevated to a Diocese (of Chotanagpur) in 1890, with Rev. J. C. Whitley as its first Bishop. In 1900, there were 14,927 baptized Christians and 1,017 inquirers. The Mission celebrated its Golden Jubilee in December 1919. In 1928, the Anglican Church of Chotanagpur became a part of the Provincial Autonomous Church of India, Burma and Ceylon, within the world-wide Anglican Communion.

Like other Missions, the Anglican Mission engaged itself not only in evangelistic and pastoral activities but also in educational, medical, literary and other philanthropic works. It also considered the growth of education as an essential part of Church development. It set up and maintained many Primary, Middle and High Schools for both boys and girls and thus contributed greatly towards the development of education in Chotanagpur. Dispensaries and hospitals were established at Ranchi, Murhu, Kamdara, Itki and Manoharpur for the treatment of the sick. While Bishop Whitley and Bishop Kennedy developed the Mundari language and literature, Rev. E. H. Whitley developed Sadri, the colloquial language of the area and Rev. W. L. Daud Singh and Rev. Abraham Bodra enriched the Ho language and literature.

8. The Santal Mission of the Northern Churches in Jharkhand (1867)

The Santal mission of the Northern Churches was formed, so to say, in a Mission field, as Rev. Edward C. Johnson (Anglican Englishman) a Baptist Mr. Hans Peter Boerresen, and a Dane (Lutheran), accidentally met in a mud-hut at Belbuni in the District of Santal Parganas and decided to start a Mission to Santals with Indian support in 1866. They sought support from their European benefactors who formed Home Boards to support this missionary venture.

On September 26, 1867, the three missionaries settled near the village of Benagaria in the District of Santal Parganas and started Mission work which they called the "Indian Home Mission to the Santals". After the sudden death of Rev. Johnson, the Mission became increasingly Lutheran in character. The period of Indian support ended in 1877. From 1878, the Mission obtained support from the supporting committees which had been formed in England, Scotland, Denmark and Norway.

Beginning with the first converts on March 28, 1869, the number of converts from Santal tribe went on increasing. There began a period of rapid expansion of work. New stations were founded. Work was extended to Assam and North Bengal. When the two founders passed away, the representatives of the supporting committees of Denmark, Norway and the United States met in

1911, framed a new Constitution and renamed the Mission as "The Santal Mission of the Northern Churches."

The third period of the Mission began in 1911. Mission work was extended among the Boros in Assam and the Bengalis of Santal Parganas and Bengal. The Golden Jubilee of the Mission was celebrated in 1917. At the beginning of the Second World War, Denmark and Norway were occupied by Germany and the Mission was in an acute financial difficulty. In 1947, the Mission had 28,703 baptized Christians. As a result of the division of the country, some areas of the Mission in Bengal, went over to East Pakistan (Bangladesh).

The Santal Mission of the Northern Churches engaged not only in evangelism and conversion, but also in educational, medical, literary, social and economic progress and welfare of the people. Its greatest achievement and service have been in the sphere of language and literature. The Mission lifted the whole Santal tribe out of the unknown dark. It 'discovered' the Santals and gave them place and honour in society. With the efforts of the two pioneer missionaries the Government of Bengal passed laws for the protection of the lands and rights of the illiterate Santals from the hands of the landlords and money-lenders. Industrial Schools were set up by the Mission to provide more avenues of employment.

The missionaries of this Mission were great lovers and patrons of the Santali language and literature. Due to their efforts, Santali became a medium of instruction in Primary Schools and a subject up to the Matriculation Standard in Santal Parganas. They reduced the Santali language to writing, primarily for the purpose of preaching and bringing the Gospel to the downtrodden tribe. By doing so, they contributed immensely towards the development of the Santali language and literature. A modern printing press was set up at Benagaria in 1890. Several schools were opened for boys and girls and the Mission spread education among the Santals and non-Santals. The Mission also founded dispensaries, leper colonies and hospitals for the treatment of different kinds of illness, and, in times of famine, conducted relief works and saved the lives of many poor people.

9. The Santal Mission of the Free Church of Scotland in Bihar and Jharkhand (1869)

The Santal Mission of the United Free Church of Scotland began its work at Pachamba in the District of Hazaribagh in 1869 by a group sent by the Free Church Mission in Calcutta. The Santals responded to their preaching and sought baptism and the first five young men received baptism in 1874. Expanding the work, the Mission set up new stations in 1879, at Bamdah in Monghyr District and Pokhuria in Manbhum District. A fourth station was opened at Tisri in Hazaribagh District in 1908.

In 1929, the Mission was renamed as the 'Santal Mission of the Church of Scotland'. Up to 1947, the Mission had four principal stations--Pachamba, Bamdah, Pokhuria and Tisri besides some small out-stations. The Mission achieved very little in the field of evangelism and conversion.

The most notable achievements of the Mission were in the fields of education, medicine and literature. Almost from the very beginning, it engaged in the education of both boys and girls. The Mission achieved much fame in medical sphere. One great feature of the Mission was its strong medical staff. Of the four pioneer missionaries, three were medical men, and up till 1934, the missionary-superintendent of the Mission was a doctor. Three Mission stations had a hospital each. The hospital at Bamdah achieved great name and fame in northern India in eye surgery.

The missionaries used and encouraged the use of Santali in Church work and contributed to its literature. They also enriched Hindi and Bengali. Dr. Andrew Campbell, did marvelous works for the progress of Santali language and literature. The Mission had a printing press of its own at Pokhuria. This Mission stressed more on social and economic service to society than on conversion and enlargement of the Christian community.

10. The Fellowship of Christian Assemblies Mission in Bihar and Jharkhand (1880)

The Fellowship of Christian Assemblies Mission began in 1880 at Jamtara in Santal Parganas District, by a Swedish seaman,

Mr. Cornelius. From Jamtara, work was extended to Mihijam, Karmatanr and Subbonpur in the same District and to some centres in Bhagalpur District. It made very few conversions. The total number of Christians in 1947 was about 330. The type of work carried on by the Mission included schools, dispensaries, leper work and village evangelism.

11. The Methodist Church of Southern Asia in Jharkhand and Bihar (1884)

The Methodist Church of Southern Asia from America started missionary work, as an extension of its work in Bengal, in 1884, at Pakur in Santal Parganas District. Mission work began with the efforts of Mr. Mcleod, who was the Sub-Divisional officer of Pakur. The early Christians were not Santals but Muslims. Through the efforts of the first Muslim convert, Sahoo Munshi, 19 Muslims received baptism in 1886. Later on Santals were more eager to be received into the Church. By 1916, the Santal converts greatly outnumbered others, that is, Muslim and Hindu Bengali converts. In Jharkhand, work was extended to Dhanbad and Gomoh and to Asansol in Bengal. In Bihar region, mission work was started at Muzaffarpur, from where it was extended to Samastipur, Arah and Buxar. The Mission successfully worked among Muslims and Bengalis Hindus and its achievements were mainly on the field of education. Schools for boys and girls were set up at various places in Bihar and Jharkhand.

12. The Zenana Bible and Medical Mission in Bihar (1890)

The Zenana Bible and Medical Mission from England which started work at Patna, in 1890, was primarily concerned with medical work and treatment of the sick. It had very little to do with conversion. The first head of the Mission was Dr. Mackinnon who founded the Duchess of Teck Hospital at Tripolia in Nuranibagh of old Patna City. With financial help from different societies, the Zenana Mission improved the medical service for women and children and expanded health care in midwifery and gynecology. It had training schools for compounders and nurses. The Zenana

Bible and Medical Mission was a ladies' Mission for the welfare of ladies and children.

13. The Dublin University Mission in Jharkhand (1892)

The Dublin University Mission to Chotanagpur from Ireland started on March 8, 1892, at Hazaribagh with the support of the Society for the Propagation of the Gospel and Rt. Rev. J. C. Whitley, the Anglican Bishop of Chotanagpur. The Mission had not to start afresh, as all the Anglican Christians of the Diocese in Hazaribagh District were placed under its care and control. The missionaries were university graduates. They gave public lectures to the educated gentlemen of Hazaribagh town but did not receive positive response from them. In 1947, its membership was only about 2,000.

Nevertheless, the Dublin University Mission was eminently successful in medical and educational fields. The Mission had a strong medical staff from the very start. Dispensaries and hospitals were built at Hazaribagh and other centres. The St. Columba's Zenana Mission Hospital achieved great name for its efficiency. It conducted a Nursing School. Being very educated, the missionaries gave much attention to imparting education. Many Primary, Middle and High Schools were opened. In 1899, the Mission started the first Christian college in undivided Bihar, St. Columba's College, at Hazaribagh. Students from North Bihar, Bengal and Orissa came to study in St. Columba's College. Thus the Dublin Mission contributed much towards higher education also.

14. The Seventh Day Adventist Mission in Jharkhand (1898)

The Seventh Day Adventist Mission from America started work first in Jharkhand at Karmatanr in Santal Parganas District, in 1898. Subsequently, sub-stations were established at Babumahal, Ranchi, Simultala, and Khunti. The work included schools, dispensaries and industries. The Mission had a fine printing press at Karmatanr. It carried on work among Santals, Bengalis, Mundas and Oraons.

15. The British Churches in Jharkhand (1909)

Mr. Paul Singh, an Indian evangelist, under the guidance of an English Christian, R. H. Parker, opened the work of the British Churches of Christ Mission in the District of Palamau, early in 1909, by establishing a small church at Daltonganj. Soon Mr. and Mrs. Percy Pittman from Australia came and worked in the Mission from 1909 to1914. Besides building a church and school at Daltonganj, two out-stations were founded at Garhwa and Laterhar, in 1912. In 1914, when the London Missionary Society relinquished its charge of the station at Dudhi in Uttar Pradesh, Mr. and Mrs. Pittman left Daltonganj to take charge of the station at Dudhi.

In early 1930s, the Mission extended further to Nawadih, Nawa Bhandaria and Baragar. Mr. Penry Pryce and his Indian colleagues made frequent visits to the tribal people of that area, whom they found in a state of extreme poverty, oppressed by landlords and without educational and medical facilities. During famines, the Mission conducted relief programmes supported by Government agencies. From time to time, special medical facilities were provided.

16. The Brethren of Christ Mission in Bihar (1914)

The Brethren of Christ Mission started work in North Bihar in 1914. Three missionaries of this Mission arrived at Madhubani, but moved to Madhepura in 1915. Further, two stations were built, at Saharsa and Supaul. The Kosi river caused much damage to Madhepura Mission. The earthquake of 1934 too damaged the Mission buildings at Saharsa and Supaul. The missionaries at Madhepura established contact with the Santals in the east of the Darbhanga District. The first Santal was baptized in April 1945 in his own village. The Mission conducted schools and orphanages at several places.

17. The Assembly of God Mission in Bihar and Jharkhand (1914)

The Assembly of God Mission came from America in 1914, first to Bihar at Chapra, in Saran District. In 1918, work was extended to Bettiah, West Champaran District. In 1922, work started at Laheriasarai in Darbhanga District. Extending to Jharkhand, Rev.

and Mrs. D. S. Mahaffey opened a Mission station at Chutupalu in Ranchi District, in 1927. Further stations were opened at Ramgarh (1938) and at Jamshedpur (1942). The Assembly of God Mission carried on Mission work, here and there, in a disconnected way. It was mainly concerned with conducting schools for both boys and girls.

18. Assessment of the Christian Missions in Bihar and Jharkhand

As noted in the beginning of this chapter, Christian Mission in Bihar began before the arrival of the British as administrators of Bengal Province in 1765. The English East India Company Government, as a matter of policy, did not permit missionaries to enter the Province till 1813, when it allowed them to impart English education. However, by 1833 the need of missionaries was realized and they were allowed to preach Christianity. Since then, a few Protestant and Catholic Missions entered Bihar, which was then under the Bengal Province of the British. These missionaries from Europe, North America and Australia, belonged to different nationalities and denominations. Over the years, the various Christian Missions founded by missionaries from abroad, took roots in Indian soil, and have been managed by their Indian successors in an eminent way. Also, most of the Missions became autonomous societies without having foreign dependence under the management of Indians especially after Indian Independence.

These missionaries tried to convert the upper class Indians, both Hindus and Muslims, in the Gangetic region. This was natural because this region was more easily accessible in those days, and, many Europeans had settled here and there, as merchants, planters, civil officers and soldiers. But they achieved very little success. After the Santal Rebellion (1855) and the 'Sepoy Mutiny' (First War of Independence) in 1857, both Roman Catholic and Protestant missionaries directed their attention and strength more towards the conversion of the hilly and aboriginal tribes of Chotanagpur Division and Santal Parganas District. Later, they evangelized the Depressed Classes (Dalits) of the plains. They achieved immediate and significant success among both Tribals and Dalits.

The missionaries generally preached, taught and healed. Some of them stressed more on teaching and healing than on preaching. As conversions increased they built churches, schools and hostels for imparting education to both boys and girls. Education was made available even to the lowest person in society. They acted as pioneers in the realm of female education in Bihar. They also founded dispensaries, hospitals and leper asylums or clinics for the treatment of the sick, men and women, of all castes and creeds. They did not discard the leprosy patients hitherto ostracized by their own kith and kin and the general society.

The Christian missionaries adopted the local languages in Mission work, studied them scientifically and committed them to writing. No such attempt had been made in this direction before their arrival. Whatever had been done so far for the tribal languages and literature, has been done by the missionaries. In the District of Santal Parganas, Santali became the medium of instruction in schools. While Lord Macaulay stood for English and rejected vernaculars as medium of instruction in schools and colleges, the Christian missionaries stood for the tribal and local languages. It may be argued that they adopted the tribal languages with the purpose of making their preaching more effective. Though they were motivated by evangelistic aims, it cannot be denied that under their patronage, tribal languages and literature made tremendous progress. Their desire to translate the Bible into every possible language resulted in the development of Hindi, Bengali, Urdu, Santali, Paharia, Mundari, Oraon and other languages and literatures in Bihar and Jharkhand.

Measures were also taken by the Christian Missions for the economic welfare of their converts and the people around them. Industrial Schools, Agricultural Schools, Lace Schools and Training Schools were founded. Missionaries helped their converts in retaining their rights on lands against the unjust claims and oppression of their landlords.

The methods of work employed by the Christian Missions were as varied as the needs of the people. They carried on a relentless war against illiteracy, disease and poverty. They effected change for the better in the mode of life of the converts. The poor and low caste people, the Dalits, the illiterate and the oppressed aboriginal people had nothing to lose except their age-long social degradation, bondage and negligence in favour of a more dignified way of life.

The Indian public generally appreciated the Christian service in the social, economic, educational and medical fields, but tended not to understand why this is linked with a desire to preach the Gospel and to baptise those who voluntarily seek to follow Christ. The missionary who dedicated his/her life was doing so because he/she was imbibed with the ideals of Christ. Naturally he/she invites others to follow Christ's ideals. It is part of the vocation of a missionary to share with others the spiritual gifts he has received from his Lord and Master in humility and love and without any ulterior motive. Looked at from this point of view, it will be seen that Christian service and evangelistic work formed an integrated whole in Christian witness. This Christian duty urged the Christian Missions, Churches and missionaries to start and continue missionary activities in Bihar, Jharkhand and other places. For this, the missionaries left their homes and countries, worked hard and had to suffer physical and mental inconveniences and pain. Some of them were brutally tortured and suffered martyrdom.

Besides, the efforts of the missionaries also seem to have led the general Indian public to introspect within in the light of the new ethical values propagated by the missionaries. This led to many internal reforms within the Hindu society. The activities and success of the Christian Missions among Dalits, aboriginals and the depressed-class people, have led the upper class Indians to change their attitude towards the latter from one of neglect and indifference to that of empathy and fellow-feeling.

The Christian Missions, whatever might have been their objectives, have shown how altruism and empathy can bring relief to the suffering humanity. The work among the leprosy patients whom the general Indian society shunned, not only helped the patients, but also changed the mindset of the general public. So also, nursing care to the sick was elevated as a noble profession, thanks to the missionaries. All the public utility institutions run by the missionaries were accessible to Christians and Non-Christians irrespective of caste or creed. Thus, the Christian Missions in Bihar and Jharkhand have contributed much to nation building. The impact of the work of the missionaries can be better assessed by studying the socio-economic, educational, occupational mobility and development achieved by the convert communities. Since the scope of this study is limited to the Missions, using mostly missionary sources, this topic needs a separate study. Indeed quite a few such studies from the perspective of the Christian communities have been done since the completion of this study.

End

Appendix-1

Note on Church Sources

The most valuable sources on Christianity in Bihar and Jharkhand are available in Church archives in India and abroad. Since the Christian Missions were founded abroad and expanded to non-Christian counties, the missionaries who were originally mostly European, kept the records both in the Mission headquarters and their offices in their home counties. It is noticed that Mission sources are definitely missionary-oriented, describing the work of the missionaries, with only peripheral mention of the native collaborators and converts. Even so, the documents in the form of letters, annual or regular reports, chronicles, registers of marriage, baptism, death, etc., are immensely valuable as practically no details of Christian activities can be obtained from Non-Christian or Government sources.

Church Sources listed here below are arranged according to their congregational origin and contents. That is, these sources can be seen as neatly falling into a church-wise category. We shall list them according to this category. The sources are various types: compiled, authored, or in the form of MSS documents written by anon, printed souvenirs, etc. Some of these are typed and unpublished.

1. The Catholic Mission in Bihar

1) Dent, Paul, S. J., (1937), *A Brief History of Patna Mission,* (cyclostyled, bound and unpublished), Patna Jesuit Archives, St. Xavier's, Patna.
   Fr. Paul Dent, S. J., an American Jesuit, jointed the Diocese of Patna in 1926. He has been a historian. He has tried to write the history of the Roman Catholic Mission at Patna, on the basis of original sources. In *A Brief History of Patna Mission* he has traced, in detail, the origin and development of the Capuchin Mission in Bihar from 1620 to about 1914.
2) Saldanha, Charles P., S.J., (1960), *Roman Catholic Mission in Bihar (Diocese of Patna),* (typed and unpublished), Patna Jesuit Archives, St. Xavier's, Patna.
3) Saldanha, Charles P., S.J., (1975), *History Sketch of Patna Diocese for our field* (typed and unpublished), Patna Jesuit Archives, St. Xavier's, Patna.
   Fr. C. P. Saldanha, S. J., joined the Patna Mission in 1936. When St. Xavier's College at Ranchi was started in July 1944, he became its first Principal for a short period. In his first article, *Roman Catholic Mission in Bihar (Diocese of Patna),* he has traced the history of the Patna Mission from 1620 to 1958. In his second article, *History Sketch of the Patna Mission for our field,* he has discussed the development of the Patna Mission from 1914 onwards. Both the articles are very authoritative and systematic.
4) Extracts from *Catholicus* (official newsletter of the Catholic Church of Allahabad Diocese) from December 1921 to January 1922, quoted in the *Patna Mission Letter,* No.2, February 1922, p. b-2a.
5) McGarry, Monsignor Urban (1960), *The Catholic Mission in the Bhagalpur District and Adjacent Santal Areas* (typed and unpublished MSS), Bhagalpur.
6) Fortelli, J. S. J. (1960), *The Catholic Mission to the Santali Land of the Districts of Purnea and Santal Parganas* (Typed and unpublished MSS).

Fr. J. Portelli, S.J., joined the Catholic Mission to the Santaliland at about 1939, and later, became its Superior. In this article, he has given the history of the origin, gradual development and works of the Mission from 1918 to 1960.

2. The Catholic Mission in Jharkhand

1) Josson, Henry (1921), *La Mission Du Bangale Occidental,* Bruges (Brussels).
   Fr. Henry Josson, S.J., joined the Roman Catholic Mission in Chotanagpur, in 1889, as a missionary and remained there as such till 1912. He compiled his book in French in two volumes from the letters and diaries of the Catholic missionaries in Chotanagpur. They are available at the Catholic archives, Ranchi. They give, in detail, the origin and development of the Catholic Mission in Chotanagpur.
2) Hoffmann, John Baptist (1923), *37 Jahre Missioner in Indien*, Innsbruck West Germany.
   Fr. John Baptist Hoffmann, S.J., was a German Catholic missionary in Chotanagpur from 1893 to 1915. He was a great Mundari scholar. In this book, written in German, he has given his experiences as a missionary and also in formations about the Roman Catholic Mission in Chotanagpur from 1878 to 1915.
3) Hoffmann, John Baptist, *Encyclopaedia Mundarica* in 13 volumes, published by Government of Bihar, Patna, during 1930-1950. It describes in a very authoritative manner, the history, customs, practices, etc., of the Mundas.
4) *Nishkalanka* (Immaculate), a Hindi Monthly, published by the Catholic Press, Ranchi, from 1922 to 1947.
5) Tucker, Victor, *The Catholic Church of Chotanagpur* (A brief sketch, typed and unpublished MSS), dated March 1, 1961).
   Fr. V. Tucker, S.J., was a very successful missionary of the Roman Catholic Mission in Chotanagpur. The article deals with the origin, development and different activities of the Catholic Mission in Chotanagpur from 1869 to 1953.

6) *A Short Historical Survey of the Catholic Mission in Chotanagpur*, Manresa House, Ranchi, dated May, 1, 1962. The article, typed and unpublished MSS, seems to have been prepared by the Jesuits in Manresa House, the official residence of the Superior of the Jesuit Mission in Chotanagpur. It narrates the history of the origin and development of the Catholic Mission in Chotanagpur from 1868 to 1961.

3. The Baptist Missionary Society in Bihar

1. *Annual Report of the Calcutta Missionary Society*, 1836, 1839 and 1857, (Baptist Mission), Calcutta.
2. *The Oriental Baptist*, July 1847 and Vol. XII, 1858.
3. *A Report of the Baptist Mission in India,* 1854.
4. *The Indian Reports of the Baptist Mission Society: North India Report* 1888, 1892, 1901, 1903-1904, 1908-1909, 1914-1916, 1920 and 1930.
5. *Minutes of the North India Conference* held at New Delhi, February 28 - March 1, 1932
6. Buyers, William, *Recollections of Northern India*, London, 1848.
   Rev. William Buyers was a missionary at Benares. He traveled in Bihar and saw by himself the life of the people, Hindus, Muslims and Christians, of the Gangetic region in the beginning of the 19th century.
7. John, Philip, *The Baptist Missionary Society in Bihar*, (typed and unpublished), 1960.
   Rev. Philip John was an Indian Priest of the Baptist Mission at Patna for many years and also the President of the Bihar Christian Council. His article gives a detailed history of the Baptist Mission in Bihar from the beginning up to 1956.

4. The Church Missionary Society in Bihar and Jharkhand

1. *Annual Reports of the Church Missionary Society, 1860, 1863-1864, 1866-1867 and 1884,* Calcutta.
2. *Calcutta Diocesan Committee of the Society Report, 1860,* Calcutta.

3. *Proceedings of the C.M.S, 1903-1904: Statistics of the Bengal Mission, 1903.*
4. Taylor, F. L. (1960), *The Church in the Diocese of Bhagalpur* (typed and unpublished, MSS).
   Ven, F. L. Taylor was a missionary, and later on, Archdeacon of the Diocese of Bhagalpur. His article deals, in detail, with the origin and growth of the Diocese of Bhagalpur, from the beginning up to 1955.
5. Taylor, F. L. (1961), *Diocese of Bhagalpur C.M.S. Santal Mission, 1860-1960*, Bhagalpur. This brochure gives a brief sketch of a hundred years' work of the C.M.S. Santal Mission.

5. The Gossner Evangelical Lutheran Church in Bihar and Jharkhand

Note:- The Gossner Mission (Church since 1919) had valuable archival documents in Berlin and Ranchi. The records in the Berlin archives were destroyed in the Second World War and most of the records in the Ranchi archives were, in course of time, lost or destroyed due to frequent internal disturbances as well as changes in the Church.

1. *Die Biene auf dem Missions felde fur Missions*, Germany. This monthly periodicals of the Gossner Mission from 1846 to 1891, contain letters of the missionaries and annual reports of the Mission.
2. *Report of the Chota Nagpore Mission* (name originally given to Gossner Mission) for the year 1866, printed at Serampore in 1867.
3. *Gossner Mission Reports* for 1870 and 1874, Ranchi.
4. *Gharbandhu*, the official monthly paper of the Mission, 1893-1912, 1916-1922, 1933-1942, Ranchi.
5. *Proceedings of the Advisory Board of the G.E.L. Church* from 1919 to 1928.
6. *Chota Nagpore Mission Quarterly Paper,* No.1, February 1874.
7. *Annual Reports of the Chotanagpur Mission*, 1895 and 1904, S.P.G. Mission, Ranchi.
8. *Chotanagpur Diocesan Report*, January 1916.

9. Mullens, Joseph (1863), *A Brief Review of Ten Years' Missionary Labour in India Between 1852 to 1861*, London. Dr. Joseph Mullens was a contemporary missionary, who came to Ranchi in April 1862 to settle the quarrel between the Curatorium and the German missionaries at Ranchi. The book gives a picture of the early activities of the Gossner Mission in Chotanagpur.
10. Cave, Brown, J., *The Chotanagpur Mission*, Calcutta, 1870.
11. Mitchell, Murray (Mrs.) (1871), *A Missionary's Wife among the Wild Tribes of South Bengal*, London.
Mrs. Murray Mitchell, wife of a Scottish missionary, Dr. Murray Mitchell, accompanied her husband in his visit to Hazaribagh and Ranchi in January 1869. Her book contains a description of the Christian worship and life of the aboriginal Christians at Singhani, near Hazaribagh, and at Ranchi.
12. Nottrott, A. (1874), *Die Gossnersche Mission unter den Kolhs (The Gossner Mission among the Kols),* Halle.
Rev. A. Nottrott came to Ranchi as a missionary of Gossner Mission in 1867. Later, he became the head of the Gossner Mission in Chotanagpur and retired in 1913. His book on the Gossner Mission in Chotanagpur, in German language, is valuable for the period it covers.
13. Sherring, M. A. (1884), *The History of the Protestant Missions in India,* Religious Tract Society, London.
Rev. M. A. Sherring was a missionary at Benares and Mirzapur during the 'Sepoy Mutiny'. His book gives details of the Mission work in Bihar, including Chotanagpur, up to the period it covers.
15. *Wueste, E., Chotanagpur Ki Masihi Mandli ka Itihas* (History of the Chotanagpur Christian Community), *1845-1870*, Ranchi.
Rev. E. Wueste was a German missionary of the Gossner Mission at Ranchi. His book in Hindi gives a brief history of the Gossner Mission from 1845 to 1870.
17. Sheetal, Kushalmay (1939), *Chotanagpur Ki Kalishya Ka Brittant* (Newsletter of the Chotanagpur Church), Ranchi.

Rev. Kushalmay Sheetal was one of the early aboriginal converts of the Gossner Mission. He was an eye-witness to the origin, development and the split in the GEL Mission. He followed the seceding German Lutheran missionaries in 1868, joined the Anglican Mission and later became a Priest. After his retirement, he wrote its history up to 1890.

6. The Anglican/S. P. G Mission in Jharkhand

1. *Report of the Chotanagpur Mission for the year 1866,* (Serampore Press, 1867), Ranchi.
2. *Annual Reports of the Chotanagpure Mission*, 1870-1947, Ranchi.
3. *Chotanagpure Mission Quarterly Paper,* No. 1, February 1874, Ranchi.
4. *Chotanagpure Mission Quarterly Paper,* No. 3, November, 1874, Ranchi.
5. *Chotanagpur Dut Patrika*, a Monthly Paper in Hindi, 1878-1947, Anglican Archives Ranchi.
6. *Chotanagpur Diocesan Paper*, a Quarterly in English, 1914-1947, Ranchi.
7. Cave-Browne, J., *The Chotanagpur Mission,* 1870, Calcutta. Rev. J. Cave-Brown was the officiating secretary of the Society for the Propagation of the Gospel in Calcutta. He came to Ranchi on April 16, 1869, along with Bishop Milman, the Metropolitan of India in Calcutta, to witness the memorable function in which the seceding German Lutheran missionaries and their native followers were admitted to the Anglican Mission. His book contains many useful information about the Gossner Mission from 1845 to 1868 and also about the establishment of the Anglican Mission in Chotanagpur.
8. Sheetal, Kushalmay (1939), op. cit.
9. Chatterton, Eyre (1901), *A Story of Fifty Years' Mission Work in Chotanagur*, London: available at Dublin University Mission, Hazaribagh.
10. Whitley, E. H. (1896), *Historical Sketches. No. II: Chota Nagpore, S.P.G. Mission*, London.

Rev. E. H. Whitley came to Ranchi in 1869 with his father Rev. (later Bishop) J.C. Whitley and became a missionary of the Anglican Mission in Chotanagpur, His sketches give, in brief, the missionary work in Chotanagpur from 1845 up to the period they cover.

7. The Santal Mission of the Northern Churches in Jharkhand

1. *Annual Reports of the Mission* 1867-1947, (Northern Churches), Benagaria.
   The first two annual reports were edited by Rev. Edward C. Johnson and they deal mostly of the period before September 26, 1867. The *15th Annual Report* for the year 1916-1917 has been very helpful in preparing this book.
2. Gausdal, Johannes (1953), *Ebeneser Evangelikal Lutheran Church,* Benagaria.
   Rev. Johannes Gausdal, a Norwegian missionary joined the Santal Mission in November 1915 and continued to serve it, even after independence, and became the first General Superintendent of the Mission, when a new constitution was adopted in 1950. His book in Santali gives the history of the origin and development of the Mission from 1867 to 1951.
3. Skrefsrud, L. O., *The Traditions and Institutions of the Santals,* (in Santali), 1st edition in 1887. Reprint with a few additions in 1916, Benagaria.
   Rev. Lars Olsen Skrefsrud, one of the three pioneer missionaries, died in 1910 after 43 years of service. He was a great scholar of Santali language and of Santals in Calcutta. His book is the most authoritative book on the traditions, customs and institutions of the Santals.

8. The Santal Mission of the United Free Church of Scotland in Bihar and Jharkhand

1. *Annual Reports of the Santal Mission of United Free Church of Scotland, 1873-1947,* Pachamba.

2. Macphail, J. M., *Missions of the United Free Church of Scotland* (also in Santali), 1904, Pokhuria.
3. Macphail, J. M., *Rev. Andrew Campbell, D. D., Missionary to the Santals*, Edinburgh: It is available at Pachamba, (n. d.)
   Dr. J. M. Macphail joined the Mission in 1889, and after forty years of service died and was buried at Bamdah. His books deal with the early history of the Mission and the life and works of Dr. Andrew Campbell.
4. Macphail, R. M., *The Santal Mission,* Pachamba, (n. d.)
   Dr. R. M. Macphail, son of Dr. J. M. Macphail was born at Bamdah and educated in Scotland. After twenty years, he returned to Bamdah in 1925 and worked as a medical missionary at Bamdah for many years. His book gives a short history of the Mission.
5. Campbell, Andrew (1902), *The Santali Dictionary,* Pokhuria.
   Rev. (Dr.) Andrew Campbell came to work in the Mission in 1872 and after about 47 years, died and was buried at Pokhuria in 1919. His dictionary depicts the life and culture of the Santals.
6. *Bamdah Christian Hospital* (1970), Bamdah, Santal Parganas.
7. *Sight for the Blind, The Story of Bamdah Hospital,* (n. d.), Bamdah, Santal Parganas.

9. The Dublin University Mission in Jharkhand

1. *Annual Reports of the Dublin University Mission to Chota Nagpore*, 1890-1947.
2. *Annual Reports of the Chotanagpur Mission*, 1892-1947, Dublin University Mission, Hazaribagh.
3. *Chotanagpur Diocesan Papers 1914-1947.*
4. Chatterton, Eyre, *A Story of Fifty Years' of Mission Work in Chotanagpur*, 1901, London.
   Rt. Rev. Eyre Chatterton was the first Head of the Dublin University Mission to Chotanagpur from 1891 to 1900. He resigned and became the Bishop of Nagpur. His book (available at the D.U. Mission, Hazaribagh) gives a history

of the Christian missionary work in Chotanagpur from 1845 up to the period it covers.

5. Kennedy, K. W. S. (1939), *Fifty Years of Chotanagpur Mission*, Ireland.
   Rev. (Dr.) K.W. Kennedy was one of the original members of the Dublin University Mission to Chotanagpur. He resigned in 1904, joined the Anglican Mission to Chotanagpur and became its Bishop from 1926 to 1936. His book gives a vivid picture of the fifty years' work of the Dublin University Mission to Chotanagpur.

10. Other Churches in Bihar and Jharkhand

10.1 Fellowship of the Christian Assemblies Mission in Jharkhand and Bihar

1. Crawford, W., *The Fellowship of Christian Assemblies in Bihar*, 1960, (typed and unpublished MSS).
   Mr. W. Crawford was the Superintendent of the Mission at Mihijam in the District of Santal Parganas. He has given a very brief history of the Mission from 1880 to 1960.

10.2 The Methodist Church of Southern Asia in Bihar

1. *Minutes of Bengal Conference,* 1897, 1926, 1941 and 1954, Calcutta.
2. *Minutes of Bengal Women's Conference*, 1913, 1919, 1921, 1924 and 1929, Calcutta.
3. *Minutes of Lucknow Conference*, 1921, Lucknow.
4. Badley, B.H., *India Missionary Directory and Memorial Volume,* 3rd edition 1886, Methodist Publishing House, Calcutta.
5. Badley, Brenton Thoburn, *Visions and Victories in Hindustan,* Methodist Publishing House, Madras, 1931.
   Bishop Brenton Thoburn Badley, eldest son of Rev. B.H. Badley, was born and brought up in India. After serving the Methodist Church in India in many capacities, he was elected a Bishop in 1924. He was a fluent and forceful speaker both in Hindustani and English.

10.3 The Zenana Bible and Medical Mission in Bihar

1. *Golden Jubilee 1895-1945*, Zenana Bible Medical Mission, The Union Press, Patna, 1945.
   The booklet, printed by the Mission, on the occasion of its Golden Jubilee in 1945, narrates the history and works of the Mission in Bihar from 1890 to 1945.

10.4 The Seventh-day Adventist Mission in Jharkhand

1. Das, R. N., (1960), *A Brief History of the Seventh-day Adventist Work in Bihar* (typed and unpublished MSS).
   Mr. R. N. Das, a senior Indian missionary of the Mission, has given a description of the origin, development and works of the Mission from 1898 to 1960.

10.5 The British Churches of Christ Mission in Jharkhand

1. Skillicorn, Keith, *History of the British Churches of the Christ Mission and Churches of Christ (National) in Palamau, Bihar,* 5th July, 1960, (typed and unpublished MSS).
   Mr. Keith Skillcorn, a senior missionary, working in the Mission at Nawa Bhandria, Palamau, has given a brief sketch of the work of the Mission in the District of Palamau from 1909 to 1960.

10.6 Brethren in Christ Mission in Bihar

1. Anon, *History of the Brethren in Christ Mission in Bihar,* 1960 (unpublished typed MSS).

10.7 The Assembly of God Mission in Bihar and Jharkhand

1. Somaiya, M. C. (1960), *The Assembly of God Mission* (typed and unpublished), Jamshedpur.
   Rev. M. C. Somaiya joined the Mission in 1942 and started work at Jamshedpur.

Appendix-2

Chronology of the Missions

A. Christian Missions in Present-day Bihar: in Chronological Order

1. Catholic Mission in Bihar, 1620.
2. Baptist Mission Society in Bihar, 1812.
3. Church Missionary Society in Bihar, 1826.
4. Gossner Evangelical Lutheran Mission in Bihar, 1838.
5. Santal Mission of the United Free Church of Scotland in Bihar, 1878.
6. Fellowship of Christian Assemblies Mission in Bihar, 1880.
7. Zenana Bible and Medical Mission in Bihar, 1882.
8. Methodist Church in Bihar, 1885.
9. Anglican Mission in Bihar, 1902.
10. Brethren of Christ Mission in Bihar, 1914.
11. Assembly of God in Bihar, 1914.

B. Christian Missions in Present-day Jharkhand: in Chronological Order

1. Anglican Mission in Jharkhand, 1842.
2. Gossner Evangelical Lutheran Mission in Jharkhand, 1845.
3. Santal Mission of the Northern Churches in Jharkhand, 1866.
4. Church Missionary Society in Jharkhand, 1868.
5. Catholic Mission in Jharkhand, 1869.
6. Santal Mission of the United Free Church of Scotland in Jharkhand, 1869.
7. Fellowship of Christian Assemblies Mission in Jharkhand, 1880.
8. Methodist Church in Jharkhand, 1884.
9. Dublin University Mission in Jharkhand, 1892.
10. Seventh Day Adventist Mission in Jharkhand, 1898.
11. British Churches of Christ's Mission in Jharkhand, 1909.
12. Assembly of God in Jharkhand, 1927.

C. Founding of the Missions in Bihar and Jharkhand till 1947: in Chronological Order

1. 1620: Catholic Mission in Bihar; Catholic Mission in Jharkhand (1869).
2. 1825: Baptist Mission Society in Bihar.
3. 1826: Church Missionary Society in Bihar and Jharkhand.
4. 1838: Gossner Evangelical Lutheran Mission in Bihar: GEL Mission in Jharkhand (1845).
5. 1842: Anglican Mission in Jharkhand and Bihar.
6. 1866: Santal Mission of the Northern Churches in Jharkhand.
7. 1869: Santal Mission of the United Free Church of Scotland in Jharkhand and Bihar.
8. 1880: Fellowship of Christian Assemblies Mission in Jharkhand and Bihar.
9. 1882: Zenana Bible and Medical Mission in Bihar.
10. 1884: Methodist Church in Jharkhand and Bihar.
11. 1892: Dublin University Mission in Jharkhand.

12. 1898: Seventh Day Adventist Mission in Jharkhand.
13. 1909: British Churches of Christ's Mission in Jharkhand.
14. 1914: Brethren of Christ Mission in Bihar.
15. 1914: Assembly of God in Bihar and Jharkhand.

D. Year of Founding of the Missions with Locations (Bihar and Jharkhand)

1. a) **Catholic Mission in Bihar**: Phase-I (1620-21) (C/o Jesuits); Catholic Mission in Bihar-Phase II (1703-1919) (C/o Capuchins); Catholic Mission in Bihar: Phase III (1919-ff.) C/o Jesuits.
   b) **Catholic Mission** in **Jharkhand:** (chaplaincy service at Hazaribagh, 1865) at Chaibasa, 1869 (C/o Jesuits).
2. **Baptist Mission Society:** preaching at Patna-Danapur, 1812; at Monghyr, 1825.
3. **Church Missionary Society in Bihar and Jharkhand:** at Bhagalpur (among *Paharias*), 1826 c/o SPG; among Santals in 1856; CMS Bihar Mission & CMS Santal Mission worked separately since mid 1850s; CMS at Pathra (Godda), 1868.
4. **Gossner Evangelical Lutheran Mission in Bihar and Jharkhand:** (Ist Mission at Patna, 1838; IInd Mission at Patna, 1840 (formed as "Ganges Valley Mission": closed down during World War I-members joined other Missions); Gossner Evangelical Lutheran Mission in Jharkhand: Ranchi, 1845.
5. **Anglican Mission in Jharkhand and Bihar:** at Hazaribagh, 1842-C/o SPG; emerged from GEL Split in 1869; at Bettiah, 1902.
6. **Santal Mission of the Northern Churches in Jharkhand:** (started as "India Home Mission" among Santals at Benagaria (Santal Parganas), 1866-1867; Santals in Assam, 1888; Boros in West Bengal, 1888.
7. **Santal Mission of the United Free Church of Scotland in Jharkhand and Bihar:** at Pachamba (Giridih), 1869; at Chakai (Monghyr-Bihar), 1878.

8. **Fellowship of Christian Assemblies Mission in Jharkhand and Bihar:** among Santals at Jamtara (Jharkhand) and Bhagalpur, 1880.
9. **Zenana Bible and Medical Mission in Bihar:** at Bhagalpur, 1882; at Jamalpur, 1887, at Tripolia (Patna City), 1890.
10. **Methodist Mission in Jharkhand and Bihar:** at Pakur (Jharkhand), 1884; at Arah, Buxar, Samastipur, 1885 + Women's Foreign Missionary Society assisted (1910s).
11. **Dublin University Mission in Jharkhand:** (at Hazaribagh (c/o Anglicans); Anglicans comprised the first members of this Mission, 1892.
12. **Seventh Day Adventist Mission in Jharkhand:** among Santals at Karmatanr (Santal Parganas), 1898.
13. **British Churches of Christ's Mission in Jharkhand:** at Daltonganj, 1909.
14. **Brethren of Christ Mission in Bihar:** at Saharsa, 1914; Madhepura (among Santals), 1915.
15. **Assembly of God Mission in Bihar and Jharkhand:** at Chapra, 1914; at Ranchi, 1927.

E. Some 'Firsts' in the Christian History of Bihar and Jharkhand

- First Christian **Mission** in undivided Bihar (including Jharkhand): Catholic (Jesuit) Mission at Patna, 1620.
- First Christian **church** in undivided Bihar (including Jharkhand): Catholic Church, Patna City, 1713.
- First **Protestant Mission** in undivided Bihar (including Jharkhand): chaplaincy service at Patna by Church Missionary Society: 1678.
- First **Protestant church** in Jharkhand: St. Stephen's Church at Hazaribagh-1842 C/o Anglican Church.
- First **Protestant Diocese** in undivided Bihar (including Jharkhand): Church Missionary Society-Bhagalpur Diocese, 1843.
- First **Catholic Diocese** in undivided Bihar (including Jharkhand): Patna Vicariate, 1845.

- First **Protestant church** in Bihar: St. Luke's Church, Danapur, 1845.
- First **Christian Mission** to work among **Tribals (Paharias)**: 1826 by the Society for the Propagation of the Gospel/ CMS.
- First Christian Mission to work among **Dalits (Chamars**: 1908; Doms: 1915) by Baptist Missionary Society.

Bibliography

A. Primary Sources

A. 1 Mission Reports

1. *A Report of the Baptist Mission in India,* 1854, Baptist Church Archives, Calcutta.
2. *Annual Reports of the Dublin University Mission to Chota Nagpore,* 1890-1947, DUM Archives, Hazaribagh.
3. *Annual Reports of the Santal Mission of United Free Church of Scotland, 1873-1947,* Pachamba.
4. *Minutes of the North India Conference* held at New Delhi, February 28-March 1, 1932,
5. *Proceedings of the Advisory Board of the G.E.L. Church* from 1919 to 1928, GEL Archives, Ranchi.
6. *Proceedings of the C.M.S, 1903-1904: Statistics of the Bengal Mission, 1903.*
7. *The Indian Reports of the Baptist Mission Society: North India Report* 1888, 1892, 1901, 1903-1904, 1908-1909, 1914-1916, 1920 and 1930, Baptist Mission Archives, Delhi.
8. *Annual Reports of the Mission* 1867-1947, (Northern Churches), Benagaria.

9. *Annual Reports of the Chotanagpure Mission*, 1870-1947, GEL Archives, Ranchi.
10. *Annual Reports of the Chotanagpur Mission*, 1892-1947, Dublin University Mission, Hazaribagh.
11. *Annual Reports of the Church Missionary Society, 1860, 1863-1864, 1866-1867 and 1884,* CMS Archives, Calcutta.
12. *Calcutta Diocesan Committee of the Society Report, 1860*, CMS Archives, Calcutta.
13. *Report of the Chotanagpur Mission for the year 1866:* GEL Archives, Ranchi.
14. *Chotanagpur Diocesan Report*, January 1916 (Gossner Mission).
15. *Minutes of Lucknow Conference*, 1921, (Methodist Church Archives), Lucknow.
16. *Annual Reports of the Calcutta Missionary Society*, 1836, 1839 and 1857 (Baptist Mission), Calcutta.
17. *Gossner Mission Reports* for 1870 and 1874, Ranchi.
18. *Annual Reports of the Chotanagpur Mission*, 1895 and 1904, S.P.G. Mission, Ranchi.
19. *Minutes of Bengal Women's Conference*, 1913, 1919, 1921, 1924 and 1929, (Methodist Church Archives, Calcutta.
20. *Minutes of Bengal Conference,* 1897, 1926, 1941 and 1954, (Methodist Church Archives), Calcutta.

A. 2 Mission Documents

1. *A Short Historical Survey of the Catholic Mission in Chotanagpur*, Manresa House, Ranchi, dated May, 1, 1962.
2. Anon, *History of the Brethren in Christ Mission in Bihar*, 1960 (unpublished typed MSS).
3. Anon, *History of Christianity in India with its Prospectus*, S.P.C.K. Press, Madras, 1895.
4. *Bamdah Christian Hospital* (1970), (United Free Church of Scotland Archives), Bamdah, Santal Parganas.

5. *Chotanagpur me Anglikan Kalishya ki Shatbarshiye Jayanti* (Birth Centenary of the Anglican Church of Chotanagpur), 1869-1969, Diocese of Chotanagpur, Ranchi (1969).

6. Crawford, W., *The Fellowship of Christian Assemblies in Bihar*, 1960 (typed and unpublished MSS).

7. Das, R. N. (1960), *A Brief History of the Seventh-day Adventist Work in Bihar* (typed and unpublished MSS).

8. *Golden Jubilee 1895-1945, Zenana Bible Medical Mission,* The Union Press, Patna, 1945.

9. Tucker, H. W. (1893), *Digest of the S. P. G. Record, London.*

10. Fortelli, J., S. J. (1960), *The Catholic Mission to the Santali Land of the Districts of Purnea and Santal Parganas* (typed and unpublished MSS).

11. Dent, Paul, S. J. (1937), *A Brief History of Patna Mission* (cyclostyled, bound and unpublished), Patna Jesuit Archives, St. Xavier's, Patna.

12. Gausdal, Johannes (1953), *Ebeneser Evangelikal Lutheran Church,* Benagaria.

13. Hoffmann, John Baptist (1923), 37 *Jahre Missioner in Indian*, Innsbruck, West Germany.

14. John, Philip, *The Baptist Missionary Society in Bihar* (typed and unpublished), 1960.

15. McGarry, Monsignor Urban (1960), *The Catholic Mission in the Bhagalpur District and Adjacent Santal Areas* (typed and unpublished MSS), Bhagalpur.

16. Saldanha, Charles P., S.J. (1960), *Roman Catholic Mission in Bihar (Diocese of Patna),* (typed and unpublished), Patna Jesuit Archives, St. Xavier's, Patna.

17. Saldanha, Charles P., S.J. (n.d.) *History Sketch of Patna Diocese for our field* (typed and unpublished), Patna Jesuit Archives, St. Xavier's, Patna.

18. *Sight for the Blind, The Story of Bamdah Hospital,* (n.d.), Bamdah, Santal Parganas.

19. Skillicorn, Keith, *History of the British Churches of the Christ Mission and Churches of Christ (National) in Palamau, Bihar,* 5th July, 1960 (typed and unpublished MSS).
20. Somaiya, M. C. (1960), *The Assembly of God Mission* (typed and unpublished), Jamshedpur.
21. Taylor, F. L. (1960), *The Church in the Diocese of Bhagalpur* (typed and unpublished, MSS).
22. Tucker, Victor, *The Catholic Church of Chotanagpur* (a brief sketch, typed and unpublished MSS), dated March 1, 1961, from December 1921 to January 1922.

A. 3 Mission Source Books.

1. Anon, *Ranchi Catholic Archdiocese* (1995), Catholic Press, Ranchi.
2. Badley, B.H., *India Missionary Directory and Memorial Volume,* 3rd edition 1886, Methodist Publishing House, Calcutta.
3. Badley, Brenton Thoburn, *Visions and Victories in Hindustan,* Methodist Publishing House, Madras, 1931.
4. Cave, Brown J., *The Chotanagpur Mission* (Gossner Mission), Calcutta, 1870.
5. Chatterton, Eyre (1901), *A Story of Fifty Years' Mission Work in Chotanagur,* SPCK, London & Dublin University Mission, Hazaribagh.
6. Chatterton, Eyre (1924), A History of the Church of England in India since the Early Days of the East India Company, S.P.C.K., London.
7. *Directory of Patna Diocese* (1998), Bishop's House, Patna.
8. *Directory of Patna Diocese* (2004), Bishop's House, Patna.
9. Gille, A., S. J. (1917), *A Record of the Inscriptions at the Catholic Church at Patna,* Bihar and Orissa, Archbishop's House Archives, Patna.
10. Holsten, D. Walter (1949), *Johannes Evangelista Gossner,* Glaube and Gemeinde, Gottingen.

11. Hollister, John N. (1956), *The Centenary of the Methodist Church in Southern Asia,* Lucknow Publishing House, Lucknow.
12. Josson, Henry (1921), *La Mission Du Bangale Occidental, Bruges* (Brussels).
13. Kennedy, K. W. S. (1939), *Fifty Years of Chotanagpur Mission*, Ireland.
14. Macphail, J. M., *Missions of the United Free Church of Scotland* (also in Santali), 1904, Pokhuria.
15. Macphail, J. M., *Rev. Andrew Campbell, D. D., Missionary to the Santals*, Edinburgh (UFCS Archives, Pachamba), (n. d.).
16. Macphail, R. M., *The Santal Mission,* Pachamba, (n. d.)
17. Marlier, A. (1929), *Een Jezuiet Missionaries, Pater C onstant Lievens,* Louvain.
18. Mitchell, Murray (Mrs.) (1871), *A Missionary's Wife among the Wild Tribes of South Bengal*, London.
19. Mullens, Joseph (1863), *A Brief Review of Ten Years' Missionary Labour in India Between 1852 to 1861*, London.
20. Nottrott, A. (1874), *Die Gossner Che Mission unter den Kokhs (The Gossner Mission unter den kols), Halle.*
21. Pascoe, C. F. (1901), *Two Hundred Years of SPG: A Historical Account of the SPG in Foreign Parts (based on the Digest of the Society's Records, 1701-1900*, SPG, London.
22. Roy, S. K. (1938), *The Church in Chotanagpur*, Ranchi.
23. Schuerren, T. Ven der, *Belgian Mission of Bengal,* 3 parts, Bengal Jesuit Archives, Calcutta, 1922-25.
24. Seeberg (1969), *Gossner Evangelical Lutheran Church: Chotanagpur Aur Assam ka Itihas (History of Chotanagpur and Assam), 1919-1969.*
25. Sherring, M. A. (1884), *The History of the Protestant Missions in India,* Religious Tract Society, London.
26. Skrefsrud, L. O., *The Traditions and Institutions of the Santals* (also in Santali), 1st edition in 1887: reprint with a few additions in 1916, Benagaria.

27. Taylor, F. L. (1961), *Diocese of Bhagalpur C.M.S. Santal Mission, 1860-1960*, Bhagalpur.

28. *The Catholic Directory of India 2005-06* (2006), Claretian Publications, Bangalore Whitley, E. H. (1896), *Historical Sketches. No. II, Chota Nagpore, S.P.G. Mission*, London.

29. Wueste, E., *Chotanagpur Ki Masihi Mandli ka Itihas* (History of the Chotanagpur Christian Community), (Gossner Church) *1845-1870*, Ranchi.

A. 4 Mission Journals

1. *Gharbandhu*, (official monthly paper of Gossner Mission), 1893-1912, 1916-1922, 1933-1942, Ranchi.

2. *Catholicus* (official newsletter of the Catholic Church of Allahabad Diocese), Allahabad.

3. *Chotanagpur Diocesan Paper*, a Quarterly in English, 1914-1947, Ranchi, (Anglican).

4. *Chotanagpur Dut Patrika* (Hindi Monthly), 1878-1947, Anglican Archives, Ranchi.

5. *Chota Nagpore Mission Quarterly Paper* No. 1, February 1874.

6. *Chotanagpure Mission Quarterly Paper* No. 1, February 1874, Ranchi.

7. *Chotanagpure Mission Quarterly Paper* No. 3, November, 1874, Ranchi.

8. Dalton, E. T. (1886), "The Kols of Chota-Nagpore", in *The Journal of the Asiatic Society of Bengal,* Vol. XXXV, Part-II , No. 3.

9. *Die Biene auf dem Missions felde fur Missions*, Germany, (Monthly periodical of the Gossner Mission, from 1846 to 1891).

10. *Gossner Pariwar* (1969), 1845-1969, GEL Archives, Ranchi.

11. *Nishkalanka*, Hindi Monthly, Catholic Press, Ranchi, (1922 to 1947).

12. Roy, S. C. (1931), "Effects on the Aborigines of Chotanagpur of their contact with Western Civilization", in *The Journal of the Bihar and Orissa Research Society,* Vol. XVI.
13. Sheetal, Kushalmay (1939), *Chotanagpur Ki Kalishya Ka Brittant* (Newsletter of the Chotanagpur Church), Ranchi.
14. "The Kols of Chota Nagpore", in the *Calcutta Review*, Vol. XLIX (1869).
15. *The Oriental Baptist*, July 1847 and Vol. XII, 1858.

A. 5 Government Sources

1. Byrne, J. (1911), *Bengal District Gazetteers: Bhagalpur,* Government Press, Calcutta.
2. Hallet, M. G. (1917), *Bihar and Orissa Gazetteers: Ranchi*, Government Press, Calcutta.
3. Hunter, W. W. (1877), *A Statistical Account of Bengal* Vol. XVI Hazaribagh and Lohardaga Districts, Trubner & Co, London, London.
4. *Imperial Gazetteer of India*, Provincial Series, Vol. I & II, Government Press, Calcutta, (1909).
5. Kumar, N. (1970), *Bihar District Gazetteers: Ranchi*, Government Press, Patna.
6. L. S. S. O'Malley (1910), *Bihar District Gazetteers: Santal Parganas,* Government Press, Calcutta.
7. Lister, E. (1917), *Bihar & Orissa District Gazetteers: Hazaribagh,* Government Press, Patna.
8. Macpherson, T. S. and Hattet, M. G. (1917), *Bihar and Orissa District Gazetteers: Ranchi,* Government Press, Patna.
9. Middleton, A. P. (1930), *Bihar and Orissa District Gazatteers: Saran*, Government Press, Patna.
10. Mukherjee, S. C. (1938), *Bihar District Gazetteers: Santal Parganas,* (Revised edition), Government Press, Patna.
11. O'Malley, L. S. S. (1907), *Bengal District Gazatteers: Muzaffarpur*, Government Press, Calcutta.

12. O'Malley, L. S. S. (1926), *Bihar and Orissa District Gazetteers: Monghyr* (Revised edition), Government Press, Patna.

13. O'Malley, L. S. S. (1926), *Bihar and Orissa District Gazetteers,* Patna, (Revised edition), Government Press, Patna.

14. O'Malley, L. S. S. (1928), *History of Bengal, Bihar and Orissa under British Rule*, Government Press, Calcutta.

15. Reid, J. (1912), *Final Report on the Survey and Settlement Operations in the District of Ranchi,* 1902-1910, Government Press, Calcutta.

B. Secondary Sources

1. Abraham, C. E. (2004), "The Rise and Growth of Christianity in India" in *Cultural-Religious Heritage-India,* Vol. 8, (ed.) Suresh K Sharma & Usha Sharma, Mittal Publications, New Delhi.

2. Albert, Vasantharaj (1992), *Bihar Church and People Groups* (Madras: Church Growth Association of India).

3. Andrews, C. F. (1908), *Handbook of English Church Expansion, North India,* A. R. Mowbray Co Ltd., London.

4. ______________(1912), *Renaissance in India: its Missionary Aspect,* Mowbray Co Ltd., London.

5. Banerjee, Mangobinda (1993), *An Historical Outline of Pre-British Chotanagpur* (Ranchi: Educational Publications).

6. Baptista, Elsie (1967), *The East Indians: Catholic Community of Bombay, Salsette and Bassein, Bandra,* The Bombay East Indian Association, Bombay.

7. Bauman, Chad M. (2011), "Indian Christian Historiography from Below, from Above, and in Between", Church History, Jan. 2011, pp. 622-629: Available at: http://works.bepress.com/chad_bauman/37.

8. Benhur, Abraham (2011), Abraham Benhur (2011), *The Jewish Background of Indian People: a Historical Study*, Jeevanist Books, Calicut.

9. Bhattacharya, Haridas (ed) (1969), *The Cultural Heritage of India*, Vol. IV, The Religions, Ramakrishna Mission, Calcutta.

10. Bhattacharya, S. K. (1999), *Christian Missions, Missionaries and Indian Society: A Socio-economic Study*, Mohit Publications, New Delhi.

11. Bogaert, Vanden Michael (1986), "Social Transformation of a Tribal Society: Fallout of Evangelization in Chotanagpur," *Sevartham,* Vol. 11, pp. 19-37.

12. Bradley-Brit, F. B. (1903), *Chota-Nagpore, a Little-known Province of the Empire*, London.

13. Buyers, William (1848), *Recollections of Northern India*, London.

14. Campbell, Andrew (1902), *The Santali Dictionary*, Pokhuria Mission Press, Pokhuria.

15. Carey, William (1888), A *Missionary Tour in the Hughli and Howrah and Districts,* Baptist Mission Press Calcutta.

16. Clarysse, L. (1985), *Father Constant Lievens,* Satya Bharti, Ranchi.

17. D' Souza, Fr. Jerome (1957), *Sardar Panikkar and Christian Missions*, St. Joseph's Industrial School Press, Trichinopoly.

18. D'souza, Daniel (n. d), *A History of the Catholic Church in North India,* (Till 1757), Mangalore, Capuchin Friary, Mangalore.

19. Daniel, K. G. (1998), *Let the Hills Rejoice: The Conversion of the Hill Arayans of Kerala and Its Effect on Evangelism*, ISPCK, Delhi.

20. Datta, K. K. (1940), *The Santal Insurrection,* University of Calcutta, Calcutta.

21. ___________(1957), *Unrest Against British Rule in Bihar*, 1832-59, Patna.

22. David, Emmanuel, (1986), "History of Christianity in India: Changing Perspective," *Indian Church History Review (ICHR)*, 30 (No. 1).

23. De Sa, Fidelis (1975), *Crisis in Chotanagpur,* Redemptorist Publications, Bangalore, India.

24. Dharmaraj, J. S. (1993), Colonialism and Christian Mission: PostColonial Reflection, ISPCK, Delhi.
25. Downs, Frederick S. (1992), op. cit., *History of Christianity in India, (North East India in the 19th and 20th Centuries)*, Vol. V, Part 5, Church History Association of India, Bangalore.
26. Dubois, Abbe (1995), *Letters on the State of Christianity in India: To which is Added A Vindication of the Hindu Male and Female*, Asian Educational Services, New Delhi.
27. Estborn, S. (1959), *Our Village Christians: A Study of the Life and Faith of Village Christians in Tamil Nadu*, Christian Literature Society, Madras.
28. Farquhar, J. N. (1921), *The Apostle St. Thomas in South India*, Rylands Library Bulletin, Manchesrer.
29. Fernandes, Walter (1981), "Caste and Conversion Movements India", *Social Action,* Vol. 31, No. 3, July-September, pp. 261-290.
30. Ferroli, D. (1951), *The Jesuits of Malabar,* Vol. I & II, The National Press, Bangalore Cant, Bangalore.
31. Fisher, George Park (1887), *History of Christian Church*, London.
32. Frykenberg, Robert E. (2008), *Christianity in India: From Beginnings to the Present*, Oxford University Press, New York.
33. Gandhi, M. K. (1941), *Christian Missions: Their Place in India,* Nawajivan Publishing House, Ahmedabad.
34. Godwin, C. J. (1972), *Change and Continuity: A Study of Two Christian Village Communities in Suburban Bombay*, Tata McGraw-Hill Publishing, Bombay.
35. Gomes, Olivinho J. F. (1987), *Village Goa, A Study of Goan Social Structure and Change*, S. Chand & Company, New Delhi.
36. Guha, Ranajit (ed.) (1982), *Subaltern Studies* 1: *Writings on South Asian History and Society*, Oxford University Press, Delhi.

37. Hasnain, Nadim (1992), *Janjatiya Bharat*: 3rd Edition (New Delhi: Jawahar Publishers & Distributors).

38. Hoffmann, John Baptist (1930), *Encyclopaedia Mundarica,* 13 volumes, Government Press, Patna.

39. Horo, P. C. (1976), "Christian Missions and Communities in Bihar", in Kali Kinkar Datta (ed), *The Comprehensive History of Bihar* Vol-III, Part-II, (Historical Research Series Vol. XIV), K. P. Jayaswal Research Institute, Patna, pp. 109-292.

40. Houlton, J. B. (1949), *Bihar the Heart of India*, Orient Longmans, Bombay.

41. Hrangkhuma, F., & C. H. Sebastian Kim (Ed.) (1999), *The Church in India: Its Missions Tomorrow*, CMS/ISPCK, Delhi.

42. Jain, P. C. (1995), *Christianity, Ideology and Social Change Among Tribals*, Rawat Publications, Jaipur.

43. James, Hough (1839, 1860), *History of Christianity in India* from the Commencement of the Christian Era, 3 Vols., R. B. Seeley and W. Burnside, London.

44. Jha, J. C. (1964), *Kol Insurrection in Chota-Nagpur,* Calcutta.

45. Josson, H. S. J.(1993), *The Mission of West Bengal or The Archdiocese of Calcutta*, Belgian Province of the Society of Jesus, Translated from the French: "La Mission Du Bengale Occidentale ou Archdiocese De Calcutta." by L. Clarysse, Catholic Press, Ranchi.

46. Kalapura, Jose (1999), *Religion and Community: The Making of the Bettiah and Ravidasi Christians in Bihar* (unpublished Ph. D Thesis), Centre for Historical Studies, Jawaharlal Nehru University, New Delhi.

47. ____________(1999), "Change of Socio-Economic Structure: A Paradigm of Dalit Mobility: A Case Study of the Ravidasis of Bihar," in *Dalits and Peasants: The Emerging Caste-Class Dynamics,* (ed) Ashish Ghosh, Gyan Sagar Publications, New Delhi, pp. 166-202.

48. _________(2000), "King, Fort, Zamindaris and Missionaries: The founding of Bihar's Oldest Christian Community, 1745,"

in *Proceedings of the Indian History Congress* (Calcutta: 61st: Session, Calcutta University), pp. 1011-1028.

49. ____________(2003), "Church in Chotanagpur: Mediating Change through Education," in (eds) Beni Ekka, H. K. Singh, V. P. Sharan, & Anirudh Prasad, *The Catholic Church in Jharkhand: A Mediator of Change,* Xavier Institute of Social Service, Ranchi, pp 197-221.

50. ____________ (2006), "Cooperatives and Community Development: A Study of Champaran in Bihar," *Jharkhand Journal of Development and Management Studies,* Vol. 4, 1, (Jan-Mar): pp. 1805-1818.

51. ____________(2006), "East-West Interaction and Development of Modern Science in India: Jesuit Mediation during 16-19th Centuries," in *Proceedings of the Indian History Congress, 66th Session*, Vishwabharati University, Santiniketan, pp. 493-513.

52. ____________(2006), "Dignity Re-discovered: Christians in Eastern India," in *Indian Christian Directory,* Rashtra Deepika Ltd., Kottayam, pp. 124-129.

53. ____________(2009), "Christianity and Marginalised Communities in India," in *Indian Church History Review,* Vol. XLIII, No. 1, June, pp 7-36.

54. ____________(2010), "Margins of Faith": Dalits and Tribal Christians in Eastern India", in *Margins of Faith: Dalit and Tribal Christianity in India*, (eds) Rowena Robinson & Joseph Marianus Kujur, Sage Publications, New Delhi, pp. 75-96.

55. ______(2011), "Christianity in Bihar: Origin, Development and Challenges", in (ed.) Joy Kaipan, sdb, *Studies on the History of the Church in India*, Kristujyoti Publications, Bangalore, pp. 77-97.

56. ____________(2011), "Church in Jharkhand: Mediating Social Transformation among Tribals", in Joy Kaipan, sdb (ed*), Studies on the History of the Church in India,* Kristujyoti Publications, Bangalore.

57. ____________(2012), "Christianity, Colonial Globalization of Culture: An Indian Experience with Special Reference to

Malabar Christians," in (eds) George Menachery & Oberland Snaitang, *Christianity and Cultural Encounter*, pp. 178-198.

58. Kamat, Pratima (1999), *Farar Far- Local Resistance to Colonial Hegemony in Portuguese Goa, 1510-1961,* Institute Menezes Braganza, Panaji.

59. __________(2013), "Priestly Protests against the Portuguese 'Pigmentocracy': The Case of the first Goan Bishop, D. Matheus de Castro" *Indian Church History Review,* Vol. XLVII, No. 2, December, pp. 118-140.

60. Kanjamala, Augustine (1981), *Religion and Modernisation: A Case Study of Northern Orissa*, Satprakashan Sanchar Kendra, Indore.

61. Kollamparambil, Jacob (1981), *The St. Thomas Christians' Revolution in 1653,* The Catholic Bishop's House, Kottayam.

62. Kooiman, Dick (1989), *Conversion and Social Equality in India: The London Missionary Society in South Travancore in the 19th Century,* Manohar Publishers, New Delhi.

63. Latourette, Kenneth Scott, (1940), A History of the Expansion of Christianity, Volume-VI, Paternoster Press, London.

64. Mac, M. R. (1989), Conversion, *Protest Movements & Change: A Select Bibliography (With Special Reference to Christianity in India),* Centre for Social Studies, Surat.

65. Mahto, Dr. S. (1971), Hundred years of Christian Missions in Chotanagpur since 1845, The Chotanagpur Christian Publication House, Ranchi.

66. Manshardt, Clifford (1933), *Christianity in a Changing India*, Calcutta.

67. Mayhew, Arthur (1929), *Christianity and Government of India: An Examination of the Christian Forces at Work in the Administration of India, 1600-1920*, Faber & Gwyer, London.

68. Mercier, Laurice and Buckendorf, Madeline (1992), *Using Oral History in Community History Projects*, Oral History Association, Pamphlet Series, No. 4, New York.

69. Mingana, A. (1926), *Early Spread of Christianity*, Manchester University Press, Manchester.

70. Mathew, George (1979), *Christian Indians and Indian Nationalism, 1885-1950.*

71. Minz, Nirmal (1998),"Christianity among the Mundas, Oraons, and Kharias of Chotanagpur" in F. Hrangkhuma(ed), Christianity in India, Delhi, pp.14-38.

72. ____________(2007), "Understanding Tribal Identities in Jharkhand," in *Pearls of Indigenous Wisdom*, eds. Joseph Marianus Kujur & Sonajharia Minz, Indian Social Institute, New Delhi, pp. 41-49.

73. Moffett, Samuel H. (1992), *A History of Christianity in Asia, Volume I*, HarperCollins, San Francisco, CA.

74. ________________(2006), *A History of Christianity in Asia, Volume 11: 1500-1900*, Orbis Books, Maryknoll, New York.

75. Moraes, George Mark (1964), *A History of Christianity in India from Early times to Sr. Francis Xavier: AD 52-1552*, Manaktalas, Bombay.

76. Munda, G. S. (2000), *Caste Dynamics and Tribal Society*, Dominant Publishers and Distributors, New Delhi.

77. Mundadan, A. M., CMI. (1984), *Indian Christians Search for Identity & Struggle for Autonomy*, Dharmaram Publications, Bangalore.

78. ______________ 2001), *History of Christianity in India*, Vol *I: From the Beginning to the Middle of the Sixteenth Century (up to 1542)*, Church History Association of India, Bangalore.

79. Nandi, Swapan Kumar (1976), "Impact of Christianity on the Chamars of Majhwaja, a Bhojpur Village," *Journal of Social Research*, Vol. 19, no. 1, (March).

80. Nedungatt, George, SJ (2008), Quest for the Historical Thomas Apostle of India: A Re-reading of the Evidence, Theological Publications in India, Bangalore.

81. Oddie, G. A. (ed) (1991), *Religion in South Asia: Religious Conversion and Revival Movements in South Asia in Medieval and Modern Times*, Manohar Publishers, New Delhi.

82. Ogilvie, J. N. (1915), *The Apostles of India*, Baird Ludure, Hodder & Stoughton, London.

83. Oommen, George & John C. B. Webster (2002), *Local Dalit Christian History*, ISPCK, Delhi.

84. Osta, A. J. (1959), *Tibet-Hindustan Mission*, Ham Sab Publications, Patna.

85. Pandey, Dr. Ravi Bhushan (2005), *Christianity and Tribes in India,* Academic Excellence, Delhi.

86. Pascual-Oiz, Henry (1991), *Blessed by the Lord, A History of the Patna Jesuits, 1921-1981*, Patna Jesuit Society, Patna.

87. Patro, S. K. & Mather, B. H. (1969), *The Anglican Church in Chotanagpur* 1869-1969, Ranchi.

88. Permalil, H. C. & E. R. Hambye (1972), *Christianity in India: A History in Ecumenical Perspective,* Prakasam Publications, Alleppey.

89. Perumalil, A. C. (1952), *The Apostles in India,* Catholic Book Crusade, Patna.

90. Picket, Waskom J. (1938), *Christian Mass Movements in India,* The Mission Press, Jabalpur.

91. Placid D. & Job, K. E. (1938), *The Syrian Church of Malabar*, Travancore.

92. Pollard, Nicholas J., (1936), "Whither Outcaste India?" *Patna Mission Letter,* (Aug-Sept.).

93. Robinson, Rowena (1998), *Conversion, Continuity and Change: Lived Christianity in Southern Goa*, Sage Publications, New Delhi.

94. Roy, S. C. (1912), *The Mundas and Their Country*, Brahmo Mission Press, Calcutta.

95. ________(1915), *The Oraons of Chotanagpur*, Brahmo Mission Press, Calcutta.

96. Sahay, K. N. (1986), *Christianity and Culture Change in India*, Inter India Publications, New Delhi.

97. Samuelkutty, Rev. T. S. (2000), *The Place and Contribution of Dalits in Select Pentecostal Churches in Central Kerala from 1922 to 1972*, ISPCK, Delhi.

98. Sarkar, S. S. & Dutta, K. K. (1934), *Text-Book of Modern Indian History*, Vol. II, Part II. Patna.

99. Satyaprakash (1986), *Christianity: A Select Bibliography*, Indian Documentation Service, Gurgaon.

100. Schuerer, T. Van Der (1928), Moral & Intellectual Uplift of the Aboriginal Races of Chotanagpur, India, East and West Ltd, London.

101. Sengupta, K. P. (1971), *The Christian Missionaries in Bengal, 1793-1833*, Firma K. L. Mukhopadhyay, Calcutta.

102. Sherring, M. A. (1884), *The History of Protestant Missions in India: From Their Commencement in 1706 to 1881*, The Religious Tract Society, London.

103. Singh, Sunil Kumar (2005), *Inside Jharkhand*, Crown Publications, Ranchi.

104. Studdert-Kennedy, George (1998), *Providence & the Raj: Imperial Mission and Missionary Imperialism,* Sage Publications, New Delhi.

105. Sundararaj, Manickam (1977), *The Social Setting of Christian Conversion in South India: The Impact of the Wesleyan Methodist Missionaries on the Trichy–Tanjore Diocese with Special Reference to the Harijan Communities of the Mass Movement Area* 1820-1947, Franz Verlag, Wiesbaden.

106. Swarno, Dasarathi (1990), *The Christian Missionaries in Orissa: Their Impact on Nineteenth Century Society*, Punthi Pustak, Calcutta.

107. Teltscher, Kate (1995), *India Inscribed: European and British Writing on India, 1600-1800*, Oxford University Press, Delhi.

108. Tete, Peter, S. J. (1986), A Missionary Social Worker in India: Fr. J. B. Hoffmann: The Chotanagpur Tenancy Act and the Catholic Co-operatives, Satya Bharati, Ranchi.

109. Thaliath Jonas (1958), *The Synod of Diamper,* Pontifica Institute Orientalium Stuiorum, Roma.

110. Thomas, V. V. (2006), *Understanding Subaltern History: Theoretical Tools*, BTESSC/SATHRI, Bangalore.

111. Thonippara, Francis, CMI (1999), *Saint Thomas Christians of India: A Period of Struggle for Unity and Self-Rule* (1775-1787), Center for Eastern and Indian Christian Studies, Bangalore.

112. Tirkey, Boniface (2001), *Jashpur mein Isaai Samudaya ka Prarambhik Itihas* (The Beginnings of the Christian Community in Jashpur, Bishop's House, Kunkuri (Chattisgarh).

113. Vadakkekara, Benedict (2007), *Origin of Christianity in India: A Historiographical Critique,* Media House, Delhi.

114. Vannini, Fulgentius(1981), *Hindustan: Tibet Mission,* Capuchin Ashram, Lucknow.

115. Webster, John C. B. (2012), Historiography of Christianity in India, Oxford University Press, New Delhi.

116. Webster, John C. B. (1976), *The Christian Community and Change in Nineteenth Century North India*, Macmillan Company of India Ltd., New Delhi.

117. ________________(1992), *The Dalit Christians: A History*, ISPCK, Delhi.

118. Weitbrecht, J. J. (1844), *Protestant Missions in Bengal Illustrated: Being the Substance of a Course of Lectures Delivered on India Missions,* John F. Shaw, London.

119. Wilfred, Felix (2009), "Historiography of Indian Christianity," *Vidyajyoti Journal of Theological Reflection*, Vol. 73, No. 10, Oct., pp. 737-751.

120. Zacharia, Dr. Scaria (Ed.), *The Acts and Decrees of the Synod of Diamper, 1599,* Indian Institute of Christian Studies, Kottayam, Kerala, 1994.

121. Zupanov, Ines G. (1998), "The Prophetic and the Miraculous in Portuguese Asia: A Hagiographical View of Colonial Culture," in Sanjay Subramaniam (ed), *Sinners and Saints: The Successors of Vasco da Gama,* Oxford University Press, Delhi, pp. 135-169.

Index

D